Teaching by Principles

An Interactive Approach to Language Pedagogy

H. Douglas Brown
San Francisco State University

Prentice Hall Regents
Englewood Cliffs, New Jersey 07632

Library of Congress Cataloging-in-Publication Data

Brown, H. Douglas, (date)
    Teaching by principles: an interactive approach to language
  pedagogy / H. Douglas Brown.
        p.   cm.
    Includes bibliographical references and index.
    ISBN 0-13-328220-1 (pbk.)
    1. Language and languages--Study and teaching. 2. English
language--Study and teaching--Foreign speakers. 3. Interaction
analysis in education. I Title.
P51.B7754 1994   93-29654
418.007--dc20   CIP

Publisher: *Tina Carver*
Director of Production and Manufacturing: *David Riccardi*
Electronic Production Coordinator: *Molly Pike Riccardi*
Creative Director: *Paula Maylahn*

Editorial Production/Design Manager: *Dominick Mosco*
Electronic production/supervision and
   interior design: *Shirley Hinkamp/Steve Jorgensen*
Copy Editor: *Janet Johnston*
Cover Photo: *George Holton*
Cover Design Coordinator: *Merle Krumper*
Production Coordinator: *Ray Keating*

Prentice-Hall International (UK) Limited, *London*
Prentice-Hall of Australia Pty. Limited, *Sydney*
Prentice-Hall Canada Inc., *Toronto*
Prentice-Hall Hispanoamericana, S.A., *Mexico*
Prentice-Hall of India Private Limited, *New Delhi*
Prentice-Hall of Japan, Inc., *Tokyo*
Simon & Schuster Asia Pte. Ltd., *Singapore*
Editora Prentice-Hall do Brasil, Ltda., *Rio de Janeiro*

Contents

Preface

As we speed toward and into the twenty-first century, we can indeed take some pride in a sophisticated accumulation of knowledge about second language learning and teaching. Such was not always the case. Language teachers in the middle part of the twentieth century witnessed the "birth" of a disciplined approach to second language learning and teaching, but the nascent profession was hard put to come up with viable answers to questions about how to teach interactive skills in the classroom. By the 1970s, second language acquisition was establishing itself as a discipline in its own right, asserting its place as not merely an offshoot of linguistics or psychology. The resulting research of this adolescent profession was beginning to provide some profound observations about communicative language teaching. As the field gathered momentum, journals, professional organizations, university departments, and research studies grew with amazing speed. And in the last two decades of the century, we are reaping the benefits of this storehouse of information about how to successfully teach foreign languages in classroom contexts.

Teaching by Principles: An Interactive Approach to Language Pedagogy (TBP) synthesizes that accumulation of knowledge into a practical, principled approach to teaching English as a second or foreign language. It is a book for prospective and new teachers who essentially need to learn how to walk into a classroom full of learners and effectively accomplish communicative objectives. It primarily addresses the needs of those in teacher education programs who have never taught before, but it secondarily serves as a refresher course for those who have had some experience in the classroom. The book speaks both to those who are in English as a second language contexts (in English-speaking countries) and to those who are in English as a foreign language situations. And the book is designed to be read and studied and enjoyed by those with little or no previous work in linguistics, psychology, or second language acquisition.

The use of the term **approach** in the subtitle of the book signals an important characteristic of current language teaching pedagogy. For a significant part of the twentieth century, teacher education programs were expected to deliver a handful of different methods—relatively homogeneous sets of classroom practices that sprang from one particular theoretical perspective. Thus, the Audiolingual Method, with its behavioristic underpinnings, was at one time touted as a method for all occasions. Or, teachers would learn how to use the Silent Way, Community Language Learning, or Suggestopedia, each with its own "formula" for success and its own theoretical bias. We have today graduated beyond such a restrictive concept of classroom practice. While we may indeed still appropriately refer to classroom "methodology," the various separately-named methods are no longer at the center of our concern. Instead, our current—and more enlightened—foundations of language teaching are built on numerous principles of language learning and teaching about which we can be reasonably secure. A principled approach to interactive language pedagogy is one that is built on such principles.

So, *TBP* is a book that helps teachers to build a repertoire of classroom techniques that are firmly embedded in well-established principles of second language acquisition. Most of these principles are treated comprehensively in my companion volume, *Principles of Language Learning and Teaching (PLLT)* (Prentice Hall, 1994), now in its third edition. Those who use the present book in their teacher-training program would benefit from (a) having first read *PLLT*, or (b) using *PLLT* as a companion text. However, *TBP* can be effectively used without its companion, since major principles on which current pedagogical practice are based are summarized here in the early chapters.

Some of the features of *TBP*:

- Practical realities of language classrooms are the primary focus, but all those pedagogical fundamentals are grounded in principles of second language acquisition. The reader is thereby led to consider why every technique might or might not work. Yet, at the same time, the reader is not dragged into long, theoretical diatribes.

- The prose is therefore deliberately light, readable, and "friendly" to those who have not had advanced courses in educational linguistics. I have avoided weighty, high-sounding, "scholarly" treatises in my objective of talking to teachers in plain, understandable language, with a minimum of distracting references to the dozens of potentially related research studies.

- Readers are given a step-by-step approach to teaching language interactively. Sometimes new teachers are quite apprehensive about the prospect of dealing with the "chaos" of a communicative classroom—one with a fair share of small group work and student participation. Will I be able to follow my lesson plan? How will I keep control? What if students are silent? What if students ask questions I can't answer? What if I give the wrong answer? What if I completely fall apart? This book will, bit by bit, help the novice teacher to become confident in directing interactive, student-centered, cooperative classrooms.

- While the four skills of listening, speaking, reading, and writing are treated separately in four different chapters, throughout this book the emphasis is on the integration of the four skills. Usually, the most effective English language teaching integrates these skills in a whole language approach, rather than assuming that one skill can be broken down, isolated, and studied for long stretches of time.

- Finally, at the end of each chapter, *TBP* has topics for discussion, action, and research, many of which model an interactive classroom by providing tasks for pairs or small groups. These tasks come out of my own experience in teacher training courses, where I have found that some of the best learning occurs when students collaborate among themselves to solve certain "problems" in language teaching. Also, suggestions for further reading at the end of each chapter are annotated to facilitate judicious choices of extra reading.

TBP is in many ways a product of my two-plus decades of instruction and research in teaching English as a second/foreign language. During that time, it has been my pleasure and challenge to teach and to learn from hundreds of students in my courses. I am grateful for all those inquisitive minds—now scattered around the world—whose insights are well represented here. I am also indebted to all those teachers out there in many countries of the world, especially in Japan, Thailand, Taiwan, the Dominican Republic, Egypt, Yugoslavia, Hong Kong, Korea, and of course the USA, with whom I have worked and talked and exchanged ideas and stories. Finally, I acknowledge the support and nurture of my own faculty colleagues at the American Language Institute and San Francisco State University. Our regular camaraderie is a source of professional stimulation and of personal affirmation that what we are all trying to do is most certainly worth the effort.

H. Douglas Brown
San Francisco, California
January 1994

Acknowledgments

Grateful acknowledgment is made to the following publishers and authors for permission to reprint copyrighted material.

American Council on Teaching Foreign Languages (ACTFL), for material from *ACTFL Proficiency Guidelines* (1986); G. Moskowitz, "Interaction analysis usage for supervisors," *Foreign Language Annals 5* (1971): 211–221.

Cambridge University Press, for material from J.C. Richards and T.S. Rodgers, *Approaches and Methods in Language Teaching* (1986); D. Nunan, *Designing Tasks for the Communicative Curriculum* (1989); G. Ellis and B. Sinclair, *Learning to Learn English* (1989).

Georgetown University Press, for material from M. Swain, "The language of French immersion students: Implications for theory and practice," in J.E. Alatis (ed.), *Georgetown University Table on Languages and Linguistics* (1990).

Heinle and Heinle Publishers, for material from R. Mackay, "Teaching the information gathering skills," in M.H. Long and J.C. Richards, *Methodology in TESOL* (1987); A.F. Kruse, "Vocabulary in context," in Long and Richards (1987); G. Crookes and C. Chaudron, "Guidelines for classroom teaching," in M. Celce-Murcia (ed.), *Teaching English as a Second or Foreign Language* (1991); P.W. Peterson, "A synthesis of models for interactive listening," in Celce-Murcia (1991); A. Chamot, J.M. O'Malley, and L. Kupper, *Building Bridges* (1992); R. Oxford, *Language Learning Strategies: What Every Teacher Should Know* (1990).

Languge Learning, for material from R.B. Kaplan, "Cultural thought patterns in intercultural education," *Language Learning 16* (1) (1966): 1–20.

Longman Publishing Group, for material from I. Boone, J. Bennett, and L. Motai, *Basics in Reading: An Introduction to American Magazines* (1988).

Oxford University Press, for material from M. Finocchiaro and C. Brumfit, *The Functional-Notational Approach: From Theory to Practice* (1983); R. Nolasco and L. Arthur, *Conversation* (1987).

Prentice Hall Regents, for material from H.D. Brown, *Vistas: An Interactive Course in English* (1992); H.D. Brown, D. Cohen, and J. O'Day, *Challenges: A Process Approach to Academic English* (1991); H.D. Brown, *Principles of Language Learning and Teaching,* third edition (1994); R. Wong, *Teaching Punctuation: Focus on English Rhythm and Stress* (CAL, 1987); D.L.F. Nilsen and A.P. Nilsen, *Pronunciation Contrasts in English* (Regents, 1971).

Simon & Schuster International, for material from D. Nunan, *Language Teaching Methodology: A Textbook for Teachers* (Cassell, 1991); D. Cross, *A Practical Handbook of Language Teaching* (Cassell, 1991); S. McKay, *Teaching Grammar: Form, Function, and Technique* (Pergamon, 1985).

Teachers of English to Speakers of Other Languages (TESOL), for material from J.C. Richards, "Listening comprehension: Approach, design, procedure," *TESOL Quarterly 17* (2) (1983): 219–239; M. Celce-Murcia, "Grammar pedagogy in second and foreign language teaching," *TESOL Quarterly 25* (3) (1991): 459–480; S. Bassano and M.A. Christison, "Teacher self-observation," *TESOL Newsletter* (August 1984), 17–19.

University of Minnesota Press, for material from B.W. Robinett, *Teaching English to Speakers of Other Languages: Substance and Technique* (1978).

Donna Jurich, Kate Kinsella, Tim Murphey, Karen Tenney, and Lauren Vanett, for unpublished material.

Part One

✳✳✳

Foundations
for
Classroom Practice

Chapter 1

Where Do I Begin?

So you've decided to be a language teacher! Welcome to a profession that will guarantee you more than your fair share of challenges, growth, joy, and fulfillment. Challenges await you at every turn in your professional path because the discipline of language teaching has only begun to solve some of the perplexing questions about how people successfully learn foreign languages. Opportunities for growth abound because, for as long as you continue to teach, you will never run out of new questions, new possibilities, new ways of looking at your students, and new ways of looking at yourself. The joy of teaching lies in the vicarious pleasure of witnessing your students' attainment of broader and broader vistas of linguistic proficiency and in experiencing the communal bond that you have been instrumental in creating in your classroom. And, ultimately, few professions can offer the fulfillment of knowing that your seemingly insignificant work really can make a difference in a world in need of communication that transcends national borders and interests.

Right now, all those lofty ideals notwithstanding, you may be a little apprehensive about what sort of a teacher you are going to turn out to be: What will it be like to be in front of a classroom full of expectant ears and eyes, hanging on my every word and action, ready and waiting, I surmise, to pounce on me if I make a false move? How will I develop the composure and poise that I've seen modeled by "master" teachers whom I have observed? Will I be able to take the sea of theoretical information about second language acquisition that I have studied and now by some miracle transform all that into practical classroom applications? How do I plan a lesson? What do I do if my lesson plan falls apart? Where do I begin?

Before you ask any more questions, which could at this stage only overwhelm you, sit back for a moment and tell yourself that you can indeed become a teacher who will fully meet the challenges ahead and who will grow in your professional expertise, thereby opening the doors of joy and fulfillment. This textbook is designed to help you to take that developmental journey one step at a time.

The first step in that journey is to come with me into a language classroom and observe what happens. Take special note, as the lesson unfolds, of each **choice** that the teacher makes: choices about how to begin the lesson, about which activity will come next, about how long to continue an activity, about who to call on, about whether to correct a student, and so on. Everything a teacher says and does in the classroom is the result of conscious or subconscious choices among many alternatives. Most of these choices are—or should be—the result of a careful consideration of a whole host of underlying principles of second language learning and teaching.

A Classroom Observation

The classroom we are about to enter is a course in English as a Second Language (ESL)[1] in a private language school in a metropolitan area in the USA. The 15 students in the course are relatively new arrivals in the country; they come from several different countries; few of them have managed to find employment thus far, but the others are searching. This is a beginning level class; students came into the class with minimal survival English proficiency. They are literate in their native languages. Their goal in the class is to be able to use English to survive in the country and to get some sort of employment. They are quite highly motivated to learn.

The course is a "whole language" course integrating the four skills of speaking, listening, reading, and writing. The textbook for the course is *Vistas: An Interactive Course in English* (Brown, 1992). At this stage, ten weeks into the course, the students have made good progress. They are able to engage in simple social conversations, numerous practical requests, uncomplicated business transactions (shopping, travel, etc.), and other routine daily uses of English.

---

[1]**ESL** is used in this book in two ways: (a) as a generic acronym to refer to instruction of English to speakers of other languages in any country under any circumstance, and (b) to refer to English as a **Second** Language taught in countries (such as the USA, the UK, or India) where English is a major language of commerce and education, a language that students often hear outside the walls of their classroom. Most instances of reference in this book to "ESL" are in the generic sense. **EFL** (English as a **Foreign** Language) always refers specifically to English taught in countries (such as Japan, Egypt, or Venezuela) where English is not a major language of commerce and education. See Chapter 8 for important pedagogical and curricular implications of each type of English language teaching.

The lesson we are about to observe is reasonably well planned, efficiently executed, and characteristic of current communicative language teaching methodology. It is not, however, necessarily "perfect" (are there ever any perfect lessons?), and so what you are about to see may have a few elements in it that you or others could take issue with. Please remember this as you read on and, if you wish, take note of aspects of the lesson that you might question, and then compare these notes with the comments following the lesson description.

We take our seats in the rear of the classroom and observe the following sequence of activities.

[1] The teacher, Ms. Miller (hereafter "T"), begins the fifty-minute class hour with some small talk with the students (hereafter "Ss"), commenting on the weather, on one S's previous evening's shopping attempts, etc.

[2] She then asks the Ss to keep their textbooks closed and directs them to the blackboard where she has already written the following:

How often do you _____**?**	
How often does he/she _____**?**	
How often do they _____**?**	
always	**= all of the time**
usually	**= generally; most of the time**
often	**= frequently; much of the time**
sometimes	**= at times; every now and then**
seldom	**= not often; rarely**
never	**= not ever; none of the time**

[3] T calls on individual Ss and asks them questions about their lives. For example:

How often do you come to class, Alberto?

Yoko, how often does Sook Mi drive to class?

Katherine, how often do you cook dinner?

etc.

[4] Ss respond with a few prompts and selected corrections from the T. In two or three cases Ss make errors (example: She usually **drive** to school) which T chooses not to correct.

[5] After a few minutes of this, T directs them to the meanings of the six adverbs of frequency listed on the board, explaining one or two of them further.

[6] Ss are then directed to work in pairs and make up some of their own questions using the three "how often" question models on the board, and responding appropriately, in complete sentences, using one of the six frequency adverbs. Before splitting Ss into pairs, T models some of the questions and responses that they have just gone over. During the pair work, T circulates and listens in, offering just one or two comments here and there.

[7] Following the pair work, Ss are told to open their textbooks to Unit 8, page 98. Here they see the following passage accompanied by a picture of a secretary typing a letter:

> Keiko is a secretary. She enjoys her work, and she always works hard. She is always on time for work. In fact, she is often early. She is never late, and she is never sick.
>
> Keiko usually types letters and answers the telephone. She sometimes files and makes copies. She seldom makes mistakes when she types or files. She always answers the phone politely.
>
> Keiko is intelligent, and she has a good sense of humor. She is never angry. Everybody in the office likes Keiko.

[8] T directs Ss to the picture of Keiko and asks questions to establish the context:

Who do you see in the picture?
Where is she?
What's she doing?
What's Keiko's occupation?

[9] Ss are then encouraged to ask each other questions about the picture. After some silence, two Ss venture to ask questions: "What's this?" (pointing to the typewriter) and "How much money she makes?" (other Ss laugh). T quickly moves on.

[10] T then calls Ss' attention to some vocabulary items in the passage: **enjoys, in fact, early, late, sick, makes copies, makes mistakes, politely, intelligent, sense of humor, angry.** T calls on Ss to attempt definitions or synonyms for each word. A couple of words are difficult to define: "politely" and "sense of humor." T clarifies these.

[11] T reads the passage aloud twice. Ss listen.

[12] Next, she makes statements about Keiko, some right and some wrong, and asks individuals to volunteer their response by saying either "that's right," or "that's wrong." If wrong, Ss are told to give the correct information. For example:

T: Keiko's a lawyer.
S1:   That's wrong. She's a secretary.
T: She enjoys her work.
S2:   That's right.

[13] T next directs Ss' attention to the next page of the textbook, on which an exercise is found:

EXERCISE 1

Read the paragraphs on page 98 again. Then choose the appropriate adverb of frequency.

1. Keiko works hard.
2. She is on time for work.
3. She is late or sick.
4. She is early for work.
5. She types letters.
6. She files.
7. She makes copies.
8. She makes mistakes when she types.
9. She answers the phone politely.
10. She is angry.

never	seldom	sometimes	often	usually	always

Now say the complete sentences.

1. Keiko always works hard.
2. She is always on time for work.

3. _____
4. _____
5. _____
6. _____

7. _____
8. _____
9. _____
10. _____

[14] T calls on a S to read aloud the directions, followed by other Ss reading aloud the ten sentences about Keiko.

[15] T calls on two other Ss to do items 1 and 2 aloud. A third S is asked to do item 3 aloud. With item 1, the S mispronounces the word *work*. (S pronounced it /wak/); T models the correct pronunciation and has the S make several attempts at a correct pronunciation. She then turns to the class and says, "Class, listen and repeat: **work**." Ss' initial cacophonous attempts to respond in unison improve by the third or fourth repetition.

[16] T tells Ss to write the responses to items 3–10 in their books, which they do in silence for a few minutes.

[17] Individual Ss are called on to read their answers aloud. Other Ss are asked to make any corrections or to ask questions.

[18] For item 5, one S says "She types usually letters." T explains that with the verb *be*, the frequency adverb usually follows the verb, but in affirmative statements with other verbs, the frequency adverb usually precedes the verb. T writes examples on the board:

Keiko is always on time.

Keiko always works hard.

[19] In the next exercise, the textbook shows six little scenes with frames of possible statements about each scene. For example, items 4 and 5 look like this:

4. Pravit is a mechanic.
   He is _____ lazy.
   He _____ wears dirty clothes.
   He _____ works in a garage.
   He _____ fixes cars.

5. Marco is a security guard.
   He is _____ busy.
   He _____ sits down.
   He _____ does dangerous work.
   He _____ works alone.

[20] T asks Ss to define or explain certain vocabulary words that may be difficult: **tired, garage, security guard, dangerous.**

[21] T tells Ss to work in pairs (same pairs as before) and to use their imagination as they fill in the blanks with different adverbs. Again T circulates during pair work and offers some assistance here and there, but most pairs seem quite able to do the activity without help from the T.

[22] T calls on pairs to say their responses aloud and in some cases, to explain why they chose a particular adverb. Ss who had different adverbs are asked to say their responses and explain. Ss display quite a bit of pleasure in noting differences in their responses and in carrying out little mock arguments to support their conclusion (for example: "Marco is **seldom** busy," claims one S, while another S—who currently works part time as a night security guard—argues that he has many duties to perform).

✳   ✳   ✳

[23] T then skips the next several exercises in the textbook, which offer practice in the use of frequency adverbs in various contexts. One pair of activities depicts a waiter in a French restaurant, who, in the first activity, "seldom does a good job, ...is never polite to his customers, ...sometimes drops food on his customers," etc. In the second activity, however, the waiter's boss is in the restaurant today, so now the waiter of course "always speaks politely, ...never drops food," etc. T later explained to us that because of time constraints (the school wants the book to be completed by the end of the session, two weeks hence), she isn't able to cover every exercise in the textbook.

[24] The next exercise of this class period shows eight different characters (see below), each with a different emotion. T asks Ss to look at the pictures and asks for volunteers to define the eight adjectives using other words or gestures.

[25] T explains that it's common to ask questions like "Are you ever nervous?" and that the response usually contains a frequency adverb.

[26] T then models several exchanges, asking Ss to repeat chorally:

> T: **Are you ever angry?**
> Ss: **Are you ever angry?**
>
> T: **Yes, I'm often angry.**
> Ss: **Yes, I'm often angry.**
>
> T: **Is Alberto ever nervous?**
> Ss: **Is Alberto ever nervous?**
>
> T: **No, he's seldom nervous.**
> Ss: **No, he's seldom nervous.**

This choral drill continues for, at most, one minute.

EXERCISE 7

Find out about different people in your class.

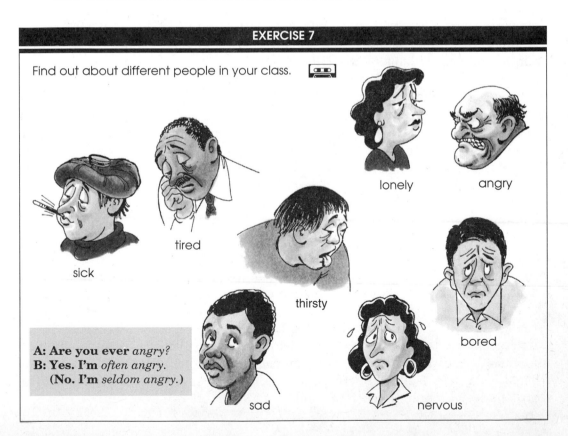

lonely

angry

tired

sick

thirsty

bored

A: **Are you ever** *angry?*
B: **Yes. I'm** *often angry.*
    (**No. I'm** *seldom angry.*)

sad

nervous

[27] T next has all the Ss get up out of their seats with a pad of paper and pencil in hand and tells them to "interview" at least 5 other people in the class and find out three things about each person (whether they are ever "angry" or "lonely") and to be prepared to give a "report" of their findings afterward.

[28] While Ss are mingling about asking questions, T circulates around the room and assists here and there with pronunciation, vocabulary, or grammar problems.

[29] The final activity consists of selected (a few volunteers to begin with and a few that T calls on) Ss to give their findings. For example, S1 says, "Yoko is often tired. She is never angry. And she is sometimes nervous, especially in the English class!" Other Ss laugh sympathetically.

[30] As the bell sounds, this activity is cut a bit short. T reminds Ss that for homework, as usual, they are to write up the Workbook exercises for Unit 8, Lesson 1. Ss scurry about to gather books and leave the classroom; one or two linger to ask the T some questions.

Beneath the Lesson

You have just observed a relatively effective class hour in which the teacher competently planned a lesson around a textbook, managed everything with no major problems, and carried out the activities with some warmth and enthusiasm. Easy, right? Well, maybe not. What you have just witnessed is the product of a teacher's experience and intuition grounded in reasonably sound theoretical principles of learning and teaching. For every tiny moment of that classroom hour, certain **choices** were made, choices that can for the most part be justified by our collective knowledge of second language acquisition and teaching. Think about those choices as you contemplate the numerous pedagogical questions that arise out of each numbered "statement" above.

[1] Why the small talk (vs. just getting straight to the lesson itself)? What teaching principle justifies such an opening? How long should such chatter continue?

[2] Why did Ms. Miller ask for closed textbooks? Isn't the written word reinforcing? Of what advantage was the blackboard material? Why did she write it on the board before class (instead of on the spot)?

[3] What are the pros and cons of asking "real" questions—about their own lives, not a fictitious textbook character—in the classroom, especially at this early stage in the lesson, before Ss have had any mechanical practice of the forms? What if a S who is called on can't respond at all?

[4] T made "selected" corrections. How did she select which errors to correct and which not to correct? Shouldn't all errors be corrected?

[5] Why weren't these words explained earlier? What if some Ss didn't know them? Or do they need explaining at all? What is the advantage to waiting until after some practice time to explain such words?

Notice, before you press on, that each question implies a **choice** that was exercised by the teacher. Among dozens of possibilities for teaching this lesson on frequency adverbs, Ms. Miller has chosen, either consciously or subconsciously, a particular set of activities, a particular order, and a particular tone for each. A relatively straightforward lesson is undergirded by a plethora of principles of learning and teaching. To further complicate matters, some of those principles are disputable. For example, the issue of when to offer a **deductive** explanation ([5]) and when to allow for **inductive** absorption of concepts is not always clearly dictated by the context.

More questions:

[6] Is this too soon for pair work? Before the pair work, why did T model questions and responses? Was that sufficient for all students, even those with lower than average proficiency? If some of the pairs are silent, what should T do? If only one person in a pair is talking, is that okay? If not, how can a T get both partners to talk? What if they talk to each other in their native language?

[7] Why did the T wait until now to "present" the paragraphs about Keiko?

[8] What purpose do the questions accomplish? Isn't it obvious who is in the picture and what she is doing?

[9] Why did the T encourage Ss' questions? Why did she quickly move on to the next step?

[10] Again, the T chose a deductive mode of dealing with vocabulary. Why? What are the advantages of encouraging students to attempt definitions?

[11] She reads the paragraphs, but why didn't she have students repeat the sentences after her in a choral drill? Or have students read the passage?

[12] What purpose did the right and wrong statements fulfill? Why did she ask Ss to volunteer here rather than calling on them?

[13] Were Ss ready for this exercise?

[14] What purpose did reading aloud serve? Why did she call on Ss rather than get volunteers? Could this just as well have been a silent activity?

[15] At this point T chooses to focus on the pronunciation error. Why now, when some other errors have gone untreated?

[16] Is it helpful to write down such responses? Why?

[17] Why did she ask students to correct each other? Under what circumstances is this appropriate (vs. the T directly correcting)?

[18] This explanation could have been made at the beginning of the lesson. Why did she wait until now?

[19] While this exercise is provided by the textbook, why did the T choose to include it? What further practice did it offer the Ss?

[20] She asks Ss to define words again. Why not just give the definitions?

[21] What is the advantage of pair work? Can a T control pair work even if classes are large (this class, of course, is not)?

[22] What research principles justify this sort of sharing and comparing? What affective and linguistic purposes did it serve?

[23] Do Ss miss vital information when Ts choose to skip certain exercises?

[24] Why volunteers here instead of calling on certain Ss?

[25] Is this explanation appropriate? Is it sufficient?

[26] What is the function of a choral drill? Shouldn't this kind of drill have come earlier in the class hour? Did it go on long enough? Too long?

[27] Why did T choose to do an activity that got everyone out of their seats? Were directions clear? Was the activity too chaotic? What if a S didn't participate?

[28] When should a T circulate like this and when is it wiser not to do so, allowing the Ss to be less inhibited? How much input should the T give at this point?

[29] What affective and linguistic purpose does this final activity serve?

[30] What do you do if an activity is cut short by the end of a period? What is the value of homework for a class like this?

You have now skimmed through some (not all!) of the many questions that one could ask about why certain choices were made about how to teach this lesson. Some of the answers are forthright with few counterarguments. Other answers would find even the best of teachers disagreeing. But the answers to all these questions can be found, in one form or another, in the huge stockpile of second language acquisition research and collective experience of language teachers around the world. And those answers will probably all appear in the chapters ahead of you in this book.

Your job, as you continue this journey, is to make the connections between research/theory/principles, on the one hand, and classrooms/teaching/practice on the other. By making those connections as you learn to teach, you will perhaps avoid some of the pitfalls of haphazard guesswork and instead engage in teaching that is enlightened by research and theory, or, teaching by principles.

TOPICS FOR DISCUSSION, ACTION, AND RESEARCH

1. Think of a typical working day in your life. Write down about a dozen **choices** you make among alternatives during that one day—things like when to get up, what to wear, what to eat, what time to leave for work/school, who to talk to, what to say, etc. Now, consider **how** you arrive at those choices, what informs and enlightens them, what stimulates them, and how predicted consequences affect them.

2. Now, with a partner, come up with a dozen instances of a teacher's choices—how to adapt an exercise, when to skip an exercise, when to correct a student, who to call on, when to do a drill, when to stop a drill, etc. Take each instance and discuss the factors that you think inform a teacher's choices in the classroom. Share these factors with the rest of the class, perhaps writing them, pair by pair, on the blackboard. You will begin to appreciate the complexity of **enlightened** teaching (as opposed to "teaching by recipe").

3. As soon as possible, arrange to observe an ESL class somewhere conveniently near you. The first time you observe, don't go in with a checklist or agenda. Just sit back and get a feel for the dynamics of the classroom. If, as you observe, some questions occur to you about **why** the teacher made certain choices, jot down your questions and discuss them later in a small group or as a whole class.

4. Find one or two currently popular textbooks in ESL and spend some time leafing through them—again, without a specific agenda. Note things that you like and don't like about each, and share those ideas with a partner or small group.

5. Consider each of the thirty numbered descriptions of the ESL class and the questions that were raised for each. Divide them up among pairs in your teacher-training class. With your partner, try to answer the question(s) assigned to you. How many of the questions can you answer with some certainty? How many do you have some intuitions about even if you can't cite certain research or principles to support your intuition?

FOR YOUR FURTHER READING

Brown, H. Douglas. 1994. *Principles of Language Learning and Teaching.* Third Edition. Prentice Hall.

This book provides a comprehensive survey of issues in second language acquisition as they apply to language teaching. In this book, you will find fuller explanations of the principles that are described in the next chapter. If you have not already read PLLT, it is strongly recommended that you read it along with this one.

Nunan, David. 1991b. *Language Teaching Methodology: A Textbook for Teachers.* Prentice Hall.

For a second perspective on language teaching methodology, you may find it useful to consult Nunan's book. Many of the same topics are covered there, but in a different way with different supporting details and information.

Celce-Murcia, Marianne. 1991. *Teaching English as a Second or Foreign Language.* Second Edition. Newbury House.

The second edition of Celce-Murcia's widely used anthology provides an updated reference for teachers. This volume is a gold mine of original and reprinted articles on a variety of topics, including general methodology, the four skills, learner variables, and practicalities of classroom teaching.

Chapter 2

Teaching by Principles

In *Principles of Language Learning and Teaching* (Brown, 1994), which perhaps you have read or are reading, I noted that these are "the best of times and the worst of times" in the language teaching profession. Best, because we have learned a great deal about language acquisition in the last two or three decades. But worst, because our information is still so slippery that just as we are about to pin down a generalization about second language acquisition, the phenomenon often eludes our grasp. By now you have perhaps already come to an appreciation of the complexity and mystery of this field. Don't lose that appreciation!

But now, as you begin your teacher education journey, it is appropriate for you to focus on what we **do** know, what we have learned, what we can say with some certainty, about second language acquisition. We can then come to grips with this notion that a great many of a teacher's **choices** spring from established **principles** of language learning and teaching. By perceiving and internalizing connections between practice (choices you make in the class-room) and theory (principles derived from research), your teaching is likely to be "enlightened." You will be better able to see why you have chosen to use a particular classroom technique (or set of techniques), to carry it out with confidence, and to evaluate its utility after the fact.

You may be thinking that such a principled approach to language teaching sounds only logical: How could one proceed otherwise? Well, I have seen many a novice language teacher gobble up teaching techniques without carefully considering the criteria that underlie their successful application in the classroom. "Just give me 101 recipes for Monday morning teaching," say some."I just want to know what to **do** when I get into the classroom." Unfortunately, this sort of quick-fix approach to teacher education will not give you that all-important ability to comprehend when to use a technique, with whom it will work, how to adapt it for your audience, or how to judge its effectiveness.

We'll now take a broad, sweeping look at twelve overarching principles of second language learning from which sound practice springs and on which your teaching can be based. It may be helpful for you, as you are reading, to refer to referenced sections of *Principles of Language Learning and Teaching* (hereafter *PLLT*) to refresh your memory of certain terms and background information.

Cognitive Principles

We will call the first set of principles "cognitive" because they relate mainly to mental and intellectual functions. It should be made clear, however, that all twelve of the principles outlined in this chapter spill across our somewhat arbitrary cognitive, affective, and linguistic boundaries.

1. Automaticity

No one can dispute the widely observed success with which children learn foreign languages, especially when they are living in the cultural and linguistic milieu of the language (see *PLLT*, Chapter 3). We commonly attribute children's success to their widely observed tendency to acquire language **subconsciously,** that is, without overtly analyzing the forms of language themselves. Through an inductive process of exposure to language input and opportunity to experiment with output, they appear to learn languages without "thinking" about them.

This childlike, subconscious processing is similar to what Barry McLaughlin (McLaughlin 1991; McLaughlin et al., 1983) called **automatic** processing with **peripheral** attention to language forms (see *PLLT*, Chapter 11). That is, in order simply to manage the incredible complexity of language—the vast numbers of bits of information—both adults and children must sooner or later move away from processing language unit by unit, piece by piece, focusing closely on each, and "graduate" to a form of high-speed, automatic processing in which language **forms** (words, affixes, word order, rules, etc.) are only on the periphery of attention. Children usually make this transition faster than adults, who tend to linger in analytical, controlled modes, focusing on the bits and pieces of language, resisting putting those bits and pieces into the "hard drive" of our minds.

We will call our first principle of language learning and teaching the Principle of Automaticity and include under this rubric the importance of:

- subconscious absorption of language through meaningful use
- efficient and rapid movement away from a focus on the forms of language to a focus on the purposes to which language is put
- efficient and rapid movement away from a capacity-limited-control of a few bits and pieces to a relatively unlimited automatic mode of processing language forms
- resistance to the temptation to analyze language forms.

The Principle of Automaticity may be stated as follows:

> **Efficient second language learning involves a timely movement of the control of a few language forms into the automatic processing of a relatively unlimited number of language forms. Overanalyzing language, thinking too much about its forms, and consciously lingering on rules of language all tend to impede this graduation to automaticity.**

Notice that this principle does not say that conscious processing is necessarily, or always, harmful. In fact adults, especially, can benefit greatly from certain conscious applications. What the principle does say is that adults can take a lesson from children here by speedily overcoming our propensity to pay too much conscious attention to the bits and pieces of language and to move on to the actual use of language for meaningful purposes.

What does this principle, which ordinarily applies to adult instruction, say to you as a teacher? Here are some possibilities:

(1) Because classroom learning normally begins with controlled, focal processing, there is no mandate to entirely avoid overt attention to language systems (of grammar, phonology, discourse). However, that attention should stop well short of blocking students from achieving a more automatic, fluent grasp of the language. Therefore, grammatical explanations or exercises dealing with what is sometimes called **usage** have a place in the adult classroom (see Principle #12), but you could overwhelm your students with grammar. If they get too heavily centered on the **formal** aspects of language, such processes can block pathways to fluency.

(2) Make sure that a large proportion of your lessons are focused on the **use** of language for purposes that are as genuine as a classroom context will permit. Students will gain more language competence in the long run if the **functional** purposes of language are the focal point.

(3) Automaticity isn't gained overnight; therefore, you need to exercise patience with students as you slowly help them to achieve fluency.

2. Meaningful Learning

Closely related to the Principle of Automaticity are cognitive theories of learning (Chapter 4, *PLLT*) which convincingly argue, as David Ausubel (1963) does, the strength of **meaningful** as opposed to **rote** learning. Meaningful learning "subsumes" new information into existing structures and memory systems, and the resulting associative links create stronger retention. Rote learning—taking in isolated bits and pieces of information that are not connected with one's existing cognitive structures—has little chance of creating long-term retention. Children are good meaningful acquirers of language (see Principle #1 above) because they associate sounds, words, structures, and discourse elements with that which is relevant and important in their daily quest for knowledge and survival.

The Principle of Meaningful Learning is quite simply stated:

> **Meaningful learning will lead toward better long-term retention than rote learning.**

The language classroom has not always been the best example of meaningful learning. In the days when the Audiolingual Method (see Chapter 4) was popular, rote learning occupied too much of the class hour as students were drilled and drilled in an attempt to "overlearn" language forms. The principle of meaningful learning tells us that some aural-oral drilling is appropriate; selected phonological elements like phonemes, rhythm, stress, and intonation, for example, can be effectively taught through pattern repetition. But drilling *ad nauseam* easily lends itself to rote learning.

Some classroom implications of the Principle of Meaningful Learning:

(1) Capitalize on the power of meaningful learning by appealing to students' interests, academic goals, and career goals.

(2) Whenever a new topic or concept is introduced, attempt to anchor it in students' existing knowledge and background so that it gets associated with something they already know.

(3) Avoid the pitfalls of rote learning:
   (a) too much grammar explanation
   (b) too many abstract principles and theories
   (c) too much drilling and/or memorization
   (d) activities whose purposes are not clear
   (e) activities that do not contribute to accomplishing the goals of the lesson or unit or course
   (f) techniques that are so mechanical or tricky that Ss get centered on the mechanics instead of the language or meanings.

3. The Anticipation of Reward

B.F. Skinner and others have clearly demonstrated the strength of rewards in both animal and human behavior (see *PLLT*, Chapter 4). There is virtually nothing that we do that is not inspired and driven by a sense of purpose or goal, and, according to Skinner, the anticipation of reward is the most powerful factor in directing one's behavior. The principle behind Skinner's operant conditioning paradigm might be briefly stated as follows:

> **Human beings are universally driven to act, or "behave," by the anticipation of some sort of reward—tangible or intangible, short term or long term—that will ensue as a result of the behavior.**

The implications for the classroom are quite obvious. At one end of the spectrum, you can appreciate the importance of the immediate administration of rewards such as the teacher's praise for correct responses ("Very good, Maria." "Nice job!"), appropriate grades or scores to indicate success, or other public recognition. At the other end, it behooves you to help students to see clearly why they are doing something, what the relevance of it is to their long-term goals in learning English.

On the other hand, a reward-driven, conditioning theory of learning has some shortcomings that ultimately have a high impact on classroom instruction. These shortcomings are summarized under Principle #4, below, but for the moment, just keep in mind that conditioning by rewards can (a) lead learners to become dependent on short-term rewards, (b) coax them into a habit of looking to teachers and others for their only rewards, and therefore (c) forestall the development of their own internally administered, intrinsic system of rewards.

Considering all sides of the reward principle, the following constructive classroom implications may be drawn:

(1) Provide an optimal degree of immediate verbal praise and encouragement to students as a form of short-term reward (just enough to keep students confident in their ability but not so much that your praise simply becomes so much verbal gush).

(2) Encourage students to reward each other with compliments and supportive action.

(3) In classes with very low motivation, short-term reminders of progress may help students to perceive their development. Gold stars and stickers (especially for young learners), issuing certain "privileges" for good work, and progress charts and graphs may spark some interest.

(4) Display enthusiasm and excitement yourself in the classroom. If you are dull, lifeless, bored, and have low energy, you can be almost sure that it will be contagious.

(5) Try to get learners to see the long-term rewards in learning English by pointing out such things as what they can do with English where they live and around the world, the prestige in being able to use English, the academic benefits of knowing English, jobs that require English, etc.

4. The Intrinsic Motivation Principle

This principle is elaborated upon in detail in the next chapter as an example of how certain complex principles underlie a surprising number of our teaching practices. Simply stated, the intrinsic motivation principle is:

> **The most powerful rewards are those that are intrinsically motivated within the learner. Because the behavior stems from needs, wants, or desires within oneself, the behavior itself is self-rewarding; therefore, no externally administered reward is necessary at all.**

If all learners were intrinsically motivated to perform all classroom tasks, we might not even need teachers! But you can perform a great service to learners and to the overall learning process by first considering carefully what the intrinsic motives of your students are and then by designing classroom tasks that feed into those intrinsic drives. Classroom techniques have a much greater chance for success if they are self-rewarding in the perception of the learner: The learners perform the task because it is fun, interesting, useful, or challenging, and not because they anticipate some cognitive or affective rewards from the teacher.

The next chapter deals extensively with intrinsic motivation and its classroom applications.

5. Strategic Investment

A few decades ago, the language teaching profession largely concerned itself with the "delivery" of language to the student: Teaching methods, textbooks, or even grammatical paradigms were cited as the primary factors in successful learning. In more recent years, in the light of many studies of successful and unsuccessful learners, language teachers are focusing more intently on the role of the **learner** in the process. The "methods" that the learner employs to internalize and to perform in the language are as important as the teacher's methods—or more so. I call this the Principle of Strategic Investment:

> **Successful mastery of the second language will be due to a large extent to a learner's own personal "investment" of time, effort, and attention to the second language in the form of an individualized battery of strategies for comprehending and producing the language.**

This principle is laid out in full detail in Chapter 12 of this book, where practical classroom applications are made. For the time being, however, ponder two major pedagogical implications of the principle: (1) the importance of recognizing and dealing with the wide variety of styles and strategies that learners successfully bring to the learning process, and, therefore, (2) the need for attention to each separate individual in the classroom.

As research on successful language learners has dramatically shown, the variation among learners poses a thorny pedagogical dilemma. Learning **styles** alone signal numerous learner preferences that a teacher needs to attend to (see *PLLT*, Chapter 5). For example, visual vs. auditory preference and individual vs. group work preference are highly significant factors in a classroom. In a related strain of research, we are finding that learners also employ a multiplicity of **strategies** for sending and receiving language and that one learner's strategies for success may differ markedly from another's.

A **variety** of techniques in your lessons will at least partially ensure that a maximum number of students will be "reached." So you would want a mixture of group work and individual work, of visual and auditory techniques, of easy and difficult exercises. Beware, however, of variety at the expense of techniques that you know are essential for the learner! If, for example, you know that three-quarters of your class prefer individual work, that should not dictate the proportion of time you devote to activities that involve silent work at their desks. They may need to be nudged, if not pushed, into more face-to-face communicative activities than their preferences would indicate.

A teacher's greatest dilemma is how to attend to each individual student in a class while still reaching the class as a whole group. In relatively large classes of 30 to 50 students, **individual attention** becomes increasingly difficult; in "extra large" classes[1] it is virtually impossible. The principle of strategic investment nevertheless is a reminder to provide as much attention as you can to each individual student. Chapters 10, 11, and 12 all address this issue to some extent.

Some aspects of the dilemma surrounding variation and the need for individualization can be solved through specific **learner strategy training**, the principal topic of Chapter 12. Meanwhile, simply as a "sneak preview" to that chapter, you might just consider the following questions as more grist for your teacher education mill:

---

[1]There are still far too many language classrooms around the world in which students number well over 50; 60 to 75 students is not uncommon. For years, I have tried to persuade administrators to lower those numbers and to understand that communicative acquisition of a language is almost impossible under such circumstances. Nevertheless, the reality of school budgets sometimes provides few alternatives. See Chapter 21 for some practical suggestions for dealing with large classes.

- Am I seizing whatever opportunity I can to let learners in on the "secrets" to develop and use strategies for learning and communication?
- Do my lessons and impromptu feedback adequately sensitize students to the wisdom of their taking responsibility for their own learning?
- What if my students don't want to put forth the effort of trying out some strategies?

Affective Principles

We now turn our attention to those principles that are more central to the emotional processing of human beings. Here, we look at feelings about self, about relationships in a community of learners, and about the emotional ties between language and culture.

6. Language Ego

The language ego principle can be summarized in a well-recognized claim:

> **As human beings learn to use a second language, they also develop a new mode of thinking, feeling, and acting—a second identity. The new "language ego," intertwined with the second language, can easily create within the learner a sense of fragility, a defensiveness, and a raising of inhibitions.**

The language ego principle might also be affectionately called the "warm fuzzy" principle: All second language learners need to be treated with affective tender loving care. Remember when you were first learning a second language and how you sometimes felt so silly, if not humiliated, when the lack of words or structure left you helpless in face-to-face communication? Otherwise highly intelligent adults can be reduced to babbling infants in a second language, and we teachers need to provide all the affective support that we possibly can.

Learners feel this fragility because the strategic arsenals of their native-language-based egos, which are normally well developed and resistant to attack, are suddenly—in the perception of the learner—obsolete. Now they must fend for their emotional selves with a paltry linguistic battery that leaves them with a feeling of total defenselessness.

How can you bring some relief to this situation? Contemplate the following possibilities:

(1) Overtly display a supportive attitude to your students. While some learners may feel quite stupid in this new language, remember that they are capable adults struggling with the acquisition of the most complex set of skills that any classroom has ever attempted to teach. Your "warm and fuzzy" patience and empathy need to be openly and clearly communicated, for fragile language egos have a way of misinterpreting intended input.

(2) On a more mechanical, lesson-planning level, your choice of techniques and sequences of techniques needs to be cognitively challenging but not overwhelming at an affective level.

(3) Considering learners' language ego states will probably help you to determine:

- who to call on
- who to ask to volunteer information
- when to correct a student's speech error
- how much to explain something
- how structured and planned an activity should be
- who to place in which small groups or pairs
- how "tough" you can be with a student

(4) If your students are learning. English as a second language (in the cultural milieu of an English-speaking country), then they are likely to experience a moderate identity crisis as they develop a "second self." Help such students to understand that the confusion if not depression of developing that second self in the second culture is a normal and natural process (see *PLLT*, Chapter 7). Patience and understanding on your part will also ease the process.

7. Self-confidence

Another way of phrasing this one is the "I can do it!" principle, or the self-esteem principle (see *PLLT*, Chapter 6, on self-esteem). At the heart of all learning is the condition that a person believes in his or her own ability to accomplish the task. While self-confidence can be linked to the language ego principle above, it goes a step further in emphasizing the importance of the learner's self-assessment, regardless of the degree of language ego involvement. Simply put, we are talking about:

> The eventual success that learners attain in a task is at least partially a factor of their belief that they indeed are fully capable of accomplishing the task.

Some immediate classroom applications of this principle emerge:

(1) Give ample verbal and non-verbal assurances to students. It helps a student to hear a teacher affirm a belief in the student's ability. Energy that the learner would otherwise direct at avoidance or at erecting emotional walls of defense is thereby released to tackle the matter at hand.

(2) Sequence techniques from easier to more difficult. As a teacher you are called on to sustain self-confidence where it already exists and to build it where it doesn't. Your activities in the classroom would therefore logically start with simpler techniques and simpler concepts. Students then can establish a sense of accomplishment that catapults them to the next, more difficult, step. In the lesson described in Chapter 1, the culminating activity (items [27]-[29]) would have been too overwhelming for most students, even if they had "known" the grammatical material, if it had occurred toward the beginning of class.

8. Risk-taking

A third affective principle interrelated with the last two principles is the importance of getting learners to take calculated risks in attempting to use language—both productively and receptively. The previous two principles, if satisfied, lay the groundwork for risk-taking. If learners recognize their own ego fragility and develop the firm belief that, yes, they can indeed do it, then they are ready to take those necessary risks. They are ready to try out their newly acquired language, to use it for meaningful purposes, to ask questions, and to assert themselves.

> **Successful language learners, in their realistic appraisal of themselves as vulnerable beings yet capable of accomplishing tasks, must be willing to become "gamblers" in the game of language, to attempt to produce and to interpret language that is a bit beyond their absolute certainty.**

This principle strikes at the heart of educational philosophy. Many instructional contexts around the world do not encourage risk-taking; instead they encourage correctness, right answers, and withholding "guesses" until one is sure to be correct. Most educational research shows the opposite to be more conducive to long-term retention and intrinsic motivation. How can your classrooms reflect the Principle of Risk-taking?

(1) Create an atmosphere in the classroom that encourages students to try out language, to venture a response, and not just to wait for someone else to volunteer language.

(2) Provide reasonable challenges in your techniques—make them neither too easy nor too hard.

(3) Help your students to understand what **calculated** risk-taking is lest some feel that they must blurt out any old response.

(4) Return students' risky attempts with positive affirmation, praising them for trying while at the same time warmly but firmly attending to their language.

9. The Language-Culture Connection

Language and culture are intricately intertwined. Anytime you successfully learn a language you will also learn something of the culture of the speakers and that language. One aspect of this principle focuses on the complex interconnection of language and culture:

> **Whenever you teach a language, you also teach a complex system of cultural customs, values, and ways of thinking, feeling, and acting.**

Classroom applications include carrying out the following:

(1) Discuss cross-cultural differences with your students, emphasizing that no culture is "better" than another, but that cross-cultural understanding is an important facet of learning a language.

(2) Include among your techniques certain activities or materials that illustrate the connection between language and culture.

(3) Teach your students the cultural connotations especially of sociolinguistic aspects of language.

(4) Screen your techniques for material that may be culturally offensive.

(5) Make explicit to your students what you may take for granted in your own culture.

A second aspect of the language-culture connection is the extent to which your students will themselves be affected by the process of **acculturation**, which will vary with the context and the goals of learning. In many second language learning contexts such as ESL in the USA, students are faced with the full-blown realities of adapting to life in a foreign country, complete with various emotions accompanying stages of acculturation (see Chapter 7 of *PLLT*). In such cases, then, acculturation, social distance, and psychological adjustment are factors to be dealt with. This aspect of the principle may be summed up in this way:

> **Especially in "second" language learning contexts, the success with which learners adapt to a new cultural milieu will affect their language acquisition success, and vice versa, in some possibly significant ways.**

From the perspective of the classroom teacher, this principle is similar to the language ego and self-confidence principles (see 6 and 7 above), and all the concomitant classroom implications apply here as well. An added dimension, however, lies in the interaction between culture learning and language learning. An opportunity is given to teachers to enhance, if not speed up, both developmental processes. Once students become aware that some of their depression or discouragement may stem from cultural sources, they can more squarely address their state of mind and emotion and do something about it.

In the classroom, you can:

(1) Help students to be aware of acculturation and its stages.

(2) Stress the importance of the second language as a powerful tool for adjustment in the new culture.

(3) Be especially sensitive to any students who appear to be depressed and do what you can to assist them.

Linguistic Principles

The last category of principles of language learning and teaching center on language itself and on how learners deal with these complex linguistic systems.

10. The Native Language Effect

It almost goes without saying that the native language of every learner is an extremely significant factor in the acquisition of a new language. Most of the time, we think of the native language as exercising an **interfering** effect on the target language, and indeed the most salient, observable effect does appear to be one of interference (see *PLLT*, Chapter 8). The majority of a learner's errors in producing the second language, especially in the beginning levels, stem from the learner's assumption that the target language operates like the native language.

But what we observe may, like an iceberg, only be part of the reality. The **facilitating** effects of the native language are surely as powerful in the process, or more so, even though they are less observable. When the native French speaker who is learning English says, "I am here since January," there is one salient native language effect, a verb tense error stemming from French. But who is to say that the learner's native French did not facilitate the production of that sentence's subject-verb-complement word order, the placement of the locative (here), the one-to-one grammatical correspondence of every other word in the sentence, rules governing prepositional phrases, and the cognate word (January)?

The principle of the native language effect stresses importance of that native system in the linguistic attempts of the second language learner:

> **The native language of learners will be a highly significant system on which learners will rely to predict the target language system. While that native system will exercise both facilitating and interfering effects on the production and comprehension of the new language, the interfering effects are likely to be the most salient.**

In dealing with the native language effect in the classroom, interference will most often be the focus of your feedback in the classroom. That's perfectly sound pedagogy. Learners' errors stand out like the tips of icebergs giving us salient signals of an underlying system at work. Errors are, in fact, windows to a learner's internalized understanding of the second language, and therefore they give us teachers something observable to react to. Their non-errors—the facilitating effects—certainly do not need to be treated. Don't try to fix something that isn't broken.

Some classroom suggestions stemming from the native language effect:

(1) Regard learners' errors as important windows to their underlying system and provide appropriate feedback on them (see Principle #11 and Chapter 15 for more information on feedback). Errors of native language interference may be repaired by acquainting the learner with the native language cause of the error.

(2) Ideally, every successful learner will hold on to the facilitating effects of the native language and discard the interference. Help your students to understand that not everything about their native language system will cause error.

(3) Thinking directly in the target language usually helps to minimize interference errors. Try to coax students into thinking directly in the second language and **not** resorting to translation as they comprehend and produce language. An occasional translation of a word or phrase here and there can actually be very helpful, especially for adults, but direct use of the second language will help to avoid the first language "crutch" syndrome.

11. Interlanguage

Just as children develop their native language in gradual, systematic stages, adults, too, manifest a systematic progression of acquisition of sounds and words and structures and discourse features (see *PLLT*, Chapter 8). The interlanguage principle tells us that:

> **Second language learners tend to go through a systematic or quasi-systematic developmental process as they progress to full competence in the target language. Successful interlanguage language development is partially a factor of utilizing feedback from others.**

While the interlanguage of second language learners **varies** considerably (see *PLLT*, Chapter 11, on variability) between systematic and unsystematic linguistic forms and underlying rules, nevertheless, one important concept for the teacher to bear in mind is that at least some of a learner's language may indeed be systematic. In other words, in the mind's eye of learners, a good deal of what they say or comprehend may be logically "correct" even though, from the standpoint of a native speaker's competence, such forms are incorrect. A learner who says, "Does John can sing?" may firmly believe it to be a correct grammatical utterance because of an internalized systematic rule that requires a pre-posed *do* auxiliary for English question formation.

Allowing learners to progress through such systematic stages of acquisition poses a delicate challenge to teachers. The collective experience of language teachers and a respectable stockpile of second language research (Doughty, 1991; Long, 1983, 1988) indicates that classroom instruction makes a significant difference in the speed and success with which learners proceed through interlanguage stages of development. This highlights the importance of the **feedback** that you give to learners in the classroom. In many settings (especially in EFL contexts where few opportunities arise outside the classroom to use the language communicatively) you are the **only** person they have real-live contact with who speaks English. All eyes (and ears) are indeed upon you as you are the authority on the English language, whether you like it or not. Such responsibility means that virtually everything you say and do will be noticed (except when they're not paying attention to you)!

Much has been written and spoken about the role of feedback in second language acquisition. In Vigil and Oller's (1976) seminal study (see *PLLT*, Chapter 8), teachers were reminded of an important distinction between **affective** and **cognitive** feedback. The former is the extent to which we value or encourage a student's attempt to communicate; the latter is the extent to which we indicate an understanding of the "message" itself. Teachers are engaged in a never-ending process of making sure that we provide sufficient positive affective feedback to students and at the same time give appropriate feedback to students about whether or not their actual language is clear and unambiguous. (See Chapter 15 for more on error feedback.)

How, then, do you know what kind of feedback to offer students? Are interlanguage errors simply to be tolerated as natural indications of systematic internalization of a language? These are important questions, which are to some extent answered in Chapter 15. For the moment, however, a number of general classroom implications deserve your attention:

(1) Try to distinguish between a student's systematic interlanguage errors (stemming from the native language or target language) and other errors; the former will probably have a logical source that the student can become aware of.

(2) Teachers need to exercise some tolerance for certain interlanguage forms that may arise out of a student's logical developmental process.

(3) Don't make a student feel stupid just because of an interlanguage error; quietly point out the logic of the erroneous form ("I can understand why you said, 'I go to the doctor yesterday,' but try to remember that in English we have to say the verb in the past tense. Okay?").

(4) Your classroom feedback to students should give them the message that mistakes are not "bad," rather that most mistakes are good indicators that innate language acquisition abilities are alive and well. Mistakes are often indicators of aspects of the new language that are still developing. Some mistakes in the classroom should be **treated** by you, but when you choose to treat them, do so with kindness and empathy so that the student will not feel thwarted in future attempts to speak.

(5) Try to get students to self-correct selected errors; the ability to self-correct may indicate readiness to regularly use that form correctly.

(6) In your feedback on students' linguistic output, make sure that you provide ample affective feedback—verbal or nonverbal—in order to encourage them to speak.

(7) As you make judicious selection of which errors to treat (see Chapter 15), make sure that your feedback doesn't thwart further student attempts to speak.

12. Communicative Competence

While communicative competence (CC) has come to convey a multiplicity of meanings depending on which teacher or researcher you consult, it is nevertheless a useful phrase to keep in your teacher's repertoire. In its skeletal form, CC consists of some combination of the following components (see *PLLT* , Chapter 9):

> Organizational competence (grammatical and discourse)
> Pragmatic competence (functional and sociolinguistic)
> Strategic competence
> Psychomotor skills

The array of studies on CC provides what is perhaps the most important linguistic principle of learning and teaching:

> **Given that communicative competence is the goal of a language classroom, then instruction needs to point toward all of its components: organizational, pragmatic, strategic, and psychomotor. Communicative goals are best achieved by giving due attention to language use and not just usage, to fluency and not just accuracy, to authentic language and contexts, and to students' eventual need to apply classroom learning to heretofore unrehearsed contexts in the real world.**

It is important to note that the CC principle still has a bit of a reactionist flavor: reacting to other paradigms that emphasized attention to grammatical forms, to "correct" language above all, to artificial, contrived language and techniques in the classroom, and to a finite repertoire of language forms and functions that might not have lent themselves to application in the world outside the classroom. But since most of our language teaching generalizations are, after all, at least partially conceived against the backdrop of previous practices, such a statement can nevertheless stand as a reasonably accurate statement of our current understanding of CC.

To attempt to list all of the applications of such a principle to the language classroom would be an exhaustive endeavor! Many such applications will become evident in Chapter 5 and in later chapters of this book. But for the sake of closure and simplicity, just consider the following six classroom teaching "rules" that might emerge:

(1) Remember that grammatical explanations or drills or exercises are just one part of a lesson or curriculum; give grammar some attention, but don't neglect the other important components of CC (e.g., functional, sociolinguistic, psychomotor, and strategic).

(2) Some of the pragmatic (functional and sociolinguistic) aspects of language are very subtle and therefore very difficult. Make sure your lessons aim to teach such subtlety.

(3) In your enthusiasm for teaching functional and sociolinguistic aspects of language, don't forget that the psychomotor skills (pronunciation) are an important component of both. Intonation alone conveys a great deal of pragmatic information.

(4) Make sure that your students have opportunities to gain some fluency in English without having to be overly wary of little mistakes all the time. They can work on errors at some other time.

(5) Try to keep every technique that you do as authentic as possible! Use language that students will actually encounter in the real world and provide genuine techniques for the actual conveyance of information of interest, not just rote techniques.

(6) Some day your students will no longer be in your classroom. Make sure you are preparing them to be independent learners and manipulators of language "out there."

※   ※   ※

The twelve principles that have just been reviewed comprise some of the major foundation stones for teaching practice. While they are not by any means exhaustive, they nevertheless can act for you as major theoretical insights on which your techniques and lessons and curricula can be based.

What I hope you have seen through this is the value of undergirding your teaching (and your teacher training process) with sound principles that help you to understand **why** you are **choosing** to do something in the classroom, what kinds of questions to ask yourself about what you are doing before the fact, how to monitor yourself while you are teaching, how to assess the effectiveness of what you did, after the fact, and then how to modify what you will do the next time around.

TOPICS FOR DISCUSSION, ACTION, AND RESEARCH

1. The twelve principles that have been summarized in this chapter are obviously all very important. If you were forced, to prioritize them, which **three** principles would you pick to be at the top of your list? Why? Share your thoughts with a partner and see if you can reach a consensus. Then, compare your top three with others in your class. You may discover how difficult it is to choose only three to be at the top of the list.

2. Are there any principles that were left out that you think should have been included? In a small group, pool your thoughts, describe any such principles, and justify their inclusion on such a list. Compare your group's conclusions with others.

3. At the end of Chapter 1, quite a number of questions were raised regarding the 30 comments about the ESL lesson that was described. (a) Divide up those 30 comments + questions into pairs, and determine which principles here justified the teacher's choice in each case. Then, (b) share your thoughts with other pairs.

4. In the same pairs (see #3 above), decide if any aspects of that lesson should have been altered and which principles support your alterations.

5. Write in your **own** words a sentence or two to describe each of the twelve principles cited here. Try doing this without looking back at the chapter, then compare your responses with a partner before referring back to the chapter.

6. Using these twelve principles as a backdrop, state—either orally or in writing—your own personal "theory" of second language learning and teaching.

FOR YOUR FURTHER READING

Brown, H. Douglas. 1991. "TESOL at twenty–five: What are the issues?" *TESOL Quarterly* 25(2), 245–260.

Major issues in the profession of teaching English as a second language are discussed: motivation, empowerment, English as an international language, content-centered education, whole language, task-based teaching, peace education, cooperative learning, and learner strategy training.

Larsen-Freeman, Diane and Long, Michael H. 1991. *An Introduction to Second Language Acquisition Research*. Longman.

This book provides a comprehensive survey of current research issues and findings in the field of second language acquisition (SLA). Topics include: research methodology, interlanguage, the role of input, factors contributing to learners' variable success, theories of SLA, and the effect of instruction on SLA.

McLaughlin, Barry. 1987. *Theories of Second Language Learning*. Edward Arnold.

Five major traditions in theories of language learning are outlined in detail here: Krashen's monitor model, interlanguage theory, linguistic universals, acculturation/pidginization theory, and cognitive theory. Critiques of each strand of theory are offered.

Chapter 3

Intrinsic Motivation in the Classroom

**For every complicated problem there is an answer
that is short, simple, and wrong.
— H.L. Mencken**

One of the more complicated problems of second language learning and teaching has been defining and applying the construct of **motivation** in the classroom. On the one hand it is an easy catchword that gives teachers a simple answer to the mysteries of language learning. "Motivation is the difference," I have heard people say, "between success and failure. If they're motivated, they'll learn, and if not, they won't." That simplification may hold some of the time. Why not all the time? Just what is motivation? Can it be acquired or is it just "there"? Can it be taught? Where does it come from? Are there different kinds of motivation? If you don't carefully face questions like these, you run the risk of passing off motivation as a short, simple answer to learner success when it is neither short nor simple. Ironically, it is indeed probably **right**, but only when its full complexity is recognized and applied appropriately in the language classroom.

In the previous chapter, the principle of intrinsic motivation was briefly defined and comments were given. In this chapter we will take a long, careful look at the the construct of motivation in general, then at intrinsic motivation in particular, and then at its classroom applications.

For quite some time research on motivation in the field of second language acquisition research was strongly influenced by Gardner and Lambert's (1972) and more recently Gardner's (1985) distinction between integrative and instrumental motivation (see *PLLT,* Chapter 6). Gardner claimed that an integrative orientation (desire to learn a language stemming from a positive affect toward a community of its speakers) is more strongly linked to success in learning a second language than an instrumental orientation (desire to learn a language in order to attain certain career, educational, or financial goals).

Perhaps because of its simplicity, the integrative-instrumental dichotomy tempted many to believe that it captures "everything you always wanted to know" about motivation. It is now clear (see Au, 1988; Crookes and Schmidt, 1992) that motivation is much too complex to be explained through one culturally related dichotomy, especially in the light of increasing numbers of people who are successfully learning "English as an International Language" (EIL), sometimes without any reference to a culture or community of English speakers.

It behooves us, then, to examine the more fundamental nature of motivation. By doing so, we can probe the issue more insightfully as teachers.

Defining Motivation

How would you define motivation? Let me offer the following "dictionary definition" drawn from a number of different sources:

Motivation is the extent to which you make choices about (a) goals to pursue and (b) the effort you will devote to that pursuit.

You can interpret this definition in varying ways, depending on the theory of human behavior you adopt. For the sake of simplicity, let us look at theories of motivation in terms of two opposing "camps." In one of these camps is a traditional view of motivation that accounts for human behavior through a behavioristic paradigm that stresses the importance of rewards and reinforcement. In the other camp are a number of cognitive psychological viewpoints that explain motivation through deeper, more unobservable phenomena. These two traditions are described below.

1. A Behavioristic Definition.

A behavioristic psychologist like Skinner or Watson would stress the role of **rewards** (and perhaps punishments) in motivating behavior. In Skinner's operant conditioning model, for example, human beings, like other living organisms, will pursue a goal because they perceive a reward for doing so. This reward serves to **reinforce** behavior: to cause it to persist. This tradition gave us what I might facetiously refer to as the "M&M theory" of behavior, derived from the now discarded practice of administering M&M candies to children for manifesting desired behavior.

A behaviorist would define motivation as "the anticipation of reinforcement." We do well to heed the credibility of such a definition. There is no question that a tremendous proportion of what we "do" is motivated by an anticipated reward. From eating to exercising to studying and even to altruistic acts of ministering to others, there is "something in it for me." The emotional overtones of the more intangible rewards must not be ignored. M&Ms, hugs, and laughter are all, at times, payoffs worth striving for.

Reinforcement theory is a powerful concept for the classroom. Learners, like the proverbial horse running after the carrot, pursue goals in order to receive externally administered rewards: praise, gold stars, grades, certificates, diplomas, scholarships, careers, financial independence, and ultimately, happiness.

2. Cognitive Definitions.

A number of cognitive psychological viewpoints offer quite a different perspective on motivation. While rewards are very much a part of the whole picture, the difference lies in the **sources** of motivation and in the power of **self-reward**. Three different theories illustrate this side of motivation.

A. Drive theory. Those who see human **drives** as fundamental to human behavior claim that motivation stems from basic innate drives. David Ausubel (1968) elaborated on six different drives:

- exploration
- manipulation
- activity
- stimulation
- knowledge
- ego enhancement

All of these drives act not so much as reinforcers, as in behavioristic theory, but as innate predispositions, compelling us, as it were, to probe the unknown, to control our environment, to be physically active, to be receptive to mental, emotional, or physical stimulation, to yearn for answers to questions, and to build our own self-esteem. Again it takes little imagination to see how motivation in the classroom is the fulfillment of these underlying drives.

B. Hierarchy of needs theory. One of the most widely cited theories of motivation comes from Abraham Maslow (1970) who, in the spirit of drive theory, elaborated further to describe a system of **needs** within each human being that propel us onward and upward to higher and higher attainment. Maslow's hierarchy is best viewed metaphorically as a pyramid of needs (see Fig. 3.1), progressing from the satisfaction of purely physical needs up through safety and communal needs, to needs of esteem, and finally to "self-actualization," a state of reaching your fullest potential.

Figure 3.1. Maslow's Hierarchy of Needs. (Maslow, 1970).

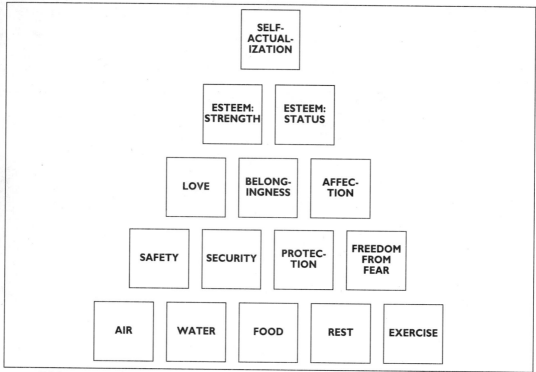

Of key importance here is that a person is not adequately energized to pursue some of the higher needs until the lower foundations of the pyramid have been satisfied. Therefore, a person who is hungry, cold, who has gotten little sleep, etc., has little motivation to see beyond those pressing physical discomforts to pursue anything higher. Likewise, needs for safety (comfort, routine, protection) and for feeling of belonging (in a group of classmates or friends) must be met in order for a person to devote full energy to the higher needs of academic attainment, achievement of recognition for successes, and to the ultimate peak of "being all that you can be."

Maslow's theory tells us that even what might be inappropriately viewed as rather ordinary classroom routines may in fact be important precursors to motivation for higher attainment. For an activity in the classroom to be considered motivating, then, it need not be something outstandingly striking, innovative, and inspirational. Even familiar classroom procedures—taking roll, checking homework, small-talk at the beginning of class, etc.—as they fulfill lower order needs can thus pave the way to meeting higher order needs.

C. Self-control theory. Certain cognitive psychologists (e.g., Hunt, 1965) center on the importance of people **deciding for themselves** what to think or feel or do. We define ourselves by making our own decisions, rather than by simply reacting to others. Motivation is highest when one can make one's own choices, whether they be in short-term or long-term contexts.

In the classroom, when learners have opportunities to make their own choices about what to pursue and what not to pursue, as in a cooperative learning context, they are fulfilling this need for autonomy. When learners get things shoved down their throats, motivation can wane, according to this branch of theory, because those learners have to yield to others' wishes and commands.

Dead Poets Society

A recent film, *Dead Poets Society*, was a classic illustration of the power of motivation in an oppressive educational institution. The boarding school, steeped in tradition and governed by intricate rules not only of behavior but of what was acceptable for a teacher to teach, provided all the impetus necessary for its young men to rebel and "seize the day"—to take every opportunity they could to fulfill their **own** needs rather than blindly submitting to the tyranny of the administration. Inspired by their literature teacher, the defiant members of the Dead Poets Society bonded together to soar well beyond their own expectations of what they could be and become.

A behavioristic theory of motivation would say that they were driven by the avoidance of aversive stimuli (punishments). However, more powerful and comprehensive explanations come from the cognitive theories of motivation:

- They were motivated by their innate drives to explore, to be stimulated, and above all to manipulate the authorities who enforced the rules.
- Their need for the security of a community of fellow human beings and to "seize the day" transcended threats of punishment.
- They needed to make their own decisions about what to learn and how to apply it rather than letting someone else determine the course of their daily lives.

Intrinsic and Extrinsic Motivation

These two traditions in motivation theory represent yet another dichotomy in our theories of language learning and teaching. The primary driving force among the members of the Dead Poets Society was an **intrinsic** set of motives within them and not the disdained **extrinsic** punishments that lay outside of them.

Edward Deci (1975:23) defined intrinsic motivation:

> **Intrinsically motivated activities are ones for which there is no apparent reward except the activity itself. People seem to engage in the activities for their own sake and not because they lead to an extrinsic reward. ...Intrinsically motivated behaviors are aimed at bringing about certain internally rewarding consequences, namely, feelings of <u>competence</u> and <u>self-determination</u>.**

Extrinsically motivated behaviors, on the other hand, are carried out in anticipation of a reward from outside and beyond the self. Typical extrinsic rewards are money, prizes, grades, and even certain types of positive feedback. Behaviors initiated solely to avoid punishment are also extrinsically motivated, even though, as in cases like the Dead Poets Society, numerous intrinsic benefits can ultimately accrue to those who, instead, view punishment avoidance as a challenge that can build their sense of competence and self-determination.

Which form of motivation is more powerful? The huge stockpile of research on motivation strongly favors intrinsic orientations, especially for long-term retention.

Jean Piaget and others would point out that human beings universally view incongruity, uncertainty, and "disequilibrium" as motivating. In other words, we seek out a reasonable challenge. Then we initiate behaviors intended to conquer the challenging situation. Incongruity is not itself motivating, but **optimal** incongruity—or what Krashen (1985) called "i+1"—presents enough of a possibility of being resolved that we will go after that resolution.

Maslow (1970) claimed that intrinsic motivation is clearly superior to extrinsic. According to his hierarchy of needs discussed above, we are ultimately motivated to achieve "self-actualization" once the basic physical, safety, and community needs are met. No matter what extrinsic rewards are present or absent, we will strive for self-esteem and fulfillment.

Jerome Bruner (1962), praising the "autonomy of self-reward," claimed that one of the most effective ways to help both children and adults to think and learn is to free them from the **control** of rewards and punishments. One of the principal weaknesses of extrinsically driven behavior is its addictive nature. Once captivated, as it were, by the lure of an immediate prize or praise, our dependency on those tangible rewards increases, even to the point that their withdrawal can then extinguish the desire to learn.

Now, you may be thinking, don't extrinsic rewards play a role in a learner's motivation? Wouldn't extrinsic rewards, coupled with intrinsic motivation, enhance the intrinsic? Not according to a surprising number of research studies. Two examples (Kohn 1990) illustrate:

(1) Subjects were asked to solve an intrinsically fascinating complex puzzle with no stated reward. Halfway through the process, the experimenter informed the subjects that there would be a monetary reward for solving the puzzle. From that point onward, intrinsic motivation (as measured by speed and correct steps toward a solution) waned.

(2) Teen-age girls were given the task of teaching some games to younger children. One group of "teachers" was simply given their task; the others were told that they would receive a reward (a free ticket to the movies) for successfully completing the teaching task. Results: The first group did their task faster, with more success, and reported greater pleasure in doing so than the second group!

Interestingly enough, the research shows one type of extrinsic reward that can indeed have an effect on intrinsic motivation: **positive** feedback that learners perceive as a boost to their feelings of competence and self-determination. No other externally administered set of rewards has a lasting effect. So, for example, sincerely delivered positive feedback in a classroom, seen by students as a validation of their own personal autonomy, critical thinking ability, and self-fulfillment, can increase or maintain intrinsic motivation.

Intrinsic motivation is of course not the only determiner of success for a language learner. Sometimes, no matter how much you want to accomplish something or how hard you try, you may not succeed for a host of other reasons. But if the learners in your classroom are given an opportunity to "do" language for their own personal reasons of achieving competence and autonomy, surely those learners will have a better chance of success than if they become dependent on external rewards for their motivation.

Intrinsic Motivation in Education

Educators like Maria Montessori, Rudolf Steiner, Paolo Freire, A.S. Neill, and Carl Rogers have all provided exemplary models of intrinsically motivated education. Traditionally, elementary and secondary schools are fraught with **extrinsically** motivated behavior. The school curriculum is dictated by institutions (sometimes politically influenced) that can be far removed from even the teacher's choice. Parents' and society's values and wishes are virtually forced onto pupils, whether they like it or not. Tests and exams, many of which are standardized and given high credence in the world "out there," are imposed on students with no consultation of the students themselves. The glorification of content, product, correctness, and competitiveness has failed to bring the learner into a collaborative process of competence building.

The consequence of such extrinsic motivators is that schools all too often teach students to play the "game" of pleasing teachers and authorities rather than developing an internalized thirst for knowledge and experience. The administration of grades and praises for being a "good child" build a dependency on immediate "M&M" gratification. Competition **against** classmates (who might otherwise be allies or partners in learning) ensues. If a communal bond is created, it runs the risk of being motivated by the need to band together **against** teachers and authorities, as in *Dead Poets Society*. Over the long haul, such dependency focuses students too exclusively on the material or monetary rewards of an education rather than instilling an appreciation for creativity and for satisfying some of the more basic drives for knowledge and exploration. Ultimately, the product of this system is a person who has been taught to fear failure above all and therefore to refrain from potentially rewarding risk-taking or innovative behavior.

Table 3.1. From Extrinsic to Intrinsic Motivation in Educational Institutions.

EXTRINSIC PRESSURES	INTRINSIC INNOVATIONS	MOTIVATIONAL RESULTS
SCHOOL CURRICULUM	learner centered personal goal setting individualization	SELF-ESTEEM SELF-ACTUALIZATION DECIDE FOR SELF
PARENTAL EXPECTATIONS	family values	LOVE, INTIMACY, ACCEPTANCE, RESPECT FOR WISDOM
SOCIETY'S EXPECTATIONS (conformity)	security of comfortable routines task-based teaching	COMMUNITY, BELONGING, IDENTITY, HARMONY, SECURITY
TESTS & EXAMS	peer evaluation, self-diagnosis level-check exercises	EXPERIENCE SELF-KNOWLEDGE
IMMEDIATE GRATIFICATION ("M & Ms")	long-term goals the big picture "things take time"	SELF-ACTUALIZATION
MAKE MONEY!	content-based teaching, ESP vocational education workplace ESL	COOPERATION HARMONY
COMPETITION	cooperative learning group work the class is a team	MANIPULATION, STRENGTH, STATUS, SECURITY
NEVER FAIL!	risk-taking, innovation creativity	LEARN FROM MISTAKES NOBODY'S PERFECT "C'EST LA VIE"

A bleak picture? Too harsh? Of course, there are many happy exceptions to such a depiction, but you don't have to look very far in any corner of the world to find major elements of the picture holding true. The question is: Can something be done to turn such a picture upside down? Or, more specifically to your quest, can your English classroom become a place where these extrinsic elements are diverted into a more positive direction? Or, better yet, can such elements be avoided entirely?

Table 3.1 depicts what can happen in an institution that takes all eight of the extrinsic elements and, while accepting their reality in virtually any society or educational institution, turns those elements in an intrinsically oriented direction. The notion here is that an intrinsically oriented school can begin to transform itself into a more positive, affirming environment not so much by revolutionizing society (which takes decades if not centuries) but by shifting its view of the student.

A school curriculum that comes from "the administration" can be modified to some extent to include student-centered learning and teaching, to allow students to set some—not all, perhaps—of their own learning goals, and to individualize lessons and activities as much as possible. The result: higher student self-esteem, greater chances for self-actualization, more deciding for oneself.

Expectations of parents and other authority figures are a reality that we cannot simply dissolve by waving a magic wand. But teachers can help to convert the perception of those expectations into a sense of the positive effect of the immediate family on a student and of the importance of tradition, not because it has been forced on them, but because its intrinsic worth is perceived. The result: an appreciation of love, intimacy, and respect for the wisdom of age.

In turn, society's expectations may, through a process of education and counseling, be seen as a means for providing comfortable routines (time schedules, customs, mores). Class discussions can focus on a critical evaluation of society so that students aren't forced to accept some way of thinking or acting but are coaxed into examining both sides of the issue. The result is a sense of belonging, a sense of the value of the wider community, of harmony.

Tests and exams can incorporate some student consultation (see Chapter 19) and peer evaluation. Teachers can help students to view tests as feedback instruments for self-diagnosis and not simply for comparing one's performance against a norm. Students thus become motivated by the experience and by achieving self-knowledge.

The otherwise extrinsic values that are given in Table 3.1. (immediate gratification, material rewards, competition, and fear of failure) can also be redirected through:

- emphasizing the "big" picture—larger perspectives
- letting students set long-term goals
- allowing sufficient time for learning
- cooperative learning activities
- group work
- viewing the class as a team
- content-centered teaching
- English for specific (vocational/professional) purposes
- English in the workplace
- allowing risk-taking behavior
- rewarding innovation and creativity

Such activities and attitudes on your part appeal to the deeper causes of motivation. They get at needs and drives, at self-control, at a balanced, realistic perception of self, and even at the simple joy of learning for its own sake!

Intrinsic Motivation in the Second Language Classroom

Turning to the role of intrinsic motivation in second language classrooms in particular, consider a few activities that capitalize on the intrinsic by appealing to learners' self-determination and autonomy:

- teaching writing as a thinking process in which learners develop their own ideas freely and openly
- showing learners strategies of reading that enable them to bring their own information **to** the written word
- language experience approaches in which students create their own reading material for others in the class to read
- oral fluency exercises in which learners talk about what interests them and not about a teacher-assigned topic
- listening to an academic lecture in one's own field of study for specific information that will fill a gap for the learner
- communicative language teaching, in which language is taught to enable learners to accomplish certain specific functions
- even grammatical explanations, if learners see their potential for increasing their autonomy in a second language

Actually, **every** technique in your language classroom can be subjected to an intrinsic motivation "litmus test" to determine the extent to which they adhere to this powerful principle. Consider the check list on the next page,

---

INTRINSICALLY MOTIVATING TECHNIQUES: A CHECK LIST

1. Does the technique appeal to the genuine interests of your students? Is it relevant to their lives?

2. Do you present the technique in a positive, enthusiastic manner?

3. Are students clearly aware of the purpose of the technique?

4. Do students have some choice in:
   (a) choosing some aspect of the technique?
   (b) determining how they go about fulfilling the goals of the technique?

5. Does the technique encourage students to discover for themselves certain principles or rules (rather than simply being "told")?

6. Does it encourage students in some way to develop or use effective strategies of learning and communication?

7. Does it contribute — at least to some extent — to students' ultimate autonomy and independence (from you)?

8. Does it foster cooperative negotiation with other students in the class? Is it a truly interactive technique?

9. Does the technique present a "reasonable challenge"?

10. Do students receive sufficient feedback on their performance (from each other or from you)?

---

the answers to which should tell you whether something you're doing in the classroom is contributing to your students' intrinsic drives.

Throughout the rest of this book, you will be reminded of the importance of the principle of intrinsic motivation in achieving your goals as a teacher. Think of yourself not so much as a teacher who must constantly "deliver" information to your students, but more as a **facilitator of learning** whose job it is to set the stage for learning, to start the wheels turning inside the heads of your students, to turn them on to their own abilities, and to help channel those abilities in fruitful directions.

Finally, the following six general guidelines should help you to infuse your ESL classroom with some intrinsically motivating dynamics:

(1) Teachers are enablers, not rewarders. Therefore, when you teach, focus less on how to administer immediate or tangible rewards and more on how to get students to tune in to their potential and to be challenged by self-determined goals.

(2) Learners need to develop autonomy, not dependence. Therefore, be careful not to let learners become dependent on your daily praise and other feedback. Rather, administer praise selectively and judiciously, helping students to recognize their own self-satisfaction in having done something well.

(3) Help learners to take charge of their own learning through setting some personal goals and utilizing learning strategies.

(4) Learner-centered, cooperative teaching is intrinsically motivating. Therefore, give students opportunities to make choices in activities, topics, discussions, etc. Sometimes a simple "either/or" choice ("Okay, class, for the next ten minutes we can either do this little cloze test or review for the test. Which do you want to do?") helps students to develop intrinsic motives. They feel less like puppets on a string if you can involve them in various aspects of looking at their needs and self-diagnosing to some extent, of planning lessons and objectives, of deciding which direction a lesson might go in, and of evaluating their learning.

(5) Content-based activities and courses are intrinsically motivating. Therefore, you might strive to focus your students on interesting, relevant subject-matter content that gets them linguistically involved with meanings and purposes and less so with verbs and prepositions.

(6) Tests, with some special attention from the teacher, can be intrinsically motivating. Allowing some student input to the test, giving well-thought-out classroom tests that are face-valid in the eyes of students, giving narrative evaluations, are just some of the topics covered in Chapter 19, on how your tests can contribute to intrinsic motivation.

✳   ✳   ✳

All of the above enthusiasm for intrinsic motivation shouldn't lure you into thinking that we now have a catch-all concept that will explain everything about learning and teaching. Clearly there are other factors affecting learning outcomes: native ability, age, context of learning, style preferences, background experience and qualifications, availability of time to give the effort needed, the quality of input that is beyond the immediate control of the learner. And clearly you will be able to use a combination of extrinsic (for more immediate concerns, for extremely low motivational contexts) and intrinsic motives to your advantage in the classroom; there is indeed a place—and a very soundly supportable place—for extrinsic motives in the language classroom.

But when all these factors are duly considered, the students' long-term goals, their deepest level of feeling and thinking, and their global assessment of their potential to be self-actualized is much, much better served by promoting intrinsic motives. Your task is to maintain these intrinsically motivating orientations on an underlying plane of awareness in your mind whenever and wherever learners are placed under your tutelage.

TOPICS FOR DISCUSSION, ACTION, AND RESEARCH

1. This chapter has provided background information, research, and classroom applications of one of the twelve principles named in Chapter 2. Now, as a limited research project, pick one of the other eleven principles and (a) do some library research (you might begin by looking through *PLLT*) to find sources on the topic and (b) draw some further practical implications for teaching. Write or orally present your report. This could be done as a collaborative project in pairs.

2. Look back once again at the ESL lesson described in Chapter 1. Make a list of aspects of that lesson that appeal to the principle of intrinsic motivation. Share your list with a partner and talk about how the lesson could have been improved by a stronger application of the principle.

3. Review Gardner's concept of integrative and instrumental motivation (see *PLLT,* Chapter 6). Explain how both of his types of motivation could actually be intrinsic **and** extrinsic. If there is no specific "community of speakers" of a language for a learner to identify (as in certain cases of English as an International Language), is it possible to be integratively oriented?

4. Look again at the six drives claimed by Ausubel to underlie human motivation. With a partner, describe classroom examples or illustrations of how each of the six drives might be fulfilled.

5. Maslow's pyramid of needs is a well-known model of motivation. With your partner, come up with some further example—beyond those already cited—of how certain "ordinary classroom routines may in fact be important precursors to motivation for higher attainment" (page 36). At what point do these ordinary routines become dull, boring, or ineffective?

6. What do the three cognitive definitions of motivation have in common?

7. In some ways, traditional, largely extrinsically inspired educational systems were harshly criticized here. Is that criticism justified? In a small group or with the rest of the class, share some examples from your own experience where extrinsically oriented practices prevailed. What did you do to survive in that atmosphere? How can your survival techniques be turned around to inspire you in your teaching?

8. Think of some counter-examples, in your experience, to the "bleak picture" of traditional education—that is, positive, intrinsically rewarding experiences in your own school experiences. Share them with a partner and analyze their high points and drawbacks.

9. If time and facilities permit, design a simple classroom experiment in intrinsic motivation, perhaps following the model of the two little studies summarized on page 39. Since motivation can't be observed, it must be inferred. Therefore, be as specific as possible in determining how you will measure intrinsic motivation. (For some background on such a study, look at Deci [1975].)

10. Look at the list of ten criteria for determining whether a technique is intrinsically motivating (page 43). As a whole class, brainstorm for a minute to come up with, say, the ten most commonly used techniques in language classrooms that you have observed recently. Then, in pairs or small groups, subject one or two of those techniques to a rigorous examination in terms of the ten criteria. What was the "report card" for each technique? Report your findings to the rest of the class.

FOR YOUR FURTHER READING

Rogers, Carl. 1983. *Freedom to Learn in the Eighties.* Charles E. Merrill Publishing Company.

Carl Rogers puts together a very practical set of essays here, all focusing on an educational model that encourages cooperative learning, collaboration between teachers and learners, discovery learning, and intrinsic motivation.

Deci, Edward L. 1975. *Intrinsic Motivation.* Plenum Press.

Edward Deci is one of the principal players in a long list of those who have conducted research on intrinsic motivation. This book, though somewhat dated, is nevertheless surprisingly applicable to current teaching practice. It explains the construct in full detail and describes supporting research.

Crookes, Graham, and Schmidt, Richard W. 1991. "Motivation: Reopening the Research Agenda." *Language Learning 41*(4), 469-512.

The authors provide a comprehensive overview of research on motivation both in general and specifically on second language acquisition.

Chapter 4

A "Methodical" History of Language Teaching

We have so far looked closely at an actual ESL class, considered twelve major principles that enlighten our teaching practices, and carefully examined one of the most powerful principles of learning and teaching. With that backdrop of classroom observation and of principled applications, you can more insightfully approach a number of questions about this language teaching profession in general. In this chapter we focus on methods as the identifying characteristics of the past century of "modern" language teaching efforts. What do we mean by the term **method** by which we tend to characterize that history? How do methods reflect various trends of disciplinary thought? How do the twelve principles of language learning and teaching help us to distinguish, in our history, between passing fads and "the good stuff"? These are some of the questions we will address in this chapter.

In the next chapter, this historical overview is culminated in a close look at the current state of the art in language teaching. Above all, you will come to see how our profession is now more aptly characterized by a unified, comprehensive **approach** rather than by competing, restricted methods. That general approach will be described in detail, along with some of the current professional jargon associated with it.

Approach, Method, Technique

In the century spanning the mid 1880s to the mid 1980s, the language teaching profession was involved in a search. That search was for what has popularly been called "methods," or ideally, a single method, generalizable across widely varying audiences, that would successfully teach students a foreign language in the classroom. Historical accounts of the profession tend therefore to describe a succession of methods each of which is more or less discarded in due course of time as a new method takes its place. We will turn to that "methodical" history of language teaching in a moment, but first, we should try to understand what we mean by method.

What is a method? Three decades ago Edward Anthony (1963) gave us a definition that has quite admirably withstood the test of time. His concept of method was the second of three hierarchical elements, namely, approach, method, and technique. An **approach**, according to Anthony, is a set of assumptions dealing with the nature of language, learning, and teaching. **Method** is an overall plan for systematic presentation of language based upon a selected approach. **Techniques** are the specific activities manifested in the classroom that are consistent with a method and therefore in harmony with an approach as well.

To this day, for better or worse, Anthony's terms are still in common use among language teachers. A teacher may, for example, at the approach level, affirm the ultimate importance of learning in a relaxed state of mental aware-ness just above the threshold of consciousness. The method that follows might resemble, say, Suggestopedia (a description follows in this chapter). Techniques could include playing Baroque music while reading a passage in the foreign language, getting students to sit in the yoga position while listen-ing to a list of words, learners adopting a new name in the classroom, or role-playing that new person.

A couple of decades later, Jack Richards and Theodore Rodgers (1982, 1986) proposed a reformulation of the concept of method. Anthony's approach, method, and technique were renamed, respectively, **approach, design,** and **procedure**, with a superordinate term to describe this three-step process now called **method**. A method, according to Richards and Rodgers, "is an umbrella term for the specification and interrelation of theory and practice." (1982:154) An approach defines assumptions, beliefs, and theories about the nature of language and language learning. Designs specify the rela-tionship of those theories to classroom materials and activities. Procedures are the techniques and practices that are derived from one's approach and design.

Through their reformulation, Richards and Rodgers made two principal contributions to our understanding of the concept of method:

(1) First, they specified the necessary elements of language teaching "designs" that had heretofore been left somewhat vague. Their schematic representation of "method" (see Fig. 4.1) reveals six important features of "designs": objectives, syllabus (criteria for selection and organization of linguistic and subject/matter content), activities, learner roles, teacher roles, and the role of instructional materials. The latter three features have occupied a significant proportion of our collective attention in the profession for the last decade or so. Already in this book you may have noted how, for example, learner roles (styles, individual preferences for group or individual learning, student input in determining curricular content, etc.) are important considerations in your teaching.

(2) Second, Richards and Rodgers nudged us into at last relinquishing the notion that separate, definable, discrete methods are the essential building blocks of **methodology**. By helping us to think in terms of an approach that undergirds our language designs (curricula), which are realized by various procedures (techniques), we could see that methods, as we still use and understand the term, are too restrictive, too pre-programmed, and too "pre-packaged." Virtually all language teaching methods make the oversimplified assumption that what teachers "do" in the classroom can be conventionalized into a set of procedures that fits all contexts. We are now all too aware that such is clearly not the case.

As we shall see in the next chapter, the whole concept of separate methods is no longer a central issue in language teaching practice. Instead, we currently make ample reference to "methodology" as our superordinate umbrella term, reserving the term "method" for somewhat specific, identifiable clusters of theoretically compatible classroom techniques.

So, Richards and Rodgers' reformulation of the concept of method was soundly conceived; however, their attempt to give new meaning to an old term has not caught on in the pedagogical literature. What they would like us to call "method" is more comfortably referred to, I think, as "methodology," in order to avoid confusion with what we will no doubt always think of as those separate entities (like Audiolingual or Suggestopedia) that are no longer at the center of our teaching philosophy.

Another terminological problem lies in the use of the term "designs"; instead, we more comfortably refer to curricula or syllabuses when we refer to design features of a language program.

Figure 4.1. Elements and Subelements of Method (Richards and Rodgers, 1986).

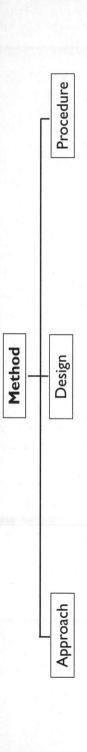

Method

Approach — **Design** — **Procedure**

Approach

a. A theory of native language
—an account of the nature of language proficiency
—an account of the basic units of language structure

b. A theory of the nature of language learning
—an account of the psycho-linguistic and cognitive processes involved in language learning
—an account of the conditions that allow for successful use of these processes

Design

a. The general and specific objectives of the method

b. A syllabus model
—criteria for the selection and organization of linguistic and/or subject-matter content

c. Types of learning and teaching activities
—kinds of tasks and practice activities to be employed in the classroom and in materials

d. Learner roles
—types of learning tasks set for learners
—degree of control learners have over the content of learning
—patterns of learner groupings that are recommended or implied
—degree to which learners influence the learning of others
—the view of the learner as processor, performer, initiator, problem solver, etc.

e. Teacher roles
—types of functions teachers fulfill
—degree of teacher influence over learning
—degree to which teacher determines the content of learning
—types of interaction between teachers and learners

f. The role of instructional materials
—primary function of materials
—the form materials take (e.g. textbook, audio visual)
—relation of materials to other input
—assumptions made about teachers and other learners

Procedure

a. Classroom techniques, practices, and behaviors observed when the method is used
—resources in terms of time, space, and equipment used by the teacher
—interactional pattern observed in lessons
—tactics and strategies used by teachers and learners when the method is being used

What are we left with in this lexicographic confusion? Interestingly, the terminology of the pedagogical literature in the field appears to be more in line with Anthony's original terms, but with some important additions and refinements. Following is a set of definitions that reflect the current usage and that will be used in this book.

Methodology: The study of pedagogical practices in general (including theoretical underpinnings and related research). Whatever considerations are involved in "how to teach" are methodological.

Approach: Theoretical positions and beliefs about the nature of language, the nature of language learning, and the applicability of both to pedagogical settings.

Method: A generalized set of classroom specifications for accomplishing linguistic objectives. Methods tend to be primarily concerned with teacher and student roles and behaviors and secondarily with such features as linguistic and subject-matter objectives, sequencing, and materials. They are almost always thought of as being broadly applicable to a variety of audiences in a variety of contexts.

Curriculum/syllabus: Designs for carrying out a particular language program. Features include a primary concern with the specification of linguistic and subject-matter objectives, sequencing, and materials to meet the needs of a designated group of learners in a defined context. (The term "syllabus" is used more customarily in the United Kingdom to refer to what is called a "curriculum" in the United States.)

Technique (also commonly referred to by other terms):[1] Any of a wide variety of exercises, activities, or devices used in the language classroom for realizing lesson objectives.

Changing Winds and Shifting Sands

A glance through the past century or so of language teaching will give an interesting picture of how varied the interpretations have been of the best way to teach a foreign language. As disciplinary schools of thought—psychology, linguistics, education, for example—have come and gone, so have language teaching methods waxed and waned in popularity. Teaching methods, as "approaches in action," are of course the practical application of theoretical findings and positions. In a field such as ours that is relatively young, it

---

[1]There is currently quite an intermingling of such terms as technique, task, procedure, activity, and exercise, often used in somewhat careless free variation across the profession. Of these terms, **task** has received the most concerted attention recently, viewed by such scholars as David Nunan (1991) as incorporating specific communicative and pedagogical principles. Tasks, according to Nunan and others, should be thought of as a special kind of technique and, in fact, may actually include more than one technique. See Chapter 5 for a full explanation.

should come as no surprise to discover a wide variety of these applications, some in total philosophical opposition to others, over the last hundred years.

Albert Marckwardt (1972:5) saw these "changing winds and shifting sands" as a cyclical pattern in which a new method emerged about every quarter of a century. Each new method broke from the old but took with it some of the positive aspects of the previous practices. A good example of this cyclical nature of methods is found in the "revolutionary" Audiolingual method (ALM) (a description follows) of the mid-twentieth century. The ALM borrowed tenets from its predecessor by almost half a century, the Direct Method, while breaking away entirely from the Grammar Translation Method. Within a short time, however, ALM critics were advocating more attention to thinking, to cognition, and to rule learning, which to some smacked of a return to Grammar Translation!

What follows is a sketch of those changing winds and shifting sands of language teaching over the years.

The Grammar Translation Method

A historical sketch of the last hundred years of language teaching really must be set in the context of a prevailing, customary language teaching "tradition." For centuries, there were few if any theoretical foundations of language learning upon which to base teaching methodology. In the western world, "foreign" language learning in schools was synonymous with the learning of Latin or Greek. Latin, thought to promote intellectuality through "mental gymnastics," was until relatively recently held to be indispensable to an adequate higher education. Latin was taught by means of what has been called the **Classical Method**: focus on grammatical rules, memorization of vocabulary and of various declensions and conjugations, translations of texts, doing written exercises.

As other languages began to be taught in educational institutions in the eighteenth and nineteenth centuries, the Classical Method was adopted as the chief means for teaching foreign languages. Little thought was given at the time to teaching someone how to speak the language; after all, languages were not being taught primarily to learn oral/aural communication but to learn for the sake of being "scholarly" or, in some instances, for gaining a reading proficiency in a foreign language. Since there was little if any theoretical research on second language acquisition in general or on the acquisition of reading proficiency, foreign languages were taught as any other skill was taught.

In the nineteenth century the Classical Method came to be known as the **Grammar Translation** Method. There was little to distinguish Grammar Translation from what had gone on in foreign language classrooms for centuries beyond a focus on grammatical rules as the basis for translating from the second to the native language. Remarkably, the Grammar Translation Method withstood attempts at the turn of the twentieth century to "reform" language teaching methodology (see Gouin's Series Method and the Direct Method, below), and to this day it is practiced in some isolated, or, shall we say, unenlightened educational contexts. Prator and Celce-Murcia (1979:3) listed the major characteristics of Grammar Translation:

(1) Classes are taught in the mother tongue, with little active use of the target language.

(2) Much vocabulary is taught in the form of lists of isolated words.

(3) Long elaborate explanations of the intricacies of grammar are given.

(4) Grammar provides the rules for putting words together, and instruction often focuses on the form and inflection of words.

(5) Reading of difficult classical texts is begun early.

(6) Little attention is paid to the content of texts, which are treated as exercises in grammatical analysis.

(7) Often the only drills are exercises in translating disconnected sentences from the target language into the mother tongue.

(8) Little or no attention is given to pronunciation.

It is ironic that this method has until very recently been so stalwart among many competing models. It does virtually nothing to enhance a student's communicative ability in the language. It is "remembered with distaste by thousands of school learners, for whom foreign learning meant a tedious experience of memorizing endless lists of unusable grammar rules and vocabulary and attempting to produce perfect translations of stilted or literary prose" (Richards and Rodgers, 1986:4).

On the other hand, one can understand why Grammar Translation is so popular. It requires few specialized skills on the part of teachers. Tests of grammar rules and of translations are easy to construct and can be objectively scored. Many standardized tests of foreign languages still do not attempt to tap into communicative abilities, so students have little motivation to go beyond grammar analogies, translations, and rote exercises. And it is sometimes successful in leading a student toward a *reading* knowledge of a second language. But, as Richards and Rodgers (1986:5) point out, "it has no advocates. It is a method for which there is no theory. There is no literature that offers a rationale or justification for it or that attempts to relate it to issues in linguistics, psychology, or educational theory." As you continue to examine language teaching methodology in this book, I think you will understand more fully the "theory-lessness" of the Grammar Translation Method.

Gouin and the Series Method

As we begin our look now at the history of "modern" foreign language teaching, beginning in the late 1800s, we look in on François Gouin, a French teacher of Latin whose insights and writings were truly remarkable. History doesn't normally think of Gouin as a founder of language teaching methodology because at the time his influence was overshadowed by that of Charles Berlitz, the popular German founder of the Direct Method. Nevertheless, some attention to Gouin's unusually perceptive observations about language teaching helps us to set the stage for the development of language teaching methods for the century following the publication of his book, *The Art of Learning and Studying Foreign Languages*, in 1880.

Gouin had to go through a very painful set of experiences in order to derive his insights. Having decided in his mid-life to learn German, he took up residency in Hamburg for one year. But rather than attempting to converse with the natives, he engaged in a rather bizarre sequence of attempts to "master" the language. Upon arrival in Hamburg he felt he should *memorize* a German grammar book and a table of the 248 irregular German verbs! He did this in a matter of only ten days, and hurried to "the academy" (the university) to test his new knowledge. "But alas!" he wrote, "I could not understand a single word, not a single word!" Gouin was undaunted. He returned to the isolation of his room, this time to memorize the German roots and to re-memorize the grammar book and irregular verbs. Again he emerged with expectations of success. "But alas!" The result was the same as before. In the course of the year in Germany, Gouin memorized books, translated Goethe and Schiller, and even memorized 30,000 words in a German dictionary, all in the isolation of his room, only to be crushed by his failure to understand German afterwards. Only once did he try to "make conversation" as a method, but this caused people to laugh at him and he was too embarrassed to continue that method. At the end of the year Gouin, having reduced the classical method to absurdity, was forced to return home, a failure.

But there is a happy ending. Upon returning home Gouin discovered that his three-year-old nephew had, during that year, gone through that wonderful stage of child language acquisition in which he went from saying virtually nothing at all to become a veritable chatterbox of French. How was it that this little child succeeded so easily, in a first language, in a task that Gouin, in a second language, had found impossible? The child must hold the secret to learning a language! So Gouin spent a great deal of time observing his nephew and other children and came to the following conclusions: Language learning is primarily a matter of transforming perceptions into conceptions. Children use language to represent their conceptions. Language is a means of thinking, of representing the world to oneself. (These insights, remember, are being formed by a language teacher over a century ago!)

So Gouin set about devising a teaching method that would follow from these insights. And thus the Series Method was created, a method that taught learners *directly* (without translation) and conceptually (without grammatical rules and explanations) a "series" of connected sentences that are easy to perceive. The first lesson of a foreign language would thus teach the following series of fifteen sentences:

I walk towards the door. I draw near to the door. I draw nearer to the door. I get to the door. I stop at the door.

I stretch out my arm. I take hold of the handle. I turn the handle. I open the door. I pull the door.

The door moves. The door turns on its hinges. The door turns and turns. I open the door wide. I let go of the handle.

The fifteen sentences have an unconventionally large number of grammatical properties, vocabulary items, word orders, and complexity. This is no simple "Voici la table" lesson! Yet Gouin was successful with such lessons because the language was so easily understood, stored, recalled, and related to reality. Unfortunately, he was a man ahead of his time, and his insights were largely lost in the shuffle of Berlitz's popular Direct Method. But as we look back now over a century of language teaching history we can appreciate the insights of this most unusual language teacher.

The Direct Method

The "naturalistic"—simulating the "natural" way in which children learn first languages—approaches of Gouin and a few of his contemporaries did not take hold immediately. A generation later, applied linguistics finally established the credibility of such approaches. Thus it was that at the turn of the century the Direct Method became quite widely known and practiced.

The basic premise of the Direct Method was similar to that of Gouin's Series Method, namely, that second language learning should be more like first language learning—lots of oral interaction, spontaneous use of the language, no translation between first and second languages, and little or no analysis of grammatical rules. Richards and Rodgers (1986:9-10) summarize the principles of the Direct Method:

(1) Classroom instruction was conducted exclusively in the target language.

(2) Only everyday vocabulary and sentences were taught.

(3) Oral communication skills were built up in a carefully traded progression organized around question-and-answer exchanges between teachers and students in small, intensive classes.

(4) Grammar was taught inductively.

(5) New teaching points were taught through modeling and practice.

(6) Concrete vocabulary was taught through demonstration, objects, and pictures; abstract vocabulary was taught by association of ideas.

(7) Both speech and listening comprehension were taught.

(8) Correct pronunciation and grammar were emphasized.

The Direct Method enjoyed considerable popularity through the end of the nineteenth century and well into this one. It was most widely accepted in private language schools where students were highly motivated and where native-speaking teachers could be employed. One of the best known of its popularizers was Charles Berlitz (who never used the term Direct Method and chose instead to call his method the Berlitz Method). To this day "Berlitz" is a household word; Berlitz language schools are thriving in every country of the world.

But almost any "method" can succeed when clients are willing to pay high prices for small classes, individual attention, and intensive study. The Direct Method did not take well in public education where the constraints of budget, classroom size, time, and teacher background made such a method difficult to use. Moreover, the Direct Method was criticized for its weak theoretical foundations. Its success may have been more a factor of the skill and personality of the teacher than of the methodology itself.

By the end of the first quarter of this century the use of the Direct Method had declined both in Europe and in the United States. Most language curricula returned to the Grammar Translation Method (see below) or to a "reading approach" that emphasized reading skills in foreign languages. But interestingly enough, by the middle of the century the Direct Method was revived and redirected into what was probably the most visible of all language teaching "revolutions" in the modern era, the Audiolingual Method (see also below). So even this somewhat short-lived movement in language teaching would reappear in the changing winds and shifting sands of history

The Audiolingual Method

In the first half of this century, the Direct Method did not take hold in the United States the way it did in Europe. While one could easily find native-speaking teachers of modern foreign languages in Europe, such was not the case in the United States. Also, European high school and university students did not have to travel far to find opportunities to put the oral skills of another language to actual, practical use. Moreover, U.S. educational institutions had become firmly convinced that a reading approach to foreign languages was more useful than an oral approach, given the perceived linguistic isolation of the United States at the time. The highly influential Coleman Report of 1929 (Coleman, 1929) had persuaded foreign language teachers that it was impractical to teach oral skills, and that reading should become the focus. Thus schools returned in the 1930s and 1940s to Grammar Translation, "the handmaiden of reading" (Bowen et al, 1985).

Then World War II broke out and suddenly the United States was thrust into a worldwide conflict, heightening the need for Americans to become orally proficient in the languages of both their allies and their enemies. The time was ripe for a language teaching revolution. The U.S. military provided the impetus with funding for special, intensive language courses that focused on the aural/oral skills; these courses came to be known as the Army Specialized Training Program (ASTP) or, more colloquially, the "Army Method." Characteristic of these courses was a great deal of oral activity—pronunciation and pattern drills and conversation practice—with virtually none of the grammar and translation found in traditional classes. Ironically, numerous foundation stones of the discarded Direct Method were borrowed and injected into this new approach. Soon, the success of the Army Method and the revived national interest in foreign languages spurred educational institutions to adopt the new methodology. In all its variations and adaptations, the Army Method came to be known in the 1950s as the Audiolingual Method.

The Audiolingual Method (ALM) was firmly grounded in linguistic and psychological theory. Structural linguists of the 1940s and 1950s were engaged in what they claimed was a "scientific descriptive analysis" of various languages; teaching methodologists saw a direct application of such analysis to teaching linguistic patterns (Fries, 1945). At the same time, behavioristic psychologists advocated conditioning and habit-formation models of learning that were perfectly married with the mimicry drills and pattern practices of audiolingual methodology.

The characteristics of the ALM may be summed up in the following list (adapted from Prator and Celce-Murcia, 1979):

(1) New material is presented in dialog form.

(2) There is dependence on mimicry, memorization of set phrases, and overlearning.

(3) Structures are sequenced by means of contrastive analysis and taught one at a time.

(4) Structural patterns are taught using repetitive drills.

(5) There is little or no grammatical explanation. Grammar is taught by inductive analogy rather than deductive explanation.

(6) Vocabulary is strictly limited and learned in context.

(7) There is much use of tapes, language labs, and visual aids.

(8) Great importance is attached to pronunciation.

(9) Very little use of the mother tongue by teachers is permitted.

(10) Successful responses are immediately reinforced.

(11) There is a great effort to get students to produce error-free utterances.

(12) There is a tendency to manipulate language and disregard content.

For a number of reasons the ALM enjoyed many years of popularity, and even to this day, adaptations of the ALM are found in contemporary methodologies. The ALM was firmly rooted in respectable theoretical perspectives at the time. Materials were carefully prepared, tested out, and disseminated to educational institutions. "Success" could be more overtly experienced by students as they practiced their dialogs in off-hours. But the popularity was not to last forever. Led by Wilga Rivers' (1964) eloquent criticism of the misconceptions of the ALM and by its ultimate failure to teach long-term communicative proficiency, its popularity waned. We discovered that language was not really acquired through a process of habit formation and overlearning, that errors were not necessarily to be avoided at all costs, and that structural linguistics did not tell us everything about language that we needed to know. While the ALM was a valiant attempt to reap the fruits of language teaching methodologies that had preceded it, in the end it still fell short, as all methods do. But we learned something from the very failure of the ALM to do everything it had promised, and we moved forward.

"Designer" Methods of the Spirited Seventies

The decade of the seventies was historically significant on two counts. First, perhaps more than in other decade, research on second language learning and teaching grew from an offshoot of linguistics to a discipline in its own right. As more and more scholars specialized their efforts in second language acquisition studies, our knowledge of how people learn languages inside and outside of the classroom mushroomed. Second, in this spirited atmosphere of pioneering research, a number of innovative if not revolutionary methods were conceived. These "designer" methods (to borrow a term from Nunan 1989a:97) were soon marketed by entrepreneurs as the latest and greatest applications of the multidisciplinary research findings of the day.

Today, as we look back at these methods, we can applaud them for their innovative flair, for their attempt to rouse the language teaching world out of its Audiolingual sleep, and for their stimulation of even more research as we sought to discover why they were **not** the godsend that their inventors and marketers hoped they would be. The scrutiny that the designer methods underwent has enabled us today to incorporate certain elements thereof in our current communicative, interactive, eclectic approach to language teaching. Let's look at five of these products of the spirited seventies.

1. Community Language Learning

The age of audiolingualism, with its emphasis on surface forms and on the rote practice of scientifically produced patterns, began to wane when the

Chomskyan revolution in linguistics turned linguists and language teachers toward the "deep structure" of language and when psychologists began to recognize the fundamentally affective and interpersonal nature of all learning. By the decade of the 1970s, as we increasingly recognized the importance of the affective domain, some innovative methods took on a distinctly affective nature. Community Language Learning was a classic example of an affectively based method.

In his "Counseling-Learning" model of education, Charles Curran (1972) was inspired by Carl Rogers' view of education in which learners in a classroom are regarded as a "group" rather than a "class"—a group in need of certain therapy and counseling. The social dynamics of such a group are of primary importance. In order for any learning to take place, as has already been noted in Carl Rogers' model, what is first needed is for the members to interact in an interpersonal relationship in which students and teacher join together to facilitate learning in a context of valuing and prizing each individual in the group. In such a surrounding each person lowers the defenses that prevent open interpersonal communication. The anxiety caused by the educational context is lessened by means of the supportive community. The teacher's presence is not perceived as a threat, nor is it the teacher's purpose to impose limits and boundaries, but rather, as a true counselor, to center his or her attention on the clients (the students) and their needs. "Defensive" learning is made unnecessary by the empathetic relationship between teacher and students. Curran's Counseling-Learning model of education thus capitalizes on the primacy of the needs of the learners—clients—who have gathered together in the educational community to be counseled.

Curran's Counseling-Learning model of education was extended to language learning contexts in the form of Community Language Learning (CLL). While particular adaptations of CLL are numerous, the basic methodology is explicit. The group of clients (learners), having first established in their native language an interpersonal relationship and trust, are seated in a circle with the counselor (teacher) on the outside of the circle. The clients may be complete beginners in the foreign language. When one of the clients wishes to say something to the group or to an individual, he or she says it in the native language (e.g., Japanese) and the counselor translates the utterance back to the learner in the second language (e.g., English). The learner then repeats that English sentence as accurately as possible. Another client responds, in English; the utterance is translated by the counselor; the client repeats it; and the conversation continues. If possible the conversation is taped for later listening, and at the end of each session, the learners inductively attempt together to glean information about the new language. If desirable, the counselor may take a more directive role and provide some explanation of certain linguistic rules or items.

The first stage of intense struggle and confusion may continue for many sessions but always with the support of the counselor and of the fellow clients. Gradually the learner becomes able to speak a word or phrase directly in the foreign language, without translation. This is the first sign of the learner's moving away from complete dependence upon the counselor. As the learners gain more and more familiarity with the foreign language, more and more direct communication can take place with the counselor providing less and less direct translation and information until after many sessions, perhaps many months or years later, the learner achieves fluency in the spoken language. The learner has at that point become independent.

CLL reflects not only the principles of Carl Rogers' view of education but also basic principles of the dynamics of counseling, in which the counselor, through careful attention to the client's needs, aids the client in moving from dependence and helplessness to independence and self-assurance.

There are advantages and disadvantages to a method like CLL. The affective advantages are evident. CLL is an attempt to put Carl Rogers' philosophy into action and to overcome some of the threatening affective factors in second language learning. The threat of the all-knowing teacher, of making blunders in the foreign language in front of classmates, of competing against peers—all threats that can lead to a feeling of alienation and inadequacy—are presumably removed. The counselor allows the learner to determine the type of conversation and to analyze the foreign language inductively. In situations in which explanation or translation seems to be impossible, it is often the client-learner who steps in and becomes a counselor to aid the motivation and capitalize on intrinsic motivation.

But there are some practical and theoretical problems with CLL. The counselor-teacher can become *too* nondirective. The student often needs direction, especially in the first stage, in which there is such seemingly endless struggle within the foreign language. Supportive but assertive direction from the counselor could strengthen the method. Another problem with CLL is its reliance upon an inductive strategy of learning. I have already noted in Chapter 5 that deductive learning is both a viable and efficient strategy of learning and that adults particularly can benefit from deduction as well as induction. While some intense inductive struggle is a necessary component of second language learning, the initial grueling days and weeks of floundering in ignorance in CLL could be alleviated by more directed, deductive learning "by being told." Perhaps only in the second or third stage, when the learner has moved to more independence, is an inductive strategy really successful. Finally, the success of CLL depends largely on the translation expertise of the counselor. Translation is an intricate and complex process that is often "easier said than done"; if subtle aspects of language are mistranslated, there could be a less than effective understanding of the target language.

Despite its weaknesses, CLL is a potentially useful method for the foreign language classroom as long as teachers are willing to adapt it to their own curricular constraints. That adaptation requires a relaxing of certain aspects of the method. For example, you might avoid the initial, complete-dependence stage by using CLL in an intermediate language class. Or you might provide more directiveness than CLL advocates. As is the case with virtually any method, if you have solid theoretical foundations—a broad, cautiously enlightened, eclectic view—you can derive valuable insights from diverse points of view and apply them creatively to your own situation.

2. Suggestopedia

Other new methods of the decade were not quite as strictly affective as CLL. Suggestopedia, for example, was a method that was derived from Bulgarian psychologist Georgi Lozanov's (1979) contention that the human brain could process great quantities of material if simply given the right conditions for learning, among which are a state of relaxation and giving over of control to the teacher. According to Lozanov, people are capable of learning much more than they give themselves credit for. Drawing on insights from Soviet psychological research on extrasensory perception and from yoga, Lozanov created a method for learning that capitalized on relaxed states of mind for maximum retention of material. Music was central to his method. Baroque music, with its 60 beats per minute and its specific rhythm, created the kind of "relaxed concentration" that led to "superlearning" (Ostrander and Schroeder, 1979:65). According to Lozanov, during the soft playing of Baroque music, one can take in tremendous quantities of material due to an increase in alpha brain waves and a decrease in blood pressure and pulse rate.

In applications of Suggestopedia to foreign language learning, Lozanov and his followers experimented with the presentation of vocabulary, readings, dialogs, role-plays, drama, and a variety of other typical classroom activities. Some of the classroom methodology did not have any particular uniqueness. The primary difference lay in a significant proportion of activity carried out in soft, comfortable seats in relaxed states of consciousness. Students were encouraged to be as "childlike" as possible, yielding all authority to the teacher and sometimes assuming the roles (and names) of native speakers of the foreign language. Students thus became "suggestible." Lozanov (1979:272) described the concert session portion of a Suggestopedia language class:

> At the beginning of the session, all conversation stops for a minute or two, and the teacher listens to the music coming from a tape-recorder. He waits and listens to several passages in order to enter into the mood of the music and then begins to read or recite the new text, his voice modulated in harmony with the musical phrases. The students follow the text in their textbooks where each lesson is translated into the mother tongue. Between the first and second part of the concert, there are several minutes of solemn silence. In some cases, even longer pauses can be given to permit the stu-

dents to stir a little. Before the beginning of the second part of the concert, there are again several minutes of silence and some phrases of the music are heard again before the teacher begins to read the text. Now the students close their textbooks and listen to the teacher's reading. At the end, the students silently leave the room. They are not told to do any homework on the lesson they have just had except for reading it cursorily once before going to bed and again before getting up in the morning.

Suggestopedia has been criticized on a number of fronts. Scovel (1979) showed quite eloquently that Lozanov's experimental data, in which he reported astounding results with Suggestopedia, were highly questionable. Moreover, the practicality of using Suggestopedia is an issue that teachers must face where music and comfortable chairs are not available. More serious is the issue of the place of memorization in language learning. Scovel (1979:260-261) noted that Lozanov's "innumerable references to... memorization... to the total exclusion of references to 'understanding' and/or 'creative solutions of problems' convinces this reviewer at least that suggestopedy... is an attempt to teach memorization techniques and is not devoted to the far more comprehensive enterprise of language acquisition."

Like some other designer methods (CLL and the Silent Way, for example), Suggestopedia became a business enterprise of its own. As such, it made claims in the advertising world that were not completely supported by research. And endorsement by *Parade* magazine (March 12, 1978) did not necessarily signify the advent of the last word in language teaching. We must, as language teachers, try to extract from such methods that which is insightful and fruitful, then adapt those insights to our own teaching contexts.

Despite its criticisms, Suggestopedia gave the language teaching profession some insights. We learned a bit about how to believe in the power of the human brain. We learned that deliberately induced states of relaxation may be beneficial in the classroom. And numerous teachers have at times experimented with various forms of music as a way to get students to sit back and relax.

3. The Silent Way

Like Suggestopedia, the Silent Way rests on more cognitive than affective arguments for its theoretical sustenance. While Caleb Gattegno, its founder, was said to be interested in a "humanistic" approach (Chamot and McKeon, 1984:2) to education, much of the Silent Way was characterized by a problem-solving approach to learning. Richards and Rodgers (1986:99) summarize the theory of learning behind the Silent Way:

(1) Learning is facilitated if the learner discovers or creates rather than remembers and repeats what is to be learned.

(2) Learning is facilitated by accompanying (mediating) physical objects.

(3) Learning is facilitated by problem solving involving the material to be learned.

"Discovery learning," a popular educational trend of the 1960s, advocated less learning "by being told" and more learning by discovering for oneself various facts and principles. In this way, students construct conceptual hierarchies of their *own* which are a product of the time they have invested. Ausubel's "subsumption" (*PLLT,* Chapter 4) is enhanced by discovery learning since the cognitive categories are created meaningfully with less chance of rote learning taking place. Inductive processes are also more encouraged in discovery learning methods.

The Silent Way capitalized on such discovery-learning procedures. Gattegno (1972) believed that learners should develop independence, autonomy, and responsibility. At the same time, learners in a Silent Way classroom had to cooperate with each other in the process of solving language problems. The teacher—a stimulator but not a hand-holder—was silent much of the time, thus the name of the method. Teachers had to resist their instinct to spell everything out in black and white—to come to the aid of students at the slightest downfall—and they had to "get out of the way" while students worked out solutions.

In a language classroom the Silent Way typically utilized as materials a set of Cuisinere rods—small colored rods of varying lengths—and a series of colorful wall charts. The rods were used to introduce vocabulary (colors, numbers, adjectives [*long, short,* and so on], verbs [*give, take, pick up, drop*]) and syntax (tense, comparatives, pluralization, word order, and the like). The teacher provided single-word stimuli, or short phrases and sentences, once or twice and then the students refined their understanding and pronunciation among themselves with minimal corrective feedback from the teacher. The charts introduced pronunciation models, grammatical paradigms, and the like.

Like Suggestopedia, the Silent Way has had its share of criticism. In one sense, the Silent Way was too harsh a method, and the teacher too distant, to encourage a communicative atmosphere. Students often need more guidance and overt correction than the Silent Way permitted. There are a number of aspects of language that can indeed be "told" to students to their benefit; they need not, as in CLL as well, struggle for hours or days with a concept that could be easily clarified by the teacher's direct guidance. The rods and charts wear thin after a few lessons, and other materials must be introduced, at which point the Silent Way can look like any other language classroom.

However, the underlying principles of the Silent Way were valid. All too often we're tempted as teachers to provide everything for our students, all neatly served up on a silver platter. We could benefit from injecting healthy doses of discovery learning into our classroom activities and from providing less teacher talk than we usually do to let the students work things out on their own.

4. Total Physical Response

James Asher (1977), the developer of Total Physical Response (TPR), actually began experimenting with TPR in the 1960s, but it was almost a decade before the method was widely discussed in professional circles. Today TPR, with its simplicity as its most appealing facet, is a household word among language teachers.

You will recall from earlier in this chapter that over a century ago Gouin designed his Series Method on the premise that a series of simple actions associated with language will be easily retained by learners. Much later, psychologists developed the "trace theory" of learning in which it was claimed that memory is increased if it is stimulated, or "traced," through association with motor activity. Over the years, language teachers have intuitively recognized the value of associating language with physical activity. So while the idea of building a method of language teaching on the principle of psychomotor associations is not at all new, it was this very idea that Asher capitalized upon in developing TPR.

TPR combines a number of other insights in its rationale. Principles of child language acquisition are important. Asher (1977) noted that children, in learning their first language, appear to do a lot of listening before they speak, and that their listening is accompanied by physical responses (reaching, grabbing, moving, looking, and so forth). He also gave some attention to right-brained learning. According to Asher, motor activity is a right-brain function that should precede left-brain language processing. Asher was also convinced that language classes were often the locus of too much anxiety and wished to devise a method that was as stress-free as possible, where learners would not feel overly self-conscious and defensive. The TPR classroom, then, was one in which students did a great deal of listening and acting. The teacher was very directive in orchestrating a performance: "The instructor is the director of a stage play in which the students are the actors" (Asher, 1977:43).

Typically, TPR heavily utilized the imperative mood, even into more advanced proficiency levels. Commands are an easy way to get learners to move about and to loosen up: Open the window, Close the door, Stand up, Sit down, Pick up the book, Give it to John, and so on. No verbal response is necessary. More complex syntax can be incorporated into the imperative: Draw a rectangle on the chalkboard, Walk quickly to the door and hit it. Humor is easy to introduce: Walk slowly to the window and jump, Put your toothbrush in your book (Asher, 1977:55). Interrogatives are also easily dealt with: Where is the book? Who is John? (students point to the book or to John). Eventually students, one by one, would feel comfortable enough to venture verbal responses to questions, then to ask questions themselves, and the process continued.

Like every other method or approach we have encountered, TPR had its limitations. It seemed to be especially effective in the beginning levels of language proficiency, but then it lost its distinctiveness as learners advanced in their competence. In a TPR classroom, after students overcame the fear of speaking out, classroom conversations and other activities proceeded as in almost any other **communicative** language classroom. In TPR reading and writing activities, students are limited to spinning off from the oral work in the classroom. Its appeal to the dramatic or theatrical nature of language learning was attractive. (See Smith, 1984, and Stern, 1983, for discussions of the use of drama in foreign language classrooms.) But soon learners' needs for spontaneity and unrehearsed language must be met.

5. The Natural Approach

Stephen Krashen's (1982, 1991) theories of second language acquisition have been widely discussed and hotly debated over the years (see *PLLT,* Chapter 9). The major methodological offshoot of Krashen's views was manifested in the Natural Approach, developed by one of Krashen's colleagues, Tracy Terrell (Krashen and Terrell, 1983). Acting on many of the claims that Asher made for TPR, Krashen and Terrell felt that learners would benefit from delaying production until speech "emerges," that learners should be as relaxed as possible in the classroom, and that a great deal of communication and "acquisition" should take place, as opposed to analysis. In fact, the Natural Approach advocated the use of TPR activities at the beginning level of language learning when "comprehensible input" is essential for triggering the acquisition of language.

There are a number of possible long-range goals of language instruction. In some cases second languages are learned for oral communication, in other cases for written communication, and in still others there may be an academic emphasis on, say, listening to lectures, speaking in a classroom context, or writing a research paper. The Natural Approach was aimed at the goal of basic personal communication skills, that is, everyday language situations—conversations, shopping, listening to the radio, and the like. The initial task of the teacher was to provide comprehensible input, that is, spoken language that is understandable to the learner or just a little beyond the learner's level. Learners need not say anything during this "silent period" until they feel ready to do so. The teacher was the source of the learners' input and the creator of an interesting and stimulating variety of classroom activities—commands, games, skits, and small-group work.

In the Natural Approach, learners presumably moved through what Krashen and Terrell defined as three stages: (1) The preproduction stage is the development of listening comprehension skills. (2) The early production stage is usually marked with errors as the student struggles with the language. The teacher focuses on meaning here, not on form, and therefore the teacher does not make a point of correcting errors during this stage (unless they are gross errors that block or hinder meaning entirely). (3) The last stage is one of extending production into longer stretches of discourse, involving more complex games, role-plays, open-ended dialogs, discussions, and extended small-group work. Since the objective in this stage is to promote fluency, teachers are asked to be very sparse in their correction of errors.

The most controversial aspects of the Natural Approach were its advocacy of a "silent period" (delay of oral production) and its heavy emphasis on comprehensible input. The delay of oral production until speech "emerges" has shortcomings (see Gibbons, 1985). What about the student whose speech never emerges? And with students all at different timetables for this so-called emergence, how does the teacher manage a classroom efficiently? And the concept of comprehensible input is difficult to pin down, as Langi noted:

> **How does one know which structures the learners are to be provided with? From the examples of "teacher talk" provided in the book (Krashen and Terrell, 1983), communication interactions seem to be guided by the topic of conversation rather than by the structures of the language. The decision of which structures to use appears to be left to some mysterious sort of intuition, which many teachers may not possess.**

But on a more positive note, most teachers and researchers agree that we are all too prone to insist that learners speak right away, and so we can take from the Natural Approach the good advice that for a period of time, while they grow accustomed to the new language, students' silence is beneficial. Through TPR and other forms of input, students' language egos are not as easily threatened, and they aren't forced into immediate risk-taking that could embarrass them. The resulting self-confidence eventually can spur a student to venture to speak out.

Innovative methods such as these five designer methods expose us to new thoughts that you can sift through, weigh, and adapt to multiple contexts. Your responsibility as a teacher is to choose the best of what others have experimented with and adapt those insights to your own situation. Those insights and intuitions can become a part of your own principled approach to language teaching.

Beyond Method: Notional-Functional Syllabuses

As the innovative methods of the seventies were being touted by some and criticized by many, some very significant foundations for future growth were being laid in what soon came to be popularly known as the **Notional-Functional Syllabus**. Beginning with the work of the Council of Europe (Van Ek and Alexander, 1975) and later followed by numerous interpretations of "notional" syllabuses (Wilkins, 1976), Notional-Functional Syllabuses (hereafter, referred to as NFS) began to be used in the United Kingdom in the 1970s.

The distinguishing characteristics of the NFS were its attention to functions (see *PLLT*, Chapter 10) as the organizing elements of English language curriculum, and its contrast with a structural syllabus in which sequenced grammatical structures served as the organizers. Reacting to methods that attended too strongly to grammatical form, the NFS sought to focus strongly—and in some of its interpretations, exclusively—on the pragmatic purposes to which we put language. As such, it was not a method at all. It was close to what we have already described as an approach, but it was more specifically focused on curricular structure than a true approach would be.

"Notions," according to Van Ek and Alexander (1975), are both general and specific. General notions are abstract concepts such as existence, space, time, quantity, and quality. They are domains in which we use language to express thought and feeling. Within the general notion of space and time, for example, are the concepts of location, motion, dimension, speed, length of time, frequency, etc. "Specific notions" correspond more closely to what we have become accustomed to calling "contexts" or "situations." Personal identification, for example, is a specific notion under which name, address, phone number, and other personal information is subsumed. Other specific notions include, travel, health and welfare, education, shopping, services, and free time.

The "functional" part of the NFS corresponds to language functions. Curricula are organized around such functions as identifying, reporting, denying, accepting, declining, asking permission, apologizing, etc. Van Ek and Alexander list some seventy different language functions.

The NFS quickly provided popular underpinnings for the development of communicative textbooks and materials in English language courses. A textbook like Coffey's (1983) *Fitting In*, for example, was organized around the following sequence of functional topics:

- Introductions, Greetings, Goodbyes
- Invitations, Apologies, Condolences
- Gratitude, Compliments, Congratulations
- Requests, Commands, Warnings, Directions
- Offers, Seeking Permission
- Advice, Intentions
- Pleasure, Displeasure
- Expressing Your Opinion
- Asking People to Repeat Themselves
- Interrupting Someone
- Changing the Topic of Conversation

A typical unit in this textbook included presentation of dialogs, conversation practice with a classmate, situations in which the student figures out "what would I say," role plays, chart work, multiple choice exercises on functional considerations, one-sided dialogs where the student fills in responses, nonverbal considerations, discussion activities, and "community exercises" for extra-class practice.

It is important for you to understand, in this historical sketch of methodology, that the NFS did not necessarily develop communicative competence in learners. First of all, it was not a method, which would specify how you would teach something; it was a syllabus. And while it was clearly a precursor to what we now call Communicative Language Teaching (see Chapter 5), as a syllabus it still presented language as an inventory of units—functional rather than grammatical units—but units nonetheless. Communicative competence implies a set of strategies for getting messages sent and received and to negotiate meaning as an interactive participant in discourse, whether spoken or written. Therefore, the danger that the NFS could simply be "structural lamb served up as notional-functional mutton" (Campbell, 1978:18) was ever present.

However, the NFS did indeed set the stage for bigger and better things. By attending to the functional purposes of language, and by providing contextual (notional) settings for the realization of those purposes, it provided a link between a dynasty of methods that was now perishing and a new era of language teaching that is the subject of the next chapter.

As an aid to your recollection of the characteristics of some of the methods reviewed above, you may wish to refer to Table 4.1 on pages 70 and 71, in which the audiolingual method, the five "designer" methods, and the Communicative Language Teaching Approach are summarized according to eight different criteria.

On looking back over this meandering history, you can no doubt see the cycles of changing winds and shifting sands alluded to earlier. In some ways the cycles were, as Marckwardt proposed, each about a quarter of a century in length or roughly a generation. In this remarkable succession of changes, however, we learned something in each generation. We did not allow history to simply deposit new dunes exactly where the old ones lay. So our cumulative history has taught us to appreciate the value of "doing" language interactively, of the emotional (as well as cognitive) side of learning, of absorbing language automatically **and** of consciously analyzing it, and of pointing learners toward the real world out there where they will use English communicatively.

In the next chapter we look at how we reaped those benefits to form an integrated, unified, communicative approach to language teaching that is no longer characterized by a series of methods.

TOPICS FOR DISCUSSION, ACTION, AND RESEARCH

1. If **approach** is a superordinate set of theories and principles from which **method** is derived, could one devise two different methods from the same (or very similar) approach? Whichever way you answer that question, illustrate your response with some practical examples either from this chapter or from your own teaching or observing.

2. Given the choice of Richards and Rodgers' model (Method: Approach/Designs/Procedures) and Anthony's earlier model (Approach/Method/Technique), which do you prefer? In a small group, explain your preference. If there is disagreement, see if you can come to a consensus. Make sure you deal with Richards and Rodgers' rationale for the change.

3. Consider the Series Method, the Direct Method, and the Audiolingual Method: In your classroom, assign a different method to each of several small groups. Of the 12 principles summarized in Chapter 2, which ones tend to **favor** the method? Then, consider which principles underscore some weaknesses or limitations in your group's method. In what way did the favorable aspects contribute to the Notional-Functional Syllabus?

4. Richards and Rodgers (1986:5) said Grammar Translation "is a method for which there is no theory." Is this too harsh a judgment? Do you agree with the theory-lessness of Grammar Translation? Explain.

5. Review the five "designer" methods. If class size permits, assign a method to each of five different small groups, where each group will "defend" its method against the others. The group task is to prepare arguments in favor of its method, questions to ask of other methods, and counter-arguments against what other groups might ask them. Using a modified debate format, then, a whole-class discussion will follow.

6. Three of those five methods (CLL, Silent Way, and Suggestopedia) were (and still are) proprietary, with their own commercial publishing and educational company. How might that fact color (a) the objectivity with which its backers promote the method and (b) public reception to it?

7. With a partner, review the cycles of "shifting sands" since Gouin's time. How did each new method borrow from previous practices? What did each reject in previous practices? Share your conclusions with the rest of the class.

Table 4.1. Approaches and Methods—an Overview (adapted from Nunan, 1989).

	Theory of language	Theory of learning	Objectives	Syllabus
Audiolingual	Language is a system of rule-governed structures heirarchically arranged.	Habit formation; skills are learned more effectively if oral precedes written; analogy not analysis.	Control of structures of sound, form, and order, mastery over symbols of the language; goal: native-speaker mastery.	Graded syllabus of phonology, morphology, and syntax. Contrastive analysis.
Total Physical Response	Basically a structuralist, grammar-based view of language.	L2 learning is the same as L1 learning; comprehension before production, is "imprinted" through carrying out commands (right brain functioning); reduction of stress.	Teach oral proficiency to produce learners who can communicate uninhibitedly and intelligibly with native speakers.	Sentence-based syllabus with grammatical and lexical criteria being primary, but focus on meaning not form.
The Silent Way	Each language is composed of elements that give it a unique rhythm and spirit. Functional vocabulary and core structure are a key to the spirit of the language.	Processes of learning a second language are fundamentally different from L1 learning. L2 learning is an intellectual, cognitive process. Surrender to the music of the language, silent awareness then active trial.	Near-native fluency, correct pronunciation, basic practical knowledge of the grammar of the L2. Learner learns *how* to learn a language.	Basically structural lessons planned around grammatical items and related vocabulary. Items are introduced according to their grammatical complexity.
Community Language Learning	Language is more than a system for communication. It involves whole person, culture, educational, developmental communicative processes.	Learning involves the whole person. It is a social process of growth from child-like dependence to self-direction and independence.	No specific objectives. Near-native mastery is the goal.	No set syllabus. Course progression is topic-based; learners provide the topics. Syllabus emerges from learners' intention and the teacher's reformulations.
The Natural Approach	The essence of language is meaning. Vocabulary not grammar is the heart of language.	There are two ways of L2 language development: "acquisition"—a natural subconscious process, and "learning"—a conscious process. Learning cannot lead to acquisition.	Designed to give beginners and intermediate learners basic communicative skills. Four broad areas; basic personal communicative skills (oral/written); academic learning skills (oral/written).	Based on selection of communicative activities and topics derived from learner needs.
Suggestopedia	Rather conventional, although memorization of whole meaningful texts is recommended.	Learning occurs through suggestion, when learners are in a deeply relaxed state. Baroque music is used to induce this state.	To deliver advanced conversational competence quickly. Learners are required to master prodigious lists of vocabulary pairs, although the goal is understanding not memorization.	Ten unit courses consisting of 1,200 word dialogues graded by vocabulary and grammar.
Communicative Language Teaching	Language is a system for the expression of meaning; primary function-interaction and communication.	Activities involving real communication; carrying out meaningful tasks; and using language which is meaningful to the learner.	Objectives will reflect the needs of the learner; they will include functional skills as well as linguistic objectives.	Will include some/all of the following: structures, functions, notions, themes, tasks. Ordering will be guided by learner needs.

70

Activity types	Learner roles	Teacher roles	Roles of materials
Dialogues and drills, repetition and memorization, pattern practice.	Organisms that can be directed by skilled training techniques to produce correct responses.	Central and active teacher dominated method. Provides model, controls direction and pace.	Primarily teacher oriented. Tapes and visuals, language lab often used.
Imperative drills to elicit physical actions.	Listener and performer, little influence over the content of learning.	Active and direct role 'the director of a stage play' with students as actors.	No basic text; materials and media have an important role later. Initially voice, action, and gestures are sufficient.
Learner responses to commands, questions, and visual cues. Activities encourage and shape oral responses without grammatical explanation or modelling by teacher.	Learning is a process of personal growth. Learners are responsible for their own learning and must develop independence, autonomy, and responsibility.	Teachers must (a) teach (b) test (c) get out of the way. Remain impassive. Resist temptation to model, remodel, assist, direct, exhort.	Unique materials: colored rods, color coded pronunciation and vocabulary charts.
Combination of innovative and conventional. Translation, group work, recording, transcription, reflection, and observation, listening, free conversation.	Learners are members of a community. Learning is not viewed as an individual accomplishment, but something that is achieved collaboratively.	Counselling/parental analogy. Teacher provides a safe environment in which students can learn and grow.	No textbook which would inhibit growth. Materials are developed as course progresses.
Activities allowing comprehensible input, about things in the here-and-now. Focus on meaning not form.	Should not try and learn language in the usual sense, but should try and lose themselves in activities involving meaningful communication.	The teacher is the primary source of comprehensible input. Must create positive low-anxiety climate. Must choose and orchestrate a rich mixture of classroom activities.	Materials come from realia rather than textbooks. Primary aim is to promote comprehension and communication.
Initiatives, question and answer, role play, listening exercises under deep relaxation.	Must maintain a passive state and allow the materials to work on them (rather than vice-versa).	To create situations in which the learner is most suggestible and present material in a way most likely to encourage positive reception and retention. Must exude authority and confidence.	Consists of texts, tapes, classroom fixtures, and music. Texts should have force, literary quality, and interesting characters.
Engage learners in communication, involve processes such as information sharing, negotiation of meaning and interaction.	Learner as negotiator, interactor giving as well as taking.	Facilitator of the communication process, participants' tasks, and texts; needs analyst, counsellor, process manager.	Primary role in promoting communicative language use; task-based materials; authentic.

FOR YOUR FURTHER READING

Anthony, Edward. 1963. "Approach, method, technique." *English Language Teaching 17:* 63-67.

In this seminal article, Anthony defines and gives examples of the three title terms. Methods are seen, perhaps for the first time, as guided by and built upon solid theoretical foundations. His definitions have prevailed to this day in informal pedagogical terminology.

Richards, Jack and Rodgers, Theodore. 1982. "Method: Approach, design, procedure." *TESOL Quarterly 16:*153-168.

The authors redefine Anthony's original conception of the terms by viewing "method" as an umbrella term covering approach, design, and procedure. Full explanations of the terms are offered and examples provided. This article also appears as a chapter in Richards and Rodgers (1986).

Richards, Jack and Rodgers, Theodore. 1986. *Approaches and Methods in Language Teaching.* New York: Cambridge University Press.

A very useful overview of a number of different methods within the rubric of approaches that support them, course designs that utilize them, and classroom procedures (techniques) that manifest them.

Larsen-Freeman, Diane. 1986. *Techniques and Principles in Language Teaching.* New York: Oxford University Press.

The author summarizes, in simplified sets of principles and characteristics, a number of methods, including the "designer" methods discussed in this chapter. This book is a useful overview for the novice teacher-trainee.

Chapter 5

The Present:
An Informed "Approach"

The "methodical" history of the previous chapter, even with our brief look at Notional-Functional Syllabuses, does not quite bring us up to the present. By the end of the 1980s, the profession had learned some profound lessons from our past wanderings. We had learned to be cautiously eclectic in making enlightened choices of teaching practices that were solidly grounded in the best of what we knew about second language learning and teaching. We had amassed enough research on learning and teaching that we could indeed formulate an integrated approach to language teaching practices. And, perhaps ironically, the **methods** that were such strong signposts of our century-old journey were no longer of great consequence in marking our progress. How did that happen?

In the seventies and early eighties, there was a good deal of hoopla about the "designer" methods described in the previous chapter. Even though they weren't widely adopted as standard methods, they were nevertheless symbolic of a profession at least partially caught up in a mad scramble to invent a new method when the very concept of method was eroding under our feet.

We didn't need a new method. We needed, instead, to get on with the business of unifying our **approach** to language teaching and of designing effective tasks and techniques that are informed by that approach.

And so, today those clearly identifiable and enterprising methods are an interesting if not insightful contribution to our professional repertoire, but few practitioners look to any one of them, or their predecessors, for a final answer on how to teach a foreign language. Method, as a unified, cohesive, finite set of design features, is now given only minor attention.[1] The profession has at last reached the point of maturity where we recognize that the complexity of language learners in multiple worldwide contexts demands an eclectic blend of tasks each tailored for a particular group of learners in a particular place, studying for particular purposes in a given amount of time. David Nunan (1991b:228) sums it up nicely: "It has been realized that there never was and probably never will be a method for all, and the focus in recent years has been on the development of classroom tasks and activities which are consonant with what we know about second language acquisition, and which are also in keeping with the dynamics of the classroom itself."

An Approach for Enlightened Eclectics

It should be clear from the foregoing that as an "enlightened, eclectic" teacher, you think in terms of a number of possible methodological options at your disposal for tailoring classes to particular contexts. Your **approach**—or theory of language and language learning—therefore takes on great importance. Your approach to language teaching methodology is your theoretical rationale that underlies everything that you do in the classroom. Your approach should include most if not all of the **principles** that were elaborated on in Chapter 2. Your approach is inspired by the interconnection of all your reading and observing and discussing and teaching.

But your approach to language pedagogy is not just a set of static principles, "set in stone." It is, in fact, a dynamic composite of energies within you that changes (or should change, if you are a growing teacher) with your experiences in your own learning and teaching. The way you understand the language learning process—what makes for successful and unsuccessful learning—may be relatively stable across months or years, but don't ever feel too

---

[1] While we may have outgrown our need to search for such definable methods, nevertheless, the term "methodology" continues to be used, as it would in any other behavioral science, to refer to the systematic application of validated principles to practical contexts. You need not therefore subscribe to a particular Method (with a capital M) in order to engage in a "methodology."

smug. There is far too much that we do not know collectively about this process, and there are far too many new research findings pouring in, to assume that you can confidently assert that you know everything you already need to know about language and language learning.

The **interaction** between your approach and your classroom practice is the key to dynamic teaching. The best teachers always take a few calculated risks in the classroom, trying new activities here and there. The inspiration for such innovation comes from the approach level, but the feedback that they gather from actual implementation then informs their overall understanding of what learning and teaching is. Which, in turn, may give rise to a new insight and more innovative possibilities, and the cycle continues.

Do you feel that you have an identifiable approach to language learning and teaching? Do you have a sense of a theoretical stance that might work for you? Try answering the questions in "Your Approach Indicator" on the next page. Checking boxes A and D indicates relatively strong agreement with the word or phrase on the left (A) or right (D). Checking boxes B or C indicates moderate agreement with one side or the other. Force yourself into one of the four boxes in each case. No neutral answers are accepted in this questionnaire!

✳   ✳   ✳

There is little doubt that you felt that quite a few of these items are loaded, especially after covering twelve basic principles in Chapter 2. Nevertheless, the very fact that you were able to make choices (you were, weren't you?) on thirteen different scales is an indication, or a beginning of an indication, of your overall approach to language learning and teaching. Your approach has been guided by a number of factors: your own experience as a learner in classrooms, whatever teaching experience you may already have had, observation experiences you have had, the principles elaborated on in Chapter 2, and other general conclusions you may have drawn from reading *Principles of Language Learning and Teaching* and other books and articles in the field.

Your approach also will differ on various issues from that of a colleague of yours, or even your teacher, just as "experts" in the field differ in their theoretical stance—in their interpretations of research on learning and teaching. There are two reasons for variation at the approach level: (1) an approach is by definition dynamic and therefore subject to some "tinkering" as a result of one's observation and experience; and (2) research in second language acquisition and pedagogy almost always yields findings that are subject to interpretation rather than giving conclusive evidence.

Your Approach Indicator: An Informal Questionnaire

A B C D

1. The main focus in a language class should be

   ON MEANING ☐ ☐ ☐ ☐ ON GRAMMAR

2. Language learners learn best by using plenty of

   ANALYSIS ☐ ☐ ☐ ☐ INTUITION

3. It is better to

   THINK DIRECTLY ☐ ☐ ☐ ☐ USE TRANSLATION
   IN THE L2 FROM L1

4. Language learners need

   IMMEDIATE REWARDS ☐ ☐ ☐ ☐ LONG-TERM REWARDS

5. Classes operate more successfully by encouraging

   INTRINSIC MOTIVATION ☐ ☐ ☐ ☐ EXTRINSIC MOTIVATION

6. With new language learners, teachers need to be

   TOUGH AND DEMANDING ☐ ☐ ☐ ☐ GENTLE AND EMPATHETIC

7. Because learners have differing learning styles, a teacher should

   GIVE INDIVIDUAL ☐ ☐ ☐ ☐ GET EVERYONE TO THINK
   ATTENTION IN THE SAME STYLE

8. The language classroom should have plenty of

   MEANINGFUL LEARNING ☐ ☐ ☐ ☐ ROTE LEARNING

9. Because different cultures have different values, my classroom should

   RESPECT DIFFERENCES ☐ ☐ ☐ ☐ BE CULTURALLY NEUTRAL

10. A teacher's feedback to the student should be given

    FREQUENTLY ☐ ☐ ☐ ☐ INFREQUENTLY, SO Ss WILL
    DEVELOP INDEPENDENCE

11. Teaching learners to use their own learning strategies is

    USEFUL AND ☐ ☐ ☐ ☐ INEFFICIENT— JUST TELL
    PRODUCTIVE THEM WHAT TO LEARN

12. Mistakes that students make in speech

    ARE INFORMATIVE ☐ ☐ ☐ ☐ SHOULD BE ERADICATED

13. A communicative class should give special attention to

    ACCURACY ☐ ☐ ☐ ☐ FLUENCY

Communicative Language Teaching

Is there a currently recognized approach that is a generally accepted norm in the field? The answer is a qualified yes. That qualified yes can be captured in the term **communicative language teaching** (CLT), and the qualifications to that answer lie in the numerous possible ways of defining CLT and a plethora of interpretations and classroom applications.

Chapter 2 summarized the all-encompassing communicative competence principle as one of the basic foundations of the profession. Chapter 4 summarized the Notional-Functional Syllabus which was a strong contributor to our "push toward communication" (Higgs and Clifford, 1982), and to what now has come to be known as CLT. Beneath this trend lies a progression of pedagogical efforts to look carefully at the properties of communicative language and language acquisition, to ask how learners can best internalize a second language, and to experiment systematically with classroom practices pointed toward accomplishing learners' communicative goals.

A quarter of a century ago we were centrally concerned with issues surrounding the linguistic description of languages and their pedagogical applications. We were quite worried about how Chomsky's generative grammar was going to fit into our language classrooms (Lamendella, 1969). We were reluctant to break away from a strong interpretation of the contrastive analysis hypothesis (see Wardhaugh, 1970). We were still almost exclusively dependent on the discipline of linguistics for our professional and bureaucratic identity. We were only just beginning to question teaching methods that advocated "overlearning" through classroom drill and memorization (Brown, 1972; Rivers, 1964). Insights from children's "natural" means of acquiring their first language were just beginning to be tapped (Cook, 1969).

Today we are benefiting from the victories and defeats of our professional march through history. But today the methodological issues are quite different and quite complex. Beyond grammatical and discourse elements in communication, we are probing the nature of social, cultural, and pragmatic features of language. We are exploring pedagogical means for "real-life" communication in the classroom. We are trying to get our learners to develop linguistic fluency, not just the accuracy that has so consumed our historical journey. We are equipping our students with tools for generating unrehearsed language performance "out there" when they leave the womb of our classrooms. We are concerned with how to facilitate lifelong language learning among our students, not just with the immediate classroom task. We are looking at learners as partners in a cooperative venture. And our classroom practices seek to draw on whatever intrinsically sparks learners to reach their fullest potential.

David Nunan (1991a:279) offers five features to characterize CLT:

1. **An emphasis on learning to communicate through interaction in the target language.**

2. **The introduction of authentic texts into the learning situation.**

3. **The provision of opportunities for learners to focus, not only on language but also on the learning process itself.**

4. **An enhancement of the learner's own personal experiences as important contributing elements to classroom learning.**

5. **An attempt to link classroom language learning with language activation outside the classroom.**

One of the most comprehensive lists of CLT features came some time ago from Finocchiaro and Brumfit (1983:91–93) in a comparison of audiolingual methodology with what they called the Communicative Approach. Because of its practicality, their list is reprinted (Table 5.1) on the next page.

In subsequent chapters, as you grapple with designing specific classroom techniques and planning lessons, you will be given chances to apply your understanding of CLT and, no doubt, to refine that understanding.

At the beginning of this section, it was noted that a "yes" to CLT needed to be qualified. Why the caution? Doesn't all the above make perfectly good sense? Haven't CLT principles been repeatedly applied, and successfully so, in classrooms around the world? Indeed you can with some assurance latch on to the CLT label and, like a member of a club, aver that you "believe in CLT," and be allowed to step inside the gates. But as with every issue in our field, there are caveats. Beware of:

(1) Giving lip service to principles of CLT (and related principles like cooperative learning, interactive teaching, learner-centered classes, content-centered education, whole language, etc.—see below) but not truly grounding your teaching techniques in such principles. No one these days would admit to a disbelief in principles of CLT; they would be marked as a heretic. But if you believe the term characterizes your teaching, then make sure you do indeed understand and practice your convictions.

(2) Overdoing certain CLT features. For example, you engage in real-life, authentic language in the classroom to the total exclusion of any potentially helpful controlled exercises, grammatical pointers, and other analytical devices. Or you simply simulate the real world out there but refrain from "interfering" in the ongoing flow of language.[2] Healthy application of CLT principles requires moderation and the common sense to take advantage of the facilitative elements in the classroom context.

---

[2]Howatt (1984), Littlewood (1981), and Nunan (1988) refer to this as the "strong" approach to CLT, noting that most practitioners would follow a "weak" version of CLT in which authenticity is coupled with structural and functional practice and other procedures of intervention.

Table 5.1. A Comparison of the Audiolingual Method and Communicative Language Teaching (Finocchario & Brumfit, 1983).

Audiolingual Method	Communicative Language Teaching
1. Attends to structure and form more than meaning.	Meaning is paramount.
2. Demands more memorization of structure-based dialogs.	Dialogs, if used, center around communicative functions and are not normally memorized.
3. Language items are not necessarily contextualized.	Contextualization is a basic premise.
4. Language learning is learning structures, sounds, or words.	Language learning is learning to communicate.
5. Mastery or "overlearning" is sought.	Effective communication is sought.
6. Drilling is a central technique.	Drilling may occur, but peripherially.
7. Native-speaker-like pronunciation is sought.	Comprehensible pronunciation is sought.
8. Grammatical explanation is avoided.	Any device which helps the learners is accepted —varying according to their age, interest, etc.
9. Communicative activities only come after a long process of rigid drills and exercises.	Attempts to communicate may be encouraged from the very beginning.
10. The use of the student's native language is forbidden.	Judicious use of native language is accepted where feasible.
11. Translation is forbidden at early levels.	Translation may be used where students need or benefit from it
12. Reading and writing are deferred till speech is mastered.	Reading and writing can start from the first day, if desired.
13. The target linguistic system will be learned through the overt teaching of the patterns of the system.	The target linguistic system will be learned best through the process of struggling to communicate.
14. Linguistic competence is the desired goal.	Communicative competence is the desired goal.
15. Varieties of language are recognized but not emphasized.	Linguistic variation is a central concept in materials and methods.
16. The sequence of units is determined solely by principles of linguistic complexity.	Sequencing is determined by any consideration of content function, or meaning which maintains interest.
17. The teacher controls the learners and prevents them from doing anything that conflicts with the theory.	Teachers help learners in any way that motivates them to work with the language.
18. "Language is habit" so error must be prevented at all costs.	Language is created by the individual often through trial and error.
19. Accuracy, in terms of formal correctness, is a primary goal.	Fluency and acceptable language is the primary goal: accuracy is judged not in the abstract but in context.
20. Students are expected to interact with the language system, embodied in machines or controlled materials.	Students are expected to interact with other people, either in the flesh, through pair and group work, or in their writings.
21. The teacher is expected to specify the language that students are to use.	The teacher cannot know exactly what language the students will use.
22. Intrinsic motivation will spring from an interest in the structure of language.	Intrinsic motivation will spring from an interest in what is being communicated by the language.

(3) Numerous interpretations of what CLT is. Because it is a catchall term, it is tempting to figure that everyone agrees on its interpretation. They don't. In fact, some of those in the profession, with good reason, feel uncomfortable using the term, even to the point of wishing to exorcise it from our jargon. As long as you are aware of many possible versions of CLT, I think it is a term that can continue to capture current language teaching approaches.

Untangling Some Current Jargon

Closely allied to CLT are half a dozen concepts that have, like CLT, become bandwagon terms without the endorsement of which (a) teachers cannot be decent human beings and (b) textbooks cannot sell! To corroborate the latter, just take a look at any recent ESL textbook catalog and try to find a book that is not "learner-centered," "cooperative," "interactive," "whole-language based," "content-centered," or, of course, "communicative."

Now, one way of looking at these terms is that they are simply expressions for the latest fads in language teaching and are therefore relatively meaningless. But another viewpoint would embrace them as legitimate attempts to label current concerns within a CLT framework, as overlapping and confusing as those concerns sometimes may be. I believe the latter is the more reasoned perspective. However, in order to take that perspective, some "demythologizing" is in order. Hence, a brief summary is appropriate.

1. Learner-centered Teaching

This term applies to curricula as well as to specific techniques. It can be contrasted to **teacher-centered**, and has received various recent interpretations. Learner-centered instruction includes:

- techniques that focus on or account for learners' needs, styles, and goals.
- techniques that give some control to the student (groupwork or strategy training, for example).
- curricula that include the consultation and input of students and that do not presuppose objectives in advance.
- techniques that allow for student creativity and innovation.
- techniques that enhance a student's sense of competence and self-worth.

Because language teaching is a domain that so often presupposes classrooms where students have very little language proficiency with which to negotiate with the teacher, some teachers shy away from the notion of giving learners the "power" associated with a learner-centered approach. Such restraint is not necessary because even in beginning level classes, teachers can offer students certain choices. All of these efforts help to give students a sense of "ownership" of their learning and thereby add to their intrinsic motivation.

2. Cooperative Learning

A curriculum or classroom that is cooperative—and therefore not **competitive**—usually involves the above learner-centered characteristics. As students work together in pairs and groups, they share information and come to each other's aid. They are a "team" whose players must work together in order to achieve goals successfully.

An added connotation to the term "cooperative," however, is its emphasis on **collaborative** efforts of students and teachers working together to pursue goals and objectives. Collaboration may be strictly among students, realized through pair and group work. Or it may involve student-teacher collaboration in choosing and carrying out techniques and in evaluating progress.

3. Interactive Learning

At the heart of current theories of communicative competence is the essential interactive nature of communication. When you speak, for example, the extent to which your intended message is received is a factor of both your production and the listener's reception. Most meaning, in a semantic sense, is a product of negotiation, of give and take, as interlocutors attempt to communicate. Thus, the communicative purpose of language compels us to create opportunities for genuine interaction in the classroom. An interactive course or technique will provide for such negotiation. Interactive classes will most likely be found:

- doing a significant amount of pair work and group work.
- receiving authentic language input in real-world contexts.
- producing language for genuine, meaningful communication.
- performing classroom tasks that prepare them for actual language use "out there."
- practicing oral communication through the give and take and spontaneity of actual conversations.
- writing to and for real audiences, not contrived ones.

4. Whole Language Education

One of the most popular terms currently sweeping through our profession, "whole language" has been so widely and divergently interpreted that it unfortunately is on the verge of losing the impact that it once had (see Rigg, 1991 for an excellent review of whole language education). Initially the term came from reading research and was used to emphasize (a) the "wholeness" of language as opposed to views that fragmented language into its bits and pieces of phonemes, graphemes, morphemes, and words; (b) the interaction and interconnections between oral language (listening and speaking) and written language (reading and writing); and (c) the importance, in literate societies, of the written code as natural and developmental, just as the oral code is.

Now the term has come to encompass a great deal more. Whole language is a label that has been used to describe:

- cooperative learning
- participatory learning
- student-centered learning
- focus on the community of learners
- focus on the social nature of language
- use of authentic, natural language
- meaning-centered language
- holistic assessment techniques in testing
- integration of the "four skills"

With all these interpretations, it is very difficult to distinguish it from CLT in general. I personally would like to see a return to its original intent, enabling us to use the term specifically to refer to the wholeness of **language** itself. Language is **not** the sum of its many dissectable and discrete parts. First language acquisition research shows us that children begin perceiving "wholes" (sentences, emotions, intonation patterns) well before its "parts." Second language teachers therefore do well to help their students attend to such wholes and not to yield to the temptation to build language from the bottom up. And since part of the wholeness of language includes the interrelationship of the "four skills" (listening, speaking, reading, writing), we are compelled to attend conscientiously to the **integration** of two or more of these skills in our classrooms.

5. Content-centered Education

Content-centered education, according to Brinton, Snow, and Wesche (1989:vii), is "the integration of content learning with language teaching aims. More specifically, it refers to the concurrent study of language and subject matter, with the form and sequence of language presentation dictated by content material." Such an approach contrasts sharply with many practices in which language skills are taught virtually in isolation from substantive content. When language becomes the medium to convey informational content of interest and relevance to the learner, then learners are pointed toward matters of intrinsic concern. Language takes on its appropriate role as a vehicle for accomplishing a set of content goals.

The recent rise of language programs in which attention to subject matter is primary has given us new opportunities and challenges. In content-centered classrooms, you can expect an increase in intrinsic motivation and empowerment. Students are pointed beyond transient extrinsic factors, like grades and tests, to their own competence and autonomy as intelligent individuals capable of actually doing something with their new language. Challenges range from a demand for a whole new genre of textbooks and other materials to the training of language teachers to teach the concepts and skills of various disciplines, professions, and occupations, and/or to teach in teams across disciplines.

6. Task-based Learning

In Chapter 4, the term "task" was referred to in passing when we dealt with the concept of "technique." In Chapters 9 and 13, we will explore the term once again. But for the moment, it is important to grapple with this last of a half-dozen high frequency professional terms.

While there is a good deal of variation among "experts" on how to describe or define **task**, Michael Breen's (1987:23) definition seems to capture its essence: "any structured language learning endeavor which has a particular objective, appropriate content, a specified working procedure, and a range of outcomes for those who undertake the task." A task is really a special form of technique. In some cases task and technique may be synonymous (a problem-solving task/technique; a role-play task/technique, for example). But in other cases, several techniques may comprise a task (for example, a problem-solving task that includes, let's say, grammatical explanation, teacher initiated questions, and a specific turn-taking procedure). Tasks are usually "bigger" in their ultimate ends than techniques.

Task-based learning is not a new method. Rather, it simply puts task at the center of one's methodological focus. It views the learning process as a set of communicative tasks that are directly linked to the curricular goals they serve, and the purposes of which extend beyond the practice of language for its own sake. Research on task-based learning attempts to identify types of tasks that enhance learning (for example, open-ended, structured, teacher-fronted, small group, pair work) and to define task-specific learner factors (roles, proficiency levels, styles), teacher roles, and other variables that contribute to successful achievement of goals.

Task-based learning is a perspective that you can take within a CLT framework that forces you to carefully consider all of the techniques that you use in the classroom in terms of a number of important pedagogical purposes:

- Do they ultimately point learners beyond the forms of language alone to real-world contexts?
- Do they specifically contribute to communicative goals?
- Are their elements carefully designed and not simply haphazardly or idiosyncratically thrown together?
- Are their objectives well specified so that you can at some later point accurately determine the success of one technique over another?
- Do they engage learners in some form of genuine problem-solving activity?

❊   ❊   ❊

Your **approach** to language teaching is obviously the keystone to all your teaching methodology in the classroom. By now, you should be able to "profess" at least major components of your own theory of language learning and teaching and have at least a beginning of an understanding of how that theory enlightens—or will enlighten—your classroom practices. Many aspects of your approach will predictably mirror those that have been espoused here, especially since you are just beginning to learn your teaching trade. That's quite acceptable. But do keep in mind the importance of the dynamic nature of the theoretical stance of even the most experienced teachers. We have much to learn, collectively, in this profession. And we will best instruct ourselves, and the profession at large, when we maintain a disciplined inquisitiveness about our teaching practices. After all, that's how we got to this point after a century of questioning.

TOPICS FOR DISCUSSION, ACTION, AND RESEARCH

1. Review the notion that your overall **approach** to language teaching can directly lead to curriculum design and lesson techniques, without subscribing to a **method** as such. Can you still comfortably use the term **methodology** to refer to pedagogical practice in general? As you read other research literature in the field of language teaching, pay special attention to how an author uses these terms. Be ready for some disparity in the various understandings of the terms.

2. Respond to the Approach Indicator on page 76. Compare your responses with a partner. Talk about items where you discovered some differences, and where you had general agreement. Discuss reasons behind both the disagreement and agreement.

3. Spinning off from #2 above, can you think of some aspect of your approach to language learning and teaching that is not firmly in place—something you are perhaps not able to come to a conclusion on? If so, why do you have ambivalent feelings? Discuss those with a partner or small group to see if the insights of others can clarify issues.

4. Look at Nunan's five features (page 78) of CLT. With a partner, come up with some practical classroom examples of each of the five ideals. Would you add any characteristics to his list? Would you change any?

5. With a partner, look again at the 22 characteristics of CLT (page 79) offered by Finocchiaro and Brumfit. Do you think they are all in keeping with general CLT principles? Are they all sufficiently balanced in their viewpoint? Would you disagree with any of them? Share your ideas with the rest of the class.

6. Observe an ESL class and use the 22 characteristics as a gauge of how closely the lesson approximates CLT. Share your observations in a small group.

7. Without looking back (no peeking!), write your own brief definitions of:

> learner centered teaching
> cooperative learning
> interactive learning
> whole language education
> content centered education
> task-based learning

Now, compare your definitions with a partner. Are you still confused by any terms? If so, try to clear up the confusion through re-reading and/or whole-class discussion.

8. Think of lessons you have observed or taught. Do any of the above (#7) six terms describe those lessons? How? Cite specific examples.

9. Is there other professional jargon that is either fuzzy or confusing in your mind? If so, try to pin them down through class discussion or research on your own.

FOR YOUR FURTHER READING

Savignon, Sandra J. 1991. "Communicative Language Teaching: State of the art." *TESOL Quarterly* 25(2), 261–277.

The author reviews the latest developments in research on communicative language teaching. This succinct survey will help you to better understand the nature of communicative language teaching as it is currently understood.

Nunan, David. 1991a. "Communicative tasks and the language curriculum." *TESOL Quarterly* 25(2), 279–295.

In this article, David Nunan summarizes the state of the art on task-based language teaching, giving definitions of terms and examples, and providing a rationale for task-based second language education.

Rigg, Pat. 1991. "Whole language in TESOL." *TESOL Quarterly* 25(3), 521–542.

Rigg provides a great deal of research and background information on whole language education. The information in this article extends well beyond the whole language approach, extending into aspects of cooperative learning, communicative language teaching, and other current approaches.

Prabhu, N.S. 1990. "There is no best method—why?" *TESOL Quarterly* *24*(2), 161–176.

In this essay on language teaching methodology, the author addresses our frequent claim that "there is no best method." He shows that we need to be sensitive to teaching/learning contexts and therefore we should not fall prey to the notion that there is in fact a method that is "best" at all. He appeals to teachers to develop a sense of "plausibility" in teaching: developing lessons and curricula that are active, alive, real, and operational enough to create a sense of involvement for both the teacher and the student.

Part Two

✳✳✳

Contexts
of
Teaching

Chapter 6

Learner Variables I:

Teaching Across Age Levels

On occasion people who are quite unaware of the language teaching field will walk into my office at the university and ask me something like, "Since English is my native language, I won't have any problem teaching it, will I?" Or they might ask, on the eve of their departure to Indonesia (without the slightest clue of who their future students will be), "Can you recommend a good textbook for my students?" Other naive inquirers who have just a little exposure to the vastness and complexity of the field still might assert, "I would like to learn how to teach ESL. Can you recommend a good workshop?" Such hopes are fueled by occasional advertisements in local newspapers that promise you lifelong employment as an English teacher (in exotic places across the seas) if only you'll attend someone's weekend seminar (or two) and, of course, cough up a fairly hefty enrollment fee.

You have already begun to get a taste of the array of questions and issues and approaches and techniques that must be included in your training as a language teacher—a complexity that can hardly be effectively covered in a weekend workshop. Part of this complexity is brought on by the multiplicity of **contexts** in which languages, and English more so than any other language, are learned and taught. Even if you could somehow pack up a suitcase full of the most current teaching resources, you would still have to face the question of **who** your learners are, **where** they are learning, and **why** they are learning.

This chapter begins to deal with contextual considerations in language teaching. In this chapter, context is addressed in terms of the learner variable of **age**. Chapter 7 deals with the learner variable of language proficiency (beginning, intermediate, and advanced). And Chapter 8 grapples with several complex variables introduced by sociopolitical contexts of teaching (country, societal expectations, cultural factors, political constraints, the status of English), by the institution one is teaching in (school, university, language school, adult education, vocational/workplace courses), and by the implied purposes for learning English (academic, technical, social, cultural immersion, enrichment, survival). Each of these considerations is essential to incorporate into your choices of techniques, lesson organization, and supporting materials.

Teaching Children

Popular tradition would have you believe that children are effortless second language learners and far superior to adults in their eventual success. On both counts, some qualifications are in order. First of all, children's widespread success in acquiring second languages belies a tremendous subconscious **effort** devoted to the task. As you have discovered in other reading (see *PLLT,* Chapters 2 and 3, for example) children exercise a good deal of both cognitive and affective effort in order to internalize both native and second languages. The difference between children and adults (that is, persons beyond the age of puberty) lies primarily in the contrast between the child's spontaneous, peripheral attention to language **forms** and the adult's overt, focal awareness and attention to those forms. Therefore, the popular notion about children holds only if "effort" refers, rather narrowly, to focal attention (sometimes thought of as "conscious" attention—see Chapter 11 of *PLLT*) to language forms.

Nor are adults necessarily less successful in their efforts. Studies have shown that adults, in fact, can be superior in a number of aspects of acquisition. They can learn and retain a larger vocabulary. They can utilize various deductive and abstract processes to shortcut the learning of grammatical and other linguistic concepts. And, in classroom learning, their superior intellect usually helps them to learn faster than a child. So, while children, with their fluency and naturalness, are often the envy of adults struggling with second languages, children in **classrooms** may have some difficulties learning a second language.

Third, the popular claim fails to differentiate very young children from pre-pubescent children and the whole range of ages in between. There are actually many instances of older (school-age) children manifesting significant difficulty in acquiring a second language for a multitude of reasons. Ranking high on that list of reasons are a number of complex personal, social, cultural, and political factors at play in elementary school teaching of second languages.

Teaching ESL to school-age children, therefore, is not merely a matter of setting them loose on a plethora of authentic language tasks in the classroom. To successfully teach children a second language requires specific skills and intuitions that differ from those that you would use for adult teaching. Five categories may help to give you some practical approaches to teaching children.

1. Intellectual development

An elementary school teacher once asked her students to take out a piece of paper and pencil and write something. A little boy raised his hand, "Teacher, I ain't got no pencil." The teacher, somewhat perturbed by his grammar, embarked on a barrage of corrective patterns: "I **don't** have **a** pencil. You **don't** have **a** pencil. **We** don't have pencils." Confused and bewildered, the child responded, "Ain't nobody got no pencils?"

Since children (up to the age of about eleven) are still in an intellectual stage of what Piaget called "concrete operations," you need to remember their limitations. Rules, explanations, and other even slightly abstract talk **about** language must be approached with extreme caution. Children are centered on the "here and now," on the functional purposes of language. They have little appreciation for our adult notions of "correctness," and they certainly cannot grasp the metalanguage we use to describe and explain linguistic concepts. Some rules of thumb for your classroom:

- **Don't explain grammar** using terms like "present progressive" or "relative clause."
- **Rules** that are stated in abstract terms ("To make a statement into a question, you add a 'do' or 'does'") should be avoided.
- Some grammatical concepts, especially at the upper levels of childhood, can be called to learners' attention by showing them certain **patterns** ("Notice the 'ing' at the end of the word.") and **examples** ("This is the way we say it when it's happening right now: 'I'm walking to the door.')
- Certain more difficult concepts or patterns require more **repetition** than adults need. For example, repeating certain patterns (without boring them) may be necessary to get the

brain and the ear to cooperate. Unlike the scene with the little boy who had no pencil, children must understand the
meaning and relevance of repetitions.

2. Attention span

One of the most salient differences between adults and children is attention span. First, it is important to understand what attention span means. Put
children in front of a TV with a favorite cartoon show on and they will stay
riveted to their seats for the duration. So, you cannot make a sweeping claim
that children have short attention spans! The short attention spans come up
only when you present stuff that to them is boring, useless, or too difficult.
Since language lessons can at times be difficult for children, your job then is
one of making them interesting, lively, and fun. How do you do that?

- Because children are focused on the immediate **here and
  now**, activities should be designed to capture their immediate interest.
- A lesson needs to have a **variety** of activities to keep interest and attention alive.
- A teacher needs to be **animated**, lively, and enthusiastic
  about the subject matter. Consider the classroom a stage in
  which you are the lead actor; your energy will be infectious
  to others. While you may think that you're overdoing it,
  children need this exaggeration to keep spirits buoyed and
  minds alert.
- A **sense of humor** will go a long way to keep children
  laughing and learning. Since children's humor is quite different from adults', remember to put yourself in their shoes.
- Children have a lot of natural **curiosity**. Make sure you tap
  into that curiosity whenever possible and you will **thereby**
  help to maintain attention and focus.

3. Sensory input

Children need to have all five senses stimulated. Your activities should
strive to go well beyond the visual and auditory modes that we usually feel
are sufficient for a classroom.

- Pepper your lessons with **physical** activity, such as having
  students act out things (role play), play games, or do Total
  Physical Response activities.
- Projects and other **hands-on activities** will go a long way
  toward helping children to internalize language. Small
  group science projects, for example, are excellent ways to
  get them to learn words and structures and to practice
  meaningful language.

- **Sensory aids** here and there will help children to internalize concepts. The smell of flowers, the touch of plants and fruits, the taste of foods, liberal doses of audio-visual aids like videos, pictures, tapes, music—all these are important elements in children's language teaching.
- Remember that your own **nonverbal language** is important as children will indeed attend very sensitively to your facial features, gestures, and touching.

4. Affective factors

A common myth is that children are relatively unaffected by the inhibitions that adults find to be such a block to learning. Not so! Children are often innovative in language forms but still have a great many inhibitions. They are extremely sensitive, especially to peers: What do others think of me? What will so-and-so think when I speak in English? Children are in many ways much more fragile than adults. Their egos are still being shaped, and therefore the slightest nuances of communication can be negatively interpreted. Teachers need to help them to overcome such potential barriers to learning.

- Help your students to **laugh with** each other at various mistakes that they all make.
- Be **patient and supportive**, to build self-esteem, yet at the same time be firm in your expectations of students.
- **Elicit** as much oral participation as possible from students, especially the quieter ones, to give them plenty of opportunities for trying things out.

5. Authentic, meaningful language

Children are focused on what this new language can actually be used for right here and now. They are less willing to put up with language that doesn't hold immediate rewards for them. Your classes can ill afford to have an overload of language that is neither authentic nor meaningful.

- Children are good at sensing language that is not **authentic**; therefore, "canned" or stilted language will simply not be accepted.
- Language needs to be firmly **context embedded**. Story lines, familiar situations and characters, real-life conversations, meaningful purposes in using language—these will establish a context within which language can be received and sent and thereby improve attention and retention. **Context reduced** language in abstract, isolated, unconnected sentences will be much less readily tolerated by children's minds.

- A **whole language** approach is essential. Don't break up language into too many bits and pieces or students won't see the relationship to the whole. And stress the interrelationships among the various skills (listening, speaking, reading, writing), otherwise they won't see important connections.

It takes a very special person to be able to teach children effectively. Along with all these guidelines, there is a certain intuition that an elementary school teacher develops with increasing months and years of experience. If you don't have the experience, you will, in due course of time. Meanwhile, you must begin somewhere, and these rules of thumb will help.

Teaching Adults

While many of the "rules" for teaching children can apply in some ways to teaching adults, the latter age group nevertheless poses some different, special considerations for the classroom teacher. Adults have superior cognitive abilities that can render them a bit more successful in certain classroom endeavors. Their need for sensory input can rely a little more on using their imagination ("imagine" smelling a rose vs. actually smelling a rose). Their level of shyness can be equal to or greater than children, but usually there is already a certain self-confidence that isn't as mature in children. And, because of adults' cognitive abilities, they can at least occasionally deal with language that isn't embedded in a "here and now" context.

So, as you consider the five variables that apply to children, keep in mind specifically some suggestions and caveats.

(1) Adults are more readily able to handle abstract rules and concepts. However, beware! As you know, too much abstract generalization about usage and not enough real-live language use can be deadly for adults, too.

(2) Adults, too, have longer attention spans for material that may not be intrinsically interesting to them. But again, the rule of keeping your activities short and sweet still applies to adult-age teaching.

(3) Sensory input need not always be quite as varied with adults, but one of the secrets of lively adult classes is their appeal to multiple senses.

(4) Adults often bring a modicum of general self-confidence (global self-esteem) into a classroom; the fragility of egos may therefore not be quite as critical as those of children. However, we should never underestimate the emotional factors that may be attendant to adult second language learning.

(5) Adults, with their more developed abstract thinking ability, are better able to take a context-reduced segment of language and understand it. Authenticity and meaningfulness are of course still highly important, but elements of adult language teaching can take temporary departures for the sake of dissecting those elements and examining them, as long as they are then readily returned to the original context.

Some implications for general classroom management (see Chapter 21 for a full treatment) can be drawn from what we know about differences between children and adults. Some management "do's"and "don'ts":

(1) Do remember that even though adults cannot express complex thinking in the new language, they are nevertheless intelligent adults with mature cognition and adult emotions. Show respect for those deeper thoughts and feelings that may be "trapped" for the moment by a low proficiency level.

(2) Don't treat adults in your class like children by:
    a. calling them "kids"
    b. using "caretaker" talk (the way parents talk to children)
    c. talking down to them

(3) Do give your students as many opportunities as possible to make **choices** (cooperative learning) about what they will do in and out of the classroom. That way, they can more effectively make an investment in their own learning process.

(4) Don't discipline adults in the same way as children. If discipline problems occur (disrespect, laughing, disrupting class, etc.), first assume that your students are adults who can be reasoned with like adults.

Teaching in Between

It is of course much too absolute to consider that a "child" ceases to be a child at the age of puberty and that all of the rules of adult teaching suddenly apply! It is therefore appropriate to consider briefly the sort of variables that apply in the teaching of what we might call "young adults," "teens," or high school age children whose ages range between 12 and 18 or so.

The "terrible teens" are an age of transition, confusion, self-consciousness, growing, and changing bodies and minds. What a challenge for the teacher! Teens are "in between" childhood and adulthood, and therefore a very special set of considerations applies to teaching them. Perhaps because of the enigma of teaching teen-agers, little is specifically said in the language teaching field about teaching at this level. Nevertheless, some thoughts are worth verbalizing, even if in the form of simple reminders:

(1) Intellectual capacity adds abstract operational thought around the age of 12. Therefore, some sophisticated intellectual processing is increasingly possible. Complex problems can be solved with logical thinking. This means that linguistic metalanguage can now, theoretically, have some impact. But the success of any intellectual endeavor will be a factor of the **attention** a learner places on the task; therefore, if a learner is attending to self, to appearance, to being accepted, to sexual thoughts, to a weekend party, or whatever, the intellectual task at hand may suffer.

(2) Attention spans are lengthening as a result of intellectual maturation, but once again, with many diversions present in a teenager's life, those potential attention spans can easily be shortened.

(3) Varieties of sensory input are still important, but again increasing capacities for abstraction lessen the essential nature of appealing to all five senses.

(4) Factors surrounding ego, self-image, and self-esteem are at their pinnacle. Teens are ultrasensitive to how others perceive their changing physical and emotional selves along with their mental capabilities. One of the most important concerns of the secondary school teacher is to keep self-esteem high by:

- avoiding embarrassment of students at all costs
- affirming each person's talents and strengths
- allowing mistakes and other errors to be accepted
- de-emphasizing competition between classmates
- encouraging small group work where risks are more easily made

(5) Secondary school students are of course becoming increasingly adult-like in their ability to make those occasional diversions from the "here and now" nature of immediate communicative contexts to dwell on a grammar point or vocabulary item. But even in teaching adults, care must be given not to insult them with stilted language or to bore them with overanalysis.

❋   ❋   ❋

This chapter was an attempt to provide a number of factors for you to consider carefully as you attend to the age of your learners. At this point, these factors have come out as a series of pointers and reminders rather than anecdotal or observational references to classrooms full of students. You can make those references yourself as you observe and as you begin to teach. The next time you're in an ESL classroom, notice how someone you're observing (or how you yourself) accounted for age variables in the overall lesson, in the type of techniques that were used, in the management of the classroom, in verbal registers as well as body language, in the teacher-student exchanges, and in the relationship that those exchanges conveyed. You may actually surprise yourself by how much of what we do and say as teachers is a factor of age!

TOPICS FOR DISCUSSION, ACTION, AND RESEARCH

1. Think back to the ESL lesson that was described in Chapter 1. That was an adult class. In a small group, talk about how you would go about teaching virtually the same grammar and discourse to children of, say, ages 7 and 8. Would the general topic fit? Would the same grammatical and communicative goals apply? What would you do differently? What would you delete and what would you add? How would you alter the various techniques?

2. Can you think of other considerations—beyond those mentioned in this chapter—that should be brought to bear on teaching ESL to children? to adults? to teenagers? In a group, brainstorm ideas then share them with the rest of the class.

3. Look again at the five major categories of things to consider as you teach children (pp. 91–94). With a partner, go through each category and come up with some specific classroom examples that illustrate the factor under consideration. For example, it was suggested that you have a sense of humor, that you use sensory aids, that you be patient and supportive, and that use context-embedded language. Give some examples of each of these and other suggestions in that section.

4. Are there any of the five factors regarding teaching ESL to children that you would like to take issue with? For example, it was noted that children do indeed have inhibitions and fragile egos. Do you agree? How do adults' and children's inhibitions differ? See if there are other factors you might want to debate. Defend your assertions with examples or research.

5. Why teach language to children at all? Aren't their innate capacities sufficient without having to be instructed? What would happen if children (in a context you specify) were just "exposed" to English with no classroom? What would they gain? What would they lose? You might want to debate this issue by assigning one group to argue for the "no-classroom" position and another group to defend the contention that language classes for children are beneficial.

6. In groups of three people each, arrange to make a series of three ESL observations: one person goes to an elementary school, another to a secondary school, and a third to a class for adults. Take careful note of the following:

   - topic or subject matter of the lesson
   - teacher talk and student talk
   - variety and type of techniques
   - discipline or behavior problems

- physical activity and sensory input
- apparent motivation and interest

After the observation, share your perceptions in your group of three. Compare differences and see what insights you garnered about teaching at the different age levels. Share your group's findings with the rest of the class.

FOR YOUR FURTHER READING

Garvie, Edie. 1990. *Story as Vehicle: Teaching English to Young Children.* Clevedon, U.K.: Multilingual Matters.

> Intended primarily for teachers and teacher-trainers, this book presents an approach to language teaching that is firmly grounded in principles of second language acquisition. The story, whether it be a published story or teacher-created or student-created, is exploited as a way of promoting intrinsic motivation, interest, and language development.

Enright, D. Scott. 1991. "Supporting children's English language development in grade-level and language classrooms." In Celce-Murcia, Marianne, *Teaching English as a Second or Foreign Language.* Second Edition. Newbury House.

> This chapter summarizes several recent developments in the education of school-age ESL students. It is especially useful as an overview of methodological considerations in teaching children. An excellent comprehensive annotated bibliography is appended to the chapter.

Rigg, Pat, and Enright, D. Scott. 1982. *Children and ESL: Integrating Perspectives.* TESOL.

> A very useful anthology of relatively recent research on teaching ESL to children, this book features articles by well-known scholars in the field: Courtney Cazden, Sarah Huddelson, Pat Rigg, Carole Urzua, and Scott Enright. Holding the articles together is a common commitment to whole language, contextual instruction of the second language.

Ventriglia, L. 1982. *Conversations with Miguel and Maria: How Children Learn a Second Language.* Reading, MA: Addison-Wesley.

> The author offers both a description of her own study of children's second language acquisition and an excellent review of the literature. This book is more research-oriented than pedagogical, but can serve as a good resource book. Among her recommendations are providing children with many sensory modalities for learning language.

Chapter 7

Learner Variables II:

Teaching Across Proficiency Levels

Hardly a teaching day goes by in this profession without someone referring to students' proficiency levels with the terms "beginning," "intermediate," or "advanced." And as long as Earth spins on its axis, I suppose, teachers will differ amongst themselves on just what those terms mean. At the American Language Institute of San Francisco State University, for example, the "beginning" level consists of students who already may know a couple of hundred English words and are able to use a few common survival phrases. In some circles these students would be labeled "false beginners" as distinguished from "true beginners." The "advanced" level, on the other hand, is not as advanced as some of the ESL writing courses offered for credit in the same university's Department of English.

So, there is a certain sense of relativity that must always be taken into account when the terms are used. What is beginning for some may not be for others. Certainly the language teaching profession does not lay unique claim to such subjectivity. Consider, for example, how "Intermediate Algebra" might be variously interpreted according to the institution in which it is offered.

Defining Proficiency Levels

Is there a standard set of guidelines by which these three mysterious terms may be uniformly understood? The answer is yes, and while textbooks and curricula do not by any means universally adhere to these guidelines, they nevertheless offer us a practical description of speaking, listening, reading, and writing proficiency at numerous gradations.

The *ACTFL Proficiency Guidelines* (1986) have come to be a widely recognized proficiency standard in language teaching circles. The current version of the guidelines is historically related to what for many years was referred to as "FSI levels" of speaking proficiency. The FSI (Foreign Service Institute) levels, now referred to as "ILR" (Interagency Language Roundtable) levels in more formal, research settings, represent points on an increasing scale of sophistication as determined by the FSI Oral Interview. The Oral Interview is a carefully designed set of structured tasks that elicit pronunciation, fluency and integrative ability, sociolinguistic and cultural knowledge, grammar, and vocabulary. The test taker is judged to possess proficiency that falls into one of the following eleven different levels:

LEVEL	DESCRIPTION
0	Unable to function in the spoken language
0+	Able to satisfy immediate needs using rehearsed utterances
I	Able to satisfy minimum courtesy requirements and maintain very simple face-to-face conversations on familiar topics
I+	Can initiate and maintain predictable face-to-face conversations and satisfy limited social demands
2	Able to satisfy routine social demands and limited work requirements
2+	Able to satisfy most work requirements with language usage that is often, but not always, acceptable and effective
3	Able to speak the language with sufficient structural accuracy and vocabulary to participate effectively in most formal and informal conversations on practical, social, and professional topics
3+	Often able to use the language to satisfy professional needs in a wide range of sophisticated and demanding tasks
4	Able to use the language fluently and accurately on all levels normally pertinent to professional needs
4+	Speaking proficiency is regularly superior in all respects, usually equivalent to that of a well-educated, highly articulate native speaker
5	Speaking proficiency is functionally equivalent to that of a highly articulate, well-educated native speaker and reflects the cultural standards of the country where the language is spoken

The *ACTFL Proficiency Guidelines* were created to expand on the FSI levels so that listening, reading, and writing would also be included. The *Guidelines* have one other important difference—they are not connected with any one proficiency test, as the FSI levels are. Instead, they were created to guide any test maker in the process of assessment. Today, numerous test designers utilize the *Guidelines* as a standard for assessment. While they were expressly not designed for assessing achievement in any one curriculum, the *Guidelines* can, with caution, provide a number of useful checkpoints for curriculum development and revision.

You will notice in the table of Speaking Guidelines (Table 7.1) that the term "novice" replaces the term "beginning" due to the difficulty of establishing a definitive beginning **point** in most language learners. For the distinction between what in ordinary conversation we might call beginners and false beginners, the *Guidelines* offer the terms novice-low and novice-mid.

Teaching Beginning Levels

Teaching beginners is considered by many to be the most challenging level of language instruction. Since students at this level have little or no prior knowledge of English on which to build, the teacher (and accompanying techniques and materials) becomes a central determiner in whether or not students accomplish their goals. This can also be the most tangibly rewarding level for a teacher because one can readily see the growth of students' proficiency in a matter of a few weeks.

At the beginning or even false-beginning level your students have very little language "behind" them. You may therefore be tempted to go along with the popular misconception that the target language cannot be taught **directly**, that you will have to resort to a good deal of talking "about" English in the students' native language. Such is clearly not the case, as beginning language courses have demonstrated for many decades. But you do have to keep well in mind that your students' capacity for taking in and retaining new words, structures, and concepts is limited. Foremost on your mind as a teacher should be the presentation of material in simple segments that don't overwhelm your students. Remember, they are just barely beginning!

The following ten factors—and the words of advice accompanying each —will help you to formulate an **approach** to teaching beginners. As you adopt a theoretical stance on each factor, you will be able to design classroom techniques that are consistent with your approach.

Table 7.1. ACTFL Proficiency Guidelines.

Generic Descriptions—Speaking

Novice
The Novice level is characterized by the ability to communicate minimally with learned material.

Novice-Low
Oral production consists of isolated words and perhaps a few high-frequency phrases. Essentially no functional communicative ability.

Novice-Mid
Oral production continues to consist of isolated words and learned phrases within very predictable areas of need, although quality is increased. Vocabulary is sufficient only for handling simple, elementary needs and expressing basic courtesies. Utterances rarely consist of more than two or three words and show frequent long pauses and repetition of interlocutor's words. Speaker may have some difficulty producing even the simplest utterances. Some Novice-Mid speakers will be understood only with great difficulty.

Novice-High
Able to satisfy partially the requirements of basic communicative exchanges by relying heavily on learned utterances but occasionally expanding these through simple recombinations of their elements. Can ask questions or make statements involving learned material. Shows signs of spontaneity although this falls short of real autonomy of expression. Speech continues to consist of learned utterances rather than of personalized, situationally adapted ones. Vocabulary centers on areas such as basic objects, places, and most common kinship terms. Pronunciation may still be strongly influenced by first language. Errors are frequent and, in spite of repetition, some Novice-High speakers will have difficulty being understood even by sympathetic interlocutors.

Intermediate
The Intermediate level is characterized by the speaker's ability to:

—create with the language by combining and recombining learned elements, though primarily in a reactive mode;

—initiate, minimally sustain, and close in a simple way basic communicative tasks;
—ask and answer questions.

Intermediate-Low
Able to handle successfully a limited number of interactive, task-oriented and social situations. Can ask and answer questions, initiate and respond to simple statements and maintain face-to-face conversation, although in a highly restricted manner and with much linguistic inaccuracy. Within these limitations, can perform such tasks as introducing self, ordering a meal, asking directions, and making purchases. Vocabulary is adequate to express only the most elementary needs. Strong interference from native language may occur. Misunderstandings frequently arise, but with repetition, the Intermediate-Low speaker can generally be understood by sympathetic interlocutors.

Intermediate-Mid
Able to handle successfully a variety of uncomplicated, basic and communicative tasks and social situations. Can talk simply about self and family members. Can ask and answer questions and participate in simple conversations on topics beyond the most immediate needs; e.g., personal history and leisure time activities. Utterance length increases slightly, but speech may continue to be characterized by frequent long pauses, since the smooth incorporation of even basic conversational strategies is often hindered as the speaker struggles to create appropriate language forms. Pronunciation may continue to be strongly influenced by first language and fluency may still be strained. Although misunderstandings still arise, the Intermediate-Mid speaker can generally be understood by sympathetic interlocutors.

Intermediate-High
Able to handle successfully most uncomplicated communicative tasks and social situations. Can initiate, sustain, and close a general conversation with a number of strategies appropriate to a range of circumstances and topics, but errors are evident.

Limited vocabulary still necessitates hesitation and may bring about slightly unexpected circumlocution. There is emerging evidence of connected discourse, particularlyor simple narration and/or description. The Intermediate-High speaker can generally be understood even by interlocutors not accustomed to dealing with speakers at this level, but repetition may still be required.

Advanced	The Advanced level is characterized by the speaker's ability to:

—converse in a clearly participatory fashion;

—initiate, sustain, and bring to closure a wide variety of communicative tasks, including those that require an increased ability to convey meaning with diverse language strategies due to a complication or an unforeseen turn of events;

—satisfy the requirements of school and work situations; and

—narrate and describe with paragraph-length connected discourse.

Advanced — Able to satisfy the requirements of everyday situations and routine school and work requirements. Can handle with confidence but not with facility complicated tasks and social situations, such as elaborating, complaining, and apologizing. Can narrate and describe with some details, linking sentences together smoothly. Can communicate facts and talk casually about topics of current public and personal interest, using general vocabulary. Shortcomings can often be smoothed over by communicative strategies, such as pause fillers, stalling devices, and different rates of speech. Circumlocution which arises from vocabulary or syntactic limitations very often is quite successful, though some groping for words may still be evident. The Advanced-level speaker can be understood without difficulty by native interlocutors.

Advanced Plus — Able to satisfy the requirements of a broad variety of everyday, school, and work situations. Can discuss concrete topics relating to particular interests and special fields of competence. There is emerging evidence of ability to support opinions, explain in detail, and hypothesize. The Advanced-Plus speaker often shows a well developed ability to compensate for an imperfect grasp of some forms with confident use of communicative strategies, such as paraphrasing and circumlocution. Differentiated vocabulary and intonation are effectively used to communicate fine shades of meaning. The Advanced-Plus speaker often shows remarkable fluency and ease of speech but under the demands of Superior-level complex tasks, language may break down or prove inadequate.

Superior — The Superior level is characterized by the speaker's ability to:

    participate effectively in most formal and informal conversations on practical, social, professional, and abstract topics; and

—support opinions and hypothesize using native-like discourse strategies.

Superior — Able to speak the language with sufficient accuracy to participate effectively in most formal and informal conversations on practical, social, professional, and abstract topics. Can discuss special fields of competence and interest with ease. Can support opinions and hypothesize, but may not be able to tailor language to audience or discuss in depth highly abstract or unfamiliar topics. Usually the Superior level speaker is only partially familiar with regional or other dialectical variants. The Superior level speaker commands a wide variety of interactive strategies and shows good awareness of discourse strategies. The latter involves the ability to distinguish main ideas from supporting information through syntactic, lexical and suprasegmental features (pitch, stress, intonation). Sporadic errors may occur, particularly in low-frequency structures and some complex high-frequency structures more common to formal writing, but no patterns of error are evident. Errors do not disturb the native speaker or interfere with communication.

1. Students' cognitive learning processes

In those first few days and even weeks of language learning, virtually all of the students' processing with respect to the second language itself is in a **focal, controlled** mode[1] (see *PLLT*, Chapter 11, for a review of McLaughlin's cognitive processes and some classroom applications). Therefore, you can expect to engage in plenty of repetition of a limited number of words, phrases, and sentences. Don't get overly frustrated if a considerable period of time goes by with little change in these learning modes.

However, even in the first few days of class, you can coax your students into some **peripheral** processing by getting them to use practiced language for genuinely meaningful purposes. For example, getting information from a classmate whom a student does not know will require using newly learned language (such as "What's your name?" or "Where do you live?") but with a focus on the purposes to which the language is put, not on the forms of language. The forms themselves, although still controlled (limited in capacity), nevertheless move into a peripheral mode as students get immersed in the task of seeking genuine information.

2. The role of the teacher

Beginning students are highly dependent on the teacher for models of language, and so a **teacher-centered** or teacher-fronted classroom is appropriate for some of your classroom time. Students are unable to initiate very many questions and comments in the classroom, and so it is your responsibility to "keep the ball rolling." However, your beginning level classes need not be devoid of a modicum of **student-centered** work. Pair work and group work (see Chapter 11) are effective techniques for taking students' focus off of you as the center of attention and for getting them into an interactive frame of mind even at the most beginning level.

It follows that the degree of **control** of classroom time also leans strongly in the direction of the teacher at the beginning levels. In a **second** language context where instruction is carried out in the target language (English), virtually all of your class time will be teacher-controlled. Since students have no means, in the English language anyway, of controlling the class period, the onus is on you for the full duration to plan topics, activity types, time-on-task, etc. As students gain in their proficiency, they will be able to initiate questions and comments of their own that may then occasionally shift the

---

[1] A quick review of *PLLT* may remind you that controlled processing is simply that which is common in any new skill where few bits of information can be managed at once. Focal attention is giving notice to something in particular: a language form, an attempted message, a person's physical appearance, a person's emotional state, etc. Automatic processing is the simultaneous management of a multitude of pieces of information. And peripheral attention refers to things that we give only incidental notice to.

locus of control. In a **foreign** language situation, where your students speak the same native language (and you speak it as well), some negotiation might be possible in the native language, allowing for a small amount of student control (see #3 below.)

3. Teacher talk

Your input in the class is crucial. Every ear and eye are indeed focused on you. Your own English needs to be very clearly articulated. It is appropriate to slow your speech somewhat for easier student comprehension, but don't slow it so much that it loses its naturalness. And remember, you **don't** need to talk any louder to beginners than to advanced students if your articulation is clear. Use simple vocabulary and structures that are at or just slightly beyond their level.

Is it appropriate to use the students' native language? As noted above, in second language situations, especially in multilingual classes, your use of a student's native language is only seldom an issue. In foreign language situations, however, it becomes an option. It is important not to let your classes go to excess in the use of the students' native language. The rule of thumb here is usually to restrict classroom language to English unless some distinct advantage is gained by the use of their native language, and then, only for very brief stretches of time. Examples of such advantages include:

- negotiation of disciplinary and other management factors
- brief descriptions of how to carry out a technique
- brief explanations of grammar points
- quick pointers on meanings of words that remain confusing after students have had a try at defining something themselves
- cultural notes and comments

4. Authenticity of language

The language that you expose your students to should, according to principles of CLT discussed in Chapters 2 and 5, be authentic language, not stilted just because students are beginners. Simple greetings and introductions, for example, are authentic and yet manageable. Make sure utterances are limited to short, simple phrases. At times such language may appear to be artificial because of all the repetition needed at this stage. Don't despair; your students will appreciate the opportunity to practice their new language.

5. Fluency and accuracy

Fluency is a goal at this level but only within the limited utterance lengths that can be considered. Fluency does not have to apply only to long utterances. The "flow" of language is important to establish, from the beginning, in reasonably short segments of language. Attention to accuracy should center on the particular grammatical, phonological, or discourse elements that are being practiced.

In teaching speaking skills, it is extremely important at this stage that you be very sensitive to students' need to practice freely and openly without fear of being corrected at every minor flaw. On the other hand, you need to give some treatment of selected grammatical and phonological errors so that students don't fall into the trap of assuming that "no news is good news" (no correction implies perfection). Pronunciation work (on phonemes, phonemic patterns, intonation, rhythm, and stress) is very important at this stage. Neglecting phonological practice now may be at the expense of later fluency. Your job, of course, is to create the perfect balance. Chapter 15 will deal in more detail with this balance.

6. Student creativity

The ultimate goal of learning a language is to be able to comprehend and produce it in **unrehearsed** situations, which demands both receptive and productive creativity. But at the beginning level, students can only be creative within the confines of a highly controlled repertoire of language. Don't expect much innovation at this level until students get more language under their control.

7. Techniques

Short, simple techniques must be used. Some mechanical techniques are appropriate—choral repetition and other drilling, for example. A good many teacher-initiated questions dominate at this level, followed only after some time by an increase in simple student-initiated questions. Group and pair activities are excellent techniques as long as they are structured and very clearly defined with specific objectives. A variety of techniques is important because of limited language capacity.

8. Listening and speaking goals

On pages 107–110 is a reproduction of the "Scope and Sequence" chart for *Vistas* (Brown, 1992) referred to in Chapter 1. Notice in that chart that the listening and speaking functions for beginners are meaningful and authentic communication tasks. They are are limited more by grammar, vocabulary, and length of utterance than by communicative function. It is surprising how many language functions can be achieved with very uncomplicated language.

TOPICS	GRAMMAR	COMMUNICATION SKILLS	
		Listening and Speaking	**Reading and Writing**
Meeting people	Subject pronouns (*I, you, he, she,* etc.)	Greeting and introducing people	Reading abbreviations
The classroom	Present tense of *be*	Getting and giving personal information	Reading for rent ads
Telephone numbers and addresses	Demonstrative adjectives and pronouns (*this, that, these, those*)	Asking how to spell something	Reading a map
The family	Definite (*the*) and indefinite (*a/an*) articles	Thanking	Reading entertainment ads
Occupations	Singular and plural noun forms	Identifying objects	Reading food ads
Physical characteristics	Possessive adjectives (*my, your, his, her,* etc.) and possessive *s*	Describing things and giving their locations	Reading recipes
Renting an apartment	Adjectives (bad, good, slow, etc.)	Correcting and confirming	Following vending machine instructions
The home and furniture	Adverbs of manner (badly, well, slowly, etc.)	Apologizing	Reading a menu
Seasons and weather	Prepositions of location (in, on, under, near, etc.)	Describing and identifying people	Reading a restaurant check
Months and dates	There is/are	Getting someone's attention	Completing a registration form
Clothes and colors	Questions with *or*	Asking someone to repeat something	Completing an I.D. card
Days of the week and daily routines	Some and any	Talking about possessions	Setting up an address book
Work and chores	Count (apples, onions, etc.), and non-count (sugar, milk, etc.), nouns	Talking about the weather and the seasons	Writing a personal description
The time	Present continuous tense	Getting and giving the time and date	Writing a postcard
Transportation	Simple present tense	Talking about the present	Writing a letter about a friend
Movies	Conjunctions and, but, and because	Talking about clothes and colors	Writing a description of one's day
Free time	Too and (not) either	Talking on the telephone	Writing a note to a friend
Cooking, shopping, and food	Clauses with before, after, and when	Talking about weekly routines and schedules	Making a shopping list
Vending machines and money	Adverbs of frequency (sometimes, always, never, etc.)	Asking about relatives and friends	
Restaurants	Have to	Offering help	
The future	Let's...	Asking for transportation information	
	A lot of, much, and many	Talk about work and school	
	How much and how many	Talking about movies	
	Quantities (dozen, can, loaf, etc.)	Agreeing	
	Affirmative and negative imperative	Talking about what people have to do	
	Need to, want to, try to, like to	Giving reasons and opinions	
	The future with the present progressive tense	Making suggestions and accepting or declining	
	Expressions of future time (later, tomorrow, tonight, etc.)	Talking about quantity and availability	
		Asking for locations in a grocery store	
		Asking about prices	
		Talking about favorite things	
		Giving and following directions	
		Talking about the future	
		Ordering in a restaurant	
		Listening to recorded movie announcements	

TOPICS	GRAMMAR	COMMUNICATION SKILLS	
		Listening and Speaking	**Reading and Writing**
Parties	Verbs that don't usually	Introducing people	Reading a store directory
Work	end in -ing (like, know,	Complimenting and	Reading sale ads
Life in the past	etc.)	accepting compliments	Reading medicine labels
History and important	Conjunctions	Agreeing and disagreeing	Reading international
dates	That and so	Apologizing and accepting	travel signs
The family	The simple past tense	an apology	Reading arrival and
Shopping for clothes	Expressions of past time	Offering, accepting, and	departure screens
Department stores	Present, past, and modal	declining food	Reading abbreviations
Bargains	tag questions (She can	Getting and giving personal	Reading help wanted ads
A robbery	swim, can't she?)	information	Getting meaning from
Illness and the body	Who as subject	Talking about the present	context
Vacations and travel	Anyone, someone, no one	and past	Writing an invitation
Applying for a job	Wh- questions with which	Talking about family and	Writing a page in a diary
Marriage	One and ones	friends	Filling out a charge account
The future, fortunetellers,	Object pronouns	Talking about people	application
and horoscopes	Would like (to)	and events	Writing a note to a teacher
Cars and driving	Compound nouns	Giving opinions	or boss
Advice	(homework, credit card,	Asking for confirmation	Writing a postcard
	etc.)	Asking for and giving	Completing a job
	The past tense of be	assistance	application form
	There was/were	Talking about clothing	Writing a résumé
	(Not) as..as	Describing people	Writing a note with only
	Adjective + to + verb	Comparing	necessary information
	(easy to clean)	Emphasizing	Taking a written driver's
	Comparative of adjectives	Talking about preferences	license examination
	Superlative of adjectives	Complaining	Writing an article about a
	The future with be going to	Making, agreeing to, and	classmate or oneself
	and will	rejecting suggestions	
	The immediate past with	Asking for and giving	
	just	advice	
	Can and could	Talking about illness	
	Have got and have got to	Making a doctor's	
	Clauses with if	appointment	
	Should	Offering sympathy	
	Must	Talking about vacations	
	Wh- questions with whose	Checking in for a flight	
	Possessive pronouns	Asking for travel	
	Too (It's too impractical.)	information	
	Had to	Talking about ability	
	A lot (of), a little, a few,	Giving reasons or excuses	
	and enough	Inviting and refusing	
	So (The movie was so	invitations	
	good.)	Making requests and	
		promises	
		Talking about the future	
		Talking about possessions	
		Talking about obligation	
		and necessity	
		Expressing surprise and	
		interest	
		Talking about quantity and	
		availability	

TOPICS	GRAMMAR	COMMUNICATION SKILLS	
		Listening and Speaking	**Reading and Writing**
Rules and public behavior	May and can for permission	Asking for confirmation	Predicting
Childhood	Present perfect with for,	Giving and denying	Scanning
Work	since, ever, already, yet,	permission	Discussing job applicants
Likes and dislikes	just	Getting and giving personal	and qualifications
A wedding	Present perfect tag questions	information	Getting the meaning of
Vacations and travel	Past time with used to	Talking about past habits,	words from contest
The use of common	Plural nouns with no article	abilities, and activities	Figuring out pronoun
machines	Verb + gerund (I enjoy	Talking about likes and	reference
Sports	working.)	dislikes	Using context to choose
Interests and abilities	Preposition + gerund	Expressing enthusiasm	synonyms
Chores around the house	Possibility with could, may,	Talking about possibility	Reading travel ads
Baking and food	and might	Drawing conclusions	Reading public signs
Geography	Conclusions with must	Congratulating	Reading a tourist guide
Trivia	Some, any, and one as noun	Expressing excitement	Reading ads and tables
Production of food and	substitutes	Making requests and offers	Reading, writing, and
goods	Verb + infinitive (plan to go)	Talking about places people	saying large numbers
Famous people, places, and	Verb + infinitive or gerund	have visited	Organizing information
things	Advice with ought to	Asking for and giving	into paragraphs
Plans for class break	Compounds with some, any,	instructions	Writing an informal
Transportation	and no (someone, anyone,	Expressing hopes	invitation
Buying cars and appliances	no one, etc.)	Making suggestions	Ordering paragraphs
	No + noun or gerund	Giving reasons and opinions	correctly
	(no exit, no smoking)	Agreeing	Making a survey and taking
	Imperative with you	Talking about health	notes
	So... (that)	Expressing reciprocity	Writing a personal letter to
	Separable two-word verbs	Talking about leisure time	bring a friend up to date
	Past continuous with when	activities	Writing a summary
	and while	Complimenting and	Writing a recipe
	Be able to	complaining	Writing a description of
	Reflexive pronouns	Talking about geography	one's country
	Reciprocal pronouns	and comparing places	Writing about the capital
	Too...to (The kitchen is too	Asking for explanations	or an important city in
	big to paint by himself.)	Expressing positive and	one's country
	Present (exhausting) and	negative feelings	Editing and writing
	past (exhausted)	Giving statistics	a postcard
	participles as adjectives	Stating rules	
	Verb + object + to/for	Talking about places and	
	Look, feel, sound, etc., +	things	
	adjective	Talking about a country's	
	Look, feel, sound, etc., +like	products	
	What a/an for compliments	Correcting	
	and complaints	Talking about how people	
	Negative yes/no questions	do things	
	Wh- questions with how	Talking about quality and	
	Comparative and	performance	
	superlative of adverbs	Asking for and giving	
	Get + adjective	advice	
	The with geographical	Giving additional	
	names	information	
	The present and past ten-	Talking about hypothetical	
	ses in the passive voice	situations	
	Had ('d) better	Convincing someone to	
	Before, during, after, and	do something	
	for + noun	Talking about future plans	
	Before, after, when + clause		
	Conditional with		
	if...would...		

TOPICS	GRAMMAR	COMMUNICATION SKILLS	
		Listening and Speaking	Reading and Writing

Shopping
Location of stores and
  services
Getting things done
Directions
Disasters and accidents
Sightseeing
Lifestyles
Careers and jobs
Bosses and employees
The circus
Television
Leisure time
Travel
Cooking and entertaining
Computers
The future
Going back to school
Politics
	The future with the simple
	  present and the present
	  continuous
	Another, the other(s), other
	Wh- noun clauses
	Causative with make, get,
	  and have
	Placement order of adverbs
	Adverbial clauses with
	  future time
	Adverbial clauses showing
	  purpose or reason
	Present perfect progressive
	Separable and inseparable
	  two-word verbs
	Relative clauses with who,
	  whom, which, and that
	Still vs. any longer
	  (anymore)
	Both...and...
	Either...or and Neither...nor
	Comparison of nouns
	Participial phrases
	Prefixes im-, in-, un-, ir-,
	  dis-, and anti-
	Such (a/an) for compli-
	  ments
	Verb + direct object +
	  infinitive
	The future, present perfect,
	  and modals in the
	  passive voice
	Result clauses with *such*
	  a...that
	Not only...but (also)
	Modals in the past
	Modals in the progressive
	Hope and wish
	Unless and only if
	Prefixes in- and re-
	Suffixes -or, -ment, -er, -
	  ent, -ion, and -ian
	Reported speech
		Making comparisons
		Making offers and requests
		Asking for and offering help
		Asking for confirmation
		Giving advice and opinions
		Asking for and giving
		  locations
		Making appointments
		Stating the purpose or
		  reason
		Asking for and giving
		  directions
		Finding out what people
		  have done recently and
		  when they did it
		Discussing what to watch
		  on TV
		Agreeing and disagreeing
		Describing people and
		  things
		Talking about jobs and
		  careers
		Expressing doubt
		Asking about likes and
		  dislikes
		Comparing places
		Talking about preferences
		Explaining how to do
		  something
		Inviting and declining an
		  invitation
		Suggesting an alternative
		  date and accepting an
		  invitation
		Proposing a toast
		Describing people's
		  behavior, personalities,
		  and actions
		Reporting a disaster
		Talking and speculating
		  about the future
		Emphasizing
		Finding out if things have
		  been done or when they
		  will be done
		Making assumptions about
		  the present and past
		Expressing hope
		Making wishes
		Complimenting and
		  complaining
		Reporting other people's
		  opinions
		Reporting what people ask
		  and say
			Reading store ads and
			  floor plans
			Getting the meaning of
			  words from contest
			Inferring
			Reading a repair bill
			Reading a checkbook
			Scanning
			Restating information from
			  a chart
			Reading sports scores
			Predicting
			Reading tour ads and
			  fact sheets
			Finding definitions in the
			  dictionary
			Reading and writing recipes
			Reading course descriptions
			Writing a comparison of
			  one's life before and now
			Writing a check
			Writing a business reply
			  letter
			Writing a personal letter to
			  give directions
			Writing descriptions of
			  sports and games
			Taking a telephone message
			Writing descriptions of
			  people and things with
			  specific details
			Writing a comparison
			Writing a personal profile
			Writing an account of
			  a disaster
			Writing a composition
			  which argues one's point
			  of view
			Rewriting an article using
			  reported speech
			Writing an article based on
			  an interview
			Writing a speech
			Writing a letter of
			  application for a job

9. Reading and writing goals

A glance at the Scope and Sequence charts (see pp. 107–110) reveals some noticeable differences between Levels 1 and 4 in reading and writing skills. In Level 1, reading and writing topics are confined to brief but nevertheless real-life written material. Advertisements, forms, and recipes are grist for the beginner's reading mill, while written work may involve forms, lists, and simple notes and letters. The most important contextual factor that you should bear in mind in teaching reading and writing to beginners is their **literacy** level in their own native language, an issue that is covered in Chapter 16.

10. Grammar

Whether a curriculum or textbook is billed as functional, communicative, structural, or whatever, grammar and grammar sequencing is an issue. As the charts show, a typical beginning level will deal at the outset with very simple verb forms, personal pronouns, definite and indefinite articles, singular and plural nouns, and simple sentences, in a progression of grammatical topics from simple to complex. (See Chapter 18 for more information on grammar sequencing in textbooks and curricula.)

Whether or not you choose to overtly "explain" grammar in the classroom is another issue (that is also dealt with in Chapter 18). If you are teaching EFL (in a non-English-speaking country), and your students all speak the same native language, you may profit from occasionally using their native language to explain simple grammatical points. In ESL situations, where you must rely only on English in the classroom, grammatical explanations of any complexity would at this level only overwhelm the students. Therefore, an inductive approach to grammar with suitable examples and patterns will be more effective.

Teaching Intermediate Levels

Now, turn your attention to that vague curricular territory that we call "intermediate" where students have progressed beyond novice stages to an ability to sustain basic communicative tasks, to establish some minimal fluency, to deal with a few unrehearsed situations, to self-correct on occasion, to use a few compensatory strategies, and generally to "get along" in the language beyond mere survival. The picture changes somewhat. Your role and the students' capacities change. Consider the same 10 factors.

1. Students' cognitive learning processes

At the intermediate stage some **automatic** processing has taken hold. Phrases and sentences and structures and conversational rules have been practiced and are increasing in number, forcing the mental processes to automatize. I like to think of automaticity as placing elements of language into the "hard drive" of our neurological computers. Our immediately controlled "desktops" (limited in capacity) are too small to contain all the information we need. One of your principal goals at this level is to get students to continue to automatize, to continue to allow the bits and pieces of language that might clutter the mind to be relegated to automaticity. There, in their linguistic hard drives, those bits and pieces are beneath the surface, as it were, yet readily available for immediate (automatic) use whenever needed.

2. The role of the teacher

You are no longer the only initiator of language. Students should be encouraged to ask questions, make comments, and negotiate certain options in learning where appropriate. More student-student interaction can now take place in pairs, small groups, and whole class activity.

Learner-centered work is now possible for more sustained lengths of time as students' language is able to maintain topics of discussion and focus. By its very nature, the intermediate level is richly diverse; that diversity can work to your advantage with carefully designed cooperative activities that capitalize on differences among students. Don't set equal expectations for all students, however, since abilities, especially speaking abilities, can vary widely.

3. Teacher talk

Most of your oral production can be sustained at a natural pace, as long as articulation is clear. Teacher talk should not occupy the major proportion of a class hour; otherwise, you are probably not giving students enough opportunity to talk.

You should be using less of the native language of the learners at this level, but some situations may still demand it.

4. Authenticity of language

At this level students sometimes get overly concerned about grammatical correctness and may want to wander into esoteric discussions of grammatical details. This penchant for analysis might get them too far afield from authentic, real language. Make sure they stay on the track.

5. Fluency and accuracy

The dichotomy between fluency and accuracy is a crucial concern here, more so than at either of the other ends of the proficiency spectrum. Some students are likely to become overly concerned about accuracy, possibly berating themselves for all the mistakes they make and demanding constant corrections for every slip-up. Others may slide into a self-satisfied rut in which they actually become quite fluent, in the technical sense of the term, but in which they become very difficult to comprehend. Be on the lookout for both types of student and be prepared to offer individualized attention to each.

In general, fluency exercises (saying or writing a steady flow of language for a short period of time without any self- or other-correction at all) are a must at this level. They help to get students over the hump of always having to say or write everything absolutely correctly. You want them in due course of time to go through the "breakthrough" stage of language learning, often thought of as a stage after which a learner looks back and says, "Wow! I just carried on a whole conversation without thinking about my grammar!" A big part of your task with most students is to maintain their "flow" with just enough attention to error to keep them growing.

6. Student creativity

The fact that some of this new language is now under control gives rise to more opportunities for the student to be "creative." Interlanguage errors like:

> **Does John can sing?**
>
> **What means this?**
>
> **I must to make a lot of money.**

are a good indication of the creative application of a system within the learner's mind. Try to recognize this form of creativity as a positive sign of language development and of the internalization of a coherent system. Students are also becoming more capable now of applying their classroom language to unrehearsed situations "out there." In EFL settings those situations may be more difficult to find, but through the various forms of media and the written word, applications to the real world, heretofore unrehearsed in the classroom, are available and should be encouraged.

7. Techniques

Because of the increasing language capacities of your students, techniques can increase in complexity. Common interactive techniques for intermediates include chain stories, surveys and polls, paired interviews, group problem solving, role plays, story telling, and many others.

8. Listening and speaking goals

The linguistic complexity of communicative listening-speaking goals increases steadily. Along with the creation of novel utterances, students can participate in short conversations, ask and answer questions, find alternative ways to convey meaning, solicit information from others, and more. The functions themselves may not be intrinsically more "complex," but the forms they use are. (For more information on teaching listening and speaking, see Chapters 14 and 15.)

9. Reading and writing goals

Increasing complexity in terms of length, grammar, and discourse now characterizes reading material as students read paragraphs, short, simple stories, and are beginning to use skimming and scanning skills. Writing is similarly more sophisticated. (For more information on teaching reading and writing, see Chapters 16 and 17.)

10. Grammar

Grammar topics such as progressive verb tenses and clauses typify intermediate level teaching. In small doses, students can benefit from short, simple explanations of points in English. Whether through English or the native language medium, such overt attention to "sore spots" in grammar can, in fact, be exceedingly helpful at this stage. Students have been known to flounder in a sea of inductivity when one cogent tip from a teacher sets them back on a straight course. I once encountered a student who for too many months (or years?), when referring to past events, would say things like

She can kept her child.

He must paid the insurance [premium].

One day, a simple explanation from his teacher about modal auxiliaries in the past tense "cured" him when all the outright corrections in the world didn't seem to make an impact.

Keep grammatical metalanguage to an ideal minimum at this level; otherwise, your students will become English grammarians instead of English speakers. Remember, **you** are interested in grammar because that is where some of your training has been, but you don't need to make budding Ph.D.s in linguistics out of your students! Overt grammatical explanation has its place, in the wings, if you will, as a prompter of sorts, but not as the dominant focus of student attention.

Teaching Advanced Levels

As students move on up the developmental ladder, getting closer and closer to their goals, developing fluency along with a greater degree of accuracy, able to handle virtually any situation in which target language use is demanded, they become "advanced" students. At the very top of this ladder is what the *ACTFL Proficiency Guidelines* describe as the "superior" level, comparable in most aspects to an educated native speaker level. Few if any ESL classes are designed for the superior level, so in order to be more in keeping with reality, we will simply focus on what the *Guidelines* describe as the "Advanced" level.

1. Students' cognitive learning processes

As competence in language continues to build, students can realize the full spectrum of processing, assigning larger and larger chunks to automatic modes and gaining the confidence to put the formal structures of language on the periphery so that focal attention may be given to the interpretation and negotiation of meaning and to the conveying of thoughts and feelings in interactive communication. Some aspects of language, of course, need focal attention for minor corrections, refinement, and other "tinkering;" otherwise, teachers would almost be unnecessary. So your task at this level is to assist in that ongoing attempt to automatize language and in that delicate interplay between focal and peripheral attention to selected aspects of language.

2. The role of the teacher

On the surface, your job may appear easier with advanced students; you can sit back and let their questions and self-generated curiosity take over. In reality, this same independence that students have acquired must be cleverly channeled into classroom routines that benefit most of the students most of the time. No mean task! The most common occurrence in advanced level teaching is that your class runs away with itself and you are left with only a quarter or half your plans fulfilled. So, while you want to take advantage of the self-starting personalities in your class, at the same time orderly plans are important. A directive role on your part can create effective learning opportunities even within a predominantly learner-centered classroom.

3. Teacher talk

Natural language at natural speed is a must at this level. Make sure your students are challenged by your choice of vocabulary, structures, idiom, and other language features. But, after all, they are still **learning** the language, so remember that they have not yet turned into native speakers. The amount of teacher talk should be commensurate with the type of activity. Make sure your students have ample opportunities to produce language so that your role as a provider of **feedback** takes prominence. For some of your students, this is the last chance they have to benefit from informed, systematic feedback on their performance; from here on out, they will be out there where people, out of politeness or respect, rarely give corrections.

Very little if any reliance on the students' native language is now justified. Discipline, explanations, and other more complex language can be carried out in English. Occasionally, a teacher of an advanced class will resort to a word or two (a definition, for example) in the native language in order to help a student who is "stuck."

4. Authenticity of language

Everything from academic prose to literature to idiomatic conversation becomes a legitimate resource for the classroom. Virtually no authentic language material ought to be summarily disqualified at this stage. Certain restrictions may come to bear, depending on how advanced your class is, of course.

5. Fluency and accuracy

At this level most if not all of your students are "fluent" in that they have passed beyond that "breakthrough" stage where they are no longer thinking about every word or structure they are producing or comprehending. At issue is a handful or two of problems that need attention. If errors are relatively rare, an occasional treatment from you or from peers may be quite helpful.

6. Student creativity

The joy of teaching at this level is in those moments of student performance when you know that they are now able to apply classroom material to real contexts beyond. Make sure that students keep their eyes fixed on those goals. Be ever wary of classroom activity that simply ends right there in the classroom.

7. Techniques

Techniques can now tap into a full range of sociolinguistic and pragmatic competencies. Typical of this level are activities like group debates and argumentation, complex role plays, scanning and skimming reading material, determining and questioning author's intent, writing essays and critiques. Often at this level students have specific purposes for which they are planning to use English. Focus on those purposes as much as possible.

8. Listening and speaking goals

At this level students can focus more carefully on all the sociolinguistic nuances of language. Pragmatic constraints are common areas needing work as students finely tune their production and comprehension in terms of register, style, the status of the interlocutor, the specific context of a conversational exchange, turn taking, topic nomination and termination, topic changing, and culturally conditioned language constraints.

9. Reading and writing goals

Reading and writing skills similarly progress closer and closer to native speaker competence as students learn more about such things as critical reading, the role of schemata in interpreting written texts, and writing a document related to one's profession (laboratory reports, records of experimental research findings, etc.).

10. Grammar

The concern at the intermediate level for basic grammatical patterns now graduates beyond some of the elements of Level 4 in the chart on page 110 to functional forms, to sociolinguistic and pragmatic phenomena, and to building **strategic competence** (see *PLLT*, Chapter 11). Linguistic metalanguage may now serve a more useful role as students perceive its relevance to refining their language. Your classes need not become saturated with language about language, but well-targeted deductive grammar has its place.

❊   ❊   ❊

You have now had a chance to contemplate quite a number of variables that change as you teach lower or higher levels of proficiency. The age and proficiency variables are two extremely important issues to incorporate into any attempt to plan and conduct language lessons. The next chapter will introduce a number of further contextual variables that come to bear on decisions that you make when you teach in a classroom.

TOPICS FOR DISCUSSION, ACTION, AND RESEARCH

1. Look again at the FSI levels (p. 100) and ACTFL Guidelines (pp. 102 and 103). For a foreign language you know (or English, if it is a second language for you), try a quick self-assessment the two scales. How confident do you feel about your self-rating? If someone else in your class knows your ability in this second language, ask them to place you on the scales, and see if you agree.

2. Let's say you have been asked to give an oral interview to a speaker of English as a second language. In a small group, collaborate to design a format and specific questions to include in such an interview, so that you could determine an FSI and/or ACTFL level of a learner. Then, compare your format with that of other groups. Finally, plan a role-played interview that your group will perform for the rest of the class, perhaps in a language other than English.

3. Think of several different ESL classes that you're familiar with, preferably ranging from beginning to advanced levels. Use the ACTFL Speaking Guidelines to determine the level of each class. Are the Guidelines sufficient? What would you need to add?

4. In a group, talk about how you would approach a class in which there are true beginners as well as "false" beginners? How would you keep the latter challenged without overwhelming the former? Share your ideas with the rest of the class.

5. Review the McLaughlin model in *PLLT,* Chapter 11, especially Table 11.2, listing some classroom examples of each of the four cells in the model. With a partner, try to come up with some additional techniques that are **controlled** with respect to language forms. Then list some where students are **automatically** attending to language forms. Where would you place each technique (both the ones given in the table and your own added ones) on the scale ranging from beginning to advanced levels?

6. It was noted on page 104 that in some EFL situations you might "negotiate" certain elements of classroom practices with students. With a

partner, identify some classroom contexts you both know, and see if you can figure out some specific examples of negotiation. How do those differ, depending on proficiency level?

7. Can **fluency** be practiced at the very beginning level? Explain and give some examples.

8. Ten criteria were offered in this chapter for considering differences across proficiency levels. In pairs or groups, look at each criterion, one by one, and discuss differences across proficiency level for each. Try to illustrate each with a specific classroom example. Then, share your thoughts with the rest of the class.

9. Design a mini-lesson of 15 minutes or so (see Chapter 20 for some guidelines on lesson planning) for **beginners** that teaches students the function of "requesting information" in the context of "transportation." Then, **change** the lesson to make it appropriate for intermediate learners. And then, change it again for advanced learners. What are the differences? Share your three versions in a small group.

FOR YOUR FURTHER READING

ACTFL Proficiency Guidelines. 1986. American Council on Teaching Foreign Languages.

These Guidelines describe proficiency levels for all four skills: speaking, listening, writing, and reading. They are reprinted in various books, one of which is Omaggio (1986). The Guidelines for one of the four skills, speaking, are reprinted on pages 101 and 102, in the current chapter.

Clark, John L.D., and Clifford, Ray T. 1988."The FSI/ILR/ACTFL proficiency scales and testing techniques." *Studies in Second Language Acquisition 10*: 129–147.

In this article, the authors survey research that led to the development of the ACTFL Proficiency Guidelines and outline some needed areas of further research.

Omaggio, Alice C. 1986. *Teaching Language in Context.* Heinle & Heinle.

In chapters 4, 5, and 6 of this book, Omaggio outlines topics, functions, and techniques appropriate at four different levels of proficiency for each of the four skills of listening, reading, speaking, and writing. Her lists provide useful starting points for teachers whose needs range from classroom techniques to curriculum development.

Chapter 8

Sociopolitical and Institutional Contexts

Age and proficiency are two major contextual variables that will affect every aspect of your lesson or curriculum. They may, in fact, be the most important variables. But two other domains also emerge for the language teacher, without consideration of which your classroom lessons may miss their mark: sociopolitical and institutional contexts. Both of these domains intertwine in such a way that it is sometimes impossible to disentangle them and examine one domain without considering the other. Then, subsumed under institutional considerations are the **general purposes** for which learners are taking a course in English.

Sociopolitical Contexts

It is easy to underestimate the importance and power of sociopolitical aspects of language. We have already seen, in looking at communicative language teaching, how dominant all of the social roles of language are. Interaction, negotiation, interpretation, intended meanings, misunderstandings, and pragmatics all underscore those roles. When such considerations are extended into communities, regions, nations, and continents, the political side of language becomes evident. Among some of the social and political issues are:

- correctness and appropriateness
- registers and styles
- acceptable speech varieties in a community
- regional and national standards of language
- national language policy
- international varieties of English

While this chapter will not attempt to treat all such issues in any detail, they come into play to a greater or lesser extent when you step into a language classroom. Three broad categories will suffice here to alert you to the possibilities: ESL and EFL contexts; English as an international language (EIL); and language policy issues.

Second and *Foreign* Language Contexts

In much of our professional musing about teaching and learning, we interchange the terms **second** and **foreign** in referring to English language teaching. (See *PLLT,* Chapter 7, for a discussion of these two terms.) But some caution is warranted when you propose to deal specifically with a curriculum or a lesson because for you and your students the difference between the two is significant.

To distinguish operationally between the two, think of what is going on outside your classroom door. That is, once your students leave your classroom, which language will they commonly hear out there in the hallways or, in case you are in the foreign language department hallway, out on the sidewalks and in the stores? **Second** language learning contexts are those in which the classroom target language is readily available out there. Teaching English in the United States or Australia clearly falls into this (ESL) category. **Foreign** language contexts are those in which students do not have readymade contexts for communication beyond their classroom. They may be obtainable through language clubs, special media opportunities, books, or an occasional tourist, but efforts must be made to create such opportunities. Teaching English in Japan or Morocco or Thailand is clearly a context of English as a foreign language (EFL).

The pedagogical implications for the two contexts of teaching are very significant. In an ESL situation, your students have a tremendous advantage. They have an instant "laboratory" available to them 24 hours a day. I often remind my students studying ESL at the American Language Institute that their classroom hours (about 25 hours a week) are only a fraction of their language learning hours. If you subtract hours spent sleeping, they are left with over 80 additional hours a week of opportunities to learn and practice English!

When you plan an ESL lesson or curriculum, you can capitalize on this advantage. Here are some ways to seize this "ESL advantage:"

- Give homework that involves
      a specific speaking task,
      listening to a radio or TV program,
      reading a newspaper article,
      writing a letter to a store or a charity.
- Encourage students to seek out opportunities for practice.
- Encourage students to seek corrective feedback from others.
- Have students keep a log or diary of their extra-class learning.
- Plan and carry out field trips (to a museum, for example).
- Arrange a social "mixer" with native English speakers.
- Invite speakers into your classroom.

Communicative language teaching in an EFL context is clearly a greater challenge for students and teachers. Often, intrinsic motivation is a big issue since students may have difficulty in seeing the relevance of learning English. Their immediate uses of the language may seem far removed from their own circumstances. Classroom hours are sometimes the only hours of the day when students are exposed to English. Therefore, the language that you present, model, elicit, and treat takes on great importance. If your class meets for, say, only 90 minutes a week, which represents a little more than one percent of their waking hours, think of what students need to accomplish!

Can it be done? Can students learn English in an EFL setting? The answer is obviously "yes" because many people have done so. Here are some guidelines to help you compensate for the lack of ready communicative situations right outside the classroom door:

- Use class time for optimal authentic language input and interaction.
- Don't waste class time on work that can be done as homework.
- Provide regular motivation-stimulating activities.
- Help them to see genuine uses for English in their own lives.
- Play down the role of tests and emphasize more intrinsic factors.
- Provide plenty of extra-class learning opportunities, such as
      assigning an English-speaking movie,
      having them listen to an English speaking TV or radio program,
      getting an English-speaking conversation partner,
      doing outside reading (news magazines, books),
      writing a journal or diary, in English, on their learning process.

- Encourage the use of learning strategies outside class.
- Form a language club and schedule regular activities.

English as an International Language

Closely related to the ES/FL distinction is the relatively new phenomenon of the role of internationalized varieties of English (see *PLLT,* Chapter 7). As English takes on more and more of a **second** language role in a country (such as India, for example), there is a greater likelihood of the growth of a **nativized** variety of English in that country. A good deal of research has been carried out on the "Indianization" of English (see Kachru, 1992), with implications for notions of acceptability and standardization in other countries like the Philippines, Singapore, or Nigeria. Two basic issues for English teachers have emerged:

(1) English is increasingly being used as a tool for interaction among **non**native speakers. Well over one half of the one billion English speakers of the world learned English as a second (or foreign) language. Most English language teachers across the globe are **non**native English speakers.

(2) English is **not** frequently learned as a tool for understanding and teaching U.S. or British cultural values. Instead, English has become a tool for international communication in transportation, commerce, banking, tourism, technology, diplomacy, and scientific research.

The multiplication of varieties of English poses some practical concerns for you. One of those concerns is the issue of grammaticalness and correctness. What standard do you accept in your classroom?

If you're teaching English in India or Nigeria or the Philippines, the practical issue boils down to the need for your open acceptance of the prevailing variety of English in use in that country. It is certainly not necessary to think of English as a language whose cultural identity can only lie with countries like the United States, the United Kingdom, New Zealand, etc. Your students will no doubt be more interested in the practical, non-stigmatized uses of English in various occupational fields in their own country than in imitating American or British English.

If you're not teaching in a country whose people use a widely accepted variety of English, you will still, no doubt, find that your teaching must keep pace with the new pragmatism. Standards of grammaticalness and of pronunciation may well need to be viewed in terms of the practice of natives who are educated, proficient English speakers. In Japan, for example, "Japanized" forms of English are becoming more widely accepted by English specialists. Your own pronunciation, especially, may not be "perfectly nativelike" if you yourself are a nonnative English speaker. The goals that you set for your students may therefore more wisely be goals of **clear, unambiguous** pronunciation of English phonology.

Even if you are teaching English in what Kachru (1988) called **inner circle** countries (United States, United Kingdom, etc.), you are well advised to base your judgments of the acceptability of students' production on the ultimate practical uses to which they will put the language: survival, social, occupational, academic, and technical uses. In a city like San Francisco, for example, we hear many varieties of English. On one occasion, as I interviewed a prospective ESL teacher, I concluded from her excellent but "Hong Kong-ized" variety of English that she was originally from Hong Kong. Upon asking her, I discovered she was a native San Franciscan!

Language Policy Issues

A final sociopolitical contextual consideration at play in your English teaching is a set of sociocultural issues: What **status** does your country accord English? Does your country have an official language **policy** toward English? How does this policy or status affect the motivation and purpose of your students?

The status of English in the United States is certainly not in question. But curiously, at the present time the United States is experiencing a language policy debate. At one end of the spectrum is the "English Only" movement that advocates the exclusive use of the English language for all educational and political contexts and that carries an implicit assumption that the use of one's "home" language will impede success in learning English. In contrast, "English Plus" advocates respond with programs in which home languages and cultures are valued by schools and other institutions, but in which ESL is promoted **and** given appropriate funding. The debate has unfortunately polarized many Americans. On one side are those who raise fears of "wild and motley throngs" of people from faraway lands creating a linguistic muddle. On the other extreme, linguistic minorities lobby for recognition in what they see as a white supremacist governmental mentality.

Yet, enrollments in ESL classes across the United States are higher than ever as recently—and not so recently—arrived immigrants appreciate the importance of English proficiency for survival and adaptation in the home, in the workplace, and in the community.

Current sociopolitical trends in the United States have created a unique challenge for some college-level ESL programs. As more and more families immigrate into the USA, children are placed into elementary and secondary schools according to their achievement in their home countries. Without adequate ESL or bilingual instruction (see below), they may get a "social pass" from one grade to the next without demonstrating mastery of the subject matter or the English proficiency necessary for that mastery. After a few years of this, they find themselves in the upper secondary school grades and in colleges with inadequate language skills to meet academic demands. They have typically gained interpersonal communication skills (see *PLLT,* Chapter 10,) that enable them to get along well socially with peers, but not the cognitive academic language skills needed to progress through a college program. They fall into neither ESL nor native-language course categories in most colleges, and so specialized courses are sometimes developed to meet their special needs. Such courses stress study skills, reading strategies, academic listening skills, and techniques for successful academic writing.

Language policies and social climates may dictate the status accorded to a native and second languages, which can, in turn, positively or negatively affect attitudes and eventual success in language learning. Two commonly used terms characterize the status of the **native** language in a society where a second language is learned. A native language is referred to as **subtractive** if it is considered to be detrimental to the learning of the second language. In some regions of the United States, for example, Spanish may be thought to be sociopolitically less desirable than English. A native Spanish-speaking child, sensing these societal attitudes, affectively feels "ashamed" of Spanish and must conquer those feelings along with learning English. **Additive** bilingual-ism occurs when the native language is held in prestige by the community or society. Children learning English in Quebec are "proud" of their native French language and traditions and can therefore more positively approach the second language.

Virtually all EFL programs are additive since the native language is the accepted norm. Moreover, as the foremost international language, the value of English as a tool for upward mobility is usually in little doubt. But in many countries English is a required subject in schools, usually secondary schools, thereby diminishing possibilities of intrinsic motivation to learn. Teachers are in a constant state of war with the "authorities" (ministries of education) on curricular goals and on the means for testing the achievement of those goals. By passing a grueling computer-scorable standardized multiple-choice exami-nation, a student's "proficiency" is determined. Unfortunately that proficien-cy turns out to be more related to the ability to cram for a standardized test than the ability to use English for communicative, meaningful purposes.

How can you teach a classroom full of students under such circum-stances? Can you focus their efforts and attention on language rather than on the exam at the end of the course? Can students develop an intrinsically ori-ented outlook on their motivation to succeed? As a start to answering such questions, go back to the principles of intrinsic motivation discussed in Chapter 3 and put them to practice, as suggested there. Beyond that, try to keep your students' vision fixed on useful, practical, reachable goals for the communicative use of English.

Institutional Contexts

One of the most salient, if not relevant, contexts of language teaching is the institution in which you are teaching. ES/FL classes are found in a wide variety of educational establishments, such a wide variety, in fact, that textbook publishers have a hard time tailoring material for the many contexts. Even within one "type" of institution, multiple goals are pursued. For example, language schools in many countries are now finely tuned to offer courses in conversation, academic skills, English for specific purposes (ESP), workplace English, vocational/technical English, test-taking strategies, and other specializations.

Institutional constraints are often allied to the sociopolitical considerations discussed above. Schools and universities cannot exist in a social vacuum. Public elementary and secondary schools are subject to official national language policy issues. In the United States and other countries, the type of second language program offered in schools is a product of legislation and governmental red tape. Students' purposes in taking English at the higher education level may be colored by institutional policies, certification and degree requirements, instructional staffing, and even immigration regulations.

Elementary and Secondary Schools

Language policies and programs in elementary and secondary schools differ greatly from country to country around the world. Within some countries like the United States, ESL requirements and offerings vary not only by state but even by school districts that may number in the hundreds in larger states. These programs of course apply to what have come to be called **Limited English Proficient** (LEP) students attending school.

In EFL countries, English is sometimes a required secondary school subject and almost always one of several foreign language options. In certain countries (Sweden and Norway, for example) English is required in elementary schools.

A number of models[1] are currently practiced in the United States for dealing with LEP students in elementary and secondary schools. Some of these models apply to other countries in varying adapted forms.

1. Submersion. The first way of treating nonnative speakers in classrooms is really no treatment at all. Pupils are merely "submerged" in regular content-area classes with no special foreign language instruction. The assumption is that they will "absorb" English as they focus on the subject

---

[1]I am grateful for Patricia Richard-Amato's (1988:221–229) summary of different types of programs and have drawn primarily on her descriptions here.

matter of the school. Research has shown that sometimes they don't succeed in either English or the content areas, especially in **subtractive** situations. So, a few schools may provide a "pull out" program in which, for perhaps one period a day, LEP students leave their regular classroom and attend special tutorials or an ESL class.

2. Immersion. Here, pupils attend specially-designed content-area classes. All of the students in a class speak the same native language and are at similar levels of proficiency in English. The teacher is not only certified in the regular content areas but also has some knowledge of the students' first language and culture. Immersion programs are found more commonly in EFL contexts than in ESL contexts. In most immersion programs pupils are in an **additive** bilingual context enjoying the support of parents and the community in this enriching experience.

3. Sheltered English. This is a specialized form of immersion program that has become popular in recent years. It differs from immersion in that students come from varying native language backgrounds and the teacher is trained in **both** subject matter content **and** ESL methodology. Also, students often have a regular ESL class as part of the curriculum. At Newcomer High School in San Francisco, for example, newly arrived immigrants are given one year of sheltered instruction that differs from other high schools in the ESL training of the teachers and the combination of content and language learning in every subject.

4. Mainstreaming. In some submersion programs, students first receive instruction in ESL before being placed into content areas. Once teachers and tests conclude that students are proficient enough to be placed into ongoing content classes, they are then "mainstreamed" into the regular curriculum. We need to remember that this ESL instruction should be content-centered so that pupils will not be at a disadvantage once they are placed in an ongoing class.

5. Transitional bilingual programs. In the United States, three different forms of bilingual education—in which students receive instruction in some combination of their first and second languages—are in common use. Transitional programs teach subject matter content in the **native** language, combined with an ESL component. When teachers and tests determine that they are ready, students are "transitioned" into regular all-English classes. This has the advantage of permitting students to build early cognitive concepts in their native language and then later to cross over to the dominant language. The major disadvantage is that students too often get mainstreamed before they are ready, before their academic and linguistics skills have been sufficiently built.

6. Maintenance bilingual programs. Here, students continue throughout their school years to learn at least a portion of their subject matter in the native language. This has the advantage of stimulating the continued development of pupils' native languages and of building confidence and expertise in the content areas. Disadvantages include discouraging the mastery of English and the high cost of staffing maintenance classes in budgetary hard times.

7. Enrichment programs. A third form of bilingual education, known as enrichment, finds students taking selected subject-matter courses in a **foreign** language while the bulk of their education is carried on in English. Students in such programs in the United States are not doing so for survival purposes but simply to "enrich" themselves by broadening their cultural and linguistic horizons.

Institutions of Higher Education

English language teaching programs exist in two-year (community) colleges, four-year colleges and universities, post-graduate universities, extended (continuing) education programs, language schools and institutes, vocational and technical schools, adult schools, and in the "workplace" (companies, corporations). And you may even be able to think of a category that has been omitted!

Cutting across those institutional contexts are a number of **purposes** for which languages are taught. Following are six broad types of **curriculum** that are designed to fit such varying student goals:

1. Pre-academic programs are designed for students who anticipate entering a regular course of study at the college level. Some such programs are **intensive** programs, that is, students are in the classroom for 20–25 hours per week, usually for the duration of a quarter or semester. The focus varies in such programs from rather general language skills at the advanced-beginner level to advanced courses in reading, writing, study skills, and research.

2. EAP (English for Academic Purposes) is a term that is very broadly applied to any course, module, or workshop in which students are taught to deal with academically related language and subject matter. EAP is common at the advanced level of Pre-Academic programs as well as in several other institutional settings.

3. ESP (English for Special Purposes) programs are specifically devoted to a professional field of study. A course in "English for Agriculture" or in "Business Writing" would fall under the general rubric of ESP. Usually ESP courses are differentiated from Vocational/Technical English in that the former apply to disciplines in which people can get university majors and degrees, and the latter (see p. 128) to trades and other non-baccalaureate certificate programs.

4. Voc/Tech (Vocational and Technical) English targets those who are learning trades (e.g., carpenters and electricians), arts (e.g., photography) and other occupations not commonly included in university programs.

5. Literacy programs are designed to teach students whose native language reading/writing skills are either non-existent or very poor. Learning to be literate in English while learning aural-oral forms as well requires energy and motivation on the part of students. Teachers need to receive special training to teach at this challenging level.

6. Survival/Social curricula run the gamut from short courses that introduce adults to conversational necessities to full-blown curricula designed to teach adults a complete range of language skills for survival in the context of the second culture. By definition such programs would not progress beyond intermediate skill levels. These courses are frequently offered in night-school adult education programs and private language schools such as Berlitz Schools.

Table 8.1 outlines eight types of institution and the above six different general types of **curriculum.** An "X" in a box indicates that an institution is likely to have such a program.

Table 8.1. Institutions and Curricula.

	Pre-Academic	EAP	ESP	Voc/Tech	Literacy	Survival
2-year college (community)	X	X		X		
4-year college (or university)	X	X	X	X		
post-graduate (university)	X	X	X	X		
language school	X	X	X	X	X	X
extended education	X	X	X	X		
technical schools		X	X	X		
adult education				X	X	X
workplace			X	X	X	X

These institutional contexts are somewhat oversimplified. In determining how to plan lessons and carry out techniques within each curriculum, quite a number of other institutional factors apply. Consider, for example:

- the extent to which institutional regulations demand a certain curriculum content
- the extent to which budgetary and bureaucratic constraints dictate class size, number of hours, etc.
- the extent to which an administrator or supervisor "forces" you to teach in a certain way
- the textbook (which you may detest) assigned to your course
- the support and feedback that you get from fellow teachers
- how other teachers in your institution teach and the extent to which they may subtly coerce you into teaching "their" way
- the number of hours you must teach in order to make a living and how that affects your energy level
- the conditions of your classroom (size of the room, lighting, furniture, etc.)
- whether or not your English course is required and the effect that has on the motivation of your students

❋ ❋ ❋

The list could go on. Institutional constraints are sometimes the biggest hurdle you have to cross. Once you have found ways to compromise with the system and yet to feel professionally fulfilled, then you can release more energy into creative teaching. Many of these issues will be dealt with in future chapters.

TOPICS FOR DISCUSSION, ACTION, AND RESEARCH

1. Think of some specific ESL and/or EFL contexts. Then, refer to the discussion on page 120 regarding the two contexts. With a partner, think of other ways (a) to seize the "ESL advantage" and (b) to compensate for the lack of ready communicative situations right outside the EFL classroom door.

2. In a small group (or as a whole class), think of some specific characteristics of a nativized variety of English such as Indianized or Africanized English (or whatever variety you may be familiar with). Which of these idiosyncrasies would you allow in the classroom as "correct?" Where, if at all, would you "draw the line?"

3. Investigate the official policy on English (and, possibly, other second languages) in the government and educational system of your country. Are there unofficial policies in business, educational, or social circles? Do they sustain or contradict the official stance? You may wish to adopt a debate format for this issue in which groups take different points of view and prepare their arguments and rebuttals.

4. With a partner, try to think of other instances of **subtractive** (p. 124) bilingualism. Describe them. What could you do as a teacher in the classroom to help students to create a more positive outlook on their native and second languages?

5. In countries where English is a compulsory subject in the schools and motivation to learn it is low, what specific steps could you take to lift the motivation level? Would those steps lead to some intrinsic motivation? Are the steps practical? Share your ideas with a small group or whole class.

6. If possible, observe ESL classes that fall into some of the models described on pages 125–127. Compare the differences and similarities in the programs. Describe what seemed to be the most effective and the least effective element in each program or class hour. Share your thoughts with the rest of the class.

7. Look at the chart showing different institutions and curricula (Table 8.1, page 128). Pick two or three types of institution that you are not familiar with and try to find a class to observe. What new approaches or techniques did you see?

8. How would you deal with each of the following scenarios:

    (a) Your administrator insists that you teach a strict ALM method when you're convinced that a form of CLT is not only appropriate but through it your students would get excited and motivated to learn.

    (b) You have been given a textbook to teach from that is boring, lifeless, outdated, with repetitious mechanical exercises throughout.

(c) You are teaching in a language school where you would like to share ideas with your teaching colleagues, but no one wants to talk with you because they all say they're too busy (and you suspect they are a bit defensive about the "rut" they're in after teaching at the same place for many years). Could you get teachers to share ideas in a non-threatening way?

9. The Brazilian educator Paolo Freire (1973) said that education *empowers* people: it enables them to become creative, productive people who will work toward political and social change. In a small group, discuss ways that you think English might empower learners? Then, share your group's ideas with the whole class.

FOR YOUR FURTHER READING

Kachru, Braj B. 1992. "World Englishes: Approaches, issues, and resources." *Language Teaching 25* (1), 1–14.

This article is the lead article for the January, 1992 issue of this abstracting journal. Kachru summarizes a sweeping array of current research and offers comments on the "state of the art" in what has come to be known as "world Englishes."

Freire, Paolo. 1970. *Pedagogy of the Oppressed.* Seabury Press.

This is the seminal work of Freire, a widely known advocate for the disenfranchised. Freire argues the importance of education as a means for empowerment for those who might otherwise be content to let others in power determine their lives.

Cazden, Courtney, and Snow, Catherine. 1990. *English Plus: Issues in Bilingual Education.* (Annals of the American Academy of Political and Social Science No. 508). Sage Publications.

This whole volume is given over to descriptions of issues and of research and practice in what is referred to as "English Plus," an alternative to the "English Only" movement that currently threatens to divide the United States. A case is made here for preserving the home languages of children in schools, and for adding English to their native language skills.

Judd, Elliot. 1987. "Teaching English to speakers of other languages: A political act and a moral question." *TESOL Newsletter 21* (1), 15–16.

In this brief article written for classroom teachers, Judd spells out the political and moral implications of teaching. Not only is every act of teaching colored by political ramifications, but English, especially, has become politicized in many countries, creating certain moral dilemmas as well.

Part Three

✳✳✳

Designing
and
Implementing Techniques

Chapter 9

Techniques and Materials

So far, as you have progressed through the first two sections of this book, you have laid some important groundwork for designing and implementing techniques in the classroom. That groundwork can be capsulized in two major categories:

1. Principled teaching. Your teaching is derived from, and gives feedback to, a set of principles that form the skeleton of an overall approach to language learning and teaching. At this stage you should have a reasonably stable and comprehensive approach, a broad understanding of how learners learn and how teachers can best facilitate that process. At the same time, your approach should be dynamic; it should change and grow as you teach students, study professional material, and observe yourself in the classroom.

2. Contexts of learning. Part of your principled approach to learning and teaching involves an understanding of who your learners are. How old are they? How proficient are they? What are their goals in language learning? What effect do sociopolitical factors have on their eventual success?

You cannot even begin to design techniques in the classroom without considering these two important backdrops that set the stage for classroom activity. The **choices** that you make about what to do in the classroom are enlightened by these two major factors.

Those choices are also enlightened by several other factors: the overall curricular plan, objectives of a particular lesson, and classroom management variables. All of these factors will be considered in detail in the next section (Part IV) once you have gained a working knowledge of the basic components or units of the language classroom: techniques.

Techniques Redefined

It is appropriate, before continuing, to make sure that certain terms are reasonably well understood. In Chapter 5, the term **technique** was introduced and defined, but it was noted in passing that there are other commonly used terms that are considered by some to be virtually synonymous. Some of these other terms include task, activity, procedure, practice, behavior, exercise, and even strategy, to name some. With the potential confusion arising from multiple terms, you will no doubt find it helpful to do some clarifying. Bear in mind, however, that experts in the field may have slightly differing points of view about the working definitions here:

1. Task

We return to the term **task** one more time. You may recall that in Chapter 5, in a discussion of task-based learning, task—depending upon whose definition you consult—usually refers to a specialized form of technique or series of techniques, closely allied with communicative curricula, and as such must minimally have communicative goals. The common thread running through half a dozen definitions of task is its focus on the authentic use of language for meaningful communicative purposes beyond the language classroom. We will return once again to the concept of task in Chapter 13.

2. Activity

A very popular term in the literature, an **activity** may refer to virtually anything that **learners** actually **do** in the classroom. Because an activity implies some sort of active performance on the part of learners, it is generally not used to refer to certain **teacher** behaviors like saying "good morning," or maintaining eye contact with students, or writing a list of words on the blackboard. The latter, however, can indeed be referred to as techniques.

3. Procedure

Richards and Rodgers (1986) used the term **procedure** to encompass "the actual moment-to-moment techniques, practices, and behaviors that operate in teaching a language according to a particular method" (p. 26). Procedures, from this definition, include techniques, but the authors appear to have no compelling objection to viewing the terms synonymously.

4. Practice, behavior, exercise, strategy...

These terms, and perhaps some others that get thrown in on occasion, all appear to refer, in varying degrees of intensity, to what is defined below as **technique.**

5. Technique

Even before Anthony (1963) discussed and defined the term, the language teaching literature widely accepted **technique** as a superordinate term to refer to various activities that either teachers or learners perform in the classroom. In other words, techniques include all tasks and activities. They are almost always planned and deliberate. They are the product of a **choice** made by the teacher. And they can, for your purposes as a teacher of ESL, comfortably refer to the pedagogical units or components of a classroom session. You can think of a lesson as consisting of a number of techniques, some teacher-centered, some learner-centered, some production oriented, some comprehension oriented, some clustering together to form a task, some as a task in and of themselves. We now turn to examine these classroom components of focus or activity.

Categorizing Techniques: A Bit of History

At last count there were 28,732 techniques for teaching language in the classroom. Okay, I'm joking. But a cursory glance at a few dozen textbooks and other teacher-activities books reveals many, many possible techniques! In one very useful teacher reference book, *ESL Teacher's Activities Kit,* Elizabeth Claire (1988) outlines 167 activities for teaching children ESL. Klippel (1986) describes 123 communicative fluency exercises. Shoemaker and Shoemaker (1991) give us 78 interactive techniques. And the list goes on.

How can you best conceptualize this multitude of techniques? Several rubrics have been used over the years to classify techniques.

1. From manipulation to communication

Techniques can be thought of as falling into a continuum of possibilities between highly manipulative and very communicative in their nature. At the extreme end of the manipulative side, a technique would be totally controlled by the teacher **and** require a predicted response from the student(s). Choral repetition and cued substitution drills are examples of oral techniques at this extreme. Other examples are dictation (listening/writing) and reading aloud.

At the communicative extreme, student responses would be completely open ended and therefore **un**predictable. Examples include story-telling, brainstorming, role-plays, certain games, etc. Teachers are usually put into a less controlled role here, as students become free to be creative with their responses and interactions with other students. However, keep in mind that a modicum of teacher control, whether overt or covert, should always be present in the classroom.

It is most important to remember that the manipulation-communication scale does **not** correspond to the beginning-advanced proficiency continuum! For too many years the language teaching profession labored under the incorrect assumption that beginners must have mechanical, unmeaningful bits and pieces of language programmed into them (typically through a memorized audiolingual drill) and that only later could "real" communication take place. The whole CLT approach accentuates a diametrically opposite philosophy: that genuine communication can take place from the very first day of a language class.

The extent to which a communicative technique can **sustain** itself in the classroom will indeed often be a factor of the overall proficiency level of your class. Communicative techniques for beginners need to have appropriately small chunks of language for students to deal with and to build in some repetition of patterns for establishing fluency. In one of the very first days of class, for example, students could be taught to ask and respond to questions like:

> **What's your name?**
>
> **Where do you live?**
>
> **How old are you (for children)? or What do you do (for adults)?**

A communicative technique would involve students in a "mixer" in which they go around the room getting information from, say, four or five other students.

At the more advanced levels, of course, a simple question or problem posed by the teacher can lead to sustained meaningful student communication between student and teacher, in pairs or in small groups.

2. Mechanical, meaningful, and communicative drills

In the decades of the 40s, 50s, and 60s, language pedagogy was consumed with the **drill**. Often great proportions of class time were spent drilling: repeating, repeating, repeating. Today, thankfully, we have developed teaching practices that make only minimal—or optimal—use of such drilling.

A drill may be defined as a technique that focuses on a minimal number (usually one or two) of language **forms** (grammatical or phonological structures) through some type of repetition. Drills are commonly done chorally (the whole class repeating in unison) or individually. And they can take the

form of simple repetition drills, substitution drills,[1] and even the rather horri-
fying aberration known as moving slot substitution drills.[2]

In referring to structural pattern drills, Paulston and Bruder (1976) used
three categories: mechanical, meaningful, and communicative. Mechanical
drills have only one correct response from a student, and have no implied
connection with reality. Repetition drills, for instance, simply require that the
student repeat a word or phrase whether the student understands it or not:

> T: **The cat is in the hat.**
>
> Ss: **The cat is in the hat.**
>
> T: **The wug is on the gling.**
>
> Ss: **The wug is on the gling.**

A meaningful drill may have a predicted response or a limited set of possible responses, but it is connected to some form of reality:

> T: **The woman is outside. [pointing out the window at a woman]
>   Where is she, Hiro?**
>
> S1: **The woman is outside.**
>
> T: **Right, she's outside. Keiko, where is she?**
>
> S2: **She's outside.**
>
> T: **Good, Keiko, she's outside. Now, class, we are inside. Hiroko, where
>   are we?**
>
> S3: **We are inside.**

---

[1]The teacher provides a sentence; students repeat; teacher cues students to change one word or
structure in the sentence; and students repeat. For example:

> T: **I went to the store yesterday.**
>
> Ss: **I went to the store yesterday.**
>
> T: **Bank.**
>
> Ss: **I went to the bank yesterday.**
>
> T: **The hospital.**
>
> Ss: **I went to the hospital yesterday.**

[2]In this case, the slot moves, as in the following example:

> T: **I went to the store yesterday.**
>
> Ss: **I went to the store yesterday.**
>
> T: **Bank.**
>
> Ss: **I went to the bank yesterday.**
>
> T: **He.**
>
> Ss: **He went to the bank yesterday.**
>
> T: **In the morning.**
>
> Ss: **He went to the bank in the morning.**
>
> T: **Will go.**
>
> Ss: **He will go to the bank in the morning.**

By this time, if students haven't thrown up their arms in the frustration of having to retain each
previous sentence alteration, they may have only accomplished the feat of overworking their
short-term memories and certainly not gained any communicative ability in the process.

And the process may continue on as the teacher reinforces certain grammatical or phonological elements. Frankly, I see no reason to refer to such a technique as a drill at all. It is quite legitimately a form of meaningful practice, useful in many communicative classrooms.

Now, while Paulston and Bruder referred to "communicative" drills almost two decades ago, as we now understand and use the term, a communicative drill is indeed an oxymoron. If the exercise is communicative, that is, if it offers the student the possibility of an open response and negotiation of meaning, then it is surely no longer a drill. So, there is what I would call **quasi**-communicative practice that might go something like this, if you were trying to get students to practice the past tense:

> T: **Good morning, class. Last weekend, I went to a restaurant and I ate salmon. Juan, what did you do last weekend?**
>
> Juan: **I went to the park and I played soccer.**
>
> T: **Ying, did you go to the park last weekend like Juan?**
>
> Ying: **No.**
>
> T: **What did you do?**
>
> Ying: **I watched a lot of TV.**
>
> T: **Great, and what did you do, Fay?**

This exercise was an attempt to force students to use the past tense, but allowed them to choose meaningful replies. Juan chose the safety of the teacher's pattern while Ying, perhaps because she was more focused on communicative reality than on past tense formation, initially broke out of the pattern before returning.

A final word about drills before moving on. A communicative approach to language teaching can make some use of drilling techniques, but only in moderation. A few short, snappy drills here and there, especially at the lower levels of proficiency, can be quite useful in helping students to establish structural patterns, rhythm, and certain pronunciation elements. But moderation is the key, especially if your drills are mechanical. There's nothing deadlier than a class hour filled with audiolingual parroting.

3. Controlled to free techniques

Perhaps the most useful classification of techniques for a teacher to use is a continuum not unlike the first one above, but in this case considering the extent to which you, the teacher, maintain control over the learning activity.

It is important to understand what is meant by **control**. In the lists on the next page are a few generalizations.

Controlled	**Free**
Teacher-centered	Student-centered
Manipulative	Communicative
Structured	Open-ended
Predicted student responses	Unpredicted responses
Pre-planned objectives	Negotiated objectives
Set curriculum	Cooperative curriculum

Clearly, the real picture is not so black-and-white as these generalizations would have you believe. For example, many controlled techniques are manipulative, as described above. But controlled techniques sometimes have communicative elements. The quasi-communicative drill just described, for example, is highly controlled in that the teacher provides set questions and each student has a short time in which to respond. But there is an opportunity for students to venture out of the mold if they wish; that's communicative. So, if you are tempted to draw a clearly defined line between controlled and free, resist that temptation.

A Taxonomy of Techniques

A comprehensive taxonomy of common techniques for language teaching, adapted from Crookes & Chaudron (1991), is found in Table 9.1 (pp. 142–143). They used the term "activity" to describe what I am calling techniques. Notice that three broad categories are used: controlled, semi-controlled, and free. Bearing in mind the somewhat slippery concept of control referred to above, you may be able to gain a broad picture, from this taxonomy, of quite a range of classroom language teaching techniques. In the chapters that follow this one, many of these techniques will be discussed with examples and analysis.

Table 9.1. Taxonomy of Language Teaching Techniques (adapted from Crookes & Chaudron, 1991:52–54).

Controlled Techniques

1. Warm-up: Mimes, dance, songs, jokes, play. This activity has the purpose of getting the students stimulated, relaxed, motivated, attentive, or otherwise engaged and ready for the classroom lesson. It does not necessarily involve use of the target language.

2. Setting: Focusing in on lesson topic. Either verbal or nonverbal evocation of the context that is relevant to the lesson point; by way of questioning or miming or picture presentation, possibly tape recording of situations and people, teacher directs attention to the upcoming topic.

3. Organizational: Managerial structuring of lesson or class activities. Includes disciplinary action, organization of class furniture and seating, general procedures for class interaction and performance, structure and purpose of lesson, etc.

4. Content explanation: Explanation of lesson content: grammatical, phonological, lexical (vocabulary), sociolinguistic, pragmatic, or any other aspects of language.

5. Role-play demonstration: Use of selected students or teacher to illustrate the procedure(s) to be applied in the lesson segment to follow. Includes brief illustration of language or other content to be incorporated.

6. Dialogue/Narrative presentation: Reading or listening passage presented for passive reception. No implication of student production or other identification of specific target forms or functions (students may be asked to "understand").

7. Dialogue/Narrative recitation: Reciting a previously known or prepared text, either in unison or individually.

8. Reading aloud: Reading directly from a given text.

9. Checking: Teacher either circulating or guiding the correction of students' work, providing feedback as an activity rather than within another activity.

10. Question-answer, display: Activity involving prompting of student responses by means of display questions (i.e., teacher or questioner already knows the response or has a very limited set of expectations for the appropriate response). Distinguished from referential questions by means of the likelihood of the questioner's knowing the response and the speaker's being aware of that fact.

11. Drill: Typical language activity involving fixed patterns of teacher and student responding and prompting, usually with repetition, substitution, and other mechanical alterations. Typically with little meaning attached.

12. Translation: Student or teacher provision of L1 or L2 translations of given text.

13. Dictation: Student writing down orally presented text.

14. Copying: Student writing down text presented visually.

15. Identification: Student picking out and producing/labeling or otherwise identifying a specific target form, function, definition, or other lesson-related item.

16. Recognition: Student identifying forms, etc., as in Identification, but without producing language as response (i.e., checking off items, drawing symbols, rearranging pictures).

17. Review: Teacher-led review of previous week/month/or other period as a formal summary and type of test of student recall performance.

18. Testing: Formal testing procedures to evaluate student progress.

19. Meaningful drill: Drill activity involving responses with meaningful choices, as in reference to different information. Distinguished from Information Exchange by the regulated sequence and general form of responses.

Semicontrolled Techniques

20. Brainstorming: A special form of preparation for the lesson, like Setting, which involves free, undirected contributions by the students and teacher on a given topic, to generate multiple associations without linking them; no explicit analysis or interpretation by the teacher.

21. Story-telling (especially when student-generated): Not necessarily lesson-based, lengthy presentation of story or even by teacher or student (may overlap with Warm-up or Narrative recitation). May be used to maintain attention, motivation, or as lengthy practice.

22. Question-answer, referential: Activity involving prompting of responses by means of referential questions (i.e., the questioner does not know beforehand the response information). Distinguished from Question-answer, Display.

23. Cued narrative/Dialog: Student production of narrative or dialog following cues from miming, cue cards, pictures, or other stimuli related to narrative/dialog (e.g., metalanguage requesting functional acts).

24. Information transfer: Application from one mode (e.g., visual) to another (e.g., writing), which involves some transformation of the information (e.g., student fills out diagram while listening to description). Distinguished from Identification in that the student is expected to transform and reinterpret the language or information.

25. Information exchange: Task involving two-way communication as in information gap exercises, when one or both parties (or a larger group) must share information to achieve some goal. Distinguished from Question-answer, Referential in that sharing of information is critical for the resolution of task.

26. Wrap-up: Brief teacher or student produced summary of point and/or items that have been practiced or learned.

27. Narration/exposition: Presentation of a story or explanation derived from prior stimuli. Distinguished from Cued Narrative because of lack of immediate stimulus.

28. Preparation: Student study, silent reading, pair planning and rehearsing, preparing for later activity. Usually a student-directed or -oriented project.

Free Techniques

29. Role-play: Relatively free acting out of specified roles and functions. Distinguished from Cued Dialogues by the fact that cueing is provided only minimally at the beginning, and not during the activity.

30. Games: Various kinds of language game activity, if not like other previously defined activities (e.g., board and dice games making words).

31. Report: Report of student-prepared exposition on books, experiences, project work, without immediate stimulus, and elaborated on according to student interests. Akin to Composition in writing mode.

32. Problem solving: Activity involving specified problem and limitations of means to resolve it; requires cooperative action on part of participants in small or large group.

33. Drama: Planned dramatic rendition of play, skit, story, etc.

34. Simulation: Activity involving complex interaction between groups and individuals based on simulation of real-life actions and experiences.

35. Interview: A student is directed to get information from another student or students.

36. Discussion: Debate or other form of grouped discussion of specified topic, with or without specified sides/positions prearranged.

37. Composition: As in Report (verbal), written development of ideas, story or other exposition.

38. A propos: Conversation or other socially oriented interaction/speech by teacher, students, or even visitors, on general real-life topics. Typically authentic and genuine.

In a taxonomy such as this, many techniques will not only be somewhat difficult to categorize in terms of the control continuum, but also you will find plenty of techniques that fit more than one category. Consider the following "warm-up" activity suggested by Klippel (1986:13–14) for use in a beginning level class:

> *Step 1:* **Each student writes his full name on a piece of paper. All the papers are collected and redistributed so that everyone receives the name of a person he does not know.**
>
> *Step 2:* **Everyone walks around the room and tries to find the person whose name he holds. Simple questions can be asked, e.g., "Is your name...?" "Are you...?"**
>
> *Step 3:* **When everyone has found his partner, he introduces him to the group.**

This exercise seems to fit into a number of possible categories: it involves **question-answer, referential** activity; there is some **information exchange** as well; and in some ways either **problem solving** or **games** may fit here. The purpose in referring to such a taxonomy, therefore, is not to be able to pinpoint every technique specifically. Rather, the taxonomy is more of a help to you as:

- an aid to raising your awareness of a wide variety of techniques available to you.
- an indicator of how techniques differ according to a continuum ranging from controlled to free.
- a resource for your own personal brainstorming process as you consider types of techniques for your classroom.

Supporting Materials

Techniques consist of the things you "do" in the classroom, but there are only a few techniques that do not in some manner involve the use of **materials** to support and enhance them. What would language classes be without books, pictures, maps, charts, audio-visuals, and realia? Yes, you could have conversations, role plays, discussions, and blackboard work, but much of the richness of language instruction is derived from supporting materials. And today such materials abound for all levels and purposes.

What kinds of materials are available to you? How do you decide what will work and what won't? Is it worthwhile to create your own materials? If so, what sorts of things can be relatively easily made? We'll look at these and related questions here in this section of the chapter.

Textbooks

The most obvious and most common form of material support for language instruction comes through textbooks. Most likely, as a relatively new teacher, your first concern will not be to choose a textbook, but rather to creatively use the textbook that has been handed to you by your supervisor. So, even though you may have idealistic thoughts about other textbooks out there that might be better, the challenge that you will be more likely to accept at the outset is to make the very best use of the textbook that you have. Sometimes new teachers, in their zeal for creating wonderful, marvelous written materials for their students, neglect the standard textbook prescribed by the school curriculum and fail to see that this resource may actually be quite useful. And you will no doubt find that, as a new teacher, you already have enough on your hands just preparing a lesson, carrying it out, monitoring its unfolding, and managing the dynamics of a classroom full of students. With all this you don't need to add more stress to your life trying to create brand new materials.

So here you are, with a textbook in hand, preparing for tomorrow's lesson. If your textbook has a teacher's edition, by all means consult it and use as many of its suggestions as you feel are appropriate. If there is no teacher's edition, then your task becomes one of devising ways to present the content and the exercises of the book to your class.

On the next three pages is a lesson from the last unit in Book 1 of *Vistas* (Brown, 1992), pitched for a high beginning level class. You will see that this lesson teaches functional language for ordering in a restaurant. Could you devise a plan (for details on planning a whole lesson, see Chapter 20) that would "teach" these six exercises? Of course, each exercise has brief directions to students, but how would you "practice the conversation" in exercise 1? Or "read... and answer" in Exercise 2? Of the techniques listed earlier in this chapter, which ones do you think would be appropriate matches for these exercises? What other techniques might you add? Would you delete any of these exercises? Change any of them?

Are you ready to order?

Look at the ads and practice the conversation.

A: **What are you doing** *later*?
B: **I'm not doing anything. Why?**
A: **Let's get something to** *eat*.
B: **That's a good idea. Where would you like to go?**
A: **How about** *the Star Restaurant*? **They have** *great hamburgers*.
B: **That's fine.**

Read the menu and answer the questions.

1. What's the special?
2. How many kinds of sandwiches are there?
3. How many kinds of soup?
4. How much is a small salad?
5. How much is a cup of soup?
6. What kind of pie does the restaurant have?

Now ask your own questions.

★ STAR RESTAURANT MENU

TODAY'S SPECIAL
Soup and sandwich with salad or French fries
$3.95

SANDWICHES
Chicken	$2.65
Egg salad	$2.50
Tuna	$1.95
Hamburger	$2.95
Cheeseburger	$3.50
Grilled cheese	$2.25

DRINKS
Coffee		$ .50
Tea		$ .50
Milk		$ .60
Soda	large	$1.00
	medium	$ .75
	small	$ .50

SALAD
Large	$1.25
Small	$ .85

SOUP
Cup	$ .85
Bowl	$1.25
Vegetable	
Chicken	

DESSERTS
Ice Cream	$1.00
Chocolate	
Vanilla	
Strawberry	
Pie	$1.50
Apple or Cherry	

Listen and complete the conversation with the kinds of food the customers order.

Waitress: Are you ready to order?
Woman: Yes, I'd like a 1_____ and a small 2_____.
Waitress: And how would you like your 3_____?
Woman: Medium.
Waitress: Anything to drink?
Woman: Just a glass of 4_____.
Waitress: And what would you like?
Man: I'll have a bowl of 5_____ soup. And what kind of 6_____ do you have?
Waitress: Apple and cherry.
Man: 7_____.
Waitress: Anything else?
Man: Yes. A cup of 8_____.
Waitress: Thank you.

Now practice the conversation.

147

Complete the check for the man's and woman's lunch. What's the total?

STAR RESTAURANT
Guest Check

Table No.	No. Persons	Check No.	Server No.
		308905	

	hamburger	2 95
	Total	

Match the questions (1–6) with the answers (a–f).

1. Are you ready to order? _____d_____
2. Would you like any dessert? _____
3. Anything to drink? _____
4. How would you like your hamburger? _____
5. What would you like? _____
6. What kind of ice cream do you have? _____

a. Medium, please.
b. I'll have a bowl of soup.
c. Vanilla, chocolate, and strawberry.
d. Yes. I'd like an egg salad sandwich.
e. Just a glass of water.
f. Cherry pie, please.

Work with a group. Use the menu on page 130 and write a conversation. Present the conversation to the class.

A: Can I help you?/Are you ready to order?
B: Yes. I'd like/I'll have a *cheeseburger* and *a small salad*.
A: How would you like your *cheeseburger*?
B: Well-done./Medium./Rare.
A: Anything to drink?/Would you like anything to drink?
B: A/Some (drink)./No thanks./Not now, thanks.
A: And what would you like?/And you?
C: I'll have/I'd like (food) and (drink).
A: Anything else?/Would you like anything else?
C: What kind of (dessert) do you have?
A: _____
C: _____

The above questions are issues of **materials adaptation** that you face every time you sit down to plan a lesson. You see to it that the way you present the textbook lesson is appropriately geared for your particular students, their level, ability, and goals and is just right for the number of minutes in your class. With this lesson, beyond the simplified directions at the head of each exercise, some of the following techniques (from the taxonomy in Table 9.1) may apply:

Exercise 1

Setting: establish context
Role-play demonstration
Dialogue presentation
Dialogue recitation
Q&A, display

Exercise 2

Review: vocabulary in menu
Cued dialog—in pairs
Q&A, referential: Ss make up
    their own questions
Drill: pronunciation of plural morpheme

Exercise 3

Reading aloud
Identification (of missing words)
Drill

Exercise 4

Information exchange
Problem solving
Exposition (of results)

Exercise 5

Identification
Recognition
Meaningful drill

Exercise 6

Meaningful drill
Cued dialog
Role-play
Drama

If your teaching situation allows you to **choose** a textbook, then you have an exciting but complex task ahead of you. In fact, the number of questions that need to be asked about a textbook can be overwhelming, indeed. (For the most comprehensive textbook evaluation checklist I have ever seen, see Skierso, 1991; this form occupies over eight printed pages!) But once you have carried out a thorough investigation of textbooks using some kind of consistent evaluation procedure, you will be rewarded by having chosen a textbook that best fits all of your criteria.

Table 9.2 provides an abridged evaluation form that might prove to be a practical set of criteria for either (a) choosing a textbook for a course, or (b) evaluating the current textbook you are using. As you read through this evaluation form, think of an ESL textbook that you are reasonably familiar with and ask yourself how well that book meets the criteria.

Table 9.2. Textbook Evaluation Checklist (adapted from Robinett, 1978: 249–251).

1. **Goals of the course** (Will this textbook help to accomplish your course goals?)
2. **Background of the students** (Does the book fit the students' background?)
    - a. age
    - b. native language and culture
    - c. educational background
    - d. motivation or purpose for learning English.
3. **Approach** (Does the theoretical approach reflected in the book reflect a philosophy that you and your institution and your students can easily identify with?)
    - a. theory of learning
    - b. theory of language
4. **Language skills** (Does the book integrate the "four skills"? Is there a balanced approach toward the skills? Does the textbook emphasize skills which the curriculum also emphasizes?)
    - a. listening
    - b. speaking
    - c. reading
    - d. writing
5. **General content**. (Does the book reflect what is now known about language and language learning?)
    - a. validity—does the textbook accomplish what it purports to?
    - b. authenticity of language
    - c. appropriateness and currency of topics, situations, and contexts
    - d. proficiency level—is it pitched for the right level?
6. **Quality of practice material**
    - a. exercises—is there a variety from controlled to free?
    - b. clarity of directions—are they clear to both students and teacher?
    - c. active participation of students—is this encouraged effectively?
    - d. grammatical and other linguistic explanation—inductive or deductive?
    - e. review material—is there sufficient spiraling and review exercises?
7. **Sequencing** (How is the book sequenced?)
    - a. by grammatical structures
    - b. by skills
    - c. by situations
    - d. by some combination of the above
8. **Vocabulary** (Does the book pay sufficient attention to words and word study?)
    - a. relevance
    - b. frequency
    - c. strategies for word analysis
9. **General sociolinguistic factors**
    - a. variety of English— American, British, dialects,or international varieties
    - b. cultural content—is there a cultural bias?
10. **Format** (Is the book attractive, usable, and durable?)
    - a. clarity of typesetting
    - b. use of special notation (phonetic symbols, stress/intonation marking, etc.)
    - c. quality and clarity of illustrations
    - d. general layout—is it comfortable and not too "busy"?

  e. size of the book and binding
  f. quality of editing
  g. index, table of contents, chapter headings
11. Accompanying materials (Are there useful supplementary materials?)
  a. workbook
  b. tapes—audio and/or video
  c. posters, flash cards, etc.
  d. a set of tests
12. Teacher's guide (Is it useful?)
  a. helpful methodological guidance
  b. alternative and supplementary exercises
  c. suitability for non-native speaking teacher
  d. answer keys

Other written texts

It needs to be made clear here how the word **text** is normally used in the profession and in this book, especially to disambiguate texts from textbooks. "Texts" are any of a wide variety of types or genres (see Chapters 14 through 17 for more on this) of linguistic forms. Texts can be spoken or written. Among written texts, the range of possibilities extends from labels and forms and charts to essays and manuals and books. "Textbooks" are one type of text, a book for use in an educational curriculum.

Among other written texts available for your use in supporting techniques in the classroom, an almost unlimited supply of real-world textual material can be part of your classroom. We daily encounter signs, schedules, calendars, advertisements, menus, memos, notes, and the list goes on (see Chapter 15 for a long list of texts). Aside from these types of text, consider two specialized texts that are invaluable storehouses of information:

(a) Teacher Resource Books. There are dozens of resource books that are specifically designed to provide ideas for teachers. Books are available on conversation (e.g., Golebiowska, 1990), role play (Ladousse, 1987), listening techniques (Ur, 1984; Rost, 1991; speaking techniques (Klippel, 1984), activities for children (Claire, 1988), and the list goes on.

(b) Other Student Textbooks. Even a small library of student textbooks other than the one you are using will yield a book or two with some additional material that you can employ as supplementary material.

Audio-visual aids: Commercially produced

A third type of support for interactive techniques in the language classroom comes from commercially produced audio-visual aids. Libraries and instructional resource centers may be able to provide a surprising variety of:

- audio cassettes with
  listening exercises
  lectures
  stories
  other authentic samples of native speaker texts
- video tape cassettes and films with
  documentaries on special topics
  specific ESL instructional modules
- slides, photographs, posters, and other illustrations

Audio-visual aids: Creating your own

If you have the equipment to do so and some time to do a good job of it, you should consider creating your own supporting materials in the form of tapes, videos, posters, charts, and magazine pictures.

- Audio tapes of conversations, especially conversations of people known to your students, can be stimulating. Or just use your tape recorder to tape radio or TV excerpts of news, speeches, talk shows, etc., for listening techniques.
- Video tapes can be created in two ways. With a VCR you can record television programs. They need not be long or complex. Sometimes a very simple advertisement or a segment of the news makes an excellent audio-visual stimulus for classroom work. With a camera, you can try your hand at creating your own "film" (a story, "candid camera," a skit, etc.), perhaps with some of your students as principal actors.
- Posters, charts, and magazine pictures. If you are artistically inclined, you should consider trying your hand at creating posters or charts for classroom use. Otherwise, a resource that no teacher should be without is an assemblage of a couple of hundred magazine pictures that you can file and cross index. Start with a pile of fairly recent magazines and pick out pictures (photos, diagrams, advertisements) that have large enough people or objects in them to be easily seen by all students in a classroom setting. A supply of mounting cardboards and either double sided tape or laminate will protect your pictures from wrinkling.

Realia

There is nothing like an "object" lesson. Objects—food items, cosmetics, tools, and other materials—always add some significant reality to the classroom. Realia are especially useful and important for teaching children.

Computer assisted language learning (CALL)

The recent advances in educational applications of computer hardware (the equipment) and software (programs) have provided a new resource for language classrooms. If your institution has computer equipment and either an existing or a potential software library, consider the following applications in your classroom:

- Tutorial programs (covering grammar, vocabulary, reading, writing) for individual work beyond the classroom. Good programs will be **interactive**; that is, they will actively engage the learner in a series of questions, answers, and feedback throughout a presentation.
- Text-building programs, which can be used individually or in pair or small group work, enable learners to do text modification (punctuate a text, change tenses, rearrange random sentences, edit an essay) and text reconstruction (cloze tests).
- Process writing (see Chapter 17) is an especially suitable application of computer word processing programs. Drafting, revising, editing, all become simpler, especially so in pair or small group peer-conferencing.
- Games and simulations, offered in a plethora of varieties and complexity, present students with stimulating problem-solving tasks that get students to use functional language to pursue the goals of the games. Carefully planned uses of such games in the classroom (e.g., for practicing certain verbs, tenses, questions, locatives, etc.) add some interest to a classroom.
- Computer adaptive **testing** is in its infancy but growing rapidly. More and more tests for textbooks and other curricula are available on computer. Students can use such tests for diagnostic purposes on their own time. Certain interactive tests are designed to steer the test taker toward items that will present an optimal challenge. During the early items, right and wrong answers are analyzed by the computer program and later items are then presented, from a bank of possible items, that will be neither too easy nor too difficult.

TOPICS FOR DISCUSSION, ACTION, AND RESEARCH

1. With a partner, review the descriptions, on pages 136 and 137, of *task, activity, procedure, technique,* etc. Are you comfortable now with the definitions? Can you easily use the term *technique* as an overall superordinate concept?

2. What is a *drill*? Review the differences among mechanical, meaningful, and quasi-communicative drills. Illustrate with more examples. What is the place of mechanical drills in an interactive, CLT curriculum?

3 Provide examples of techniques that fall along the continuum of manipulation to communication. Look at the taxonomy of techniques in Table 9.1 (pp. 142, 143). In small groups, see if you can agree on where certain techniques should be placed on the scale.

4. There is an important difference between the manipulation-communication scale and the controlled-free scale. With a partner, ascertain this difference, and then take the same taxonomy (Table 9.1) and decide where each technique falls on the manipulation-communication continuum.

5. As you work with the taxonomy of techniques referred to in #3 and #4 above, ask your instructor to clarify any questions you might have about what each category includes. If time permits, divide some or all of the techniques among pairs in the classroom, and you and your partner figure out how to demonstrate the technique to the rest of the class.

6. On page 145 some questions were asked about the six exercises reprinted from the *Vistas* series. Could you devise a plan that would "teach" these six exercises? For example, how would you "practice the conversation" in exercise 1? Or "read… and answer" in exercise 2? Of the techniques listed earlier in this chapter, which ones do you think would be appropriate matches for these exercises? What other techniques might you add? Would you delete any of these exercises? Change any of them? Work with a partner if possible.

7. Refer to the list of evaluative factors for a textbook (page 150) and convert them into questions that you could answer on a scale of 1 (poor) to 5 (excellent). Use your newly devised questionnaire to evaluate a textbook that is available to you. Write a brief review (or make an oral report in class) of the textbook based on your evaluation.

8. Find a **teacher's resource book** in a library or bookstore. Present its strengths and weaknesses (as you view them) to your class in a three- to five-minute presentation.

9. With a partner, video tape (if you have a VCR) two different versions (from different channels) of a top news story. How do they differ? What do the differences tell you about what you should teach students to listen for in newscasts? Present your findings to the rest of the class. (If no VCR is available, do the same with two newspapers.)

10. For a lesson on "foods and drugs," select 10 magazine pictures. Think of some ways that you might actually use them in a lesson. Share your thoughts in a small group or present them to the rest of the class.

FOR YOUR FURTHER READING

Cross, David. 1991. *A Practical Handbook of Language Teaching.* Cassell (Prentice Hall).

Doff, Adrian. 1988. *Teach English: A Training Course for Teachers.* Teacher's Handbook. Cambridge University Press.

Jerald, Michael, and Clark, Raymond C. 1989. *Experiential Language Teaching Techniques.* Pro Lingua Associates.

There are a number of other similarly organized books; these are but a few that provide a storehouse of various techniques for teaching English as a second language. They are categorized according to the type of technique and/or the skill areas they highlight. They are a useful reference for a teacher's personal library.

Claire, Elizabeth. 1988. *ESL Teacher Activities Kit.* Prentice Hall.

For the teacher's reference library, a very practical compendium of many different techniques that you can use to teach ESL to children. The techniques are organized into categories of TPR, using realia, games of various kinds, songs and chants, projects, subject-matter techniques, pictures, and tape recorder activities. Directions for each technique are clearly spelled out.

Skierso, Alexandra. 1991. "Textbook selection and adaptation." In Celce-Murcia, Marianne (Ed.), *Teaching English as a Second or Foreign Language,* Second Edition (pp. 432–453). Newbury House.

The author provides a comprehensive look at the many factors to be considered in selecting an appropriate textbook. The rationale behind each factor is clearly spelled out. An eight-page check list follows in the appendix.

Kenning, Marie-Madeleine. 1990. "Computer assisted language learning." *Language Teaching 23* (2), 67–76.

A wealth of information and references on the state of the art in computer assisted language learning (CALL). This summary article reviews the last decade of work in CALL, summarizes current research and practice, and points toward new "growth" areas in the field. An excellent bibliography is included.

Chapter 10

Interactive Language Teaching I: Initiating Interaction

The quiet buzz of voices from the classroom echoes down the hallway. The thirty some odd students in an intermediate English class in a Bangkok high school are telling stories, joking, gossiping, talking about the latest popular songs. As the teacher walks in, the students suddenly fall silent, face uniformly forward, and open their textbooks in anticipation of another English lesson, another day of reciting, repeating, copying, reading aloud, translating sentences, and answering multiple-choice questions.

But today their usual teacher is absent and a substitute teacher sits down at the front of the class and asks the students to rearrange their desks into concentric semicircles. Surprised, the students comply. Then the teacher speaks:

T: Kavin, what's your favorite movie?

K: [after some silence] I'm sorry. Please repeat.

T: What movie do you like best?

K: [long silence, furtive glances to classmates] Best?

T: Yeah, your favorite movie?

K: [more silence] I like best Rambo III.

T: Okay. Arunee, what about you?

A: [embarrassed, giggles] About me?

T: Yeah, what about you? What's your favorite movie?

A: Oh, uh, favorite movie is Ghost.

T: Great. Now, Salinee, what's your favorite food?

This line of questioning continues for several minutes, with an increasing degree of ready participation by the students. Then the teacher changes the format a little:

T: Now, Anchalee, ask Pravit what his favorite sport is.

A: [silence] What your favorite sport?

P: Uh, soccer.

T: Okay, Pravit, now ask Salinee a question.

P: [long silence] What sport you like?

T: Okay, Pravit, good try. Now, say it this way: "What is your favorite sport?"

P: What is favorite sport?

Slowly, the students warm up to asking each other questions. The teacher then has students pair off, continuing to ask about favorite movies, songs, sports, and food.

The teacher then asks the students to make four columns on a blank sheet of paper with the headings, "Singer, TV program, Actress, Actor." This time dividing the class into groups of four students each, the teacher directs each group to fill in their sheets with the favorites of the other members of the group—in English! Initial silence is gradually replaced by buzz of voices in the groups as the teacher circulates and encourages the more reticent to participate. The exercise ends with "reports" of findings from appointed group leaders.

The last few minutes of the class hour are spent with the teacher pointing out certain grammatical reminders ("His favorite movie is ____." "I like ____ best.").

What Is Interaction?

This class, accustomed to recitation and mechanical output, had just become—perhaps for the first time—**interactive**. Interaction is an important word for language teachers. In the era of communicative language teaching, interaction is, in fact, the heart of communication; it is what communication is all about. We send messages; we receive them; we interpret them in a context; we negotiate meanings; and we collaborate to accomplish certain purposes. And after several decades of research on teaching and learning languages, we have discovered that the best way to learn to interact is through interaction itself.

Interaction is the collaborative exchange of thoughts, feelings, or ideas between two or more people resulting in a reciprocal effect on each other. Theories of communicative competence emphasize the importance of interaction as human beings use language in various contexts to "negotiate" meaning, or simply stated, to get one idea out of your head and into the head of another person and vice versa.

From the very beginning of language study, classrooms should be interactive. Wilga Rivers puts it this way:

> Through interaction, students can increase their language store as they listen to or read authentic linguistic material, or even the output of their fellow students in discussions, skits, joint problem-solving tasks, or dialogue journals. In interaction, students can use all they possess of the language—all they have learned or casually absorbed—in real-life exchanges. ...Even at an elementary stage, they learn in this way to exploit the elasticity of language (1987:4–5).

Interactive Principles

Most of the 12 Principles listed and discussed in Chapter 2 form foundation stones for structuring a theory of interaction in the language classroom. Consider the following selected relationships:

Automaticity: True human interaction is best accomplished when focal attention is on meanings and messages and not on grammar and other linguistic forms. Learners are thus freed from keeping language in a controlled mode and can more easily proceed to automatic modes of processing.

Intrinsic motivation: As students become engaged with each other in speech acts of fulfillment and self-actualization, their deepest drives are satisfied. And as they more fully appreciate their own competence to use language, they can develop a system of self-reward.

Strategic investment: Interaction requires the use of strategic language competence both to make certain decisions on how to say or write or interpret language, and to make repairs when communication pathways are blocked. The spontaneity of interactive discourse requires judicious use of numerous strategies for production and comprehension.

Risk-taking: Interaction requires a certain degree of risk of failing to produce intended meaning, of failing to interpret intended meaning (on the part of someone else), of being laughed at, of being shunned or rejected. The rewards of course are great and worth the risks.

The language-culture connection: The cultural loading of interactive speech as well as writing requires that interlocutors be thoroughly versed in the cultural nuances of language.

Interlanguage: The complexity of interaction entails a long developmental process of acquisition. Numerous errors of production and comprehension will be a part of this development. And the role of teachers' feedback is crucial to the developmental process.

Communicative competence: All of the elements of communicative competence (grammatical, discourse, sociolinguistic, pragmatic, strategic) are involved in human interaction. All aspects must work together for successful communication to take place.

Roles of the Interactive Teacher

Teachers can play many roles in the course of teaching. Just as parents are called upon to be many things to their children, neither can teachers be satisfied with one role. Following is a spectrum of possibilities, some of which are more conducive to creating an interactive classroom and others less so.

The teacher as controller

A role that is sometimes expected in traditional educational institutions is that of "master" controller, always in charge of every moment in the classroom. Master controllers determine what the students do, when they should speak, and what language forms they should use. They can often **predict** virtually all student responses because everything is mapped out ahead of time, with no leeway for going on tangents. In some respects, such control may sound admirable. But for interaction to take place, the teacher must create a climate in which spontaneity can thrive, in which unrehearsed language can be performed, and in which the freedom of expression given over to students makes it impossible to predict everything that they will say and do.

Nevertheless, some control on your part is actually an important element of successfully carrying out interactive techniques. In the planning phase especially, a wise controller will carefully project how a technique will proceed, map out the initial input to students, specify directions to be given, and gauge the timing of a technique. So, granted that allowing for spontaneity of expression involves yielding certain elements of control over to students, nevertheless, even in the most cooperative of interactive classrooms, the teacher must maintain some control simply to organize the class hour.

The teacher as director

Some interactive classroom time can legitimately be structured in such a way that the teacher is like a conductor of an orchestra or a director of a drama. As students engage in either rehearsed or spontaneous language performance, it is your job to keep the process flowing smoothly and efficiently. The ultimate motive of such direction, of course, must always be to enable students eventually to engage in the real-life drama of improvisation as each communicative event brings its own uniqueness.

The teacher as manager

This metaphor captures your role as one who plans lessons and modules and courses, one who structures the larger, longer segments of classroom time, but who then allows each individual player to be creative within those parameters. Managers of successful corporations, for example, retain control of certain larger objectives of the company, keep employees pointed toward goals, engage in ongoing evaluation and feedback but give freedom to each person to work in their own individual areas of expertise. A language class should not be markedly different.

The teacher as facilitator

A less directive role might be described as facilitating the process of learning, of making learning easier for students, helping them to clear away roadblocks, to find shortcuts, to negotiate rough terrain. The facilitating role requires that you step away from the managerial or directive role and allow students, with your guidance and gentle prodding here and there, to find their own pathways to success. A facilitator capitalizes on the principle of intrinsic motivation by allowing students to discover language through using it pragmatically rather than telling them about language.

The teacher as resource

Here you take the least directive role. In fact, the implication of the resource role is that the student takes the initiative to come to you. You are "there" for advice and counsel when the student seeks it. It is of course not practical to push this metaphor to an extreme where you would simply walk into a classroom and say something like "Well, what do you want to learn today?" Some degree of control, of planning, of managing the classroom is essential. But there are appropriate times when you can literally take a back seat and allow the students to proceed with their own linguistic development.

As an interactive teacher, you should be able to assume all five of the above roles on this continuum of **directive** to **nondirective** teaching. But the key to interactive teaching is to play toward the upper, nondirective end of the continuum, gradually enabling your students to move from their roles of total dependence (upon you, the class activities, the textbook, etc.) to relatively total independence. The proficiency level of your class will determine to some extent which roles will dominate. But even at the lowest levels, some genuine interaction can take place, and your role must be one that releases your students to try things for themselves.

We turn now to a more empirical and practical consideration of interaction in the communicative language classroom. In the remainder of this chapter you will get a sense of what you can do to **initiate** interaction in the classroom, that is, how your input can stimulate student interaction. In the next chapter (12), you will be given some guidance on **maintaining** interaction through effective group work techniques.

Foreign Language Interaction Analysis

One way to begin to look at your role as an initiator of interaction in the classroom is to look at yourself (and other teachers) in terms of a well-known taxonomy for describing classroom interaction. Over two decades ago, the work of Flanders (1970) and, more specific to foreign language teaching, of Gertrude Moskowitz (1971, 1976) gave us some categories for observation of classes known as the FLINT (**F**oreign **L**anguage **Int**eraction) model (see Table 10.1).

TEACHER TALK	**INDIRECT INFLUENCE**	1.	**Deals with Feelings:** In a nonthreatening way, accepting, discussing, referring to, or communicating understanding of past, present, or future feelings of students.
		2.	**Praises or Encourages:** Praising, complimenting, telling students why what they have said or done is valued. Encouraging students to continue, trying to give them confidence, Confirming answers are correct.
		2a.	**Jokes:** Intentional joking, kidding, making puns, attempting to be humorous, providing the joking is not at anyone's expense. Unintentional humor is not included in this category.
		3.	**Uses Ideas of Students:** Clarifying, using, interpreting. summarizing the ideas of students. The ideas must be rephrased by the teacher but still recognized as being student contributions.
		3a.	**Repeats Student Response Verbatim:** Repeating the exact words of students after they participate.
		4.	**Asks Questions:** Asking questions to which the answer is anticipated. Rhetorical questions are not included in this category.
	DIRECT INFLUENCE	5.	**Gives information:** Giving information, facts, own opinion or ideas, lecturing, or asking rhetorical questions.
		5a.	**Corrects without Rejection:** Telling students who have made a mistake the correct response without using words or intonations which communicate criticism.
		6.	**Gives Directions:** Giving directions, requests, or commands which students are expected to follow. Directing various drills. Facilitating whole-class and small-group activity.
		7.	**Criticizes Student Behavior:** Rejecting the behavior of students; trying to change the non-acceptable behavior; communicating anger, displeasure, annoyance, dissatisfaction with what students are doing.
		7a.	**Criticizes Student Response:** Telling the student his response is not correct or acceptable and communicating by words or intonation criticism, displeasure, annoyance, rejection.
STUDENT TALK		8.	**Student Response, Specific:** Responding to the teacher within a specific and limited range of available or previously practiced answers. Reading aloud, dictation, drills.
		9.	**Student Response, Open-ended or Student-initiated:** Responding to the teacher with students own ideas, opinions, reactions, feelings. Giving one from among many possible answers which have been previously practiced but from which students must now make a selection. Initiating the participation.
		10.	**Silence:** Pauses in the interaction. Periods of quiet during which there is no verbal interaction.
		10a.	**Silence—AV:** Silence in the interaction during which a piece of audio-visual equipment, e.g., a tape recorder, filmstrip projector, record player, etc., is being used to communicate.
		11.	**Confusion, Work-Oriented:** More than one person at a time talking, so the interaction cannot be recorded. Students calling out excitedly, eager to participate or respond, concerned with the task at hand.
		11a.	**Confusion, Non-Work-Oriented:** More than one person at a time talking, so the interaction cannot be recorded. Students out-of-order, not behaving as the teacher wishes, not concerned with the task at hand.
		12.	**Laughter:** Laughing, giggling by the class, individuals, and/or the teacher.
		13.	**Uses the Native Language:** Use of the native language by the teacher or the students. This category is always combined with one of the categories from 1 to 9.
		14.	**Nonverbal:** Nonverbal gestures or facial expressions by the teacher or the student which communicate without the use of words. This category is always combined with one of the categories of teacher or student behavior.

Table 10.1. Foreign Language Interaction Analysis (FLint) System (adapted from Moskowitz, 1971).

How is a model like this helpful in developing interactive language teaching? There are several practical uses.

First, it gives you a taxonomy for observing other teachers. Moskowitz recommends using a chart or grid to note instances of each category. You can also calculate how much time a teacher spends with each. Then you can evaluate the wisdom of certain choices made by the teacher or look at the overall distribution of time and ask yourself (or your teacher trainer) about the appropriateness of such a distribution.

Second, it gives you a framework for evaluating and improving your own teaching. For example, how well do you balance teacher talk and student talk? While the FLINT model includes seven categories for teacher talk and only two for student talk, don't let that fool you into believing that your own talk should dominate. Depending on the objectives of the lesson, the level of the students, and other contextual factors, the proportions will vary, but most of the time we teachers tend to talk too much, not allowing enough time for students to respond to you or to initiate talk. A careful consideration of all seven of the teacher-talk categories can also serve as a blueprint for your teaching behavior in the classroom: Am I accepting a student's feelings in a non-threatening way? Am I offering sufficient praise? Am I lecturing too much? Do I give my students opportunities to initiate language on their own?

Third, the FLINT model, especially the first seven categories, helps to set a learning climate for interactive teaching. In Chapter 3, under the rubric of intrinsically motivating classrooms, we discussed the importance of learners being brought into the decision-making process. You can establish a climate of cooperation by recognizing and openly accepting your students' emotional ups and downs, by recognizing each individual student in the class as special in his or her own way, by soliciting their ideas, and by careful framing of questions. We now turn to an extensive look at the latter.

Questioning Strategies for Interactive Learning

The most important key to creating an interactive language classroom is the initiation of interaction by the teacher. However non-directive your teaching style is, the onus is on you to provide the stimuli for continued interaction. These stimuli are important in the initial stage of a classroom lesson as well as throughout the lesson. Without such **ongoing** teacher guidance, classroom interaction may indeed be communicative, but it can easily fall prey to tangential chitchat and other behavior that is off-course from the class objectives.

One of the best ways to develop your role as an initiator and sustainer of interaction is to develop a repertoire of **questioning strategies**. In second language classrooms, where learners often do not have a great number of tools for initiating and maintaining language, your questions provide necessary stepping stones to communication. Appropriate questioning in an interactive classroom can fulfill a number of different functions (adapted from Christenbury and Kelly, 1983, and Kinsella, 1991):

(1) Teacher questions give students the impetus and opportunity to produce comfortably language without having to risk initiating language themselves. It's very scary for students to have to initiate conversation or topics for discussion. Appropriately pitched questions can give more reticent students an affective "green light" and a structured opportunity to communicate in their second language.

(2) Teacher questions can serve to initiate a chain reaction of student interaction among themselves. One question may be all that is needed to start a discussion among students; without the initial question, however, students will be reluctant to initiate the process.

(3) Teacher questions give the instructor immediate feedback about student comprehension. After posing a question, a teacher can use the student response to diagnose linguistic or content difficulties. Grammatical or phonological problem areas, for example, may be "exposed" through the student's response and give the teacher some specific information about what to treat.

(4) Teacher questions provide students with opportunities to find out what they think by hearing what they say. As they are nudged into responding to questions about, say, a reading or a film, they can discover what their own opinions and reactions are. This self-discovery can be especially useful for a prewriting activity.

There are many ways to classify what kinds of questions are effective in the classroom. Perhaps the simplest way to conceptualize the possibilities is to think of a range of questions, beginning with **display** questions, that attempt to elicit information already known by the teacher, all the way to highly **referential** questions that request information not known by the questioner; often the latter responses involve judgment about facts that are not clear or a statement of values. Following are seven categories of questions, ranging from display to referential, with typical classroom question words associated with each category (adapted from Kinsella, 1991, and Bloom, 1956).

1. **Knowledge questions:** Eliciting factual answers, testing recall and recognition of information.

   <u>Common question words:</u> Define. Tell. List. Identify. Describe. Select. Name. Point out. Label. Reproduce. Who? What? Where? When? Answer "yes" or "no."

2. **Comprehension questions:** Interpreting, extrapolating.

   <u>Common question words:</u> State in your own words. Explain. Define. Locate. Select. Indicate. Summarize. Outline. Match.

3. **Application questions:** Applying information heard or read to new situations.

   <u>Common question words:</u> Demonstrate how. Use the data to solve. Illustrate how. Show how. Apply. Construct. Explain. What is _____ used for? What would result? What would happen?

4. **Inference questions:** Forming conclusions that are not directly stated in instructional materials.

   <u>Common question words:</u> How? Why? What did _____ mean by? What does _____ believe? What conclusions can you draw from?

5. **Analysis questions:** Breaking down into parts, relating parts to the whole.

   <u>Common question words:</u> Distinguish. Diagram. Chart. Plan. Deduce. Arrange. Separate. Outline. Classify. Contrast. Compare. Differentiate. Categorize. What is the relationship between? What is the function of? What motive? What conclusions? What is the main idea?

6. **Synthesis questions:** Combining elements into a new pattern.

   <u>Common question words:</u> Compose. Combine. Estimate. Invent. Choose. Hypothesize. Build. Solve. Design. Develop. What if? How would you test? What would you have done in this situation? What would happen if? How can you improve? How else would you?

7. **Evaluation questions:** Making a judgment of good and bad, right or wrong, according to some set of criteria, and stating why.

   <u>Common question words:</u> Evaluate. Rate. Defend. Dispute. Decide which. Select. Judge. Grade. Verify. Choose why. Which is best? Which is more important? Which do you think is more appropriate?

All of these types of questions have their place in the interactive classroom. Even those that are more on the display end of the continuum are very useful in eliciting both content and language from students. Usually, the higher the proficiency level you teach the more you can venture into the upper, referential end of the continuum. One interesting study of high intermediate pre-university ESL students (Brock, 1986) found that teachers who incorporated more referential questions into their classes stimulated student responses that were longer and more grammatically complex. Make sure, then, that you challenge your students sufficiently but without overwhelming them.

Asking a lot of questions in your classroom will not by any means guarantee stimulation of interaction. Certain types of questions may actually discourage interactive learning. Beware of the following (adapted from Kinsella, 1991):

- too much class time spent on display questions—students can easily grow weary of artificial contexts that don't involve genuine seeking of information.
- questions that insult students' intelligence by being so obvious to everyone in the class that students will think it's too silly a question to bother answering.
- vague questions that are worded in abstract or ambiguous language (e.g., "Do you pretty much understand more or less what to do?").
- questions stated in language that is too complex or too wordy for aural comprehension (e.g., "Given today's discussion, and also considering your previous experience in educational institutions, what would you say are the ramifications of, or the potential developmental impacts on children functioning in an educational system in which assessment procedures largely consist of multiple-choice, paper and pencil instrumentation?").
- too many rhetorical questions (that you intend to answer yourself) that students think you want them to answer, then get confused when you answer the question yourself.
- random questions that don't fall into a logical, well-planned sequence, sending students' thought patterns into chaos.

There are, of course, other teacher strategies, besides questioning, that promote interaction. Pair work and group work obviously give rise to interaction. Giving directions ("Open your books." "Do the following exercise.") can stimulate interaction. Organizational language ("Get into small groups.") is important. Reacting to students (praise, recognition, or a simple "uh-huh") cannot be dispensed with. Responding genuinely to student initiated questions is a must. Encouraging students to develop their own strategies is an excellent means of stimulating the learner to develop tools of interaction. Even "lecturing" (and other forms of orally providing information) and having students read texts are part of the process of creating and maintaining an interactive classroom.

Most of these strategies are dealt with in subsequent chapters; pair and group work is given extensive coverage in the next chapter. For the moment, however, as you build some tools for creating an interactive classroom, consider your questioning strategies as one of the most important teaching behaviors for you to master.

❊   ❊   ❊

This chapter focused on the first step in creating an interactive classroom: your role as an initiator of the interaction. What you do and say to get students started, to prime them, to stimulate them to further communication, is crucial to the success of interactive techniques. We now turn to the intricate process of managing what has come to be a hallmark of interactive language teaching: group work.

TOPICS FOR DISCUSSION, ACTION, AND RESEARCH

1. Define interaction in your own words (without looking back at the beginning of the chapter). How does an interactive classroom differ from a "traditional" classroom? List the factors and discuss them in a small group.

2. Consider the **other** principles not mentioned on pages 159–160 (anticipation of reward, meaningful learning, language ego, self-confidence, the native language effect). In a group, go through them one by one and discuss how they support the notion of interactive learning? Do any of them speak to the importance of "individual study" as opposed to interaction with classmates?

3. Of the five teacher roles described on pages 160–162, which one(s) do you think might come most naturally to you? Why? Which would come least naturally? Do your natural inclinations reflect the kind of balancing of roles that you think is appropriate for an interactive language classroom? Compare your thoughts with a partner, then with the rest of the class.

4. How would those roles change depending on (a) the proficiency level of your students, (b) the age of your students, and (c) the culture of your students?

5. Observe an ESL class using the FLINT taxonomy as a guide in which you note teacher and student behavior. Did the taxonomy reveal anything new or interesting to you? Discuss your observation in a small group and/or with the rest of the class.

6. As you observe the same or another class, try to attend also to the kinds of **questions** the teacher asks. Write them down. How many were display

questions and how many were referential questions? Do you think the teacher should have had a different proportion of display and referential questions? Justify your response.

7. With a partner, list some specific examples of questions that **discourage** interaction. Why do you think your examples fail to promote interaction? Share your thoughts with other members of your class.

8. On page 167, other teacher strategies for stimulating interaction, besides questioning, are alluded to. Make lists of specific things a teacher can say or do to (a) give directions, (b) organize the class, and (c) react to students. Pool your list with others in a small group and then with the whole class.

FOR YOUR FURTHER READING

Wright, Tony. 1987. *Roles of Teachers and Learners.* Oxford University Press.

A number of different teacher and learner roles are described with no less than 71 specific classroom techniques that illustrate those roles. This "teacher-friendly" book provides simple theoretical justification for the adoption of various roles.

Rivers, Wilga. 1987. *Interactive Language Teaching.* Cambridge University Press.

This anthology of articles by foreign language practitioners and researchers includes a number of articles supporting an emphasis on greater interaction in the classroom. Rivers herself makes a strong case in the lead article.

Long, Michael H., and Sato, Charlene. 1983. "Classroom foreigner talk discourse: Forms and functions of teacher questions." In Seliger, Herbert W., and Long, Michael H. (Eds.), *Classroom Oriented Research in Second Language Acquisition.* Newbury House.

This is a seminal empirical study of the forms and functions of teachers' questions in ESL classrooms. Categories examined included display vs. referential questions, temporal and non-temporal reference, and the use of certain grammatical categories. Comments are made about the advisability of emphasis placed on display questions in the sample of teachers studied here.

Brock, Cynthia A. 1986. "The effects of referential questions on ESL classroom discourse." *TESOL Quarterly 20* (1), 47–59.

In this fascinating study, the author studied the effect on learners' language of higher frequencies of referential questions (as opposed to display questions). Results of the experiment indicated that students in classes with more referential questions produced sentences that were longer, more syntactically complex, and that contained a greater number of connectives.

Chapter 11

Interactive Language Teaching II:

Sustaining Interaction Through Group Work

The teacher of the community college ESL class of about 15 students has just played a cassette tape of an oceanographer describing the ecology of the ocean. The language of this 10-minute mini-lecture was comprehensible, but the subject matter itself offered a heavy cognitive load. Now, the teacher asks the students to get into groups of four students each to answer a set of comprehension questions. His directions are:

T: Get into groups now and answer the questions on the handout.

He then gives each student a handout with ten comprehension questions—items like, "What is the role of shrimp in ocean ecology?" and "According to the lecture, in what three ways are human beings dependent on the ocean for survival?"

The students comply with the first part of the directive by getting into previously arranged groups. Then, silence. Students spend a good three to four minutes silently reading the questions. Some students in some groups jot down answers to some of the questions. Others look up occasionally to see what other groups are doing or look at each other and then go back to studying the handout.

Finally, in one group a student says to another:

S1: **You figure out number 3?**

S2: **Um, no, and you?**

S1: **No. How about number 6?**

S2: **Well, answer is "plankton," I think.**

Whereupon the group falls back into silence and more individual work.

In another group, one student has apparently finished jotting down answers to the questions, and a second student says:

S3: **You got them all?**

S4: **Yes, I think so.**

S3: **So, what you write down?**

S4: **Number 1 is …**

And S4 continues to read off his answers one by one, as other Ss in the group fill in the answers in silence.

A third group seizes upon the latter group's method and queries one of their members who appears to have all the answers. And the fourth group works on in silence; students occasionally glance at each other's papers, mumble a comment or two, and make emendations. Meanwhile the teacher has circulated around once to watch the students, only responding if a student initiates a question directly. He then returned to his desk to record attendance and grade some papers.

After about fifteen minutes, the teacher asks the class to report on their responses, question by question, students individually volunteering answers. For each question the teacher asks if anyone disagrees, then indicates whether the answer is right or wrong, then asks if everyone in the class understands.

❋   ❋   ❋

There is something wrong with this picture! If the fifteen-minute time period in which students were in small groups is **group work,** then the language teaching profession is in serious trouble. Fortunately, the description you have just read demonstrates just about everything that you should **not** do in conducting group work techniques in your classroom. Before reading on in this chapter, jot down (a) problems with the above lesson, and (b) what you think the teacher should have done to make a successful group activity following a 10-minute mini-lecture.

In this chapter, we will look at group work as central to **maintaining** linguistic interaction in the classroom. In so doing, you will get some answers to questions like: What are the advantages of group work? What are some problems to overcome in successful group work? What different kinds of tasks are appropriate for group work? What are some steps for implementing group work? What are some rules for successful group work?

Advantages of Group Work

What is group work? It is a generic term covering a multiplicity of techniques in which two or more students are assigned a **task** that involves collaboration and self-initiated language. Note that what we commonly call **pair work** is simply group work in groups of two. It is also important to note that group work usually implies "small" group work, that is, students in groups of perhaps six or fewer. Large groupings defeat one of the major purposes for doing group work: giving students greater opportunities to speak.

Group work is solidly grounded in research principles (see Long and Porter, 1985, for an overview). Consider the twelve principles cited in Chapter 2. You can think of other theoretical foundations of successful language teaching and learning already discussed in this and other books on second language learning and teaching. And consider the importance of interaction in the language classroom discussed in the previous chapter. An integration of these principles and issues yields a number of advantages of group work for your English language classroom.

1. Group work generates interactive language.

In so-called traditional language classes, teacher talk is dominant. Teachers lecture, explain grammar points, conduct drills, and at best lead whole-class discussions in which each student might get a few seconds of a class period to talk. Group work helps to solve the problem of classes that are too large to offer many opportunities to speak. By one estimate (Long and Porter, 1985), if just half of your class time were spent in group work, you could increase individual practice time five-fold over whole-class traditional methodology.

Closely related to the sheer **quantity** of output made possible through group work is the variety and **quality** of interactive language. With traditional methods, language tends to be restricted to initiation only by the teacher in an artificial setting where the whole class becomes a "group interlocutor." Small groups provide opportunities for student initiation, for face to face give and take, for practice in negotiation of meaning, for extended conversational exchanges, and for student adoption of roles that would otherwise be impossible.

2. Group work offers an embracing affective climate.

The second important advantage offered by group work is the security of a smaller group of students where each individual is not so starkly on public display, vulnerable to what the student may perceive as criticism and rejection. In countless observations of classes, I have seen the magic of small groups. Quite suddenly, reticent students become vocal participants in the process. The small group becomes a community of learners cooperating with each other in pursuit of common goals.

A further affective benefit of small group work is an increase in student motivation. With Maslow's "security/safety" level satisfied through the cohesiveness of the small group, learners are thus freed to pursue higher objectives in their quest for success.

3. Group work promotes learner responsibility and autonomy.

Even in a relatively small class of 15 to 20 students, whole-class activity often gives students a screen to hide behind. I remember a college French class I took in which the teacher's single teaching technique was to call on students one by one to translate a sentence in our reading passage of the day. My way of playing that game was simply to keep one sentence ahead of the teacher so that when my name came up, I was ready. I paid no attention to what was currently being translated, to the meaning of the whole passage, to comments by the teacher, or to fellow classmates. An extreme case, to be sure! But even in less deadly classroom climates, students can "relax" too much in whole-class work. Group work places responsibility for action and progress upon each of the members of the group somewhat equally. It is difficult to "hide" in a small group.

4. Group work is a step toward individualizing instruction.

Each student in a classroom has needs and abilities that are unique. Usually the most salient individual difference that you observe is a range of proficiency levels across your class and, even more specifically, differences among students in their speaking, listening, writing, and reading abilities. Small groups can help students with varying abilities to accomplish separate goals. (See pages 178–179, for some suggestions on implementation of small group work.) The teacher can recognize and capitalize upon other individual differences (age, cultural heritage, field of study, cognitive style, to name a few) by careful selection of small groups and by administering different tasks to different groups.

Excuses for Avoiding Group Work

Some teachers are afraid of group work. They feel they'll lose control or students will just use their native language, and so they shy away from it. Some of these apprehensions are understandable; group work does **not** mean simply putting students into groups and having them do what you would otherwise do as a whole class. But the limitations or drawbacks to group work are all surmountable obstacles when group work is used appropriately, that is, for objectives that clearly lend themselves to group work. Let's look at these limitations—or, "myths," perhaps—and try to understand how to deal with them.

1. The teacher is no longer in control of the class.

Now, you may be thinking, "Well, I don't mind giving control over to the students." But, depending on the context of your teaching, control could be a very important issue. If you are...

- teaching in an institution where the administrator in charge requires that you teach through a traditional, whole-class methodology,
- teaching in a culture where "good teaching" is defined as students quietly working in orderly fashion, speaking only when spoken to by the teacher,
- teaching very large classes (of 75 or more) where a plethora of small groups becomes difficult to manage,
- teaching a group of unruly students—possibly of secondary school age—where discipline is a major issue,
- yourself a non-native speaker of English without the confidence to "let your students go" in small groups,

...then control may be an issue. There is no doubt that group work requires some yielding of control to the students. In numerous cultures, students are indeed primed to be under the complete control and authority of the teacher, and group work therefore is a very strange activity to engage in. In such contexts the teacher must be very clever to orchestrate successful small group work.

But this is still a "drawback" rather than a reason to avoid group work. By quietly introducing small doses of group work into your otherwise traditional classroom, you may be able to convince administrators and students of the advantages. With careful attention to guidelines for implementation of group work, administrative or managerial dilemmas should be able to be solved. And if you are unsure of your own English language ability, take heart in the fact that you are still quite a few steps ahead of your students.

As we noted earlier in Chapter 10, control, if it is thought of as **predicting** everything that is going to transpire in a class hour, then you do not want "control" because you will be thwarting virtually all possibility of an interactive language classroom. Group work still allows you to play the roles of director, manager, facilitator, and resource. In those roles, there is still an adequate degree of control; the class will not necessarily run away with you.

2. Students will use their native language.

In ESL settings where a multiple number of languages are often represented in a single classroom, teachers can avoid the native language syndrome by placing students in heterogeneous language groups. But in EFL situations, where all of the students have a common native language, it is indeed possible, if not probable, that students in small groups will covertly use their native language. In fact, this is usually the primary reason teachers give to me for shying away from group work. How can it be overcome?

Judicious following of guidelines for implementation (next section, this chapter) will help. If students feel that the task is too hard (or too easy), or that directions are not clear, or that the task is not interesting, or that they are not sure of the purpose of the task, then you may be inviting students to take shortcuts via their native language. The most important factor, however, is setting the climate for group work. Here are some suggestions:

(1) Impress upon your students the importance of **practice** in the second language for eventual success. Make sure—in whatever way you see fit—that they clearly understand that successful learners consistently practice using the target language in face to face contexts.

(2) Appeal to various **motivational** factors affecting them so that they can see some real uses for English in their own lives. Try to hone in on their **intrinsic** motivation to learn.

(3) Demonstrate how **enjoyable** the various small group tasks and games and activities are. Careful selection and administration of group activities helps to insure such pleasure. Your own overt display of enthusiasm will help to set a tone.

(4) Inform them of the **security** offered by the smaller groups. Get the groups to think of themselves as teams, the members of which are all working together. Remind them that, in the process, they can try out language without feeling that the whole class (and the teacher!) is watching and criticizing.

(5) For students who argue that the only reason they are in your class is to pass an examination, remind them that research has shown that people do better on **tests** if they dive into the language itself rather than just study test items. If they can be convinced that small groups help to build their **intuitions** about language, they may also understand that those intuitions will be their ally in a test situation.

3. Students' errors will be reinforced in small groups.

Teachers are usually concerned about the fact that, especially in large classes, students will simply reinforce each other's errors and the teacher won't get a chance to correct them. This concern can really be laid to rest. There is now enough research on errors and error correction to tell us that (a) levels of accuracy maintained in unsupervised groups is as high as that in teacher-monitored whole-class work, and that (b) as much as you would like not to believe it, teachers' overt attempts to correct speech errors in the classroom have a negligible effect on students' subsequent performance. (For more discussion and further references on this issue, see Long and Porter, 1985.) Errors are a "necessary" manifestation of interlanguage development and we do well not to become obsessed with their constant correction. Moreover, well-managed group work can encourage spontaneous peer feedback on errors within the small group itself.

4. Teachers cannot monitor all groups at once.

Related to the issue of control is the sometimes misguided belief that a teacher should be "in on" everything a student says or does during the class hour. Interactive learning and teaching principles counter with the importance of meaningful, purposeful language and real communication, which in turn must allow the student to give vent to creative possibilities. Yes, the effective teacher will circulate among the groups, listen to students, offer suggestions and criticisms, but it is simply not necessary—for reasons cited above in #3—to be a party to all linguistic intercourse in the classroom.

5. Some learners prefer to work alone.

It is true that many students, especially adult-age students, prefer to work alone because that is the way they have operated ever since they started going to school. As a successful manager of group work, you need to be sensitive to such preferences, acknowledging that some if not many of your students will find group work frustrating because they may simply want you just to give them the answers to some problem and then move on. Help your students to see that language learning is not a skill where you can simply bone up on rules and words in isolation. Language is for communicating with people (whether through oral or written modes) and the more they engage in such face to face communication the more their overall communicative competence will improve.

Related to the work style issue are numerous other **learning** style variations among students that get magnified in small groups. Because the teacher isn't present within the group at all times, groups are often left to derive their own dynamic inductively. In the process, individual differences become more salient than they are in whole-class work. On the following page are several of many possible scenarios:

- A highly left-brain oriented student is put off by the otherwise more right-brain members of the group.
- Quicker (impulsive) thinkers tend to blurt out their ideas, overwhelming the slower (reflective) thinkers, or,
- Impulsive learners get easily frustrated with the group process, which they perceive as circuitous.
- Competitive members of a group are reluctant to share information with others.
- "Talkative" students dominate the process.

While such problems can and do occur in group work, virtually every problem that is rooted in learning-style differences can be solved by careful planning and management. In fact, when the group members know their task and know their roles in the group, learning style differences can be efficiently utilized and highly appreciated—much more so than in whole-class work.

Implementing Group Work in Your Classroom

As you saw in the scene opening this chapter, group work can go wrong if it is not carefully planned, well executed, monitored throughout, and followed up on in some way. We'll now look at practical steps to take to carry out successful group work in your classroom.

Selecting Appropriate Group Techniques

So far in this chapter, as your attention has been focused on group work, differences between **pair work** and **group work** have not been emphasized. There are, in fact, some important distinctions. Pair work is more appropriate than group work for tasks that are (a) short, (b) linguistically simple, and (c) quite controlled in terms of the structure of the task. Appropriate pair activities (that are **not** recommended for groups of more than two) include:

1. practicing dialogues with a partner
2. simple question and answer exercises
3. performing certain meaningful substitution "drills"
4. quick (one minute or less) brainstorming activity
5. checking written work with each other
6. preparation for merging with a larger group
7. any brief activity for which the logistics of assigning groups, moving furniture, and getting students into the groups is distractive

Pair work enables you to get students engaged in interactive (or quasi-interactive) communication for a short period of time with a minimum of logistical problems. But don't misunderstand the role of pair work. It is not to be used exclusively for the above types of activity; it is **also** appropriate for many group work tasks (listed below).

The first step in promoting successful group work, then, is to select an appropriate task. In other words, choose something that lends itself to the group process. Lectures, drills, dictations, certain listening tasks, silent reading, and a host of other activities are obviously **not** suitable for small group work. Typical group tasks include:

1. Games
2. Role-play and simulations
3. Drama
4. Projects
5. Interview
6. Brainstorming
7. Information gap
8. Jig saw
9. Problem-solving and decision-making
10. Opinion exchange

Each of these types of task is defined and briefly characterized below. For further examples and information, I highly recommend that you consult a few of a wide variety of teacher resource books that offer a multitude of tasks for you to consider. Here are some of the most useful books of this type:

Claire, Elizabeth. 1988. *ESL Teacher's Activities Kit*. Prentice Hall. Especially suitable for teaching children.

Klippel, Friederike. 1986. *Keep Talking: Communicative Fluency Activities for Language Teaching*. Cambridge University Press. For adults, coded by proficiency level.

Shoemaker, Connie L., and Shoemaker, F. Floyd. 1991. *Interactive Techniques for the ESL Classroom.* Newbury House. Includes techniques involving reading and writing.

1. Games

A game could be any activity that formalizes a technique into units that can be scored in some way. Several of the other group tasks outlined below could thus become "games." Guessing games are common language classroom activities. "Twenty questions," for example, is easily adapted to a small group. One member secretly decides that he or she is some famous person; the rest of the group have to find out who within 20 yes/no questions, each member of the group taking turns asking questions. The person who is "it" rotates around the group and points are scored.

2. Role-play and simulations

Role-play minimally involves (a) giving a role to one or more members of a group and (b) assigning an objective or purpose that participants must accomplish. In pairs, for example, student A is an employer; student B is a prospective employee; the objective is for A to interview B. In groups, similar dual roles could be assumed with assignments to others in the group to watch for certain grammatical or discourse elements as the roles are acted out. Or a group role-play might involve a discussion of a political issue with each person assigned to represent a particular political point of view.

Simulations usually involve a more complex structure and often larger groups (of 6 to 20) where the entire group is working through an imaginary situation as a social unit, the object of which is to solve some specific problem. A common genre of simulation game specifies that all members of the group are shipwrecked on a "desert island." Each person has been assigned an occupation (doctor, carpenter, garbage collector, etc.) and perhaps some other mitigating characteristics (a physical disability, an ex-convict, a prostitute, etc.) Only a specified subset of the group can survive on the remaining food supply so the group must decide who will live and who will die.

3. Drama

Drama is a more formalized form of role-play or simulation, with a pre-planned story line and script. Sometimes small groups may prepare their own short dramatization of some event, writing the script and rehearsing the scene as a group. This may be more commonly referred to as a "skit." Longer, more involved dramatic performances have been shown to have positive effects on language learning, but they are time consuming and rarely can form part of a typical school curriculum.

4. Projects

For learners of all ages, but perhaps especially for younger learners who can greatly benefit from hands-on approaches to language, certain projects can be rewarding indeed. If you were to adopt an environmental awareness theme in your class, for example, various small groups could each be doing different things: Group A creates an environmental bulletin board for the rest of the school; Group B develops fact sheets; Group C makes a three-dimensional display; Group D puts out a newsletter for the rest of the school; Group E develops a skit. And we could go on. As learners get absorbed in purposeful projects, both receptive and productive language is used meaningfully.

5. Interview

A popular activity for pair work, but also appropriate for group work, interviews are useful at all levels of proficiency. At the lower levels, interviews can be very structured, both in terms of the information that is sought and the grammatical difficulty and variety. The goal of an interview could at this level be limited to using requesting functions, learning vocabulary for expressing personal data, producing questions, etc. Students might ask each other questions like

- What's your name?
- Where do you live?
- What country (city) are you from?

and learn to give appropriate responses. At the higher levels, interviews can probe more complex facts, opinions, ideas, and feelings.

6. Brainstorming

Brainstorming is a technique whose purpose is to initiate some sort of thinking process. It gets students' "creative juices" flowing without necessarily focusing on specific problems or decisions or values. Brainstorming is often put to excellent use in preparing students to read a text, to discuss a complex issue, or to write on a topic. Brainstorming involves students in a rapid-fire, free-association listing of concepts or ideas or facts or feelings relevant to some topic or context.

Suppose you were about to read a passage on future means of transportation. You might ask small groups to brainstorm (a) different forms of transportation, past and present, and (b) current obstacles to more efficient means of transportation. The groups' task would be to make a composite list of everything they can think of within the category, **without evaluating** it. In brainstorming, no discussion of the relative merits of a thought takes place; everything and anything goes. This way, all ideas are legitimate, and students are released to soar the heights and plum the depths, as it were, with no obligation to defend a concept. In whatever follow-up to brainstorming you plan, at that point evaluation and discussion can take place.

7. Information gap

These last four types of technique are quite commonly used in adult classes around the world, up and down the proficiency continuum.

The term information gap covers a tremendous variety of techniques in which the objective is to convey or to request information. The two focal characteristics of information gap techniques are (a) their primary attention to information and not to language forms and (b) the necessity of communicative interaction in order to reach the objective. The information that students must seek can range from very simple to complex.

At the beginning level, for example, each member of a small group could be given the objective of finding out from the others their (a) birthday, (b) address, (c) favorite food, etc. and filling in a little chart with the information. In intermediate classes you could ask groups to collectively pool information about different occupations: their qualifications, how long it takes to prepare for an occupation, how much the preparation costs, what typical job condi-tions are, what salary levels are, etc. In advanced classes, a small group dis-cussion on determining an author's message, among many other possibilities, would be an information gap technique.

8. Jigsaw

Jigsaw techniques are a special form of information gap in which each member of a group is given some specific information and the goal is to pool all information to achieve some objective. Imagine four members of a group each with a [fictitious] application form, and on each form different informa-tion is provided. As students ask each other questions (without showing any-one their own application form), they eventually complete all the information on the form. Or, you might provide maps to students in small groups, each student receiving different sets of information (where the bank is, where the park is, etc.). The goal for beginners might be simply to locate everything cor-rectly, and for intermediate learners to give directions on how to get from one place on the map to another, requiring a collaborative exchange of informa-tion in order to provide complete directions.

One very popular jigsaw technique that can be used in larger groups is known as a "strip story." The teacher takes a moderately short written narra-tive or conversation and cuts each sentence of the text into a little strip, shuf-fles the strips, and gives each student a strip. The goal is for students to deter-mine where each of their sentences belongs in the whole context of the story, to stand in their position once it is determined, and to read off the reconstruct-ed story. Students enjoy this technique and almost always find it challenging.

9. Problem solving and decision making

Problem solving group techniques focus on the group's solution of a specified problem. They might or might not involve jigsaw characteristics, and the problem itself might be relatively simple (such as giving directions on a map), moderately complex (such as working out an itinerary from train, plane, and bus schedules) or quite complex (such as solving a mystery in a "crime story" or dealing with a political or moral dilemma). Once again, problem solving techniques center students' attention on meaningful cogni-tive challenges and not so much on grammatical or phonological forms.

Decision making techniques are simply one kind of problem solving where the ultimate goal is for students to make a decision. Some of the prob-lem solving techniques alluded to above (say, giving directions to someone and solving a mystery) don't involve a decision about what to **do**. Other prob-lem solving techniques do involve such decisions. For example, students pre-sented with several profiles of applicants for a job may be asked to decide who they would hire. The "bomb shelter" simulation game referred to earlier involves a decision. Or a debate on environmental hazards might reveal several possible causes of air pollution, but if decision-making is the goal, then the group would have to decide now what they would actually do to reduce toxics in our air.

10. Opinion exchange

An opinion is usually a belief or feeling that might not be founded on empirical data or that others could plausibly take issue with. Opinions are difficult for students to deal with at the beginning levels of proficiency, but by the intermediate level, certain techniques can effectively include the exchange of various opinions. Many of the above techniques can easily incorporate beliefs and feelings. Sometimes opinions are appropriate; sometimes they are not, especially when the objective of a task is to deal more with "facts."

Moral, ethical, religious, and political issues are usually "hot" items for classroom debates, arguments, and discussions. Students can get involved in the content-centered nature of such activity and thus pave the way for more automatic, peripheral processing of language itself. Just a few of the plethora of such issues:

- women's rights
- choosing a marriage partner
- cultural taboos
- economic theories
- political candidates and their stands
- abortion
- euthanasia
- worldwide environmental crises
- war and peace

One warning: You play an important and sensitive role when you ask students to discuss their beliefs. Some beliefs are deeply ingrained from childhood rearing or from religious training, among other factors. So, it is easy for a student to be offended by what another student says. In such exchanges, do everything you can to assure everyone in your class that, while there may be disagreement on issues, **all** opinions are to be valued, not scorned, to be respected, and not ridiculed.

Planning Group Work

Possibly the most common reason for the breakdown of group work is an inadequate introduction and lead-in to the task itself. Too often, teachers assume that purposes are clear, directions are understood, and then have to spend an inordinate amount of time clarifying and redirecting groups. Once you have selected an appropriate type of activity, your planning phase should include the following eight "rules" for introducing a group technique.

1. Introduce the technique

The introduction may simply be a brief explanation. For example, "Now, in groups of four, you're each going to get different transportation schedules (airport limo, air, train, and bus) and your job is to figure out, as a group, which combination of transportation services will take the least amount of time." The introduction almost always should include a statement of the ultimate **purpose** so that students can apply all other directions to that objective.

2. Justify the use of small groups for the technique

You may not need to do this all the time with all your classes, but if you think your students have any doubts about the significance of the upcoming task, then tell them explicitly why the small group is important for accomplishing the task. Remind them that they will get an opportunity to practice certain language forms or functions, and that if they are reluctant to speak up in front of the whole class, now is their chance to do so in the security of a small group.

3. Model the technique

In simple techniques, especially those that your students have done before, modeling may not be necessary. But for a new and potentially complex task, it never hurts to be too explicit in making sure students know what they are supposed to do. After students get into their groups, you might for example, show them (possibly on an overhead projector) four transportation schedules (not the ones they will see in their groups). Then select four students to simulate a discussion of meshing arrival and departure times; your guidance of their discussion will help.

4. Give explicit detailed instructions

Now that students have seen the purpose of the task and have had a chance to witness how their discussion might proceed, give them specific instructions on what they are to do. Include:
  (1) a restatement of the purpose
  (2) rules they are to follow (e.g., Don't show your schedule to anyone else in your group. Use "if" clauses as in, "If I leave at 6:45 AM, I will arrive at the airport at 7:25.")
  (3) establish a time frame (e.g., You have 10 minutes to complete the task.)
  (4) assign roles (if any) to students (e.g., The airport limo person for each group is the "chair." The airplane person will present your findings to the rest of the class. The train person is the timekeeper, etc.)

5. Divide the class into groups

This element is not as easy as it sounds. In some cases you can simply number off (e.g., 1,2,3,4...) and specify which area of the room to occupy. But to ensure participation or control you may want to preassign groups in order to account for one or two of the following:

- native language (especially in ESL classes with varied native language backgrounds)
- proficiency levels
- age or gender differences
- culture or subcultural group
- personality types
- cognitive style preferences
- cognitive/developmental stages (for children)
- interests
- prior learning experience
- target language goals

In classes of under 30 people, preassigning groups is quite manageable if you come to class with the preassignments, having thought through the variables that you want to control. Just put the group names up on the blackboard and tell people to get into their groups.

6. Check for clarification

Before students start moving into their groups, check to make sure they all understand their assignment. Do **not** do this by asking, "Does everyone understand?"[1] Rather, test out certain elements of your lead-in by asking questions like, "Keiko, please restate the purpose of this activity."

7. Set the task in motion

This part should now simply be a matter of saying something like, "Okay, get into your groups and get started right away on your task." Some facilitation may be necessary to ensure smooth logistics.

Monitoring the Task

Your job now becomes one of Facilitator and Resource. To carry out your role, you need to tread the fine line between inhibiting the group process and being a helper or guide. The first few times you do group work, you may need to establish this sensitive role, letting students know you will be available for help and that you may make a suggestion or two here and there to keep them

---

[1]Teachers are often tempted to assume that asking a blanket question like this provides an informal assessment of how well students comprehended something. Usually, whether students understood or not, a small minority of them will nod their heads affirmatively while the rest of the class shows no response. The few nodding heads must not be taken as a measure of comprehension by all. It is better, therefore, never (or rarely) to say such things as, "Does everyone understand?" because it can lead to a false sense of satisfaction on the part of the teacher.

on task but that they are to carry out the task on their own. There may actually be a few moments at the outset where you do not circulate among the groups so that they can establish a bit of momentum. The rest of the time it is very important to circulate so that, even if you have nothing to say to the group, you can listen to students and get a sense of the groups' progress and of individuals' language production.

A few don'ts:

- Do **not** sit at your desk and grade papers.
- Do **not** leave the room and take a break.
- Do **not** spend an undue amount of time with one group at the expense of others.
- Do **not** correct students' errors unless asked to do so.
- Do **not** assume a dominating or disruptive role while monitoring groups.

Debriefing

Almost all group work can be brought to a beneficial close by some sort of whole-class debriefing, once the group task is completed. This debriefing, or "processing," as some would refer to it, has two layers:

1. Reporting on task objectives

If groups were assigned a reporter to present something to the class, or if the task implicitly lends itself to some discussion of the "findings" of the groups, then make sure that you leave enough time for this to take place. As reporters or representatives of each group bring their findings, you may entertain some brief discussion but be sure not to let that discussion steal time from other groups. This whole-class process gives each group a chance to perceive differences and similarities in their work. Some group work involves different assignments to different groups, and in these cases the reporting phase is interesting to all and provides motivation for further group work.

2. Establishing affective support

A debriefing phase also serves the purpose of exploring the group process itself and of bringing the class back together as a whole community of learners. If you or some students have questions about how smoothly the task proceeded, how comfortable people were with a topic or task, or problems they encountered in reaching their objective, now is an excellent time to encourage some whole-class feedback. This gives **you** feedback for your next group work assignment. Ultimately, even a very short period of whole-class discussion reminds students that everyone in the room is a member of a team of learners and that the groups, especially if any inter-group competition arose, are but temporary artifacts of classroom learning.

❋   ❋   ❋

It is possible that this chapter on group work has been so explicit in its description that you feel overwhelmed or put off by the prospect of doing group work in your classroom. If so, that need not be the case! All of the guidelines and reminders and dos and don'ts included in this chapter will in due course of time become a part of your subconscious intuitive teaching behavior. You won't have to process every minute of your class hour in terms of whether you've done all the "right" things. In the meantime, just remember that conscientious attention to what makes for successful group work will soon pay off.

TOPICS FOR DISCUSSION, ACTION, AND RESEARCH

1. With a partner, look again at the lesson described at the beginning of the chapter. Pick it apart: list the things about it that were problematic, and why they were problems. Can you put the lesson back together in a way that would promote successful group work? What would you do differently? Compare your findings with other pairs.

2. What is "control"? Is control an issue for you? How might you do group work and still stay in control? Specifically, at what points should you relinquish control?

3. What if, after all the precautions, students **still** use their native language in small groups? In a small group or with a partner, brainstorm further solutions. Then, discuss their feasibility.

4. In a group, brainstorm other examples (besides those given in the book) of each of the ten categories of small group work starting on page 179. Describe them carefully, and if possible, demonstrate selected techniques to your classmates.

5. Start collecting a resource file of group techniques. Consult resource books and other teachers for examples. Share your collection with your classmates.

6. With a partner, think of other "hot topics" for opinion exchange (p. 183). Which ones would be too "hot" to include in classroom discussion? Why? Share your thoughts with the rest of the class.

7. Try to observe an ESL class with several instances of group work. Use the criteria on pages 184–187 to evaluate the effectiveness of the group work that you observe. Report your findings back to your classmates.

8. On page 185 some criteria were listed for pre-assigning group membership. Justify the use of those criteria, that is, under what circumstances and for what reasons would you pre-assign small group membership? Can you think of other criteria?

9. In a small group or with a partner, pick a specific group technique within one of the categories (or two) and devise a "blow-by-blow" plan for implementing it. Demonstrate it to your classmates. Have them criticize it. Then respond to the criticism as constructively as possible.

FOR YOUR FURTHER READING

Long, Michael H., and Porter, Patricia. 1985. "Group work, interlanguage talk, and second language acquisition." *TESOL Quarterly 19* (2), 207–228.

> In this seminal article on group work, the authors review the research relating to the effectiveness of group work in the second language classroom. They examine some "myths" about group work and encourage teachers to employ interactive small group work in their classrooms. This article is a "must" for teachers wishing to understand the importance of group work in second language classrooms.

Brown, Raymond. 1991. "Group work, task difference, and second language acquisition." *Applied Linguistics 12* (1), 1-12.

> The author takes a careful look at the effect of different kinds of group work tasks, including the open-endedness of group tasks He suggests that we be very careful in the way we frame group tasks in order to encourage creative language use and not just rote practice.

Doughty, Catherine, and Pica, Teresa. 1986. "'Information gap' tasks: Do they facilitate second language acquisition?" *TESOL Quarterly 20*(2), 305–325.

> In yet another empirical study of classroom group work, the authors suggest that group tasks with a requirement for information exchange is crucial to the generation of conversational interaction.

DiPietro, Robert J. 1987. *Strategic Interaction. Learning Languages through Scenarios*. Cambridge University Press.

> A particular genre of group work is advocated here: the development of little "scenarios" by small groups of students. As students negotiate an appropriate conversation to fit a prescribed situation, creative language is employed and principles of grammar and discourse are inductively learned. The "performance" brings the whole class together as audience and critic.

Shoemaker, Connie L. and Shoemaker, F. Floyd. 1991. *Interactive Techniques for the ESL Classroom*. Newbury House.

Hendrick, Judith Carl, and Butler, Marilyn Smith. 1992. *Interaction Activities in ESL*. Second Edition. University of Michigan Press.

> Both of these books can serve as useful resources for your personal professional reference library. They contain many different interaction techniques, divided into various categories for easy reference.

Chapter 12

Learner Strategy Training

Did you ever see one of those enticing advertisements for a quick and easy foreign language course? It may have read something like this:

> ## SPEAK GERMAN LIKE A NATIVE!
> Haven't you often wished you could speak a foreign language fluently and effortlessly? Well, now you can! With our programmed cassettes and just 20 hours of listening, you too will join the ranks of hundreds who have learned a foreign language from our course. All you have to do is...

The advertisement might have gone on to make other guarantees and promises if only you will write your check for, say, $150.

You know from your own experiences in learning and/or teaching a foreign language that there is no single magic formula for successful foreign language learning. One set of tapes may indeed be a good start, a good refresher, or a good back-up. But with the vast complexity of second language learning, a great deal more than this is necessary for ultimate mastery and the "fluency" that the advertisements promise.

What is required for such success is the persistent use of a whole host of **strategies** for language learning, whether the learner is in a regular language classroom or working on a self-study program. Sometimes these strategies are subconsciously applied as certain learners seem to have a "knack" for language learning that they are not consciously aware of. But often, successful learners have achieved their goals through conscious, systematic application of a battery of strategies.

Strategic Investment

In recent years language teaching methodology has seen a dramatic increase in attention to what I like to call the **strategic investment** that learners can make in their own learning process. The learning of any skill involves a certain degree of "investment" of one's time and effort into the process. Every complex set of skills—like learning to play a musical instrument or tennis—is acquired through an investment of considerable observing, focusing, practicing, monitoring, correcting, and redirecting. And so one develops strategies for perceiving others and for singling out relevant elements of language and all the other necessary behaviors essential for ultimate mastery. A language is probably the most complex set of skills one could ever seek to acquire; therefore, an investment is necessary in the form of developing multiple layers of strategies for getting that language into one's brain.

In Chapter 2 (Principle #5) the principle of strategic investment was introduced. Here we probe its implications for your teaching methodology in the classroom, namely, how can your language classroom techniques encourage, build, and sustain effective language learning strategies in your students?

All twelve of the other principles outlined in Chapter 2 have a bearing on this issue. If one's language learning should sustain a modicum of automatic processing (Principle #1), what kind of strategies can students use to assist in converting controlled processes into automatic? If meaningful learning (Principle #2) is important, how can learners maximize meaning in their linguistic input and output? What kind of immediate, extrinsic rewards (#3) and long range, intrinsic motives (#4) are necessary to keep learners pointed toward goals? And as you run down the list of principles yourself, it becomes apparent how learning strategies are germane to the eventual success of learners. Strategies are, in essence, learners' techniques for capitalizing on the principles of successful learning.

In an era of interactive, intrinsically motivated, learner-centered teaching, learner strategy training simply cannot be overlooked. All too often, language teachers are so consumed with the "delivery" of language to their students that they neglect to spend some effort preparing learners to "receive" the language. In an effort to fill class hours with fascinating material, they might overlook their mission of enabling learners to eventually become **independent** of classrooms. And students, mostly unaware of the tricks of successful language learning, simply do whatever the teacher tells them to do, with no means to question the wisdom thereof.

One of your principal goals as an interactive language teacher is to equip your students with a sense of what successful language learners do to achieve success and to aid them in developing their own unique individual pathways to success. Because by definition interaction is unrehearsed, mostly unplanned discourse, students need to have the necessary **strategic competence** to hold their own in the give and take of meaningful communication.

One could compare language learners to participants in an elaborate wine-tasting party. The color and sweetness of our linguistic corkage are enticing. But how are students to fully appreciate this event without some education on how to partake of the libations spread before them? Tips on what to look for and what goes with what and how to get the most out of something—these are necessary elements of our methodology. When students are taught how to look at themselves and how to capitalize on their talents and experiences, they learn lessons that carry them well beyond any language classroom. That's what learner strategy training is all about.

Good and Bad Language Learners

Learner strategy training had its early roots a number of years ago in studies of "good" and "bad" language learners. Research in this area tended first to identify certain successful language learners and then to extract—through tests of psycholinguistic factors, interviews, and other data analysis—relevant factors believed to be contributing to their success. Some generalizations were drawn by Rubin and Thompson (1982) that will give you a sense of the flavor of this line of research. Good language learners...

(1) find their own way, taking charge of their learning

(2) organize information about language

(3) are creative, developing a "feel" for the language by experimenting with its grammar and words

(4) make their own opportunities for practice in using the language inside and outside the classroom

(5) learn to live with uncertainty by not getting flustered and by continuing to talk or listen without understanding every word

(6) use mnemonics and other memory strategies to recall what has been learned

(7) make errors work for them and not against them

(8) use linguistic knowledge, including knowledge of their first language, in learning a second language

(9) use contextual cues to help them in comprehension

(10) learn to make intelligent guesses

(11) earn chunks of language as wholes and formalized routines to help them perform "beyond their competence"

(12) learn certain tricks that help to keep conversations going

(13) learn certain production strategies to fill in gaps in their own competence

(14) learn different styles of speech and writing and learn to vary their language according to the formality of the situation.

It is important to remember that some of the above characteristics are not based on empirical findings, rather on the collective observations of teachers and learners themselves. Therefore, do not assume that **all** successful learners exhibit **all** of these characteristics. Nor is this list of 14 an exhaustive one; in fact, later in this chapter, you will find a much more detailed taxonomy (Oxford, 1990) of successful learning strategies.

The good language learner studies are of obvious interest to teachers. The more your classroom activity can model the behavior exhibited by successful language learners, the better and more efficient your students will be, especially in developing their own autonomy as learners.

Styles of Successful Language Learning

One step in understanding learner strategy training is to make a distinction between **styles** and strategies (see *PLLT,* Chapter 5). Styles, whether related to personality (e.g., extroversion, self-esteem, anxiety) or to cognition (e.g., left/right brain orientation, ambiguity tolerance, field sensitivity) characterize the consistent and rather enduring **traits,** tendencies, or preferences that may differentiate you from another person. You might, for example, tend to be extroverted or right-brain oriented (while someone else might be introverted and left-brain oriented) These styles are an appropriate characterization of how you **generally** behave, even though you may for a multitude of reasons consciously or subconsciously adopt more introverted or left-brain behavior in specific contexts.

Strategies, on the other hand, are specific methods of approaching a problem or task, modes of operation for achieving a particular end, or planned designs for controlling and manipulating certain information. Strategies vary widely **within** an individual, while styles are more constant and predictable. You may almost simultaneously utilize a dozen strategies for figuring out what someone just said to you, for example. You may use strategies of "playback" (imagine an instant taped replay of the conversation), key word identification, attention to nonverbal cue(s), attention to context, dictionary look-up, grammatical analysis, numerous direct requests for repetition, rephrasing, word definition, or turning to someone else for interpretation. And the list could go on.

Successful second language learners are usually people who know how to manipulate style (as well as strategy) levels in their day to day encounters with the language. This means that they are first aware of general personality and cognitive characteristics or tendencies that usually lead to successful acquisition and strive to develop those characteristics. For example, a successful learner who is not a risk-taker (personality trait), quite left-brain dominant and somewhat intolerant of ambiguity (cognitive traits), recognizes her dominant traits and resolves to force herself to take more risks, to balance her brain, and to adopt a more tolerant attitude toward language she doesn't understand. Why? Because she has been informed of the importance of the latter styles for most language learning contexts.

In other words, styles are not by any means immutable tendencies. Learners can, through a program of self-awareness, understand who they are and take steps to change what may be inhibiting traits within their general style. At this point in our collective knowledge about language acquisition, the number of personality and cognitive styles that lead toward successful learning is finite. In fact, the "ten commandments" listed on page 199 may sufficiently identify chief style factors that a language learner needs to worry about.

Developing Student Self-awareness of Style Tendencies

How do you help learners to develop the self-awareness necessary to work toward successful language learning styles? Several means are available to you as a teacher.

1. Informal self-check lists

One effective way to instill student awareness of successful styles is through an informal self-check list (you might devise it yourself) that students fill out and then discuss. Such check-lists are usually not formally scored or tallied; rather, they serve as focal points for discussion and enlightenment.

Figure 12.1 (p. 195) is an example of a check list that has been used with ESL students. (For lower proficiency levels, the vocabulary was simplified.) You could adapt the following procedure for use in your classroom:

(1) Hand out check lists to each student and tell them to fill it in on their own.

(2) When they finish, put students into groups of four. Their objective is to compare answers, to justify individual responses, and to determine if anyone feels compelled to change their response category after discussion. The ultimate objective is to get students to talk openly about their own styles.

(3) In whole-class activity, groups can be asked to share any major agreements **and** disagreements. You should direct this discussion toward some conclusions about the best styles for successful language learning.

(4) Summarize by explaining that no one side is necessarily good or bad, but that (a) if they are too dominant on one side, they may profit from allowing the other side of a continuum to operate, and (b) that most learners tend to lean too far to the right side of the chart, which is usually **not** the best learning style.

2. Formal personality and cognitive style tests.

If formal personality or cognitive style tests are available to you, you might try using them in your class—but with caution! Often these tests are culturally biased, have difficult language, and need to be interpreted with a grain of salt. Many tests designed for North American English speakers are loaded with cultural references that learners from other countries may easily misinterpret. And if the language is too difficult, your attempts to paraphrase may destroy a test's validity. And always remember that any self-check test, however formal, is a product of a test taker's own self-image; often they will simply want to see themselves in a good light, and therefore their responses may reflect a bit of self-flattery.

Nevertheless, a few simple scorable tests may be feasible for the second language classroom. Certain versions of the Myers-Briggs Type Inventory (MBTI) have been attempted with learners, especially the Keirsey Temperament Sorter (Keirsey & Bates, 1984), in order to give a measure of personality indices (see *PLLT*, Chapter 6). There is now enough research (Ehrman, 1990) to indicate that personality styles as measured by the MBTI (e.g., extroversion, intuition, logic, etc.) correspond to language learning styles and that learners can benefit from knowing both the assets and liabilities of each style. For example, an extroverted style is beneficial for face-to-face conversation, but it can also entail dependency on outside stimulation and work against self-sufficiency.

Two other examples of formal tests are provided in Figures 12.2 and 12.3. The first is an extroversion test and the second a left/right-brain dominance test. Tests like these can be administered and treated in the same way (or variations thereof) as was suggested for self-check test above. In this way students can become aware of their possible style tendencies, consider the relationship between such styles and success in their language learning goals, and take positive steps to capitalize on their assets and to overcome any liabilities.

Figure 12.1. Learning Styles Check List.

Check one box in each item that best describes you. Boxes A and E indicate that the sentence is very much like you . Boxes B and D would indicate that the sentence is somewhat descriptive of you. Box C would indicate that you have no inclination one way or another.

	A	**B**	**C**	**D**	**E**	
1. I don't mind if people laugh at me when I speak.	❏	❏	❏	❏	❏	I get embarassed if people laugh at me when I speak.
2. I like to try out new words and structures that I'm not completely sure of.	❏	❏	❏	❏	❏	I like to use only language that I am certain is correct.
3. I feel confident in my ability to succeed in learning this language.	❏	❏	❏	❏	❏	I feel quite uncertain about my ability to succeed in learning this language.
4. I want to learn this language because of what I can personally gain from it.	❏	❏	❏	❏	❏	I am learning this language only because someone else is requiring it.
5. I really enjoy working with other people in groups	❏	❏	❏	❏	❏	I would much rather work alone than with other people.
6. I like to "absorb" language and get the general "gist" of what is said or written.	❏	❏	❏	❏	❏	I like to analyze the many details of language and understand exactly what is said or written.
7. If there is an abundance of language to master, I just try to take things one step at a time.	❏	❏	❏	❏	❏	I am very annoyed by an abundance of language material presented all at once.
8. I am not overly conscious of myself when I speak.	❏	❏	❏	❏	❏	I "monitor" myself very closely and consciously when I speak.
9. When I make mistakes, I try to use them to learn something about the language.	❏	❏	❏	❏	❏	When I make a mistake, it annoys me because that's a symbol of how poor my performance is.
10. I find ways to continue learning the language outside of the classroom.	❏	❏	❏	❏	❏	I look to the teacher and the classroom activities for everything I need to be successful.

Figure 12.2. Extroversion/Introversion Test.

Take the following self-test and score yourself according to the directions at the end. You must circle either *a* or *b*, even if you have a hard time placing yourself into one or the other.

1. I usually like
   a. mixing with people
   b. working alone

2. I'm more inclined to be
   a. fairly reserved
   b. pretty easy to approach

3. I'm happiest when I'm
   a. alone
   b. with other people

4. At a party, I
   a. nteract with many, including stranger
   b. interact with a few people I know

5. In my social contacts and groups, Iusually
   a. get behind on the news
   b. keep abreast of what's happening with others

6. I can usually do something better by
   a. figuring it out on my own
   b. talking with others about it

7. My usual pattern when I'm with other people is
   a. to be open and frank, and take risks
   b. to keep to myself and not be very open

8. When I make friends, usually
   a. someone else makes the first move
   b. I make the first move

9. I would rather
   a. be at home on my own
   b. go to a boring party

10. Interaction with people I don't know
    a. stimulates and energizes me
    b. taxes my reserves

11. In a group of people I usually
    a. wait to be approached
    b. initiate conversation

12. When I'm by myself I usually feel a sense of
    a. solitude and peacefulness
    b. loneliness and uneasiness

13. In a classroom situation I prefer
    a. group work, interacting with others
    b. individual work

14. When I get into a quarrel or argument, I prefer to
    a. be silent, hoping the issue will resolve itself or blow over
    b. "have it out" and settle the issue right then and there

15. When I try to put deep or complex thoughts into words, I usually
    a. have quite a hard time
    b. do so fairly easily

Scoring procedure:

Mark an X corrresponding to your choices in the grid below.

	(a)	b		a	(b)		a	(b)
1			2			3		
4			5			6		
7			8			9		
10			11			12		
13			14			15		
Totals			+			+			=

Add up the number of X's in ONLY three of the columns, as indicated.
(Ignore all other X's.) Total those three numbers to get a grand total and write it in the box at the right. This is your score for the test. Here's how to interpret your score:

13 and above:	**quite extroverted**
9 to 12:	**moderately extroverted**
7 or 8:	**moderately introverted**
6 and below:	**quite introverted**

Figure 12.3. Right/Left Brain Dominance Test.

In this test, each item has two contrasting statements. Between the two statements is a scale of five points on which you are to indicate your perception of which statement best describes you. Boxes 1 and 5 indicate that a statement is very much like you; boxes 2 and 4 indicate that one statement is somewhat more like you than the other statement; box 3 indicates no particular leaning one way or the other. See next page for scoring directions.

	1	2	3	4	5	
I prefer speaking to large audiences.	❏	❏	❏	⊠	❏	I prefer speaking in small group situations.

Box number 4 has been checked to indicate a moderate preference for speaking in small group situations.

	1	2	3	4	5	
1. I remember names.	❏	❏	❏	❏	❏	1. I remember faces.
2. I respond better to verbal instructions.	❏	❏	❏	❏	❏	2. I respond better to demonstrated, illustrated, symbolic instructions.
3. I am intuitive.	❏	❏	❏	❏	❏	3. I am intellectual.
4. I experiment randomly and with little restraint.	❏	❏	❏	❏	❏	4. I experiment systematically and with control.
5. I prefer solving a problem by breaking it down into parts, then approaching the problem sequentially, using logic.	❏	❏	❏	❏	❏	5. I prefer solving a problem by looking at the whole, the configurations, then approaching the problem through patterns using hunches.
6. I make objective judgments, extrinsic to person.	❏	❏	❏	❏	❏	6. I make subjective judgments, intrinsic to person.
7. I am fluid and spontaneous.	❏	❏	❏	❏	❏	7. I am planned and structured.
8. I prefer established, certain information.	❏	❏	❏	❏	❏	8. I prefer elusive, uncertain information.
9. I am a synthesizing reader.	❏	❏	❏	❏	❏	9. I am an analytical reader.
10. I rely primarily on language in thinking and remembering.	❏	❏	❏	❏	❏	10. I rely primarily on images in thinking and remembering.
11. I prefer talking and writing.	❏	❏	❏	❏	❏	11. I prefer drawing and manipulating objects.
12. I get easily distracted trying to read a book in noisy or crowded places.	❏	❏	❏	❏	❏	12. I can easily concentrate on reading a book in noisy or crowded places.
13. I prefer work and/ or studies that are open ended.	❏	❏	❏	❏	❏	13. I prefer work and/or studies that are carefully planned.
14. I prefer hierarchical (ranked) authority structures.	❏	❏	❏	❏	❏	14. I prefer collegial (participative) authority structures.
15. I control my feelings.	❏	❏	❏	❏	❏	15. I am more free with my feelings.
16. I respond best to kinetic stimuli (movement, action).	❏	❏	❏	❏	❏	16. I respond best to auditory, visual stimuli.

Continue on next page

Adapted from E. Paul Torrance, *Your Style of Learning and Thinking*, 1987. Bensonville, IL.: Scholastic Testing Service, Inc.

	I	2	3	4	5	
17. I am good at interpreting body language.	❑	❑	❑	❑	❑	17. I am good at paying attention to people's exact words.
18. I frequently use metaphors and analogies.	❑	❑	❑	❑	❑	18. I rarely use metaphors or analogies.
19. I favor logical problem solving.	❑	❑	❑	❑	❑	19. I favor intuitive problem solving.
20. I prefer multiple-choice tests.	❑	❑	❑	❑	❑	20. I prefer open-ended questions.

Scoring directions.
Score each item as follows: Some of the items are scored according to the numbers at the top of each column of boxes, others are *reversed*. For the following items use the indicated numbers on the test page:

1 2 5 6 8 10 11 14 15 19 20 ⬜1⬜ ⬜2⬜ ⬜3⬜ ⬜4⬜ ⬜5⬜

The rest of the items are reversed in their scoring. Score the following as indicated below.

3 4 7 9 12 13 16 17 18 ⬜5⬜ ⬜4⬜ ⬜3⬜ ⬜2⬜ ⬜1⬜

Now total up all scores: ▭

This was a test of left- and right-brain preference. A score of 60 is the midpoint. The scoring chart below indicates that a score of 60 plus or minus 3 is a toss-up:

Above 70   Quite right-brain oriented
64-70   Moderately right-brain oriented
57-63   No particular dominance on either side
50-56   Moderately left-brain oriented
Below 50   Quite left-brain oriented

3. Readings, lectures, discussions

Yet another way of encouraging self-awareness of styles in your classroom is through occasional readings, lectures, or "lecturettes" delivered by others or by you, followed by discussions about successful learning styles. A significant number of ESL reading books include a chapter on successful language learners. Your own knowledge of this domain could be enhanced by consulting books like:

Brown, H. Douglas. 1991. *Breaking the Language Barrier*. Intercultural Press.

Cohen, Andrew. 1990. *Language Learning: Insights for Learners, Teachers, and Researchers*. Newbury House.

Marshall, Terry. 1990. *The Whole World Guide to Language Learning*. Intercultural Press.

Oxford, Rebecca. 1990. *Language Learning Strategies: What Every Teacher Should Know*. Newbury House.

Wenden, Anita, and Rubin, Joan. 1987. *Learner Strategies in Language Learning*. Prentice Hall International.

Table 12.1. "Ten Commandments" for Good Language Learning.

	TEACHER'S VERSION	**LEARNER'S VERSION**
1.	Lower inhibitions	Fear not!
2.	Encourage risk-taking	Dive in
3.	Build self-confidence	Believe in yourself
4.	Develop intrinsic motivation	Seize the day
5.	Engage in cooperative learning	Love thy neighbor
6.	Use right-brain processes	Get the BIG picture
7.	Promote ambiguity tolerance	Cope with the chaos
8.	Practice intuition	Go with your hunches
9.	Process error feedback	Make mistakes work FOR you
10.	Set personal goals	Set your own goals

4. Impromptu teacher-initiated advice

Yet another form of instilling self-awareness in students is through frequent impromptu reminders of "rules" for good language learning and encouragement of discussion or clarification. Sometimes the little comments you make here and there have the effect of subtly urging students to take charge of their own destiny by understanding their own styles of learning and capitalizing on their abilities.

A set of successful styles for language learning might be appropriately capsulized in the form of ten rules or "commandments," as I have on occasion facetiously called them. In Table 12.1, they are given in a teacher's version and a learner's version. The former are stated in more technical terms; the latter uses words and cliches that are designed to catch the attention of learners. The learners' version, in the right hand column, with appropriate explanations, might be something useful for a classroom bulletin board, for class discussions, or for student journal writing topics.

It is extremely important to remember here that the directionality of these style continua does not always fit all learners. These rules encompass what **most** learners need to point to **most** of the time in **most** language learning contexts. That is, most learners come to a language class with too many inhibitions, not enough willingness to take risks, relatively low self-confidence in their ability to learn a language, etc. Your mission to 90% of your students is to pull them away from this potentially interfering side of the continuum and to get them to grapple with these "problems" and overcome them. Ten percent (this is just a rough guess—it could be a higher or lower proportion depending on the makeup of your classroom and on the particular style tendency in question) of your students could lean the **other** way. For them your job is to put the brakes on things like high (and haphazard) risk-taking, excessive impulsiveness, overinflated self-confidence, an approach that is too "laid back," and so forth. Further comments on this issue follow later in this chapter.

How to Teach Strategies in the Classroom

Just what are all these tricks of the trade that we're calling "strategies"? Rebecca Oxford (1990) provides the most comprehensive taxonomy of learning strategies currently available. These strategies are divided into what has come to be known as **direct** or **cognitive** strategies, which learners apply directly to the language itself, and **indirect** or **metacognitive** strategies in which learners manage or control their own learning process. Direct strategies include a number of different ways of

- remembering more effectively
- using all your cognitive processes
- compensating for missing knowledge

Indirect strategies, according to Oxford's taxonomy, include

- organizing and evaluating your learning
- managing your emotions
- learning with others

A list of 50 specific strategies falling into these six general categories is contained in Oxford's (1990) Strategy Inventory for Language Learning (SILL), reprinted on pages 203–208 in this chapter. It would be appropriate to turn to that inventory now, before reading on, in order to become familiar with some specific strategies for successful language learning.

Strategies, like styles, can be taught, and because of their specificity, even more easily than styles. There are at least four different approaches you can take to teaching strategies in the language classroom.

1. Teach strategies through interactive techniques

Many strategies are related to, and actually become the outward manifestation of styles. For example, a risk-taking style would result in seeking practice opportunities, making conversation even when it isn't "necessary," trying out language you're not sure of, asking for correction, making guesses about what someone said, etc.

One way to familiarize your students with this plethora of possible strategies is to promote the ten "commandments" above through your own classroom techniques. Some techniques will be the ones you would utilize anyway. Other techniques will perhaps be specifically geared toward building **strategic** competence. Table 12.2 offers some suggestions for creating an atmosphere in your classroom in which students feel comfortable and encouraged to develop their own strategies.

One of the best teacher resource books to appear in recent years on the subject of learner strategy training is Rebecca Oxford's (1990) aforementioned *Language Learning Strategies: What Every Teacher Ought to Know*. In this book the author recommends many different techniques and shows which strategies they encourage. For example, an information gap listening tech-

Table 12.2. Building Strategic Techniques.

1. **to lower inhibitions:** play guessing games and communication games; do role plays and skits; sing songs; use plenty of group work; laugh **with** your students; have them share their fears in small groups.

2. **to encourage risk-taking:** praise students for making sincere efforts to try out language; use fluency exercises where errors are not corrected at that time; give outside-of-class assignments to speak or write or otherwise try out the language.

3. **to build students' self-confidence:** tell students explicitly (verbally and nonverbally) that you do indeed believe in them; have them make lists of their strengths, of what they know or have accomplished so far in the course.

4. **to help them to develop intrinsic motivation:** remind them explicitly about the rewards for learning English; describe (or have students look up) jobs that require English; play down the final examination in favor of helping students to see rewards for themselves beyond the final exam.

5. **to promote cooperative learning:** direct students to share their knowledge; play down competition among students; get your class to think of themselves as a team; do a considerable amount of small group work.

6. **to encourage them to use right-brain processing:** use movies and tapes in class; have them read passages rapidly; do skimming exercises; do rapid "free writes"; do oral fluency exercises where the object is to get students to talk (or write) a lot without being corrected.

7. **to promote ambiguity tolerance:** encourage students to ask you, and each other, questions when they don't understand something; keep your theoretical explanations very simple and brief; deal with just a few rules at a time; occasionally you can resort to translation into a native language to clarify a word or meaning.

8. **to help them use their intuition:** praise students for good guesses; do not always give explanations of errors—let a correction suffice; correct only selected errors, preferably just those that interfere with learning.

9. **to get students to make their mistakes work FOR them:** tape record students' oral production and get them to identify errors; let students catch and correct each other's errors; do not always give them the correct form; encourage students to make lists of their common errors and to work on them on their own.

10. **to get students to set their own goals:** explicitly encourage or direct students to go beyond the classroom goals; have them make lists of what they will accomplish on their own in a particular week; get students to make specific time commitments at home to study the language; give "extra credit" work.

---

nique is explained (p. 109–110) in which students listen to a conversation on a tape and then, in groups, fill in an information grid (with blank spaces for name, profession, address, age, and appearance) for each of four people mentioned in the conversation. Oxford explains that such a task involves direct strategies like practicing naturalistically, guessing, note-taking, focusing attention, and cooperating with co-learners.

2. Use compensatory techniques

A related avenue for learner strategy training is in the specific identification of techniques that aim to compensate for certain style weaknesses. Over a decade ago Alice Omaggio (1981) published a little book that classified some 55 different techniques according to numerous cognitive style "problems" that might be preventing students from reaching their highest potential. For example, "excessive reflectiveness/caution" is one such problem that might apply to certain students in your class: they are unwilling to take risks; they pause too long before responding orally; they want to get everything right before they attempt to speak or write something. Several dozen techniques are then "prescribed" to help such students overcome their problem. Here are some typical cognitive style "problems" and a few of the sorts of things one might prescribe to help overcome each problem.

(1) low tolerance of ambiguity: brainstorming, retelling stories, role-play, paraphrasing, finding synonyms, jigsaw techniques, skimming tasks

(2) excessive impulsiveness: making inferences, syntactic or semantic clue searches, scanning for specific information, inductive rule generalization

(3) excessive reflectiveness/caution: small group techniques, role play, brainstorming, fluency techniques

(4) too much field <u>dependence</u>: syntactic or semantic clue searches, scanning for specific information, proofreading, categorizing and clustering activities, information gap techniques

(5) too much field <u>independence</u>: integrative language techniques, fluency techniques, retelling stories, skimming tasks

3. Administer a strategy inventory

Earlier in this chapter you were offered some suggestions for using a self-check list and formal style tests in the classroom. Following the same format, you could introduce a strategy inventory. The best and most comprehensive of such instruments is Rebecca Oxford's *Strategy Inventory for Language Learning* (1990), an extensive questionnaire covering (in its ESL version) fifty separate strategies in six major categories. The SILL has now been used with learners in a number of different countries including the USA, and has proven to be exceptionally enlightening to learners as they are exposed, perhaps for the first time, to so many different strategic options. The SILL (Figure 12.4) is reprinted on pages 203–208.

The SILL can be used in class for developing awareness of strategies in the same way suggested earlier for the self-check list on styles. Or, it could become an out-of-class assignment for later class discussion. Its scoring and interpretation can be tricky, however, so make sure that in either case students are fully aware of how to score it.

The SILL can do double duty as an instrument that enlightens **you** about fifty different ways that your learners could become a little more successful in their language learning endeavor.

Figure 12.4. Oxford's SILL (Oxford, 1990).

Strategy Inventory for Language Learning (SILL)
Version for Speakers of Other
Languages Learning English

Directions

This form of the STRATEGY INVENTORY FOR LANGUAGE LEARNING (SILL) is for students of English as a second or foreign language. You will find statements about learning English. Please read each statement. On the separate Worksheet, write the response (1, 2, 3, 4, or 5) that tells HOW TRUE OF YOU THE STATEMENT IS.

  1. **Never or almost never true of me**
  2. **Usually not true of me**
  3. **Somewhat true of me**
  4. **Usually true of me**
  5. **Always or almost always true of me**

NEVER OR ALMOST NEVER TRUE OF ME means that the statement is <u>very rarely</u> true of you.

USUALLY NOT TRUE OF ME means that the statement is true <u>less than half the time.</u>

SOMEWHAT TRUE OF ME means that the statement is true of you <u>about half the time.</u>

USUALLY TRUE OF ME means that the statement is true <u>more than half the time.</u>

ALWAYS OR ALMOST ALWAYS TRUE OF ME means that the statement is true of you <u>almost always.</u>

Answer in terms of <u>how well the statement describes you.</u> Do not answer how you think you <u>should</u> be, or what <u>other</u> people do. <u>There are no right or wrong answers to these statements.</u> Put your answers on the separate Worksheet. Please make no marks on the items. Work as quickly as you can without being careless. This usually takes about 20-30 minutes to complete. If you have any questions, let the teacher know immediately.

  EXAMPLE
  1. **Never or almost never true of me**
  2. **Usually not true of me**
  3. **Somewhat true of me**
  4. **Usually true of me**
  5. **Always or almost always true of me**

Read the item, and choose a response (1 through 5 as above), and write it in the space after the item.

  I actively seek out opportunities to talk with native speakers of English_____

You have just completed the example item. Answer the rest of the items on the Worksheet.

1. **Never or almost never true of me**
2. **Usually not true of me**
3. **Somewhat true of me**
4. **Usually true of me**
5. **Always or almost always true of me**
   (Write answers on Worksheet)

Part A

1. I think of relationships between what I already know and new things I learn in English.
2. I use new English words in a sentence so I can remember them.
3. I connect the sound of a new English word and an image or picture of the word to help me remember the word.
4. I remember a new English word by making a mental picture of a situation in which the word might be used.
5. I use rhymes to remember new English words.
6. I use flashcards to remember new English words.
7. I physically act out new English words.
8. I review English lessons often.
9. I remember new English words or phrases by remembering their location on the page, on the board, or on a street sign.

Part B

10. I say or write new English words several times.
11. I try to talk like native English speakers.
12. I practice the sounds of English.
13. I use the English words I know in different ways.
14. I start conversations in English.
15. I watch English language TV shows spoken in English or go to movies spoken in English.
16. I read for pleasure in English.
17. I write notes, messages, letters, or reports in English
18. I first skim an English passage (read over the passage quickly) then go back and read carefully.
19. I look for words in my own language that are similar to new words in English.
20. I try to find patterns in English.
21. I find the meaning of an English word by dividing it into parts that I understand.
22. I try not to translate word-for-word
23. I make summaries of information that I hear or read in English.

Part C

24. To understand unfamiliar English words, I make guesses.
25. When I can't think of a word during a conversation in English, I use gestures.
26. I make up new words if I do not know the right ones in English.
27. I read English without looking up every new word.
28. I try to guess what the other person will say next in English.
29. If I can't think of an English word, I use a word or phrase that means the same thing.

Part D

30. I try to find as many ways as I can to use my English.
31. I notice my English mistakes and use that information to help me do better.
32. I pay attention when someone is speaking English.
33. I try to find out how to be a better learner of English.

1. **Never or almost never true of me**
2. **Usually not true of me**
3. **Somewhat true of me**
4. **Usually true of me**
5. **Always or almost always true of me**
   (Write answers on Worksheet)

34. I plan my schedule so I will have enough time to study English.
35. I look for people I can talk to in English.
36. I look for opportunities to read as much as possible in English.
37. I have clear goals for improving my English skills.
38. I think about my progress in learning English.

Part E

39. I try to relax whenever I feel afraid of using English.
40. I encourage myself to speak English even when I am afraid of making a mistake.
41. I give myself a reward or treat when I do well in English.
42. I notice if I am tense or nervous when I am studying or using English.
43. I write down my feelings in a language learning diary.
44. I talk to someone else about how I feel when I am learning English.

Part F

45. If I do not understand something in English, I ask the other person to slow down or say it again.
46. I ask English speakers to correct me when I talk.
47. I practice English with other students.
48. I ask for help from English speakers.
49. I ask questions in English.
50. I try to learn about the culture of English speakers.

STRATEGY INVENTORY FOR LANGUAGE LEARNING

Your Name_____Date_____

Worksheet for Answering and Scoring

1. The blanks (_____) are numbered for each item on the SILL.
2. Write your response to each item (that is, write 1, 2, 3, 4, or 5) in each of the blanks.
3. Add up each column. Put the result on the line marked SUM.
4. Divide by the number under SUM to get the average for each column. Round this average off to the nearest tenth, as in 3.4.
5. Figure out your overall average. To do this, add up all the SUMs for the different parts of the SILL. Then divide by 50.
6. When you have finished, your teacher will give you the Profile of Results. Copy your averages (for each part and for the whole SILL) from the Worksheet to the Profile.

Part A	Part B	Part C	Part D	Part E	Part F	Whole SILL
1._____	10._____	24._____	30._____	39._____	45._____	SUM Part A_____
2._____	11._____	25._____	31._____	40._____	46._____	SUM Part B_____
3._____	12._____	26._____	32._____	41._____	47._____	SUM Part C_____
4._____	13._____	27._____	33._____	42._____	48._____	SUM Part D_____
5._____	14._____	28._____	34._____	43._____	49._____	SUM Part E_____
6._____	15._____	29._____	35._____	44._____	50._____	SUM Part F_____
7._____	16._____		36._____			
8._____	17._____		37._____			
9._____	18._____		38._____			
	19._____					
	20._____					
	21._____					
	22._____					
	23.					

SUM____	**SUM**____	**SUM**____	**SUM**____	**SUM**____	**SUM**____	**SUM**____
÷ 9=____	÷14=____	÷6=____	÷9=____	÷6=____	÷6=____	÷50=____
						(OVERALL AVERAGE)

STRATEGY INVENTORY FOR LANGUAGE LEARNING

Your Name_____Date_____

Profile of Results on the Strategy Inventory for Language Learning (SILL)

You will receive this Profile after you have completed the Worksheet. This Profile will show your SILL results. These results will tell you the kinds of strategies you use in learning English. There are no right or wrong answers.

To complete this profile, transfer your averages for each part of the SILL, and your overall average for the whole SILL. These averages are found on the Worksheet.

Part	What Strategies Are Covered	Your Average on This Part
A.	Remembering more effectively	_____
B.	Using all your mental processes	_____
C.	Compensating for missing knowledge	_____
D.	Organizing and evaluating your learning	_____
E.	Managing your emotions	_____
F.	Learning with others	_____
	YOUR OVERALL AVERAGE	_____

STRATEGY INVENTORY FOR LANGUAGE LEARNING

Your Name_____Date_____

Key to Understanding Your Average

High	Always or almost always used	4.5 to 5.0
	Usually used	3.5. to 4.4
Medium	Sometimes used	2.5 to 3.4
Low	Generally not used	1.5 to 2.4
	Never or almost never used	1.0 to 1.4

Graph Your Averages Here

If you want, you can make a graph of your SILL averages. What does this graph tell you? Are you very high or very low on any part?

```
5.0 -
4.5 -
4.0 -
3.5 -
3.0 -
2.5 -
2.0 -
1.5 -
1.0 -
```

A	B	C	D	E	F	YOUR
Remembering more effectively	Using all your mental processes	Compensating for missing knowledge	Organizing and evaluating your learning	Managing your emotions	Learning with others	OVERALL AVERAGE

What These Averages Mean to You

The overall average tells how often you use strategies for learning English. Each part of the SILL represents a group of learning strategies. The averages for each part of the SILL show which groups of strategies you use the most for learning English.

The best use of strategies depends on your age, personality, and purpose for learning.
If you have a very low average on one or more parts of the SILL, there may be some new strategies in these groups that you might want to use. Ask your teacher about these.

4. Impromptu teacher-initiated advice

Finally, as you may recall from the discussion of developing style aware-ness, learners can benefit greatly from your daily attention to the many little tricks of the trade that you can pass on to them. Think back to your own lan-guage learning experiences and note what it was that you now attribute your success (or failure!) to, and pass these insights on. Did you use flash cards? Did you practice a lot? Did you see subtitled movies? Read books? Pin rules and words up on your wall? When those appropriate moments present them-selves in your class, seize the opportunity to teach your students **how to learn**. By doing so you will increase their opportunities for strategic invest-ment in their learning process.

"Packaged" Models of Learner Strategy Training

Most of your opportunities for strategy training in the classroom will be "methodological." That is, you will opt for one of the four possible means suggested above. There remain three more formalized models of strategy training; these are growing in popularity as more educational administrators (and budgetary managers!) appreciate the value of strategy training for suc-cess.

1. Textbook-embedded training

A few content-centered ESL textbooks are now appearing in which the **content** itself is the study and utilization of learning strategies. In *Learning to Learn English,* Ellis and Sinclair (1990) get intermediate EFL learners to look systematically at successful learning strategies through readings, check lists, and various techniques in all four skills of listening, speaking, reading, and writing. In one chapter, for example, students are taught what to do when they don't know the word for something (see Figure 12.5). Chamot, O'Malley, and Kupper's (1992) series, *Building Bridges: Content and Learning Strategies for ESL*, takes a similar approach. One of their lessons recommends keeping a daily log for one week and checking how many times a student uses any of fourteen different strategies. A grid is provided for easy checking (see Figure 12.6).

Step 6 Do you need to build up your confidence?

What can you do when you don't know a word?

Listen to three people in a shop describing an objcct they want to buy but don't know the word for. Can you guess what the object is?

In a situation like this, there are several strategies you can use if you don't know the word. Can you think of any? Look at the chart below to see some examples.

—Listen again to the people on the cassette and tick (✓) the strategies you hear them using.

—Which strategy or combination of strategies do you think was the most effective and why?

—Can you think of any other strategies that may be effective? Add them to the list.

Strategies	Speaker 1	Speaker 2	Speaker 3
i) using a foreign word			
ii) describing what it is for			
iii) describing what it looks like and what it is made of			
iv) using a word that is close in meaning			
v) inventing a new word or expression			
vi) using substitute words e.g., 'thingy'			
vii) other			

Figure 12.6. Self-help Learning Strategies (Chamot, O'Malley and Kupper, 1992:98).

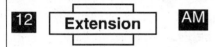

12   **Extension**   AM

Keep a notebook about your learning

A. For the next week, keep a notebook about your learning. Pay attention to what you do in school. This includes: what you think, how you read, how you listen, when you take notes, when you listen hard, or when you don't listen. Use the chart below to help you.

WHAT I DO TO HELP MYSELF LEARN					
STRATEGIES	DAY 1	DAY 2	DAY 3	DAY 4	DAY 5
I paid attention to the teacher.					
I took notes when I listened.					
I took notes when I read.					
I read the questions before I listened.					
I read the questions before I read.					
I looked at my notes later.					
I repeated new words aloud.					
I used new words in a sentence.					
I looked for information in a reference book.					
I did all my homework.					
I helped a friend with homework.					
I asked the teacher questions					
I asked a friend questions about schoolwork.					
I guessed at new words.					

2. Adjunct self-help guides

A second pre-packaged way of enlightening students about strategies is through the assignment or recommendation of a self-help study guide, several of which are currently available. Such "how to" guides tend to have short, easy-to-understand chapters with information, anecdotes, tips, and exercises that will help learners to use strategies successfully. They can be offered to students as recommended reading over and above their regular course assignments. Following are a few of this genre of strategy training books:

Brown, H. Douglas. 1989. *A Practical Guide to Language Learning.* McGraw Hill. (Translated editions are available in Japanese and Thai; forthcoming are translations in Spanish and Chinese.)

Rubin, Joan, and Thompson, Irene. 1983. *How to Be a More Successful Language Learner.* Heinle and Heinle.

Marshall, Terry. 1991. *The Whole World Guide to Language Learning.* Intercultural Press.

One drawback to books like these for English learners is that they are written in English, and one could argue that if students are proficient enough to read the book, they may not need all the strategies suggested therein! However, it has been found that intermediate level learners of English have profited from reading such books by simply skipping over some of the beginner level strategies. The one exception above, the *Practical Guide,* has been translated into four languages.

3. Learning centers

In spite of declining budgets in many schools and universities, there are nevertheless a considerable number of learning centers around the world that have an ESL-related component. Such centers typically make available to learners a number of possible types of extra-class assistance in writing, reading, academic study skills, pronunciation, and other oral production. Assistance can include diagnostic testing and interpretation, one-on-one tutorials, small-group tutorials, audio and video teaching programs, and computer programs ranging from grammatical brush-up to writing self-help.

A few progressive institutions view such learning centers not merely as a place to offer "remedial" help but as a resource for all learners for the improvement of their strategic competence in language learning. One such center at the Defense Language Institute of Monterey, California, is now in the piloting stage. Students seeking assistance at the Learning Strategies Center get an initial interview to determine what kind of resources can benefit them the most. Then a number of diagnostic tests can be chosen—tests of right/left brain preference, ambiguity tolerance, self-esteem, extroversion, motivation, Oxford's *SILL,* and others. The test results identify areas needing attention, such as using both sides of style continua, motivation, strategy use, language-specific problems, and stress and time management. Numerous treatments are "prescribed": workshops, self-instructional programs, tutorials, clinics, and the like. Periodic evaluative instruments indicate progress.

❈   ❈   ❈

Interactive language teachers must not underestimate the importance of getting students strategically invested in their language learning process. Perhaps the most powerful principle of learning of all kinds is the principle of intrinsic motivation. One of the best ways of getting students intrinsically involved in their language learning is to offer them the opportunity to develop their own set of strategies for success. Having thus invested their time and effort into the learning of English, they can take responsibility for a good deal of their own learning. This, in turn, generates more motivation as they "seize the day."

TOPICS FOR DISCUSSION, ACTION, AND RESEARCH

1. Look through some travel magazines and try to find an advertisement for a foreign language self-study program. What kinds of promises does it make? In view of what you know about principles of language learning and teaching, do you think those promises are justified? In a group, create an advertisement for an imaginary new program or school that you have started. How would you advertise it? What would the major features of the program be? After creating the ad, in your group discuss whether or not you could "sell" your program and still be true to the unpredictability of success in language learning?

2. Among members of your class, in pairs, divide up the eleven *other* principles (besides strategic investment) outlined in Chapter 2. Discuss how your principle contributes to or relates to the strategic investment principle. Then, share your thoughts with the rest of the class.

3. Look at the list of characteristics of "good language learners" (Rubin and Thompson) on pages 191 and 192 and the "ten commandments" for learners on page 199. Of that combined list, which *three or four* principles or characteristics would you place at the top of the list as most important? In a group, compare your choice with others and discuss the reasons behind your choice. After the discussion, decide whether or not you might change any of your choices.

4. Fill out the check list on page 195, based on a second language you have learned. How many D and E categories did you fall into? How many A and B? With a partner, see if you both agree that, in each case, A & B categories are more indicative of successful learning styles. If you fell into some D and E categories, talk about what steps you might take to change your learning style. How would you teach these changes in an ESL classroom?

5. Take the two style tests on pages 196 and 197. Did the results seem to be indicative of the "real you?" What are some drawbacks to tests like these? Do you see any cross-cultural problems in their structure, conceptualization, or wording?

6. Following some of the guidelines in this chapter, prepare a "lecturette" on successful learning strategies for ESL learners. Deliver it to your classmates (pretending they are ESL students) and then have them critique you.

7. Look at Table 12.2 on page 201. In a small group, discuss the list and add, subtract, or change some of the items to fit contexts that you are familiar with. Observe an ESL class and use the ten items as a check list to see how much the teacher instilled strategic competence in the learners. Share your conclusions with the group after observing.

8. In pairs or small groups, look at the "compensatory techniques" on page 202. Discuss ways in which each "prescription" could be an effective antidote to poor learning styles and strategies.

9. Take the *SILL.* Discuss how it could be used, in your context, an ESL classroom that you're familiar with. Could any of the 50 items be practiced in the classroom? In a group, select a few items and work out the details of how you might teach those strategies.

10. Of the three "packaged" models of learner strategy training (p. 209, and 212), which one is the most feasible in contexts that you know? Why? What aspects of the other two models would you be able to incorporate with some modification? Justify your choices.

FOR YOUR FURTHER READING

Oxford, Rebecca. 1990. *Language Learning Strategies: What Every Teacher Should Know.* Newbury House.

This is an excellent resource for teachers wishing to understand how they might incorporate strategy training in their language classrooms. Background theoretical information on learning strategies is provided along with carefully specified classroom techniques and materials.

Wenden, Anita. 1992. *Learner Strategies for Learner Autonomy.* Prentice Hall.

The principle of autonomous learning—which underlies all learner strategy training—is explored in depth. Research on the issue is reviewed, and practical suggestions are offered for the classroom.

Stevick, Earl. 1989. *Success with Foreign Languages.* Prentice Hall.

This fascinating book chronicles the learning processes of seven foreign language learners who were interviewed in depth about the strategies they used—or failed to use—in their attempt to become successful in reaching their goals.

Brown, H. Douglas. 1989. *A Practical Guide to Language Learning.* McGraw Hill.

This little book is designed for native English speakers who are learning foreign language. Fifteen easy-to-read chapters inform students of possibilities open to them and provide exercises for self-monitoring and self-improvement. Three translated versions are available for native speakers of Thai, Japanese, and Spanish who are learning ESL.

Brown, H. Douglas. 1991. *Breaking the Language Barrier.* Intercultural Press.

This is a book for non-specialist readers to learn a bit about principles of language learning and strategies for success. In some ways, it provides a simplified overview of the material covered in *Principles of Language Learning and Teaching (PLLT)* (Brown, 1994).

Chapter 13

Integrating
the "Four Skills"

For almost six decades now research and practice in English language teaching has identified the "four skills"—listening, speaking, reading, and writing—as of paramount importance. In textbooks and curricula in widely varying contexts, ESL classes around the world tend to focus on one or two of the four skills, sometimes to the exclusion of the others. And a visit to the most recent TESOL Convention will offer you a copious assortment of presentations indexed according to the four skills.

It is perfectly appropriate to so identify language performance. The human race has fashioned two forms of productive performance, oral and written, and two forms of receptive performance, aural (or auditory) and reading. There are of course offshoots of each mode. Lumped together under non-verbal communication are various visually perceived messages delivered through gestures, facial expressions, proximity, and so forth. Graphic art (drawings, paintings, diagrams) is also a powerful form of communication. And we could go on. But for learners of a second language, some attention to the four different skills does indeed pay off as learners discover the differences among these four primary modes of performance along with their interrelationships.

With all our history of treating the four skills in separate segments of a curriculum, there is nevertheless a more recent trend toward skill **integration**.

That is, rather than designing a curriculum to teach the many aspects of one skill, say, reading, curriculum designers are taking more of **whole language** approach whereby reading is treated as one of two or more interrelated skills. A course that deals with reading skills, then, will also deal with related listening, speaking, and writing skills. A lesson in a so-called reading class, under this new paradigm, might, for example, include:

(1) A pre-reading **discussion** of the topic to activate schemata.

(2) **Listening** to a lecture or a series of informative statements about the topic of a passage to be read.

(3) A focus on a certain **reading** strategy, say, scanning.

(4) **Writing** a paraphrase of a section of the reading passage.

This class, then, models for the students the real-life integration of language skills, gets them to perceive the relationship among several skills, and provides the teacher with a great deal of flexibility in creating interesting, motivating lessons.

Why Integration?

Some may wish to argue that the integration of the four skills diminishes the importance of the rules of listening, of speaking, of reading, and of writing that are unique to each separate skill. Such an argument rarely holds up under careful scrutiny of integrated-skill courses. If anything, the added richness of the latter gives students greater motivation that converts to better retention of principles of effective speaking, listening, reading, and writing. Rather than being forced to plod along through a course that limits itself to one mode of performance, they are given a chance to diversify their efforts in more meaningful tasks. Such integration can, of course, still utilize a strong principled approach to the separate, unique characteristics of each separate skill.

So you may be wondering why courses weren't always integrated in the first place. There are several reasons:

(1) In the pre-CLT days of language teaching, the focus on the **forms** of language almost predisposed curriculum designers to segment courses into the separate language skills. It seemed logical to fashion a syllabus that dealt with, say, pronunciation of the phonemes of English, stress and intonation, oral structural patterns (carefully sequenced according to presumed grammatical difficulty), and variations on those patterns. These "language-based" classes tended to be courses in "baby linguistics" where a preoccupation with rules and paradigms taught students a lot **about** language but sometimes at the expense of teaching language itself.

(2) Administrative considerations still make it easier to program separate courses in "reading" and "speaking," etc., as a glance at current intensive and

university English courses reveals. Such divisions can indeed be justified when one considers the practicalities of coordinating three-hour-per-week courses, hiring teachers for each, ordering textbooks, and placing students into the courses. It should be noted, however, that a proficient teacher who professes to follow principles of CLT would never conduct, say, a "Reading" class without extensive use of speaking, listening, and writing in the class.

(3) Which leads to a third reason that not all classes are integrated: There are certain specific purposes for which students are studying English that may best be labeled by one of the four skills, especially at the high-intermediate to advanced levels. In an academic setting such as a university, for example, specialized workshops, modules, tutorials, or courses may be constructed explicitly to improve certain specialized skills. Thus a module in listening comprehension might include instruction on listening effectively to academic lectures, to fellow students in the classroom, to audio programs where there are no visual cues, to the consultative register used in the professor's office, and even to fellow students in casual conversation. Such a course might encompass phonological, morphological, syntactic, lexical, semantic, and discourse elements.

Aside from the above caveats, the integration of the four skills is the only plausible approach to take within a communicative, interactive framework. Most of the interactive techniques already described or referred to in this book involve the integration of skills. The following observations support such techniques.

(1) Production and reception are quite simply two sides of the same coin; one cannot split the coin in two.

(2) Interaction means sending **and** receiving messages.

(3) Written and spoken language often (but not always!) bear a relationship to each other; to ignore that relationship is to ignore the richness of language.

(4) For literate learners, the interrelationship of written and spoken language is an intrinsically motivating reflection of language and culture and society.

(5) By attending primarily to what learners can **do** with language, and only secondarily to the forms of language, we invite any or all of the four skills that are relevant into the classroom arena.

(6) Often one skill will reinforce another; we learn to speak, for example, in part by modeling what we hear, and we learn to write by examining what we can read.

How can you maintain an integrated-skills focus in your teaching? The following five models are in common use. They all pull the direct attention of the student away from the separateness of the skills of language and toward the meaningful purposes for which we use language.

Content-based Teaching

The first of the five models of integrated-skills approaches is **content-based** instruction. Quite simply, content-based (also known as "content-centered") language teaching integrates the learning of some specific subject-matter content with the learning of a second language. The overall structure of a content-based curriculum, in contrast to many traditional language curricula, is dictated more by the nature of the subject matter than by language forms and sequences. The second language, then, is simply the medium to convey informational content of interest and relevance to the learner.

Here are some examples of content-based curricula:

- Immersion programs for elementary school children
- Sheltered English programs (mostly found at elementary and secondary school levels)
- Writing across the curriculum (where writing skills in secondary schools and universities are taught within subject-matter areas like biology, history, art, etc.)
- English for specific purposes (ESP) (e.g., for engineering, agriculture, medicine)

It is perhaps already clear that content-based teaching allows learners to acquire knowledge and skills that transcend all the bits and pieces of language that may occupy hours and days of analyzing in a traditional language classroom. Research on second language acquisition at various ages indicates the ultimate strength of learning that is pointed toward practical non-language goals. The meaningful learning principle applies well here. Learners are focused on very useful, practical objectives as the subject matter is perceived to be relevant to long term goals. This also increases the intrinsic motivation that is so important to learning of any kind.

Can content-based teaching take place at all levels of proficiency, even beginning levels? While it is possible to argue that certain basic survival skills, for example, are themselves content-based skills and that a beginning level class could therefore be content-based, such an argument seems to extend the content-based notion beyond its normal bounds. Content-based instruction usually pertains to academic or occupational instruction over an extended period of time at intermediate to advanced proficiency levels. Talking about renting an apartment one day, shopping the next, getting a driver's license the next, and so on, is certainly **useful** and **meaningful** for beginners, but would be more appropriately called task-based rather than content-based.

Content-based teaching presents some challenges to language teachers. Allowing the subject matter to control the selection and sequencing of language items means that you have to view your teaching from an entirely different perspective. You are first and foremost teaching geography or math or culture; secondarily you are teaching language. So you may have to become a double expert! There are some team-teaching models of content-based teaching, however, that alleviate this potential drawback. In some schools, for example, a subject-matter teacher and a language teacher link their courses and curriculum so that each complements the other. Such an undertaking is not unlike what Brinton, Snow, and Wesche (1989) describe as an "adjunct" model of content-based instruction.

Content-based instruction allows for the complete integration of language skills. As you plan a lesson around a particular sub-topic of your subject matter area, your task becomes one of how best to present that topic or concept or principle. In such lessons it would be difficult **not** to involve at least three of the four skills as you have students reading, discussing, solving problems, analyzing data, writing opinions and reports.

Theme-based Teaching

In order to distinguish theme-based teaching from content-based, it is important to distinguish between what I will call "strong" and "weak" versions of content-based teaching (not to be confused in any way with "good" and "bad"). In the strong version, the **primary** purpose of a course is to instruct students in a subject-matter area. Of secondary and subordinate interest is language. All four of the examples of content-based instruction named above are good illustrations of the strong version. English for Specific Purposes (ESP) at the university level, for example, gathers engineering majors together in a course designed to teach terminology, concepts, and current issues in engineering. Because students are ESL students, they must of course learn this material in English, which the teacher is prepared to help them with. Immersion and sheltered programs, along with programs in writing across the curriculum are similarly focused.

A weak form of content-based teaching actually places an **equal** value on content and language objectives. While the curriculum, to be sure, is organized around subject-matter area, both students and teachers are fully aware that language skills do not occupy a subordinate role. Students have no doubt chosen to take a course or curriculum because their language skills need improvement, and they are now able to work toward that improvement without being battered with linguistically based topics. The ultimate payoff is that their language skills are indeed enhanced, but through focal attention to topic, and peripheral attention to language.

This weak version is actually very practical and very effective in many instructional settings. It typically manifests itself in what has come to be called **theme-based**, or topic-based teaching. Theme-based instruction provides an alternative to what would otherwise be traditional language classes by structuring a course around themes or topics. Theme-based curricula can serve the multiple interests of students in a classroom and can offer a focus on content while still adhering to institutional needs for offering a language course, *per se.* So, for example, an intensive English course for intermediate pre-university students might deal with topics of current interest such as public health, environmental awareness, world economics, etc. In the classroom students read articles or chapters, view video programs, discuss issues, propose solutions, and carry out writing assignments on a given theme. "English for Academic Purposes" (EAP) in a university is an appropriate instance of theme-based instruction.

Granted, there is a fuzzy line of distinction between theme-based instruction and "traditional" language instruction. You could easily argue that many existing reading and writing courses, for example, are theme-based in that they offer students substantial opportunities to grapple with topics of relevance and interest. I do not think it is important, or necessary, to dichotomize here. What **is** important is to put **principles** of effective learning into action. The major principles underlying both theme-based and content-based instruction are:

- the automaticity principle
- the meaningful learning principle
- the intrinsic motivation principle
- the communicative competence principle

All these principles are well served by theme-based instruction and/or by courses that are successfully able to get students excited and interested in some topic, issue, idea, or problem rather than bored or weary of overanalyzing linguistic rules.

Numerous current ESL textbooks, especially at the intermediate to advanced levels, offer theme-based courses of study. Such textbooks catch the curiosity and motivation of students with challenging topics and as they grapple with a whole array of real-life issues ranging from simple to complex, they can also focus on improving their linguistic skills.

Consider just one of an abundance of possible topics that has been used as a theme through which language is taught: environmental awareness and action. (For a collection of environmentally theme-based ESL activities, see Hockman, et al., 1991). With this topic, you are sure to find immediate intrinsic motivation—we all want to survive! Here are some possible theme-based activities:

(1) Use environmental statistics and facts for classroom reading, writing, discussion, and debate. You don't have to look very far to find information about the environmental crisis, research on the issues, and pointers on what individuals can do to forestall a global disaster. Following are some things that students can do with such material:

[for intermediate to advanced students]

- scan [reading selections] for particular information
- do "compare-and-contrast" exercises
- detect biases in certain statistics
- use statistics in argument
- learn the discourse features of persuasive writing
- write personal opinion essays
- discuss issues
- engage in formal debates

[for beginning students]

- use imperatives ("Don't buy aerosol spray cans.")
- practice verb tenses ("The ozone layer is vanishing.")
- develop new vocabulary
- learn cardinal and ordinal numbers
- work with simple conversations/dialogs like:

A: **Why do you smoke?**

B: **Because I like it.**

A: **You shouldn't smoke.**

B: **Well, it makes me less nervous.**

A: **But it's not good for your health.**

B: **I don't care.**

A: **Well, you will die young.**

(2) Conduct research and writing projects. When your ESL syllabus calls for a research project, one very intrinsically motivating possibility is to assign an environmental topic. Libraries, bookstores, newsstands, television and radio, and even political campaigns are fruitful sources of information. While individual projects are suitable, why not encourage students to work in pairs or teams, each assigned to a different aspect of an issue. Data are sought, gathered, synthesized, counter-arguments explored, and finally presented orally and/or in writing to the rest of the class.

(3) Have students create their own environmental awareness material. Whether you are teaching adults or children, beginning or advanced students, you can get a great deal of language and content material out of a "language experience approach" (see Chapter 16) in which students may create leaflets, posters, bulletin boards, newsletter articles, or even a booklet that outlines practical things you can do to "save the earth." If time and equipment permit, some exciting things can be done with a video camera, for example, an information program, a drama, interviews, news reports, etc.

(4) Conduct field trips that involve a pre-trip module (of perhaps several days) of reading, researching, and other fact finding and a post-trip module of summary and conclusions. Field trips can be made to recycling centers, factories that practice recycling, wildlife preserves, areas that need litter removed (abandoned lots, beaches, parks), etc.

(5) A growing number of simulation games are being created that use the environmental crisis as a theme around which to build various scenarios for the gaming process. Some games can get quite elaborate, with countries of the world and their respective resources represented by objects like egg cartons, bottles, cans, newspapers, and the like, and players charged to resolve problems of unequal distribution of wealth as well as environmental controls.

Experiential Learning

Closely related to and overlapping content-based and theme-based instruction is the concept of **experiential** language learning. Experiential learning includes activities that engage both left and right brain processing, that contextualize language, that integrate skills, and that point toward authentic, real-world purposes. So far, as Eyring (1991) points out, experiential learning is a word describing everything in the last five chapters of this book. But what experiential learning highlights for us is giving students **concrete experiences** through which they "discover" language principles (even if subconsciously) by trial and error, by processing feedback, by building hypotheses about language, and revising these assumptions in order to become fluent (Eyring, 1991:347). That is, teachers do not simply tell students about how language works; instead, they give students opportunities to use language as they grapple with the problem-solving complexities of a variety of concrete experiences.

According to Keeton and Tate (1978:2), in experiential learning,

the learner is directly in touch with the realities being studied. It is contrasted with learning in which the learner only reads about, hears about, talks about, or writes about these realities but never comes in contact with them as part of the learning process. ...It involves direct encounter with the phenomenon being studied rather than merely thinking about the encounter or only considering the possibility of doing something with it.

Experiential learning is not so much a novel concept as it is an emphasis on the marriage of two substantive principles of effective learning, principles espoused by the famous American educator, John Dewey: (1) one learns best by "doing," by active experimentation, and (2) inductive learning by discovery activates strategies that enable students to "take charge" of their own learning progress. As such it is an especially useful concept for teaching children, whose abstract intellectual processing abilities are not yet mature.

Experiential learning techniques tend to be learner-centered by nature. But some teacher controlled techniques may be considered experiential:

- using props, realia, visuals, "show and tell" sessions
- playing games (which often involve strategy) and songs
- utilizing media (television, radio, movies)

Examples of student-centered experiential techniques would include:

- hands-on projects (e.g., nature projects)
- computer activities (especially in small groups)
- research projects
- cross-cultural experiences (camps, dinner groups, etc.)
- field trips and other "on-site" visits (e.g., to a grocery store)
- role-plays and simulations

Experiential learning tends to put an emphasis on the psychomotor aspects of language learning by involving learners in physical actions into which language is subsumed and reinforced. Through action, students are drawn into a utilization of multiple skills.

The Episode Hypothesis

Over a hundred years ago, François Gouin, if you will recall from Chapter 4, designed a method of language teaching called the Series Method. One of the keys to the success of the method lay in the presentation of language in an easily followed story line. You may remember the sequence of sentences about opening a door. In another lesson, Gouin teaches a number of verbs, verb forms, and other vocabulary in a little story about a girl chopping wood:

> **The girl goes and seeks a piece of wood.**
>
> **She takes a hatchet.**
>
> **She draws near to the block.**
>
> **She places the wood on this block.**
>
> **She raises the hatchet.**
>
> **She brings down the hatchet.**
>
> **The blade strikes against the wood.**
>
> **etc.**

In easily visualized steps, the students are led through the process of chopping and gathering wood, all at a very elementary level of the language.

In some ways, Gouin was utilizing a psychological device that, a hundred years later, John Oller called the **episode hypothesis**. According to Oller (1983:12), "text (i.e., discourse in any form) will be easier to reproduce, understand, and recall, to the extent that it is structured **episodically**." By this he meant that the presentation of language is enhanced if students do **not** get disconnected series of sentences thrown at them, but rather sentences that are interconnected in an interest-provoking episode.

The episode hypothesis goes well beyond simply "meaningful" learning. Look at the following dialogue:

> Jack: Hi, Tony. What do you usually do on weekends?
>
> Tony: Oh, I usually study, but sometimes I go to a movie.
>
> Jack: Uh huh. Well, I often go to movies, but I seldom study.
>
> Tony: Well, I don't study as much as Greg. He always studies on the weekends. He never goes out.
>
> etc.

You can see that this conversation, while easily understood, clearly presented, and perhaps quite relevant to students learning English, lacks a certain sense of drama—of "what's going to happen next?" Most of our communicative textbooks have many Jack & Tony types of presentation. They often illustrate certain grammatical or discourse features, but they hardly grip the learner with suspense.

But consider the following conversation (Brinton & Neuman, 1982:33), and notice how it differs from the above:

> Darlene: I think I'll call Bettina's mother. It's almost five and Chrissy isn't home yet.
>
> Meg: I thought Bettina had the chicken pox.
>
> Darlene: Oh, that's right. I forgot. Chrissy didn't go to Bettina's today. Where is she?
>
> Meg: She's probably with Gary. He has Little League practice until five.
>
> Darlene: I hear the front door. Maybe that's Gary and Chrissy.
>
> Gary: Hi.
>
> Darlene: Where's Chrissy? Isn't she with you?
>
> Gary: With me? Why with me? I saw her at two after school, but then I went to Little League practice. I think she left with her friend.
>
> Darlene: Which one?
>
> Gary: The one next door ... the one she walks to school with every day.
>
> Darlene: Oh, you mean Timmy. She's probably with him.
>
> Gary: Yeah, she probably is.
>
> Darlene: I'm going next door to check.

This conversation uses a familiar setting and ordinary characters to whet the curiosity of the reader. Because the outcome is not clear, learners are motivated to continue reading and to become more involved in the content than in the language, therefore increasing its episodic flavor. Oller notes that the interaction of cognition and language enables learners to form "expectancies" as they encounter either logically or episodically linked sentences. Moreover, "stories" are universal, and therefore students from many different cultures can understand their organizational structure and identify with the characters.

You may be wondering how the Episode Hypothesis contributes or relates to integrated-skills teaching. Here are some possible ways:

- Stories or episodes challenge the teacher and textbook writer to present interesting, natural language to the student, whether the language is viewed as written discourse or oral discourse.
- Episodes can be presented in either written and/or spoken form, thus requiring reading and/or writing skills on the student's part.
- Episodes can provide the stimulus for spoken or written questions that students respond to, in turn, by speaking or writing.
- Students can be encouraged to write their own episodes, or to complete an episode whose resolution or climax is not presented (such as the above conversation).
- Those written episodes might then be dramatized in the classroom by the students.

Now, it must be noted that the reality of the language classroom is such that not every aspect of language can be embedded in gripping dramatic episodes which have students yearning for the next day's events, as they perhaps do with a favorite soap opera! Linguistic samples like the conversation between Jack and Tony above are really quite respectable and pedagogically useful. Drills, writing practice, grammar explanations, essays on the world economy, and many other non-episodic activities still have a viable place in the classroom. But to the extent that a curriculum allows it, episodic teaching and testing may offer quite a rewarding alternative to sprinkle into your daily diet of teaching techniques.

Task-based Teaching

Task-based learning was defined and briefly discussed in Chapters 5 and 9. As you will recall, there are a number of different interpretations in the literature on what, exactly, a **task** is. What these various understandings all emphasize, however, is the centrality of the task itself in a language course and, for task-based teaching as an overall **approach**, the importance of organizing a course around communicative tasks that learners need to engage in outside the classroom. David Nunan (1991a:279) gives us five characteristics of a task-based approach to language teaching:

(1) **An emphasis on learning to communicate through interaction in the target language.**

(2) **The introduction of authentic texts into the learning situation.**

(3) **The provision of opportunities for learners to focus, not only on language, but also on the learning process itself.**

(4) **An enhancement of the learner's own personal experiences as important contributing elements to classroom learning.**

(5) **An attempt to link classroom language learning with language activation outside the classroom.**

Task-based teaching makes an important distinction between **target tasks,** which students must accomplish beyond the classroom, and **pedagogical tasks**, which form the nucleus of the classroom activity. Target tasks are not unlike the **functions** of language that are listed in notional-functional syllabuses (see Chapter 4, here, and Chapter 10 of *PLLT*); however, they are much more specific and more explicitly related to classroom instruction. If, for example, "giving personal information" is a communicative function for language, then an appropriately stated target task might be "giving personal information in a job interview." Notice the task specifies a context. Pedagogical tasks include any of a series of techniques designed ultimately to teach students to perform the target task; the climactic pedagogical task actually involves students in some form of simulation of the target task itself (say, through a role-play simulation in which certain roles are assigned to pairs of learners).

Pedagogical tasks are distinguished by their specific goals that point beyond the language classroom to the target task. They may, however, include both **formal** and **functional** techniques. A pedagogical task designed to teach students to give personal information in a job interview might, for example, involve:

1. exercises in comprehension of *wh*-questions with *do*-insertion

   (**"When do you work at Macy's?"**)

2. drills in the use of frequency adverbs

   (**"I usually work until five o'clock."**)

3. listening to extracts of job interviews

4. analyzing the grammar and discourse of the interviews

5. modeling an interview: teacher and one student

6. role-playing a simulated interview: students in pairs

While you might be tempted only to consider the climactic task (#6) as the one fulfilling the criterion of pointing beyond the classroom to the real world, all five of the other techniques build toward enabling the students to perform the final technique.

A task-based curriculum, then, specifies what a learner needs to **do** with the English language in terms of target tasks and organizes a series of pedagogical tasks intended to reach those goals. Be careful that you do not look at task-based teaching as a hodge-podge of useful little things that the learner should be able to do, all thrown together haphazardly into the classroom. In fact, a distinguishing feature of task-based curricula is their insistence on pedagogical soundness in the development and sequencing of tasks. The teacher and curriculum planner are called upon to consider carefully the following dimensions of communicative tasks:

- goal
- input from the teacher
- techniques
- the role of the teacher
- the role of the learner
- evaluation

In task-based instruction, the priority is not the bits and pieces of language but rather the functional purposes for which language must be used. While content-based instruction focuses on subject-matter content, task-based instruction focuses on a whole set of real-world tasks themselves. Input for tasks can come from a variety of authentic sources:

• speeches	• interviews
• conversations	• oral descriptions
• narratives	• media extracts
• public announcements	• games and puzzles
• cartoon strips	• photos
• letters	• diaries
• poems	• songs
• directions	• telephone directories
• invitations	• menus
• textbooks	• labels

And the list goes on and on. The pedagogical task specifies exactly what learners will do with the input, what the respective roles of the teacher and learners are, and the evaluation thereof forms an essential component that determines its success and offers feedback for performing the task again with another group of learners at another time.

Task-based curricula differ from content-based, theme-based and experiential instruction in that the course objectives are somewhat more unabashedly language-based. While there is an ultimate focus on communication and purpose and meaning, nevertheless goals are linguistic in nature. They are not linguistic in the traditional sense of just focusing on grammar or phonology, but by maintaining the centrality of functions like greeting people, expressing opinions, requesting information, etc., the course goals center on learners' **pragmatic** language competence.

So we have in task-based teaching a well integrated approach to language teaching that asks you to organize your classroom around those practical tasks that language users engage in "out there" in the real world. These tasks virtually always imply several skill areas, not just one, and so by pointing toward tasks, we disengage ourselves from thinking only in terms of the separate four skills. Instead, principles of listening, speaking, reading, and writing become appropriately subsumed under the rubric of what it is our learners are going to do with this language.

❊   ❊   ❊

We have considered five different ways to approach the integration of the four skills. The principal idea here is for you **not** to assume that all your techniques should be identified with just one of the four but rather that most successful **interactive** techniques will include several skill areas.

In the next four chapters, we will look at those four components but not with a view to programming your language teaching into compartments. Instead, these next chapters should help you to become aware of goals and problems and issues and trends that relate to each of the four modes of communication.

TOPICS FOR DISCUSSION, RESEARCH, AND ACTION

1. Review the reasons for **not** integrating skills in ESL courses given on pages 218–219. Can you add others? If you know of certain courses that are not integrated, can these three—or any other—justifications be advanced for keeping them non-integrated?

2. Look at the six observations (p. 219) in support of integrated-skills classes. With a partner, discuss whether or not they apply to contexts you are familiar with. Would you be able to add any more justification of integrating the skills?

3. Write brief definitions of each of the five types of integrated skill instruction discussed in this chapter: content-based, theme-based, experiential, the episode hypothesis, and task-based teaching. Share your definitions with a partner and revise them, if necessary. Now, make a list of various institutions that teach ESL and discuss the extent to which each model does or does not fit the institution.

4. Suppose you are asked to employ a teacher for a content-centered curriculum. What qualifications would you draw up for such a teacher?

5. In a group or in pairs, define an audience and context, then design a theme based lesson or module on environmental action and awareness. As you plan the techniques, discuss any "political" implications of what you might ask students to do. Share your lesson with the rest of your class.

6. Look in a library or resource center for books that could be classified as theme-based. Select one to evaluate, perhaps with a partner. Are both language and content goals fulfilled? Are the four skills well integrated? Will students be intrinsically motivated to study the book? Are the other three principles (cited on page 222) evident in the design of the book? Share your thoughts with the rest of the class.

7. With a partner, design an "episodic" activity. Share your activity with the rest of the class.

8. Once again, the term "task-based" is presented in this chapter. Define it again without referring to the chapter. With a partner, design a task that involves several techniques. Share your task with the rest of the class, and give your rationale for your design.

FOR YOUR FURTHER READING

Brinton, Donna M., Snow, Marguerite Ann, and Wesche, Marjorie B. 1989. *Content-based Second Language Instruction.* Newbury House.

Three different content-based approaches—theme-based, sheltered, and adjunct—are examined. The book presents profiles of several exemplary programs, and explores the contexts appropriate for the different models. Guidelines for designing a content-based curriculum are offered.

Nunan, David. 1991a. "Communicative tasks and the language curriculum." *TESOL Quarterly 25*(2), 279–295.

Nunan takes a long, careful look at task-based language teaching, with its focus on task as a significant building block in the development of language curricula. The article reviews and summarizes research on the influence of the communicative task on our current teaching approaches.

Long, Michael H. and Crookes, Graham. 1992. "Three approaches to task-based syllabus design." *TESOL Quarterly 26* (1), 27–56.

Three task-based syllabus types are described and analyzed: procedural, process, and task. All three types reject linguistic elements as the unit of analysis and opt instead for some conception of task. All three are different, however, in ways which are explained in this article.

Legutke, Michael, and Thomas, Howard. 1991. *Process and Experience in the Language Classroom.* Longman.

Communicative language teaching is seen in this book as an experiential and task-driven process. The authors describe practical   attempts to utilize project tasks, especially, both as a means of realizing task-based language learning and of redefining the roles of teacher and learner within a jointly constructed curriculum.

Chapter 14

Teaching Listening Comprehension

Three people were on a train in England. As they approached what appeared to be Wemberly Station, one of the travelers said, "Is this Wemberly?" "No," replied a second passenger, "it's Thursday." Whereupon the third person remarked, "Oh, I am too, let's have a drink!"

The importance of listening in language learning can hardly be overestimated. Through reception, we internalize linguistic information without which we could not produce language. In classrooms, students always do more listening than speaking. Listening competence is universally "larger" than speaking competence. Is it any wonder, then, that in recent years the language teaching profession has placed a concerted emphasis on listening comprehension?

Listening comprehension has not always drawn the attention of educators that it now has. Perhaps human beings have a natural tendency to look at speaking as the major index of language proficiency. Consider for example our commonly used query, "Do you speak Japanese?" Of course we don't mean to exclude comprehension when we say that, but when we think of foreign language learning, we first think of speaking. In the decades of the 1950s and '60s, language teaching methodology was preoccupied with the spoken language as classrooms full of students could be heard performing their oral drills. It was not uncommon for students to orally practice phrases they didn't even understand!

Listening Comprehension in Pedagogical Research

Listening as a major component in language learning and teaching first hit the spotlight in the late 1970s with James Asher's (1977) work on Total Physical Response (see Chapter 4), in which the role of comprehension was given prominence as learners were given great quantities of language to listen to before they were encouraged to respond orally. Similarly, the Natural Approach (see also Chapter 4) recommended a significant "silent period" during which learners were allowed the security of listening without being forced to go through the anxiety of speaking before they were "ready" to do so.

Such approaches were an outgrowth of a variety of research studies that showed evidence of the importance of **input** in second language acquisition. (see *PLLT,* Chapter 11) Stephen Krashen (1982), for example, borrowing insights from first language acquisition, stressed the significance of "comprehensible input," or the aural reception of language that is just a little beyond the learner's present ability. About the same time, researchers were also stressing the crucial importance of whatever mental processes were brought to bear on the learner's converting input into **intake,** or that which is actually stored in a learner's competence. In other words, you could be "exposed" to great quantities of input, but what counts is the linguistic information that you ultimately glean from that exposure through conscious and subconscious attention, through cognitive strategies of retention, through feedback, and through interaction.

The conversion of input into intake is absolutely crucial in considering the role of listening in language learning, as we shall see. As you consider the role of listening techniques in your classes, you ultimately want to ask yourself about what students have **taken in** from perhaps a whole array of comprehension activity. This issue prompts teachers to consider some specific questions about listening comprehension:

- What are listeners "doing" when they listen?
- What factors affect good listening?
- What are the characteristics of "real-life" listening?
- What are the many things listeners listen for?
- What are some principles of designing listening techniques?
- How can listening techniques be interactive?
- What are some common techniques for teaching listening?

These and other related questions will be addressed in this chapter.

An Interactive Model of Listening Comprehension

Listening is not a one way street. It is not merely the process of a unidirectional receiving of audible symbols. One facet—the first step—of listening comprehension is the psychomotor process of receiving sound waves through the ear and transmitting nerve impulses to the brain. But that is just the beginning of what is clearly an **interactive** process as the brain acts on the impulses, bringing to bear a number of different cognitive and affective mechanisms.

The following eight processes (adapted from Clark & Clark, 1977, and Richards, 1983) are all involved in comprehension. With the exception of the initial and final processes below, no sequence is implied here; they all occur, if not simultaneously, then in extremely rapid succession. Neurological time must be viewed in terms of microseconds.

(1) The hearer processes what we'll call "raw speech" and holds an "image" of it in short-term memory. This image consists of the constituents (phrases, clauses, cohesive markers, intonation and stress patterns) of a stream of speech.

(2) The hearer determines the type of speech event that is being processed. The hearer must, for example, ascertain whether this is a conversation, a speech, a radio broadcast, etc., and then appropriately "color" the interpretation of the perceived message.

(3) The hearer infers the objectives of the speaker through consideration of the type of speech event, the context, and content. So, for example, one determines whether the speaker wishes to persuade, to request, to exchange pleasantries, to affirm, to deny, to inform, and so forth. Thus the **function** of the message is inferred.

(4) The hearer recalls background information (or **schemata**—see Chapter 16 for more on this) relevant to the particular context and subject matter. A lifetime of experiences and knowledge are used to perform cognitive **associations** in order to bring a plausible interpretation to the message.

(5) The hearer assigns a literal meaning to the utterance. This process involves a set of semantic interpretations of the surface strings that the ear has perceived. In many instances, literal and intended (see #6 below) meanings match. So, for example, if one of your students walks into your office as you are madly grading papers and says she has a question that she would appreciate your answering, then says, "Do you have the time?" the literal meaning (do you possess enough time now to answer me) is appropriate. However, this process may take on a peripheral role in cases where literal meanings are irrelevant to the message, as in metaphorical or "idiomatic" language. If, for example, a stranger sitting beside you in a bus has been silent for a period of time and then says, "Do you have the time?" the appropriate response is not a "yes" or a "no" but rather "It's quarter to nine," or whatever. Second language learners must, in such cases, learn to go "beneath" the surface of such language in order to interpret correctly.

(6) The hearer assigns an intended meaning to the utterance. The person on the bus intended to find out what time of day it was, even though the literal meaning didn't directly convey that message. How often do misunderstandings stem from false assumptions that are made on the hearer's part about the intended meaning of the speaker? A key to human communication is the ability to match **perceived** meaning with **intended** meaning. This match-making, of course, can extend well beyond simple metaphorical and idiomatic language. It can apply to short and long stretches of discourse, and its breakdown can be caused by careless speech, inattention of the hearer, conceptual complexity, contextual miscues, psychological barriers, and a host of other performance variables.

(7) The hearer determines whether information should be retained in short-term or long-term memory. Short-term memory—a matter of a few seconds—is appropriate, for example, in contexts that simply call for a quick oral response from the hearer. Long-term memory is more common when, say, you are processing information in a lecture. There are, of course, many points in between.

(8) The hearer deletes the **form** in which the message was originally received. The words and phrases and sentences themselves are quickly forgotten—"pruned"—in 99 percent of speech acts. You have no need to retain this sort of cognitive "clutter." Instead the important information, if any, (see #7 above) is retained conceptually. (See also *PLLT,* Chapter 4.)

It should be clear from the foregoing that listening comprehension is an **interactive** process. After the initial reception of sound, we human beings perform at least seven other major operations on that set of sound waves. In conversational settings, of course, immediately after the listening stage, further interaction takes place as the hearer then becomes speaker in a response of some kind. All of these processes are important for you to keep in mind as you teach. They are all relevant to a learner's purpose for listening, to performance factors that may cause difficulty in processing speech, to overall principles of effective listening techniques, and to the choices you make of what techniques to use and when to use them in your classroom.

Types of Spoken Language

Much of our language teaching energy is devoted to instruction in mastering English **conversation**. However, numerous other forms of spoken language are also important to incorporate into a language course, especially in teaching listening comprehension. As you plan lessons or curricula, the classification shown in Fig. 14.1 of types of oral language should enable you to see the big picture of what teaching aural comprehension entails.

Figure 14.1. Types of Oral Language (adapted from Nunan, 1991b:20–21).

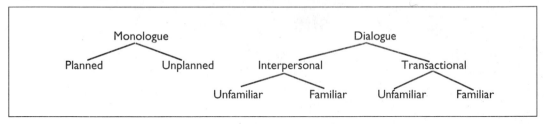

In monologues, when one speaker uses spoken language for any length of time, as in speeches, lectures, readings, news broadcasts, and the like, the hearer must process long stretches of speech without interruption—the stream of speech will go on whether or not the hearer comprehends. Planned, as opposed to unplanned monologues, differ considerably in their discourse structures. Planned monologues (e.g., speeches and other pre-written material) usually manifest little redundancy and are therefore relatively difficult to comprehend. Unplanned monologues (impromptu lectures and long "stories" in conversations, for example) exhibit more redundancy, which makes for ease in comprehension, but the presence of more performance variables and other hesitations (see below) can either help or hinder comprehension.

Dialogues involve two or more speakers and can be subdivided into those exchanges that promote **social relationships** (interpersonal) and those for which the purpose is to convey **propositional** or factual information (transactional). In each case, participants may have a good deal of shared knowledge (background information, schemata); therefore, the familiarity of the interlocutors will produce conversations with more assumptions, implications, and other meanings hidden "between the lines." In conversations between or among participants who are unfamiliar with each other, references and meanings have to be made more explicit in order for effective comprehension to take place. When such references are not explicit, misunderstandings can easily follow.

One could have also subdivided dialogues between those in which the hearer is a participant and those in which the hearer is an "eavesdropper." In both cases, the above conversational descriptions apply, but the major—and highly significant—difference is that in the latter the hearer is, as in monologues, unable to interrupt or otherwise to participate vocally in the negotiation of meaning.

In all cases, remember that these categories are really not discrete, mutually exclusive domains; rather, each dichotomy, as usual, represents a **continuum** of possibilities. For example, everyday social conversations can easily contain elements of transactional dialogues, and vice versa. Similarly, "familiar" participants may on a particular topic share very little common knowledge. If each category, then, is viewed as an end point, you can aim your teaching at appropriate ranges in between.

What Makes Listening Difficult?

As you contemplate designing lessons and techniques that are exclusively for teaching listening skills, or that have listening components in them, a number of special characteristics of spoken language need to be taken into consideration. Second language learners need to pay special attention to such factors because they highly influence the processing of speech and can often block comprehension if they are not attended to. In other words, they can make the listening process difficult. The following eight characteristics of spoken language are adapted from several sources (Dunkel, 1991; Richards, 1983; Ur, 1984).

1. Clustering

In written language we are conditioned to attend to the sentence as the basic unit of organization. In spoken language, due to memory limitations and our predisposition for "chunking," or clustering, we break down speech into smaller groups of words. Clauses are common constituents, but phrases within clauses are even more easily retained for comprehension. In teaching listening comprehension, therefore, you need to help students to pick out manageable clusters of words; sometimes second language learners will try to retain overly long constituents (a whole sentence or even several sentences), or they will err in the other direction in trying to attend to every word in an utterance.

2. Redundancy

Spoken language, unlike most written language, has a good deal of redundancy. The next time you're in a conversation, notice the rephrasings, repetitions, elaborations, and little insertions of "I mean" and "you know" here and there. Such redundancy helps the hearer to process meaning by offering more **time** and **extra information**. Learners can train themselves to profit from such redundancy by first becoming aware that not every new sentence or phrase will necessarily contain new information and by looking for the signals of redundancy. Consider the following excerpt of a conversation.

> **Amos: Hey, Andy, how's it going?**
>
> **Andy: Pretty good, Amos. How was your weekend?**
>
> **Amos: Aw, it was terrible, I mean the worst you could imagine. You know what I mean?**

> Andy: Yeah, I've had those days. Well, like what happened?
>
> Amos: Well, you're not gonna believe this, but my girlfriend and I— you know Rachel? I think you met her at my party—any- way, she and I drove up to Point Reyes, you know, up in Marin County? So we were driving along minding our own business, you know, when this dude in one of those four- wheelers, you know, like a Bronco or something, comes up like three feet behind us and like tailgates us on these crazy mountain roads up there—you know what they're like. So, he's about to run me off the road, and it's all I can do to just concentrate. Then...

You can easily pick out quite a few redundancies in Amos's recounting of his horrendous experience. Learners might initially get confused by this, but with some training, they can learn to take advantage of redundancies as well as other markers that provide more processing time.

3. Reduced forms

While spoken language does indeed contain a good deal of redundancy, it also has many reduced forms. Reduction can be phonological ("Djeetyet?" for "Did you eat yet?"), morphological (contractions like "I'll"), syntactic (elliptical forms like "When will you be back?" "Tomorrow, maybe."), or pragmatic (Phone rings in a house, child answers, cups the telephone and yells to another room in the house, "Mom! Phone!"). These reductions pose significant difficulties especially to classroom learners who may have initial- ly been exposed to the full forms of the English language.

4. Performance variables

In spoken language, except for planned discourse (speeches, lectures, etc.), hesitations, false starts, pauses, and corrections are common. Native lis- teners are conditioned from very young ages to "weed out" such performance variables whereas they can easily interfere with comprehension in second language learners. Imagine listening to the following verbatim excerpt of a sportsman talking about his game:

> But, uh—I also—to go with this of course if you're playing well—if you're playing well then you get uptight about your game. You get keyed up and it's easy to concentrate. You know you're playing well and you know... in with a chance then it's easier, much easier to—to you know get in there and—and start to... you don't have to think about it. I mean it's gotta be automatic.

In written form this looks like gibberish but it's the kind of language we hear and process all the time. Learners have to train themselves to listen for meaning in the midst of all these distracting performance variables.

Everyday casual speech by native speakers also commonly contains ungrammatical forms. Some of these forms are simple performance slips. For example, "We arrived in a little town that there was no hotel anywhere" is something a native speaker could easily self-correct. Other ungrammaticality arises out of dialect differences ("I don't get no respect") that second language learners are likely to hear sooner or later.

5. Colloquial language

Learners who have been exposed to standard written English and/or "textbook" language sometimes find it surprising and difficult to deal with colloquial language. Idioms, slang, reduced forms, shared cultural knowledge are all manifested at some point in conversations. Colloquialisms appear in both monologues and dialogues.

6. Rate of delivery

Virtually every language learner initially thinks that native speakers speak too fast! Actually, as Richards (1983) points out, the number and length of pauses used by a speaker is more crucial to comprehension than sheer speed. Learners will nevertheless eventually need to be able to comprehend language delivered at varying rates of speed and, at times, delivered with few pauses. Unlike reading, where a person can stop and go back to reread something, in listening the hearer may not always have the opportunity to stop the speaker. Instead, the stream of speech will continue to flow!

7. Stress, rhythm, and intonation

The prosodic features of the English language are very important for comprehension. As a stress-timed language, English speech can be a terror for some learners as mouthfuls of syllables come spilling out between stress points. The sentence, "The PREsident is INTerested in eLIMinating the emBARgo." with four stressed syllables out of 18, theoretically takes about the same amount of time to utter as "Dead men wear plaid." Also, intonation patterns are very significant (see Chapter 15) not just for interpreting such straightforward elements as questions and statements and emphasis but more subtle messages like sarcasm, endearment, insult, solicitation, praise, etc.

8. Interaction

Unless a language learner's objective is exclusively to master some specialized skill like monitoring radio broadcasts or attending lectures, interaction will play a large role in listening comprehension. Conversation is especially subject to all the rules of interaction: negotiation, clarification, attending signals, turn taking, and topic nomination, maintenance, and termination (see Chapter 10 of *PLLT*). So, to learn to listen is also to learn to respond and to continue a chain of listening and responding. Classroom techniques that include listening components must at some point include instruction in the two-way nature of listening. Students need to understand that good listeners (in conversation) are good responders. They know how to **negotiate meaning**, that is, to give feedback, to ask for clarification, to maintain a topic, so that the process of **comprehending** can be complete rather than being aborted by insufficient interaction.

A fourth century Chinese proverb says it more eloquently:

> **Not to let a word get in the way of its sentence**
> **Nor to let a sentence get in the way of its intention,**
> **But to send your mind out to meet the intention as a guest;**
> **THAT is understanding.**

Microskills of Listening Comprehension

Jack Richards (1983), in his seminal article on teaching listening skills, provided a comprehensive taxonomy of aural skills involved in conversational discourse. Such lists are very useful in helping you to break down just what it is that your learners need to **do** as they acquire effective interactive listening strategies. Through a checklist of microskills, you can get a good idea of what your techniques need to cover in the domain of listening comprehension. As you plan a specific technique or listening module, such a list helps you to focus on clearly conceptualized objectives. And, in your evaluation of listening, these microskills can become testing criteria. Following is just such a checklist, adapted from Richards and other sources:

1. **Retain chunks of language of different lengths in short-term memory.**
2. **Discriminate among the distinctive sounds of English.**
3. **Recognize English stress patterns, words in stressed and unstressed positions, rhythmic structure, intonational contours, and their role in signaling information.**
4. **Recognize reduced forms of words.**
5. **Distinguish word boundaries, recognize a core of words, and interpret word order patterns and their significance.**
6. **Process speech at different rates of delivery.**
7. **Process speech containing pauses, errors, corrections, and other performance variables.**
8. **Recognize grammatical word classes (nouns, verbs, etc.), systems (e.g., tense, agreement, pluralization), patterns, rules, and elliptical forms.**

9. Detect sentence constituents and distinguish between major and minor constituents.

10. Recognize that a particular meaning may be expressed in different grammatical forms.

11. Recognize cohesive devices in spoken discourse.

12. Recognize the communicative functions of utterances, according to situations, participants, goals.

13. Infer situations, participants, goals using real world knowledge.

14. From events, ideas, etc., described, predict outcomes, infer links and connections between events, deduce causes and effects, and detect such relations as main idea, supporting idea, new information, given information, generalization, and exemplification.

15. Distinguish between literal and implied meanings.

16. Use facial, kinesic, "body language," and other nonverbal clues to decipher meanings.

17. Develop and use a battery of listening strategies, such as detecting key words, guessing the meaning of words from context, appeal for help, and signaling comprehension or lack thereof.

It is important to note that these 17 microskills apply to conversational discourse. Less interactive forms of discourse, such as listening to monologues like academic lectures, include further, more specific microskills. Students in an academic setting need to be able to perform such things as identifying the structure of a lecture, weeding out what may be irrelevant or tangential, detecting the possible biases of the speaker, critically evaluating the speaker's assertions, and developing means (through notetaking, for example) of retaining the content of a lecture.

Types of Classroom Listening Performance

With literally hundreds of possible techniques available for teaching listening skills, it will be helpful for you to think in terms of several kinds of listening performances, that is, what your students **do** in a listening technique. Sometimes these types of performance are embedded in a broader technique or task, and sometimes they are themselves the sum total of the activity of a technique.

1. Reactive

Sometimes you simply want a learner to listen to the surface structure of an utterance for the sole purpose of repeating it back to you. While this kind of listening performance requires little meaningful processing, it nevertheless may be a legitimate, even though a minor, aspect of an interactive, communicative classroom. This role of the listener as merely a "tape recorder" (Nunan, 1991b:18) must be very limited, otherwise the listener as a generator of meaning does not reach fruition. About the only role that reactive listening can play in an interactive classroom is in brief choral or individual drills that focus on pronunciation.

2. Intensive

Techniques whose only purpose is to focus on components (phonemes, words, intonation, discourse markers, etc.) of discourse may be considered to be intensive—as opposed to extensive—in their requirement that students single out certain elements of spoken language. They include the bottom-up skills (see page 246) that are important at all levels of proficiency. Examples of intensive listening performance include:

- students listen for cues in certain choral or individual drills
- the teacher repeats a word or sentence several times to "imprint" it in the student's mind
- the teacher asks students to listen to a sentence or a longer stretch of discourse and to notice a specified element, e.g., intonation, stress, a contraction, a grammatical structure, etc.

3. Responsive

A significant proportion of classroom listening activity consists of short stretches of teacher language designed to elicit immediate responses. The students' task in such listening is to process the teacher talk immediately and to fashion an appropriate reply. Examples include:

- asking questions ("How are you today?" "What did you do last night?")
- giving commands ("Take out a sheet of paper and a pencil.")
- seeking clarification ("What was that word you said?")
- checking comprehension ("So, how many people were in the elevator when the power went out?")

4. Selective

In longer stretches of discourse such as monologues of a couple of minutes or considerably longer, the task of the student is not to process everything that was said but rather to **scan** the material selectively for certain information. The purpose of such performance is not to look for global or general meanings, necessarily, but to be able to find important information in a field of potentially distracting information. Such activity requires **field independence** on the part of the learner. Selective listening differs from intensive listening in that the discourse is in relatively long lengths. Examples of such discourse include:

- speeches
- media broadcasts
- stories and anecdotes
- conversations in which learners are "eavesdroppers"

Techniques promoting selective listening skills could ask students to listen for:

- people's names
- dates
- certain facts or events
- location, situation, context, etc.
- main ideas and/or conclusion

5. Extensive

This sort of performance, unlike the intensive processing (#2) described above, aims to develop a top-down, global understanding of spoken language. Extensive performance could range from listening to lengthy lectures to listening to a conversation and deriving a comprehensive message or purpose. Extensive listening may require the student to invoke other interactive skills (e.g., notetaking, discussion) for full comprehension.

6. Interactive

Finally, there is listening performance that can include all five of the above types as learners actively participate in discussions, debates, conversations, role-plays, and other pair and group work. Their listening performance must be intricately integrated with speaking (and perhaps other) skills in the authentic give and take of communicative interchange.

Principles for Designing Listening Techniques

Several decades of research and practice in teaching listening comprehension have yielded some practical principles for designing techniques that include aural comprehension. These principles are summarized below. Some of them, especially the first two, actually apply to any technique; the others are more germane to listening.

1. **In an interactive, four-skills curriculum, make sure that you don't overlook the importance of techniques that specifically develop listening comprehension competence.**

If your curriculum is strongly content-based, or otherwise dedicated to the integration of skills, remember that each of the separate skills deserves special focus in appropriate doses. It is easy to adopt a philosophy of just letting students "experience" language without careful attention to component skills. Because aural comprehension itself cannot be overtly "observed" (see #4 below), teachers sometimes incorrectly assume that the **input** provided in the classroom will always be converted into **intake**. The creation of effective listening techniques requires studied attention to all the principles of listening already summarized in this chapter.

2. Techniques should be intrinsically motivating.

Appeal to listener's personal interests and goals. Since background information (schemata) is an important factor in listening, take into full account the experiences and goals and abilities of your students as you design lessons. Also, remember that the cultural background(s) of your students can be both facilitating and interfering in the process of listening. Then, once a technique is launched, try to construct it in such a way that students get caught up in the activity and feel self-propelled toward its final objective.

3. Techniques should utilize authentic language and contexts.

Authentic language and real-world tasks enable students to see the relevance of classroom activity to their long term communicative goals. By introducing natural texts (for a list of real-world texts, see page 229) rather than concocted, artificial material, students will more readily dive in to the activity.

4. Carefully consider the form of listeners' responses.

Comprehension itself is not externally observable. We cannot peer into a learner's brain through a little window of some kind and empirically observe exactly what is stored there after someone else has said something. We can only **infer** that certain things have been comprehended through students' overt **responses** (verbal or nonverbal) to speech. It is therefore important for teachers to design techniques in such a way that students' responses indicate whether or not their comprehension has been correct. Lund (1990) offers nine different ways that we can check listeners' comprehension:

- doing—the listener responds physically to a command
- choosing—the listener selects from alternatives such as pictures, objects, texts
- transferring—the listener draws a picture of what is heard
- answering—the listener answers questions about the message
- condensing—the listener outlines or takes notes on a lecture
- extending—the listener provides an ending to a story heard

- duplicating—the listener translates the message into the native language or repeats it verbatim
- modeling—the listener orders a meal, for example, after listening to a model order
- conversing—the listener engages in a conversation that indicates appropriate processing of information

5. Encourage the development of listening strategies.

Most foreign language students are simply not aware of **how** to listen. One of your jobs is to equip them with listening strategies that extend well beyond the classroom. Draw their attention to the value of such strategies as:

- looking for keywords
- looking for nonverbal cues to meaning
- predicting a speaker's purpose by the context of the spoken discourse
- associating information with one's existing cognitive structure (activating schemata)
- guessing at meanings
- seeking clarification
- listening for the general gist.
- for tests of listening comprehension, various test-taking strategies

As you "teach learners how to learn" by helping them to develop their overall strategic competence (look back at Chapter 12), strategies for effective listening can become a highly significant part of their chances for successful learning.

6. Include both bottom-up and top-down listening techniques.

Speech processing theory distinguishes between two types of processing in both listening and reading comprehension. **Bottom-up** processing proceeds from sounds to words to grammatical relationships to lexical meanings, etc., to a final "message." **Top-down** processing is evoked from "a bank of prior knowledge and global expectations" (Morley, 1991:87) and other background information that the listener brings to the text. Bottom-up techniques typically focus on sounds, words, intonation, grammatical structures, and other components of spoken language. Top-down techniques are more concerned with the activation of schemata, with deriving meaning, with global understanding, and with the interpretation of a text. It is important for learners to operate from both directions since both can offer keys to determining the meaning of spoken discourse. However, in a communicative, interactive context, you don't want to dwell too heavily on the bottom-up, for to do so may hamper the development of a learner's all-important automaticity in processing speech.

Listening Techniques from Beginning to Advanced

Techniques for teaching listening will vary considerably across the proficiency continuum. Chapter 7 has already dealt with general characteristics. Listening techniques are no exception to the general rule. What follows here are three lists of techniques (adapted from Peterson, 1991:114–121), for each of three proficiency levels. Each list is broken down into bottom-up, top-down, and interactive types of activity.

Techniques for Teaching Listening Comprehension

Exercise Types for Beginning-Level Listeners

Bottom-Up Exercises

1) Goal: *Discriminating between Intonation Contours in Sentences*
   Listen to a sequence of sentence patterns with either rising or falling intonation. Place a check in column 1 (rising) or column 2 (falling), depending on the pattern you hear.

2) Goal: *Discriminating between Phonemes*
   Listen to pairs of words. Some pairs differ in their final consonant (stay/steak), and some pairs are the same (laid/laid). Circle the word "same" or "different," depending on what you hear.

3) Goal: *Selective Listening for Morphological Endings*
   Listen to a series of sentences. Circle "yes" if the verb has an -ed ending, and circle "no" if it does not.
   Listen to a series of sentences. On your answer sheet are three verb forms. Circle the verb form that is contained in the sentence that you hear.

4) Goal: *Selecting Details from the Text (Word Recognition)*
   Match a word that you hear with its picture.
   Listen to a weather report. Look at a list of words and circle the words that you hear.
   Listen to a sentence that contains clock time. Circle the clock time that you hear, among three choices (5:30, 5:45, 6:15).
   Listen to an advertisement, select out the price of an item, and write the amount on a price tag.
   Listen to a series of recorded telephone messages from an answering machine. Fill in a chart with the following information from each caller: name, number, time, and message.

5) Goal: *Listening for Normal Sentence Word Order*
   Listen to a short dialog and fill in the missing words that have been deleted in a partial transcript.

Top-Down Exercises

6) Goal: *Discriminating between Emotional Reactions*
   Listen to a sequence of utterances. Place a check in the column that describes the emotional reaction that you hear: interested, happy, surprised, or unhappy.

7) Goal: *Getting the Gist of a Sentence*
   Listen to a sentence describing a picture and select the correct picture.

8) Goal: *Recognize the Topic*
   Listen to a dialog and decide where the conversation occurred. Circle the correct location among three multiple choice items.
   Listen to a conversation and look at a number of greeting cards that are pictured. Decide which of the greeting cards was sent. Write the greeting under the appropriate card.
   Listen to a conversation and decide what the people are talking about. Choose the picture that shows the topic.

Interactive Exercises

9) Goal: **Build a Semantic Network of Word Associations**

Listen to a word and associate all the related words that come to mind.

10) Goal: **Recognize a Familiar Word and Relate It to a Category**

Listen to words from a shopping list and match the words to the store that sells it.

11) Goal: **Following Directions**

Listen to a description of a route and trace in on a map.

Exercise Types for Intermediate-Level Listeners

Bottom-Up Exercises

12) Goal: **Recognizing Fast Speech Forms**

Unstressed function words. Listen to a series of sentences that contain unstressed function words. Circle your choice among three words. Circle your choice among three words on the answer sheet—for example: "up," "a," "of".

13) Goal: **Finding the Stressed Syllable**

Listen to words of two (or three) syllables. Mark them for word stress and predict the pronunciation of the unstressed syllable.

14) Goal: **Recognizing Words with Reduced Syllables**

Read a list of polysyllabic words and predict which syllabic vowel will be dropped. Listen to the words read in fast speech and confirm your prediction.

15) Goal: **Recognize Words as They Are Linked in the Speech Stream**

Listen to a series of short sentences with consonant/vowel linking between words. Mark the linkages on your answer sheet.

16) Goal: **Recognizing Pertinent Details in the Speech Stream**

Listen to a short dialog between a boss and a secretary regarding changes in the daily schedule. Use an appointment calendar. Cross out appointments that are being changed and write in new ones.

Listen to announcements of airline arrivals and departures. With a model of an airline information board in front of you, fill in the flight numbers, destinations, gate numbers, and departure times.

Listen to a series of short dialogs. Before listening, read the questions that apply to the dialogs. While listening, find the answers to questions about prices, places, names, and numbers. Example: "Where are the shoppers?" "How much is whole wheat bread?"

Listen to a short telephone conversation between a customer and a service station manager. Fill in a chart which lists the car repairs that must be done. Check the part of the car that needs repair, the reason, and the approximate cost.

Top-Down Exercises

17) Goal: **Analyze Discourse Structure to Suggest Effective Listening Strategies**

Listen to six radio commercials with attention to the use of music, repetition of key words, and number of speakers. Talk about the effect these techniques have on the listeners.

18) Goal: **Listen to Identify the Speaker or the Topic**

Listen to a series of radio commercials. On your answer sheet, choose among four types of sponsors or products and identify the picture that goes with the commercial.

19) Goal: **Listen to Evaluate Themes and Motives**

Listen to as series of radio commercials. On your answer sheet are listed four possible motives that the companies use to appeal to their customers. Circle all the motives that you feel each commercial promotes: escape from reality, family security, snob appeal, sex appeal.

20) Goal: **Finding Main Ideas and Supporting Details**

Listen to a short conversation between two friends. On your answer sheet are scenes from television programs. Find and write the name of the program and the channel. Decide which speaker watched which program.

21) Goal: **Making Inferences**

Listen to a series of sentences, which may be either statements or questions. After each sentence, answer inferential questions, such as: "Where might the speaker be? " "How might the speaker be feeling?" "What might the speaker be referring to?"

Listen to a series of sentences. After each sentence, suggest a possible context for the sentence (place, situation, time, participants).

Interactive Execises

22) Goal: *Discriminating between Registers of Speech and Tones of Voice*

Listen to a series of sentences. On your answer sheet, mark whether the sentence is polite or impolite.

23) Goal: *Recognize Missing Grammar Markers in Colloquial Speech*

Listen to a series of short questions in which the auxiliary verb and subject have been deleted. Use grammatical knowledge to fill in the missing words: ("Have you) got some extra?"

Listen to a series of questions with reduced verb auxiliary and subject and identify the missing verb (does it/is it) by checking the form of the main verb. Example: "`Zit come with anything else? `Zit arriving on time?"

24) Goal: *Use Knowledge of Reduced Forms to Clarify the Meaning of an Utterance*

Listen to a short sentence containing a reduced form. Decide what the sentence means. On your answer sheet, read three alternatives and choose the alternative that is the best paraphrase of the sentence you heard. Example: You hear, "You can't be happy with that." You read: "(a) Why can't you be happy? (b) That will make you happy. (c) I don't think you are happy".

25) Goal: *Use Context to Build Listening Expectations*

Read a short want-ad describing job qualifications in the employment section of a newspaper. Brainstorm additional qualifications that would be important for that type of job.

26) Goal: *Listen to Confirm Your Expectations*

Listen to short radio advertisements for jobs that are available. Check the job qualifications against your expectations.

27) Goal: *Use Context to Build Expectations. Use Bottom-Up Processing to Recognize Missing Words. Compare Your Predictions to What You Actually Heard*

Read some telephone messages with missing words. Decide what kinds of information are missing so you know what to listen for. Listen to the information and fill in the blanks. Finally, discuss with the class what strategies you used for your predictions.

28) Goal: *Use Incomplete Sensory Data and Cultural Background Information to Construct a More Complete Understanding of a Text*

Listen to one side of a telephone conversation. Decide what the topic of the conversation might be and create a title for it.

Listen to the beginning of a conversation between two people and answer questions about the number of participants, their ages, gender, and social roles. Guess the time of day, location, temperature, season, and topic. Choose among some statements to guess what might come next.

Exercise Types for Advanced-Level Learners

Bottom-Up Exercises

29) Goal: *Use Features of Sentence Stress and Volume to Identify Important Information for Note Taking*

Listen to a number of sentences and extract the content words, which are read with greater stress. Write the content words as notes.

30) Goal: *Become Aware of Sentence Level Features in Lecture Text*

Listen to a segment of a lecture while reading a transcript of the material. Notice the incomplete sentences, pauses, and verbal fillers.

31) Goal: *Become Aware of Organizational Cues in Lecture Text*

Look at a lecture transcript and circle all the cue words used to enumerate the main points. Then listen to the lecture segment and note the organizational cues.

32) Goal: *Become Aware of Lexical and Suprasegmental Marker for Definitions*

Read a list of lexical cues that signal a definition; listen to signals of the speaker's intent such as rhetorical questions; listen to special intonation patterns and pause patterns used with appositives.

Listen to short lecture segments that contain new terms and their definitions in context. Use knowledge of lexical and intonational cues to identify the definition of the word.

33) Goal: **Identify Specific Points of Information**

Read a skeleton outline of a lecture in which the main categories are given but the specific examples are left blank. Listen to the lecture, and find the information that belongs in the blanks.

Top-Down Exercises

34) Goal: **Use the Introduction to the Lecture to Predict Its Focus and Direction**

Listen to the introductory section of a lecture. Then read a number of topics on your answer sheet and choose the topic that best expresses what the lecture will discuss.

35) Goal: **Use the Lecture Transcript to Predict the Content of the Next Section**

Read a section of a lecture transcript. Stop reading at a juncture point and predict what will come next. Then read on to confirm your prediction.

36) Goal: **Find the Main Idea of a Lecture Segment**

Listen to a section of a lecture that describes a statistical trend. While you listen look at three graphs that show a change over time and select the graph that best illustrates the lecture.

Interactive Exercises

37) Goal: **Use Incoming Details to Determine the Accuracy of Predictions about Content**

Listen to the introductory sentences to predict some of the main ideas you expect to hear in the lecture. Then listen to the lecture as it is played. Note whether or not the instructor talks about the points you predicted. If she/he does, note a detail about the point.

38) Goal: **Determine the Main Ideas of a Section of a Lecture by Analysis of the Details in that Section**

Listen to a section of a lecture and take notes on the important details. Then relate the details to form an understanding of the main point of that section. Choose from a list of possible controlling ideas.

39) Goal: **Make Inferences by Identifying Ideas on the Sentence Level That Lead to Evaluative Statements**

Listen to a statement and take notes on the important words. Indicate what further meaning can be inferred from the statement. Indicate the words in the original statement. Indicate the words in the original statement that serve to cue the inference.

40) Goal: **Use Knowledge of the Text and the Lecture Content to Fill In Missing Information**

Listen to a lecture segment to get the gist. Then listen to a statement from which words have been omitted. Using your knowledge of the text and of the general content, fill in the missing information. Check your understand by listening to the entire segment.

41) Goal: **Use Knowledge of the Text and the Lecture Content to Discover the Lecturer's Misstatements and to Supply the Ideas That He Meant to Say**

Listen to a lecture segment that contains an incorrect term. Write the incorrect term and the term that the lecturer should have used. Finally, indicate what clues helped you find the misstatement.

The importance of listening comprehension in language learning should by now be quite apparent. As we move on to look at speaking skills, always remember the ever-present relationship among all four skills, and the necessity in authentic, interactive classes to integrate these skills even as you focus from time to time on the specifics of one skill area.

TOPICS FOR DISCUSSION, RESEARCH, AND ACTION

1. What is the difference between *input* and *intake*? How does input get converted into intake? Try to illustrate this conversion with classroom examples. What hints or ideas or techniques could you recommend for helping students to maximize the conversion of input to intake? Discuss in a group.

2. Give specific language examples of each of the eight processes of listening referred to on pages 235–236. How are factors 2 through 8 interactive by definition?

3. Look at the chart on page 237 and make sure you understand each category. With a partner, devise an illustration of each, then compare your illustrations with some other pairs.

4. Pick an English language news program and audio-tape record a two or three minute segment. In a small group listen to the tape and identify the "clusters" of words which form thought groups. What hints would you give to ESL students to help them to listen to such clusters rather than each separate word?

5. Specifically identify the redundant words/phrases in the conversation between Amos and Andy (pp. 238–239). How would you teach students either to use such redundancies for comprehension or to overlook them when comprehension is already sufficient?

6. If possible, tape record a casual conversation in English, between two native speakers of English. In a small group, listen to the tape and pick out as many "performance variables" as you can. How do these performance variables differ from those of a learner of English? Can students be taught to overlook or to compensate for such naturally-occurring performance variables?

7. Look again at the taxonomy of listening microskills (p. 241). In a group go through the taxonomy and make sure you understand each item by offering an example. Then look at the six types of classroom listening performance (pp. 242–244) and, in your group, share examples of each and discuss their appropriateness in the classroom.

8. Consider the listening strategies referred to on p. 244. With a partner, define each strategy. Then, sketch out some techniques that you could use to teach such strategies to students. Share your techniques with the rest of the class.

9. Review the six principles for effective listening techniques on pages 242–244. Then, as a class, divide up the 41 techniques outlined on pages 247–250, and, with a partner systematically evaluate the techniques you have been given. Your evaluation should be based on the seven principles.

10. One type of listening technique (combined with writing) not considered in this chapter is *dictation*. How useful is dictation? What are the pros and cons of using this technique in a classroom?

FOR YOUR FURTHER READING

Richards, Jack C. 1983. "Listening comprehension: Approach, design, procedure." *TESOL Quarterly 17*(2), 219–239.

In a comprehensive treatment of the nature of listening, Jack Richards uses his approach/design/procedure model to discuss numerous theoretical and practical issues in teaching listening skills. This article is reprinted in Long & Richards (1987).

Dunkel, Patricia. 1991. "Listening in the native and second/foreign language: Toward an integration of research and practice." *TESOL Quarterly 25*(3), 431–457.

This excellent review article makes a case for the importance of listening in second language acquisition. The author discusses factors that influence success and failure to comprehend a language, stresses the pivotal role of listening in second language curricula, and looks at related models and taxonomies.

Ur, Penny. 1984. *Teaching Listening Comprehension.* Cambridge University Press.

Rost, Michael. 1991. *Listening in Action: Activities for Developing Listening in Language Teaching.* Prentice Hall.

Both of these highly useful teacher reference books are gold mines of ideas on many different kinds of techniques that can be used to teach listening comprehension, from listening for perception only to interactive "real-life" listening.

Lund, R. 1990. "A taxonomy for teaching second language listening. *Foreign Language Annals 23*(1), 105–115.

A broad, conceptual framework for understanding the teaching of listening is offered here. The author lists a number of "listener function" tasks (related to the message that the listener attempts to process) and "listening response tasks" (such as choosing, answering, extending, modeling, and conversing). Aspects of the taxonomy are illustrated, among other things, through classroom tasks.

Chapter 15

Teaching Oral Communication Skills

From a communicative, pragmatic view of the language classroom, listening and speaking skills are closely intertwined. More often than not, ESL curricula that treat oral communication skills will simply be labeled as "Listening/Speaking" courses. The interaction between these two modes of performance applies especially strongly to the most popular discourse category in the profession: conversation. And, in the classroom, even relatively unidirectional types of spoken language input (speeches, lectures, etc.,) are often followed or preceded by various forms of oral production on the part of students.

Some of the components of teaching spoken language were covered in the previous chapter as we looked closely at teaching listening comprehension: types of spoken language, idiosyncrasies of spoken language that make listening difficult, and listening microskills that are a factor of the oral code. This chapter will build on those considerations as we investigate the teaching of oral communication skills.

Oral Communication Skills in Pedagogical Research

A review of some of the current issues in teaching oral communication will help to provide some perspective to the more practical considerations that follow in this chapter.

1. The place of pronunciation teaching

This issue will be covered in some detail later in the chapter. For the time being, some introductory remarks are in order. There has been some controversy over the role of pronunciation work in a communicative, interactive course of study. Because the overwhelming majority of adult learners will never acquire an "accent free" command of a foreign language, then, should a language paradigm that emphasizes whole language, meaningful contexts, and subconscious acquisition focus on these tiny pronunciation details of language? The answer is "yes" but in a different way from what was perceived to be essential a mere decade or two ago. More on this later in the chapter.

2. Accuracy and fluency

An issue that pervades all of language performance centers on the distinction between accuracy and fluency. In spoken language the question we face as teachers is: How shall we prioritize the two clearly important speaker goals of accurate (clear, articulate, grammatically and phonologically correct) language and fluent (flowing, natural) language?

In the mid to late 70s, egged on by a somewhat short-lived anti-grammar approach, some teachers turned away from accuracy issues in favor of providing a plethora of "natural" language activity in their classrooms. The argument was, of course, that adult second language acquisition should simulate the child's first language learning processes. Our classrooms must not become linguistics courses but rather the locus of meaningful language involvement, or so the argument went.

Unfortunately, such classrooms so strongly emphasized the importance of fluency—with a concomitant playing down of the bits and pieces of grammar and phonology—that many students managed to produce fairly fluent but barely comprehensible language. Something was lacking.

It is now very clear that **both** fluency **and** accuracy are important goals to pursue in CLT. While fluency may in many communicative language courses be an **initial** goal in language teaching, accuracy is achieved to some extent by allowing students to focus on the elements of phonology, grammar, and discourse in their spoken output. If you were learning to play tennis instead of a second language, this same philosophy would initially get you out on the tennis court to feel what it's like to hold a racquet, to hit the ball, to serve, etc., and then have you focus more cognitively on certain fundamentals. Fluency is probably best achieved by allowing the "stream" of speech to "flow," then, as some of this speech spills over beyond comprehensibility, the "river banks" of instruction on some details of phonology, grammar, or discourse will channel the speech on a more purposeful course.

The fluency/accuracy issue often boils down to the extent to which our techniques should be **message oriented** (or, as some call it, teaching language **use**) as opposed to **language oriented** (also known as teaching language **usage**). Current approaches to language teaching lean strongly toward message orientation with language usage offering a supporting role.

3. Affective factors

One of the major obstacles learners have to overcome in learning to speak is the anxiety generated over the risks of blurting things out that are wrong, stupid, or incomprehensible. Because of the language ego (see *PLLT* Chapters 3 and 6) that informs people that "you are what you speak," learners are reluctant to be judged by hearers. Language learners can put a new twist on Mark Twain's quip that "it's better to keep your mouth closed and have others think you are ignorant than to open it and remove all doubt." Our job as teachers is to provide the kind of warm, embracing climate that encourages students to speak however halting or broken those attempts may be.

4. The interaction effect

The greatest difficulty that learners have in learning to speak is not in the multiplicity of sounds, words, phrases, and discourse forms that characterize any language, but rather in the interactive nature of most communication. Conversations are collaborative as participants are engaged in a process of negotiation of meaning. So, for the learner, the matter of **what** to say—a tremendous task, to be sure—is often eclipsed by conventions of **how** to say things, **when** to speak, and other discourse constraints. Among the many possible grammatical sentences, for example, that a learner could produce in response to a comment, how does that learner make a choice?

David Nunan (1991b:47) notes a further complication in interactive discourse: what he calls the "interlocutor effect," or the difficulty of a speaking task as gauged by the skills of one's interlocutor. In other words, one learner's performance is always colored by that of the person (interlocutor) he or she is talking with.

Types of Spoken Language

In the previous chapter, several categories were defined for understanding types of spoken language (see especially Figure 14.1, page 237). In beginning through intermediate levels of proficiency, most of the efforts of students in oral production come in the form of conversation, or dialogue. As you plan and implement techniques in your interactive classroom, make sure your students can deal with both types of dialogue and that they are able to converse with a total stranger as well as someone with whom they are quite familiar.

What Makes Speaking Difficult?

Again, Chapter 14 outlined some idiosyncrasies of spoken language that make listening skills somewhat difficult to acquire. These same characteristics must be taken into account in the productive generation of speech but with a slight twist, in that the learner is now the producer. Bear in mind that characteristics of spoken language can make oral performance easy as well as, in some cases, difficult.

1. Clustering

Fluent speech is phrasal, not word by word. Learners can organize their output both cognitively and physically (in breath groups) through such clustering.

2. Redundancy

The speaker has an opportunity to make meaning clearer through the redundancy of language. Learners can capitalize on this feature of spoken language.

3. Reduced forms

Contractions, elisions, reduced vowels, etc. all form special problems in teaching spoken English (see below, section on Pronunciation). Students who don't learn colloquial contractions can sometimes develop a stilted, bookish quality of speaking that in turn stigmatizes them.

4. Performance variables

One of the advantages of spoken language is that the process of thinking as you speak allows you to manifest a certain number of performance hesitations, pauses, backtracking, and corrections. You can actually **teach** learners how to pause and hesitate. For example, in English our "thinking time" is not silent, but rather we insert certain "fillers": uh, um, well, you know, I mean, like, etc. One of the most salient differences between native and nonnative speakers of a language is in their hesitation phenomena.

5. Colloquial language

Make sure your students are reasonably well acquainted with the words and idioms and phrases of colloquial language and that they get practice in producing these forms.

6. Rate of delivery

Another salient characteristic of fluency is rate of delivery. One of your tasks in teaching spoken English is to help learners to achieve an acceptable speed along with other attributes of fluency.

7. Stress, rhythm, and intonation

This is **the** most important characteristic of English pronunciation, as will be explained below. The stress-timed rhythm of spoken English and its intonation patterns convey important messages.

8. Interaction

As noted in the previous section, learning to produce waves of language in a vacuum—without interlocutors—would rob speaking skill of its richest component: the creativity of conversational negotiation.

Microskills of Oral Communication

In the previous chapter, 17 microskills for listening comprehension (adapted from Richards, 1983) were presented. Here, many of the same microskills apply, but because of major cognitive and physical differences between listening and speaking, some noticeable alterations have been made.

1. Produce chunks of language of different lengths.
2. Orally produce differences among the English phonemes and allophonic variants.
3. Produce English stress patterns, words in stressed and unstressed positions, rhythmic structure, and intonational contours.
4. Produce reduced forms of words and phrases.
5. Use an adequate number of lexical units (words) in order to accomplish pragmatic purposes.
6. Produce fluent speech at different rates of delivery.
7. Monitor your own oral production and use various strategic devices—pauses, fillers, self-corrections, backtracking—to enhance the clarity of the message.
8. Use grammatical word classes (nouns, verbs, etc.), systems (e.g., tense, agreement, pluralization), word order, patterns, rules, and elliptical forms.

9. Produce speech in natural constituents—in appropriate phrases, pause groups, breath groups, and sentence constituents.

10. Express a particular meaning in different grammatical forms.

11. Use cohesive devices in spoken discourse.

12. Appropriately accomplish communicative functions according to situations, participants, and goals.

13. Use appropriate registers, implicature, pragmatic conventions, and other sociolinguistic features in face-to-face conversations.

14. Convey links and connections between events and communicate such relations as main idea, supporting idea, new information, given information, generalization, and exemplification.

16. Use facial features, kinesics, "body language," and other nonverbal cues along with verbal language in order to convey meanings.

17. Develop and use a battery of speaking strategies, such as emphasizing key words, rephrasing, providing a context for interpreting the meaning of words, appealing for help, and accurately assessing how well your interlocutor is understanding you.

One implication of such a list is the importance of focusing on both the **forms** of language as well as the **functions** of language. In teaching oral communication, we don't limit students' attention to the whole picture, even though that whole picture is important. We also help students to see the pieces—right down to the small parts—of language that make up the whole. Just as you would instruct a novice artist in composition, the effect of color hues, shading, and brush stroke techniques, so language students need to be shown the details of how to convey and negotiate the ever elusive meanings of language.

Teaching Pronunciation: Then and Now

Views on teaching pronunciation have changed dramatically over the last half-century of language teaching. In the heyday of audiolingualism and its various behavioristic methodological variants, the pronunciation component of a course or program was a mainstay. Language was viewed as a hierarchy of related structures and at the base of this hierarchy was the articulation of phonemes and their contrasts within English and between English and native languages. Pronunciation classes consisted of imitation drills, memorization of patterns, minimal pair exercises, and explanations of articulatory phonetics. (For a chart of English vowels and consonants, see the Appendix to this chapter.)

In the 1970s, as the language teaching profession began to experience a revolution of sorts (see Chapter 4), explicit pedagogical focus on **anything** that smacked of linguistic nuts and bolts was under siege by proponents of the various non-directive, "let-it-just-happen" approaches to language teaching. As we became more concerned with authenticity, real-world tasks, natural-ness, non-directive teaching, and process, we became less concerned with the product: language itself. Pronunciation instruction became somewhat inci-dental to a course of study. It was not ignored entirely, but in the interest of promoting fluency-based instruction, accuracy-based focus on English phonology became, for many, an afterthought.

By the mid 1980s, the cutting edge of the profession turned in a different direction. With greater attention to grammatical structures as important elements in discourse, to a balance between fluency and accuracy, and to the explicit specification of pedagogical tasks that a learner should accomplish, it became clear that pronunciation was a key to gaining full communicative competence.

But the current approach to pronunciation starkly contrasts with the early approaches. Rather than attempting only to build a learner's articulatory competence from the bottom up, and simply as the mastery of a list of phonemes and allophones, a top-down approach is taken in which the most **relevant** features of pronunciation—stress, rhythm, and intonation—are given high priority. Instead of teaching only the role of articulation within words, or at best, phrases, we teach its role in a whole stream of discourse. Rita Wong (1987:21) reminds us that

> ...contemporary views [of language] hold that the sounds of language are less crucial for understanding than the way they are organized. The rhythm and intonation of English are two major organizing structures that native speakers rely on to process speech. ...Because of their major roles in communication, rhythm and intonation merit greater priority in the teaching program than attention to individual sounds.

Wong's comments reflect an approach that puts all aspects of English pronunciation into the perspective of a communicative, interactive, whole-language view of human speech. Once again, history has taught us the lesson of maintaining balance.

Factors Affecting Pronunciation Learning

Many learners of foreign languages feel that their ultimate goal in pro-nunciation should be "accent free" speech that is undistinguishable from that of a native speaker. Such a goal is not only unattainable (see *PLLT*, Chapter 3) for virtually every adult learner, but in a multilingual, multicultural world, "accents" are quite acceptable. With English as an International Language growing by leaps and bounds, a **native** accent is extremely difficult to define, and even genuine native speakers of English are often mistakenly identified as "foreigners." Moreover, as the world community comes to appreciate and value people's heritage, one's accent is just another symbol of that heritage.

Our goal as teachers of English pronunciation should therefore be more realistically focused on **clear, comprehensible** pronunciation. At the beginning levels, we want learners to surpass that threshold beneath which pronunciation detracts from their ability to communicate. At the advanced levels, pronunciation goals can focus on elements that enhance communication: intonation features that go beyond basic patterns, voice quality, phonetic distinctions between registers, and other refinements that are far more important in the overall stream of clear communication than rolling the English /r/ or getting a vowel to perfectly imitate a "native speaker."

What are the factors within learners that affect pronunciation and how can you deal with each of them? Below is a list (adapted from Kenworthy, 1987:4-8) of variables that you should consider:

1. Native language

Clearly, the native language will be the most influential factor affecting a learner's pronunciation (see *PLLT*, Chapter 8). If you are familiar with the sound system of a learner's native language, you will be better able to diagnose student difficulties. Many L1-L2 carryovers can be overcome through a focused awareness and effort on the learner's part.

2. Age

Generally speaking, children under the age of puberty stand an excellent chance of "sounding like a native" if they have continued exposure in authentic contexts. Beyond the age of puberty, while adults will almost surely maintain a "foreign accent," there seems to be no particular advantage attributed to age. A fifty-year-old can be as successful as an eighteen-year-old if all other factors are equal. Remind your students, especially if your students are "older," that youth has no special advantage.

3. Exposure

It is difficult to define exposure. One can actually live in a foreign country for some time but not take advantage of being "with the people." Research seems to support the notion that the quality and intensity of exposure is more important than the mere length of time. If class time spent focusing on pronunciation demands the full attention and interest of your students, then they stand a good chance of reaching their goals.

4. Innate phonetic ability

Often referred to as having an "ear" for language, some people manifest a phonetic coding ability that others do not. In many cases, if a person has had exposure to a foreign language as a child, this "knack" is present whether the early language is remembered or not. Others are simply more attuned to phonetic discriminations. Some people would have you believe that you either have such a knack, or you don't. Learner strategy training (see Chapter 12), however, has proven that some elements of learning are a matter of an awareness of your own limitations combined with a conscious focus on **doing** something to compensate for those limitations. Therefore, if pronunciation seems to be naturally difficult for some students, they should not despair; with some effort and concentration, they can improve their competence.

5. Identity and language ego

Yet another influence is one's attitude toward speakers of the target language and the extent to which the language ego identifies with those speakers. Learners need to be reminded of the importance of positive attitudes toward the **people** who speak the language (if such a target is identifiable), but more importantly, students need to become aware of—and not afraid of—the second identity that may be emerging within them.

6. Motivation and concern for good pronunciation

Some learners are not particularly concerned about their pronunciation while others are. The extent to which their intrinsic motivation propels them toward improvement will be perhaps the strongest influence of all six of the factors in this list. If that motivation and concern is high, then the necessary effort will be expended in pursuit of goals. You can help learners to perceive or develop that motivation by showing, among other things, how clarity of speech is significant in shaping their self-image and ultimately, in reaching some of their higher goals.

All six of the above factors suggest that **any** learner who really wants to can learn to pronounce English clearly and comprehensibly. You can assist in the process by gearing your planned and unplanned instruction toward these six factors.

In the last section of this chapter, you will find that a number of techniques for teaching aspects of English pronunciation are mingled in with techniques for teaching various other aspects of spoken language. Take note of how those techniques may capitalize on the positive benefits of the six factors above, and how they reflect the current, discourse-based view of pronunciation teaching. A significant factor for you in the success of such techniques lies in the extent to which you can, through an ongoing concern for students' progress, instill the motivation that students need to put forth the effort needed to develop clear, comprehensible pronunciation.

A Model for Correction of Speech Errors

One of the most frequently posed questions by teachers who are new to the trade is: When and how should I correct the speech errors of learners in my classroom? This happens also to be one of the most complex questions in the profession! Some guidelines are offered here.

One of the keys, but not the only key, to successful second language learning lies in the *feedback* that a learner receives from others. Chapter 9 of *PLLT* described Vigil and Oller's (1976) model of how affective and cognitive feedback affects the message-sending process. Figure 15.1 depicts, metaphorically at least, what happens in Vigil and Oller's model.

Figure 15.1. Affective and Cognitive Feedback.

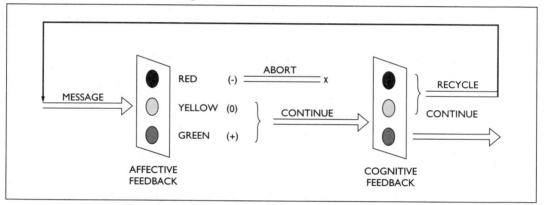

The "green light" of the affective feedback mode allows the sender to continue attempting to get a message across; a "red light" causes the sender to abort such attempts. (The metaphorical nature of such a chart is evident in the fact that affective feedback does not precede cognitive feedback, as this chart may lead you to believe; both modes can take place simultaneously.) The traffic signal of cognitive feedback is the point at which error correction enters in. A green light here symbolizes noncorrective feedback that says "I understand your message." A red light symbolizes corrective feedback that takes on a myriad of possible forms (outlined below) and causes the learner to make some kind of alteration in production. To push the metaphor further, a yellow light could represent those various shades of color that are interpreted by the learner as falling somewhere in between a complete green light and a red light, causing the learner to adjust, to alter, to recycle back, to try again in some way. Note that fossilization may be the result of too many green lights when there should have been some yellow or red lights.

The most useful implications of Vigil and Oller's model for a theory of error correction is that cognitive feedback must be **optimal** in order to be effective. Too much negative cognitive feedback—a barrage of interruptions—shuts off students' attempts at communication. They perceive that so much is wrong with their production that there is little hope to get anything right. On the other hand, too much positive cognitive feedback—willingness of the teacher-hearer to let errors go uncorrected, to indicate understanding when understanding may not have occurred—serves to reinforce the errors of the speaker-learner. The result is the persistence, and perhaps the eventual fossilization, of such errors. Your job as a teacher is to discern the optimal tension between positive and negative cognitive feedback: providing enough green lights to encourage continued communication, but not so many that crucial errors go unnoticed, and providing enough red lights to call attention to those crucial errors, but not so many that the learner is discouraged from attempting to speak at all.

We do well to recall at this point the application of Skinner's operant conditioning model of learning. The affective and cognitive modes of feedback are *reinforcers* to speakers' *responses*. As speakers perceive "positive" reinforcement, or the "green lights" of Figure 15.1, they will be led to internalize certain speech patterns. Corrective feedback can still be "positive" in the Skinnerian sense, as we shall see below. However, ignoring erroneous behavior has the effect of a positive reinforcer; therefore teachers must be very careful to discern the possible reinforcing consequences of neutral feedback. What we must avoid at all costs is the administration of *punitive* reinforcement, or, correction that is viewed by learners as an affective red light—devaluing, dehumanizing, or insulting their personhood.

Against this theoretical backdrop we can evaluate some possibilities of when and how to treat errors in the language classroom. Long (1977:288) suggested that the question of *when* to treat an error (that is, which errors to provide some sort of feedback on) has no simple answer.

> **Having noticed an error, the first (and, I would argue, crucial) decision the teacher makes is whether or not to treat it at all. In order to make that decision the teacher may have recourse to factors with immediate, temporary bearing, such as the importance of the error to the current pedagogical focus on the lesson, the teacher's perception of the chance of eliciting correct performance from the student if negative feedback is given, and so on. Consideration of these ephemeral factors may be preempted, however, by the teacher's beliefs (conscious or unconscious) as to what a language is and how a new one is learned. These beliefs may have been formed years before the lesson in question.**

In a most practical and clearly written article on error correction, Hendrickson (1980) advised teachers to try to discern the difference, in learners' language, between "global" and "local" errors. Global errors hinder communication; they prevent the hearer from comprehending some aspect of the message. Local errors, because they usually only affect a single element of a sentence, do not prevent a message from being heard; context provides keys to meaning. Once a learner of English was describing a quaint old hotel in Europe and said, "There is a French widow in every bedroom." The local error is clearly, and humorously, recognized. Hendrickson recommended that local errors usually need not be corrected since the message is clear and correction might interrupt a learner in the flow of productive communication. Global errors need to be corrected in some way since the message may otherwise remain garbled. A Spanish-speaking student who said, "I saw their department" (and meant "apartment") would most likely need correcting if the hearer is confused about the final word in that sentence.

Many erroneous utterances fall somewhere between global and local, and it is difficult to discern the necessity for corrective feedback. A learner once wrote, "The grammar is the basement of every language." While this witty little proclamation may indeed sound more like Chomsky than Chomsky does, it behooves the teacher to ascertain just what the learner meant here (no doubt "basis" rather than "basement"), and to provide some feedback to clarify the difference between the two. The bottom line is that we simply must not stifle our students' attempts at production by smothering them with corrective feedback.

The matter of *how* to correct errors gets exceedingly complex. Research on error correction methods is not at all conclusive on the most effective method or technique for error correction. It seems quite clear that students in the classroom generally want and expect errors to be corrected. However, some methods recommend no direct treatment of error at all (Krashen and Terrell 1983). In "natural," untutored environments nonnative speakers generally get corrected by native speakers on only a small percentage of errors that they make; native speakers will attend basically just to global errors and then usually not in the form of interruptions but at transition points in conversation. Balancing these various perspectives, I think we can safely conclude that a sensitive and perceptive language teacher should make the language classroom a happy optimum between some of the overpoliteness of the real world and the expectations that learners bring with them to the classroom.

Error treatment options can be classified in a number of possible ways, but one useful taxonomy is recommended by Kathleen Bailey (1985). Seven "basic options" are complemented by eight "possible features" within each option (Bailey 1985:111). (For a comprehensive taxonomy of such options and features, you might look at Chaudron's chart in Allwright and Bailey [1991], pp. 220–221.)

Basic Options

1. **To treat or to ignore**
2. **To treat immediately or to delay**
3. **To transfer treatment [to, say, other learners] or not**
4. **To transfer to another individual, a subgroup, or the whole class**
5. **To return, or not, to original error maker after treatment**
6. **To permit other learners to initiate treatment**
7. **To test for the efficacy of the treatment**

Possible Features

1. **Fact of error indicated**
2. **Location indicated**
3. **Opportunity for new attempt given**
4. **Model provided**
5. **Error type indicated**
6. **Remedy indicated**
7. **Improvement indicated**
8. **Praise indicated**

All of the basic options and features within each option are conceivably viable modes of error correction in the classroom. The teacher needs to develop the intuition, through experience and solid eclectic theoretical foundations, for ascertaining which option or combination of options is appropriate at given moments. Principles of optimal affective and cognitive feedback, of reinforcement theory, and of communicative language teaching, all combine to form those intuitions.

At least one general conclusion that can be drawn from the study of learners' errors is that learners are indeed creatively operating on a second language—constructing, either consciously or subconsciously, a system for understanding and producing utterances in the language. That system should not necessarily be treated as an imperfect system; it is such only insofar as native speakers compare their own knowledge of the language to that of the learners. It should rather be looked upon as a flexible, dynamic system, reasonable to a great degree in the mind of the learners, albeit idiosyncratic. Learners are processing language on the basis of knowledge of their own interlanguage, which ought not to have the value judgments of either language placed upon it. Your task as a teacher is to value learners, prize their attempts to communicate, and then to provide optimal feedback for the system to evolve in successive stages until learners are communicating more clearly.

Types of Classroom Speaking Performance

In the previous chapter, six types of listening performance were listed. With the obvious connection between listening and speaking, six similar categories apply to the kinds of oral production that students are expected to carry out in the classroom.

1. Imitative

A very limited portion of classroom speaking time may legitimately be spent in the human "tape recorder" speech, where learners are, for example, practicing an intonation contour, trying to pinpoint a certain vowel sound, etc. Imitation of this kind is carried out not for the purpose of meaningful interaction, but for focusing on some particular element of language form.

A question that new teachers in the field always want to have answered is: Is **drilling** a legitimate part of the communicative language classroom? The answer is a qualified yes. Drills offer students an opportunity to listen and to orally repeat certain strings of language that may pose some **linguistic** difficulty—either phonological or grammatical. Drills are to language teaching what the pitching machine is to baseball. They offer limited practice through repetition. They allow one to focus on one element of language in a controlled activity. They can help to establish certain psychomotor patterns (to "loosen the tongue") and to associate selected grammatical forms with their appropriate context.

Here are some useful guidelines for successful drills:
- Keep them short (a few minutes of a class hour only).
- Keep them simple (preferably just **one** point at a time).
- Keep them "snappy".
- Make sure students know why they are doing the drill.
- Limit them to phonology or grammar points.
- Make sure they ultimately lead to communicative goals.
- Don't overuse them.

Failure to follow these guidelines could result in students becoming parroting tape recorders, incapable of batting the ball during the real ball game.

2. Intensive

Intensive speaking goes one step beyond imitative to include any speaking performance that is designed to practice some phonological or grammatical aspect of language. Intensive speaking can be self-initiated or it can even form part of some pair work activity, where learners are "going over" certain forms of language.

3. Responsive

A good deal of student speech in the classroom is responsive: short replies to teacher or student initiated questions or comments. These replies are usually sufficient and do not extend into dialogues (categories 4 and 5 below). Such speech can be meaningful and authentic:

    T: **How are you today?**

    S: **Pretty good, thanks, and you?**

    T: **What is the main idea in this essay?**

    S: **The United Nations should have more authority.**

    S1: **So, what did you write for question number one?**

    S2: **Well, I wasn't sure, so I left it blank.**

4. Transactional (dialogue)

Transactional language, carried out for the purpose of conveying or exchanging specific information, is an extended form of responsive language. Conversations, for example, may have more of a negotiative nature to them than merely responsive speech:

    T: **What is the main idea in this essay?**

    S: **The United Nations should have more authority.**

    T: **More authority than what?**

    S: **Than it does right now.**

    T: **What do you mean?**

    S: **Well, for example, the UN should have the power to force a country like Iraq to destroy its nuclear weapons.**

    T: **You don't think the UN has that power now?**

    S: **Obviously not. Iraq is still manufacturing nuclear bombs.**

Such conversations could readily be part of group work activity as well.

5. Interpersonal (dialogue)

The other form of conversation mentioned in the previous chapter was interpersonal dialogue, carried out more for the purpose of maintaining social relationships than for the transmission of facts and information. These conversations are a little trickier for learners because they can involve some or all of the following factors:

- a casual register
- colloquial language
- emotionally charged language
- slang
- ellipsis
- sarcasm
- a covert "agenda"

For example:

Amy: Hi, Bob, how's it going?

Bob: Oh, so-so.

Amy: Not a great weekend, huh?

Bob: Well, far be it from me to criticize, but I'm pretty miffed about last week.

Amy: What are you talking about?

Bob: I think you know perfectly well what I'm talking about.

Amy: Oh, that.... How come you get so bent out of shape over something like that?

Bob: Well, whose fault was it, huh?

Amy: Oh, wow, this is great. Wonderful. Back to square one. For crying out loud, Bob, I thought we'd settled this before. Well, what more can I say?

6. Extensive (monologue)

Finally, students at intermediate to advanced levels are called on to give extended monologues in the form of oral reports, summaries, or perhaps short speeches. Here the register is more formal and deliberative. These monologues can be planned or impromptu.

Principles for Designing Speaking Techniques

1. Techniques should cover the spectrum of learner needs, from language-based focus on accuracy to message-based focus on interaction, meaning, and fluency.

In our current zeal for interactive language teaching, we can easily slip into a pattern of providing zesty content-based, interactive activities that don't capitalize on grammatical pointers or pronunciation tips. When you do a jigsaw group technique, play a game, or discuss solutions to the environmental crisis, make sure that your tasks include techniques designed to help students to perceive and use the building blocks of language. At the same time, don't bore your students to death with lifeless, repetitious drills. As already noted above, make any drilling you do as meaningful as possible.

2. Techniques should be intrinsically motivating.

Try at all times to appeal to students' ultimate goals and interests, to their need for knowledge, for status, for achieving competence, autonomy, and for "being all that they can be." Even in those techniques that don't send students into ecstasy, help them to see how the activity will benefit them.

Many times students don't know **why** we ask them to do certain things; it usually pays to tell them why.

3. Techniques should encourage the use of authentic language in meaningful contexts.

This theme has been played time and again in this book, but one more reminder shouldn't hurt! It is not easy to keep coming up with meaningful interaction. We all succumb to the temptation to do, say, disconnected little grammar exercises where we go around the room calling on students one by one to pick the right answer. It takes energy and creativity to devise authentic contexts and meaningful interaction, but with the help of quite a storehouse of teacher resource material now (see recommended books and articles at the end of this chapter) it can be done. Even drills (see page 275) can be structured to provide a sense of authenticity.

4. Provide appropriate feedback and correction.

In most EFL situations, students are totally dependent on the teacher for useful linguistic feedback. (In ESL situations, they may get such feedback "out there" beyond the classroom, but even then you are in a position to be of great benefit.) It is important that you take advantage of your knowledge of English to inject the kinds of corrective feedback that are appropriate for the moment.

5. Capitalize on the natural link between speaking and listening.

Many interactive techniques that involve speaking will also of course include listening. Don't lose out on opportunities to integrate these two skills. As you are perhaps focusing on speaking goals, listening goals may naturally coincide, and the two skills can reinforce each other. Skills in producing language are often initiated through comprehension.

6. Give students opportunities to initiate oral communication.

A good deal of typical classroom interaction is characterized by teacher initiation of language. We ask questions, give directions, provide information, and students have been conditioned only to "speak when spoken to." Part of oral communication competence is the ability to initiate conversations, to nominate topics, to ask questions, to control conversations, and to change the subject. As you design and use speaking techniques, ask yourself if you have allowed students to initiate language.

7. Encourage the development of speaking strategies.

The concept of strategic competence (see Chapter 12 and *PLLT*, Chapter 10) is one that few beginning language students are aware of. They simply have not thought about developing their own personal strategies for accomplishing oral communicative purposes. Your classroom can be one in which students become aware of, and have a chance to practice such strategies as:

- asking for clarification (What?)
- asking someone to repeat something (Huh? Excuse me?)
- using fillers (Uh, I mean, Well) in order to gain time to process
- using conversation maintenance cues (Uh huh, Right, Yeah, Okay, Hm)
- getting someone's attention (Hey, Say, So)
- using paraphrases for structures one can't produce
- appealing for assistance from the interlocutor (to get a word or phrase, for example)
- using formulaic expressions (at the survival stage) (How much does ____ cost? How do you get to the ____?)
- using mime and nonverbal expressions to convey meaning

Techniques for Teaching Oral Communication Skills

Many of the interactive techniques already described or referred to in Chapters 10 and 11 involve oral communication as a key skill. What follows here is set of brief descriptions of just a **few samples** of the hundreds of different techniques you could use to teach various speaking skills.

1. Pronunciation: Rhythm and thought groups (Wong, 1987:46–47)

The following sentences, all on the topic of contemporary superstitions and popular beliefs, illustrate the use of pauses to separate prepositional phrases and clauses. These sentences can be used with advanced level students; for students of intermediate proficiency, more appropriate sentences should be selected. Have students listen as you read the sentences that follow and pause only at the points marked by a slash. Then have them practice in pairs with the listener monitoring for pauses only at the places marked.

1. In Illinois,/ driving around the house in low gear/ is said to cure a family member's illness./
2. In North Carolina,/ if the first bird seen on New Year's morning is flying high,/ there will be good health during the year./
3. Many superstitions follow the formula:/ if A/ then B/ with an optional C./
4. If you break a mirror,/ then you will have seven years bad luck,/ unless you throw the broken pieces in a moving stream./
5. If you spill salt,/ then you will have bad luck,/ unless you throw some over your left shoulder./

Ask the students to discuss, in small groups, superstitions from their countries and then report on their findings to the large group, monitoring themselves for placing pauses between phrases and clauses.

2. Pronunciation: Intonation (Wong, 1987:61–64)

Listening for Pitch Changes Exercise No. 1

Record the following conversation and play it for the students. Establish the participants, the setting, and the event by asking the students to guess who and what they are.

Conversation A

He: **Ready?** ↗

She: **No.** ↘

He: **Why?** ↘

She: **Problems.** ↘

He: **Problems?** ↗

She: **Yes.** ↘

He: **What?** ↘

She: **Babysitter.** ↘

The typical scenario that students come up with is as follows: A husband and wife are preparing to go out to a party or dinner, but the babysitter has just phoned to say she could not make it, and so now they may not be able to go out after all. Another scenario proposed is that a young man has come to pick up his date, but she cannot go because the babysitter didn't show up so she would have to stay home and babysit.

After the students have figured out what is going on, you can then play the conversation again. This time put the transcription of the conversation on the board or on an overhead projector and ask the students to try to determine for each utterance whether the speaker's voice ends with a rising or falling pitch. Students will be confused at first, especially with falling intonation on monosyllabic words; some students will identify these as rising. Draw arrows next to each utterance and play the conversation once more. To isolate pitch from the words, you can use a kazoo, which can be purchased at a toy store (see Gilbert, 1978). By humming into it, you can demonstrate rising and falling pitch to the amusement and illumination of your students. If your budget allows it, buy a kazoo for each student so they can all try it for themselves.

Ask the students to explain what each utterance means, Then point out that a change in pitch can indicate a change in meaning. *Ready?* with a rising pitch means *Are you ready?* but *Ready?* with a falling pitch means *I am ready. Why?* with a falling pitch means *I want a specific answer to my question,* while *Why?* with a rising pitch might mean *I want a specific answer to my question, but I don't want to sound too insistent.*

Listening for Pitch Changes Exercise No. 2

List the following words on the board. Make your own list and mark the words for either a rise or fall in pitch, Read them one at a time as marked and ask the students to point up if they hear a rise in pitch down if they hear a fall. Confirm or inform their responses by marking the words on the board with an arrow pointing up or down,

↘	↘
ready	no
↗	↗
problems	yes
↗	↗
babysitter	no
↗	↗
ready	yes
↘	↘
problems	what
↘	↗
yes	why

Have the students pronounce each word with you, checking for the appropriate rise or fall in pitch.

Rising and Falling Pitch Exercise No. 1

Divide the students into pairs to practice the first conversation. Additional practice dialogues are provided here. Make up more for your particular students. Follow the procedure described for the first conversation. making sure the students know or have some idea of who is speaking, what the circumstances are, and what roles the speakers have in relation to one another.

Conversation B	**Conversation C**	**Conversation D**
A: Single?	A: Good?	A: Locked?
B: Double.	B: Delicious.	B: Locked.
A: Double?	A: More?	A: Key?
B: Yes.	B: Please.	B: Key?
A: Cone?		A: Key.
B: Cup.		B: Oh-oh.

Rising and Falling Pitch Exercise No. 2

In this next exercise, a variation on the previous one was created by Epstein (1983). Pair up students and give each pair an index card with the following instructions: "This conversation is out of order. Rearrange the sentences in the correct order on a separate piece of paper and mark the pitch as rising ⏶ or falling ⏷."

Here are some sample scrambled conversations. You can make up more of your own, try unscrambling them yourself; some of them are not as easy as they appear.

Conversation #1	Conversation #2	Conversation #3
Sure	Apple?	Five.
Cup of coffee?	Starved.	Please.
Milk?	Thanks.	Nonsmoking?
Pardon?	Hungry?	Reservations?
Black, please.	Sure?	This way.
Coffee?	Take it.	How many?
No.		

Once the students have unscrambled the phrases and marked the pitch patterns, give them time to practice. Then ask each pair to put their conversation on the board, explain the situation, and perform it for the class. Other students can comment on the arrangement and propose other possibilities. The whole class can practice the final versions of each conversation.

38 I want a blue one!

LEVEL Elementary to Intermediate

TIME 10-15 minutes

AIM To give students stress practice in the context of a drill.

PREPARATION Prepare twenty-seven little cards with a picture on each to cover all the possible permutations of the following colours, fabrics, and items of clothing. The items can be increased and/or varied if required:

red	woolen	dress
blue	cotton	shirt
black	nylon	sweater

The cards should look like this:

PROCEDURE

1 Set up a shop situation. Show students the cards to indicate what they can buy, and write a substitution table on the board like this:

I'd like a	red woolen dress, blue cotton sweater, black nylon shirt,	please.

2 Take the role of the shop assistant, and ask the students to take turns to ask for something in the shop. Whenever a student asks for something you should hand over a picture making an error in either the colour, the fabric, or the item of clothing. The student then has to correct the error using appropriate stress and intonation. The dialogue should go like this:

Student I'd like a red cotton dress, please.
Teacher Here you are.
Student No. I asked for a *red* cotton dress not a *blue* one.
or
Student I'd like a black woolen shirt, please.
Teacher Here you are.
Student No. I said a black woolen *shirt*, not a black woolen *skirt*.

3 When they have got the hang of the exercise divide the cards out among pairs of students so that they can practise on their own.

REMARKS This activity could be used with other objects and adjectives.

4. Pronunciation: Meaningful minimal pairs

Traditional minimal-pair drills, used for decades in language teaching, go something like this:

> T: Okay, class, on the board, picture #1 is a "pen", and picture #2 is a "pin." Listen: Pen [points to #1]. Pin [points to #2] [several repetitions]. Now, I'm going to say either #1 or #2. You tell me which. Ready?[pause] Pin.

> Ss: #2

> T: Good. Ready. Pin.

> Ss: #2

> T: Okay. [pause] Pen.

> Ss: #1

Communicative language teaching principles prod us to be a little more meaningful. In the following examples, (see Celce-Murcia & Goodwin, 1991; Bowen, 1972) you can see that a little contextualization goes a long way:

1. T: This pen leaks.
   S: Then don't write with it.
   T: This pan leaks.
   S: Then don't cook with it.
2. T: Where can I buy cold *cream*?
   S: At the dairy.
   T: Where can I buy *cold* cream?
   S: At the drugstore.
3. T: The sun is hot on my head!
   S: Then get a cap.
   T: Oh, no, I missed the bus. I'm going to be late!
   S: Then get a cab.

These are good examples of drilling techniques that have been modified to bring context, interest, and a bit of authenticity to what would otherwise be a very mechanical task.

5. Grammar (Nolasco & Arthur, 1987: 45, 46)

Je ne regrette rein

LEVEL — **Intermediate and above**

TIME — **15-20 minutes**

AIM — To give students practice in hypothetical *would*.

PREPARATION — None.

PROCEDURE —
1 Put the following list on the board or on an OHT:

—*Your school.*

—*Your job or occupation.*

—*Your friends.*

—*Your habits, e.g. smoking, exercise, eating,* etc.

—*Your hobbies, e.g playing the piano, stamp collecting,* etc.

—*Your skills, e.g. languages, carpentry,* etc.

2 Ask the students to write a personal entry for each heading, i.e. the name of their school, job, etc. They should then decide which of these they would or would not change if they were to live their lives again.

3 Once they have done this, encourage them to share their thoughts in small groups of three or four.

4 Ask the students to take it in turns to tell others in the group what they would change if they had their life again. The others can ask questions or comment.

5 Wind up the activity by seeing if there are any areas that most of the class would want to change.

REMARKS — The title of the activity comes from an Edith Piaf song, there is an English version called "No regrets." It would make a lively and stimulating start to this activity.

6. Discourse (Nolasco & Arthur, 1987: 40, 41)

Is that right?

LEVEL   Elementary and above

TIME   10-15 minutes

AIM   To help students recognize gambits.

PREPARATION   Find a short cassette or video recording of two or three people chatting naturally. Identify examples of short responses being used and put them in random order on a task sheet, blackboard or OHT, along the following lines. You can add distractors if you wish. The task sheet might look like this:

TASK SHEET

Read the following list of expressions, Listen to the tape. Tick (✔) any of the expressions you hear. You may hear some expressions more than once:

Is that right?	_____	*That's great!*	_____
Really….?	_____	*Oh, dear.*	_____
How interesting !	_____	*What a shame!*	_____
Er… hum.	_____	*Oh, no!*	_____
Fine.	_____	*You're joking!*	_____
I see.	_____		

PROCEDURE

1 Give a task sheet to each student and ask them to tick off the examples they hear on the tape.

2 When they have done this, choose two or three examples to focus on and see if the students can recall the utterances which precede or follow them on the tape.

7. Strategy consciousness raising (Nolasco & Arthur, 1987: 105, 106)

Plan your time

LEVEL
Intermediate or above

TIME
30-35 minutes

AIM
For students to consider ways in which they can learn English outside the classroom.

PREPARATION
Make photocopies of the task sheet over the page for your class.

PROCEDURE

1 Arouse student interest in the planning task.

2 Set up the initial pair work and give the students five to ten minutes to discuss, add to or modify the list of suggestions.

3 When the initial discussion is over you should facilitate the setting up of groups. Allow the groups a maximum of twenty minutes to complete the planning task.

4 Chair the report back session in which each group presents its suggestions. Make OHTs or posters available to help the groups present their ideas.

TASK SHEET

Here is a list of techniques which people use to help them learn English outside the classroom:
—memorizing a list of words;
—reading a grammar book;
—doing grammar exercises;
—reading a book or magazine in English;
—re-copying things from their class notebook;
—correcting mistakes made in written work;
—preparing the next unit of the coursebook

Work with a partner and add any others of your own. Tell each other which ones in the list you find helpful, if any, then tell the class about the new ones you have added.

Arrange yourselves in groups and take a time period from this list:
—thirty minutes per day for six days a week;
—one hour a day for five days a week;
—two hours per day for four days a week.

In your group plan a programme to show how you could make use of the time to do extra work on your English. Use the ideas from the earlier list, as well as any others you can think of. Choose one person to present your plan to the rest of the class.

REMARKS
If students agree to experiment with a study plan, some time should be allowed in class for them to discuss how they are getting on.

8. Interactive techniques

Interactive techniques are almost impossible to categorize, but here are few of possible types, gleaned simply from the table of contents of Friederike Klippel's highly practical little resource book, *Keep Talking: Communicative Fluency Activities for Language Teaching* (1984):

- Interviews
- Guessing games
- Jigsaw tasks
- Ranking exercises
- Discussions
- Values clarification
- Problem-solving activities
- Role-play
- Simulations

9. Individual practice: Oral dialogue journals

For extra-class practice, aside from recommending that your students seek out opportunities for authentic use of English, several teacher trainers (Celce-Murcia and Goodwin, 1991; MacDonald, 1989) recommend using oral dialog journals. Written dialog journals (where the student records thoughts, ideas, reactions, and the teacher reads and responds with written comments) have been in use for some time. Why not use the convenience of a tape recorder for audiotaped journals? With large classes, such a technique is too time consuming for the teacher, but for individual students, tutees, or very small classes, it offers students a way to express themselves (without risking ridicule from peers) orally, to convey real concerns and thoughts, to practice speaking, and to get feedback from the teacher on both form and content.

❊   ❊   ❊

Listening and speaking are the two skills that are most widely used for classroom interaction. By now you have at least encountered many different parameters of these two skills, what they are, types of each, issues, and some idea of the kinds of techniques that help to focus on either one or both of them. We now move on to another very important set of skills, reading and writing.

TOPICS FOR DISCUSSION, ACTION, AND RESEARCH

1. Define fluency in a phrase or two. Now, give an operational definition (in which measurable factors are specified) of fluency through such variables as rate, pronunciation accuracy, colloquial language, errors, clarity, etc. What does the operational definition say about what you should teach your students?
2. Explain the difference between accuracy and fluency. Which should come first in a curriculum? Under what circumstances? With a partner, think of some examples of how both fluency and accuracy might get attention within one technique.

3. On p. 255 the "interlocutor effect" was described. Think of some specific examples of this interlocutor effect and share them with a partner. How might this effect help you formulate certain plans for grouping or pairing students?

4. Review the 8 factors (pp. 256–257) that make spoken language difficult. Which is more difficult, speaking or listening (compare pp. 238-241)? Can you justify your response?

5. In pairs, briefly name some common hesitation phenomena. With your partner figure out how you might actually teach students to strategically use hesitation phenomena. Share your ideas with the rest of the class.

6. Observe a class in which there is a considerable amount of oral activity. Using the list of microskills (pp. 257–258) as a check list, take some notes that would enable you to report back to your class on how various microskills manifested themselves.

7. Look again at the conversation between Bob and Amy (p. 268) and, with a partner, identify the seven factors of interpersonal exchange (cited just prior to the conversation). Decide how you would teach these factors. Then share your ideas with the rest of the class.

8. Principles of error correction are outlined on page 265. In your own words, restate the principles in a short list of "error correction maxims." Compare your maxims with others in a small group, and make any changes you might want to. Then use those maxims as guidelines for observing a class in which you try to understand (a) why the teacher chose to correct something or not, and (b) how the correction was made.

9. How, exactly, could you teach the speaking strategies (pp. 268–270) to an audience you specify? Devise a plan for teaching one of the strategies, then peer teach it to your classmates.

10. Carefully review all the speaking techniques outlined on pages 266–268. Divide them up among class members and, perhaps in pairs, demonstrate each technique to the rest of the class. Evaluate each on the extent to which it conforms to the seven principles for designing speaking techniques on pages 268–270.

FOR YOUR FURTHER READING

Brown, Gillian, and Yule, George. 1983. *Teaching the Spoken Language.* Cambridge University Press.

This is one of the best complete treatments of teaching oral production in the second language classroom. The authors carefully deal with both theoretical issues and with practical pedagogical practices.

Pennington, Martha C., and Richards, Jack C. 1986. "Pronunciation revisited." *TESOL Quarterly 20*(2), 207–225.

The authors contrast the traditional, phonemic-based view of pronunciation with a broader, discourse-based view that is more in line with principles of communicative language teaching. Voice setting, stress, intonation, and other prosodic features are seen as important features in interactive oral production.

Morley, Joan. 1991. "The pronunciation component in teaching English to speakers of other languages. *TESOL Quarterly 25*(3), 481–520.

This important review article looks at the nature of changing patterns in pronunciation teaching over a quarter-century of practices. Issues such as the role of pronunciation teaching in a communicative curriculum are carefully analyzed. Practical classroom principles and techniques are also described.

Wong, Rita. 1987. *Teaching Pronunciation: Focus on English Rhythm and Intonation.* Prentice Hall Regents.

This little book (89 pages) is a gold mine of information for the classroom teacher who wishes solid theoretical grounding but practical classroom techniques in teaching the prosodic features of English in a communicative framework.

Klippel, Friederike. 1984. *Keep Talking: Communicative Fluency Activities for Language Teaching.* Cambridge University Press.

Golebiowska, Aleksandra. 1990. *Getting Students to Talk: A Resource Book for Teachers.* Prentice Hall.

Both of these books provide a compendium of techniques designed to stimulate oral production: conversations, tasks, games, role-plays, and much more. They are useful references for your personal professional library.

Appendix: consonant/vowel charts

English Consonants

	two lips	top lip/bottom teeth	tongue tip/top teeth	tongue tip/tooth ridge	tongue tip/hard palate	tongue mid/hard palate	tongue back/soft palate	not localized	
									STOPS
p			t			k			Voiceless
b			d			g			Voiced
									CONTINUANTS
hw	f	θ	s	r	š		h		Voiceless
w	v	]	z/y/l		ž				Voiced (Oral)
m			n			ŋ			Voiced (Nasal)
									AFFRICATES
					č				Voiceless
					j				Voiced

English Vowels

		Front	Central	Back
High	Tense	iy		uw
	Lax	i		u
Mid	Tense	ey		ow
	Lax	e	ə	
Low	Tense	æ		
	Lax		a	ɔ

Diphthongs
ay
aw
oy

From: Nilsen, Don L.F. & Nilsen, Aleen Pace. *Pronunciation Contrasts in English.*
Simon & Schuster/Regents. 1971.

Chapter 16

Teaching Reading

The written word surrounds us daily. It confuses us and enlightens us, it depresses us and amuses us, it sickens us and heals us. At every turn, we who are members of a **literate** society are dependent on twenty-some-odd letters and a handful of other written symbols for significant, even life-and-death, matters in our lives. How do we teach second language learners to master this written code? What do we teach them? What are the issues?

As you read this chapter, keep well in mind that once again, interactive, integrated-skills approaches to language teaching emphasize the interrelationship of skills. Reading ability will best be developed in association with writing, listening, and speaking activity. Even in those courses that may be labeled "reading," your goals will be best achieved by capitalizing on the interrelationship of skills, especially the reading-writing connection. So, we focus here on reading as a component of general second language proficiency, but only in the perspective of the whole picture of interactive language teaching.

Research on Reading a Second Language

By the 1970s, first language reading research had been flourishing for a couple of decades, as solutions were sought to problems of why some children couldn't read. But research on reading in a second language was almost nonexistent. Then, with the work of Kenneth Goodman (1970) and others, second language specialists began to tackle the unique issues and questions facing second language reading pedagogy. A glance through those two decades of research reveals some significant findings that will affect you and your approach to teaching reading skills. These findings are briefly summarized here.

1. Reading: A psycholinguistic guessing game

This title of Goodman's (1970) seminal work on reading captures the spirit of the **bottom-up** side of the process of decoding meaning from the printed page. Readers must first recognize a multiplicity of linguistic signals (letters, morphemes, syllables, words, phrases, grammatical cues, discourse markers) and use their linguistic data processing mechanisms to impose some sort of order on these signals. This **data-driven** processing obviously requires a sophisticated knowledge of the language itself. Then, the reader selects from among all this information those data that make some sense, that cohere, that "mean." Virtually all reading involves a risk — a guessing game, in Goodman's words — because readers must, through this puzzle-solving process, infer meanings, decide what to retain and not to retain, and move on.

2. Schema theory and background knowledge

How do readers construct these meanings? How do they decide what to hold on to, and having made that decision, how do they infer a writer's message? These are the sorts of questions addressed by what has come to be known as **schema theory**, the hallmark of which is that a text does not by itself carry meaning. The reader brings information, knowledge, emotion, experience, and culture **to** the printed word. Clarke and Silberstein (1977:136–137) capture the essence of schema theory:

> **Research has shown that reading is only incidentally visual. More information is contributed by the reader than by the print on the page. That is, readers understand what they read because they are able to take the stimulus beyond its graphic representation and assign it membership to an appropriate group of concepts already stored in their memories. ...Skill in reading depends on the efficient interaction between linguistic knowledge and knowledge of the world.**

Schema theory emphasizes this other side of the reading process, the **conceptually driven**, or **top-down** processing that brings a whole host of **background information** into the arena of making decisions about what something "means."

A good example of the role of schemata in reading is found in the following little anecdote:

> **A fifteen-year-old boy got up the nerve one day to try out for the school chorus, despite the potential ridicule from his classmates. His audition time made him a good 15 minutes late to the next class. His hall permit clutched nervously in hand, he nevertheless tried surreptitiously to slip into his seat, but his entrance didn't go unnoticed.**

"And where were you?" bellowed the teacher.

Caught off guard by the sudden attention, a red-faced Harold replied meekly, "Oh, uh, er, somewhere between tenor and bass, sir."

A full understanding of this little story and its humorous punchline requires that the reader know the following **content** schemata:

- how fifteen-year-old boys might be embarrassed about singing in a choir
- how being late to class without a permit is "forbidden"
- how embarrassing it is to be singled out in a class
- something about music parts
- that fifteen-year-olds' voices are often "breaking"

Formal schemata about discourse structure also reveal some implied connections:

- The audition spilled over into the next class period.
- He did indeed have a permit to be late.
- His nervousness made him forget to give the permit to the teacher.
- The teacher, at least, did indeed notice his entry.
- The teacher's question referred to location, not a musical part.

3. Adult literacy training

As ESL materials and methods continue to apply both bottom-up and top-down models of reading to programs and curricula, one particularly challenging focus of effort for researchers and teachers has been literacy-level teaching of adults. A significant number of immigrants arriving on the shores of the United States are non-literate in their native languages, posing special issues in the teaching of English. Both "skills-based" (bottom-up) and "strategy-based" (top-down) approaches are used in adult literacy training.

Teaching literacy is a specialized field of research and practice that derives insights from a number of psycholinguistic and pedagogical domains of inquiry. In order to become familiar with basic principles and practices at this level, you might carefully consult some of the excellent material now available. Below are two enlightening possibilities:

Bell, J., and Burnaby, B. 1984. *A Handbook for ESL Literacy.* Agincourt, Ontario: Dominie Press.

Haverson, Wayne, and Haynes, J. 1982. *Literacy Training for ESL Adult Learners.* Englewood Cliffs, NJ: Prentice Hall (Center for Applied Linguistics).

The material in the remainder of this chapter will not attempt to deal specifically with adult literacy training.

Aside from the three major issues touched on above, a multitude of other topics are grist for current researchers' mills:

- the effect of culture on reading
- the role of cognition in reading
- the role conscious strategies in learning to read a second language
- effective techniques for activating schemata
- relationships of reading to writing

And the list goes on. At this stage in your professional career when you are learning to teach, rather than getting immersed in oceans of research data, it is perhaps more important to lay some basic foundations for the development of an effective teaching approach, which we now turn to.

Types of Written Language

In the previous two chapters we looked at types of spoken language so that you could identify the kinds of language your listening and speaking techniques should include. Here, we do the same for reading and writing.

In our highly literate society, there are literally hundreds of different **types** of written text, much more of a variety than found in spoken texts. Each of the types listed below represents, or is an example of, a **genre** of written language. Each has certain rules or conventions for its manifestation, and we are thus able immediately to identify a genre and to know what to look for within the text. Consider the following, inexhaustive list:

- non-fiction
    - reports
    - editorials
    - essays, articles
    - reference (dictionaries, encyclopedias)
- fiction
    - novels
    - short stories
    - jokes
    - drama
    - poetry
- letters
    - personal
    - business
- greeting cards
- diaries, journals
- memos (e.g., interoffice memos)
- messages (e.g., phone messages)
- announcements
- newspaper "journalese"

- academic writing
    short answer test responses
    reports
    essays, papers
    theses, books
- forms, applications
- questionnaires
- directions
- labels
- signs
- recipes
- bills (and other financial statements)
- maps
- manuals
- menus
- schedules (e.g., transportation information)
- advertisements
    commercial
    personal ("want ads")
- invitations
- directories (e.g., telephone, yellow pages)
- comic strips, cartoons

And I'm sure you could name a few more! Interestingly, every literate adult knows what the distinctive features of each of these genres are. You can immediately distinguish a menu from a map, an interoffice memo from a telephone message, and a bill from an invitation—well, okay, some bills are invitations to pay! When you encounter one of the above, you usually know what your purpose is in reading it, and therefore you know what to select and what not to select for short- and long-term memory—in other words, you bring various **schemata** to bear on the message that you have chosen to derive. What would happen if you didn't know some of these differences? That is what some of your students encounter when they read English, so part of your job as a teacher is to enlighten your students on features of these genres and to help them to develop strategies for extracting necessary meaning from each.

Characteristics of Written Language

There are quite a number of salient and relevant differences between spoken and written language. Students already literate in their native languages will of course be familiar with the broad, basic characteristics of written language; however, some characteristics of English writing, especially certain rhetorical conventions, may be so different from their native language that reading efforts are blocked. The characteristics listed below will also be of some help for you:

(a) to diagnose certain reading difficulties arising from the idiosyncrasies of written language,

(b) to point your techniques toward specific objectives,

(c) and to remind students of some of the advantages of the written language over spoken.

1. Permanence

Spoken language is fleeting. Once you speak a sentence, it vanishes (unless there is a tape recorder around). The hearer, therefore, is called upon to make immediate perceptions and immediate storage. Written language is permanent (or, as permanent as paper and computer disks are!), and therefore the reader has an opportunity to return again and again, if necessary, to a word or phrase or sentence or even a whole text.

2. Processing time

A corollary to the above is the processing time that the reader gains. Most reading contexts allow readers to read at their own rates. They aren't forced into following the rate of delivery, as in spoken language. A good deal of emphasis is placed on reading speed in our fast-paced, time-conscious society, which is good news and bad news. The good news is that readers can indeed capitalize on the nature of the printed word and develop very rapid reading rates. The bad news is that many people who are "slow" readers are made to feel inferior. In practice, except for the time factor itself, fast readers do not necessarily achieve an advantage over slow readers.

3. Distance

The written word allows messages to be sent across two dimensions: physical distance and temporal distance. The pedagogical significance of this centers on interpretation. The task of the reader is to interpret language that was written in some other place at some other time with only the written words themselves acting as contextual clues. Readers can't confront an author and say, "Now, what exactly did you mean by **that**?" Nor can they suddenly transport themselves back through a time machine and "see" the surrounding context as we can in face-to-face conversations. This **decontextualized** nature of writing is one of the things that makes reading difficult.

4. Orthography

In spoken language, we have phonemes that correspond to writing's graphemes. But we also have stress, rhythm, juncture, intonation, pauses, volume, voice quality settings, and nonverbal cues, all of which enhance the message. In writing we have graphemes — that's it! Yes, sometimes pictures or charts add a lending hand. And, yes, a writer can **describe** the aforementioned phonological cues, as in,

> **With loud, rasping grunts, punctuated by roars of pain, he slowly dragged himself out of the line of enemy fire.**

But, these written symbols stand alone as the one set of signals that the reader must perceive. Because of the frequent ambiguity that therefore is present in a good deal of writing, readers must do their best to infer, to interpret, and to "read between the lines."

English orthography itself, in spite of its reputation for being "irregular," is highly predictable from its spoken counterpart, especially when one considers morphological information as well. For literate learners of English, our spelling system presents only minor difficulties, even for those whose native languages have quite different systems. Actually most of the irregularity in English manifests itself in high frequency words (of, to, have, do, done, was, etc.) and once those words are in place, the rest of the system can usually be mastered without special instruction.

5. Complexity

You might be tempted to say that writing is more complex than speech, but in reality, that would be difficult to demonstrate. Writing and speech represent different modes of complexity, and the most salient difference is in the nature of **clauses**. Spoken language tends to have shorter clauses connected by more coordinate conjunctions while writing has longer clauses and more subordination. The shorter clauses are often a factor of the **redundancy** we build into speech (repeating subjects and verbs for clarity). Look at the following pair:

(1) Because of the frequent ambiguity that therefore is present in a good deal of writing, readers must do their best to infer, to interpret, and to "read between the lines."

(2) There's frequent ambiguity in a lot of writing.
And so, readers have to infer a lot.
They also have to interpret what they read.
And sometimes they have to "read between the lines."

The cognitive complexity of version 1, the written version, is no greater than version 2, the spoken version. But structurally, four clauses were used in 2 to replace the one long clause in 1.

Readers—especially second language readers who may be quite adept in the spoken language—have to retool their cognitive perceptors in order to extract meaning from the written code. The linguistic differences between speech and writing are another major contributing cause to difficulty.

6. Vocabulary

It is true that written English typically utilizes a greater variety of lexical items than spoken conversational English. In our everyday give and take with family, friends, and colleagues, vocabulary is limited. Because writing allows the writer more processing time, because of a desire to be precise in writing, and simply because of the formal conventions of writing (see #7 below), lower frequency words often appear. Such words can present stumbling blocks to learners. However, because the meaning of a good many unknown words can be predicted from their context and because sometimes the overall meaning of a sentence or paragraph is nevertheless still clear, learners should refrain from the frequent use of a bilingual dictionary.

7. Formality

Writing is quite frequently more formal than speech. What do we mean by that? Formality refers to prescribed **forms** that certain written messages must adhere to. The reason that you can both recognize a menu and decide what to eat fairly quickly is that menus conform to certain conventions. Things are categorized (appetizers, salads, entrees, desserts, etc.) in logical order and subcategorized (all seafood dishes are listed together), exotic or creative names for dishes are usually defined, prices are given for each item, and the menu isn't so long that it overwhelms you. We have **rhetorical**, or **organizational** formality in essay writing that demands a writer's conformity to conventions like paragraph topics, logical order for, say, comparing and contrasting something, openings and closings, preference for non-redundancy and subordination of clauses, etc. Until a reader is familiar with the formal features of a written text, some difficulty in interpretation may ensue.

Microskills for Reading Comprehension

An adaptation of the models of microskills offered in the previous two chapters follows on the next page, this time a breakdown of what students of ESL need to do in order to become efficient readers.

1. Discriminate among the distinctive graphemes and orthographic patterns of English.
2. Retain chunks of language of different lengths in short-term memory.
3. Process writing at an efficient rate of speed to suit the purpose.
4. Recognize a core of words, and interpret word order patterns and their significance.
5. Recognize grammatical word classes (nouns, verbs, etc.), systems (e.g., tense, agreement, pluralization), patterns, rules, and elliptical forms.
6. Recognize that a particular meaning may be expressed in different grammatical forms.
7. Recognize cohesive devices in written discourse and their role in signalling the relationship between and among clauses.
8. Recognize the rhetorical forms of written discourse and their significance for interpretation.
9. Recognize the communicative functions of written texts, according to form and purpose.
10. Infer context that is not explicit by using background knowledge.
11. From events, ideas, etc., described, infer links and connections between events, deduce causes and effects, and detect such relations as main idea, supporting idea, new information, given information, generalization, and exemplification.
12. Distinguish between literal and implied meanings.
13. Detect culturally specific references and interpret them in a context of the appropriate cultural schemata.
14. Develop and use a battery of reading strategies, such as scanning and skimming, detecting discourse markers, guessing the meaning of words from context, and activating schemata for the interpretation of texts.

Strategies for Reading Comprehension

For most second language learners who are already literate in a previous language, reading comprehension is primarily a matter of developing appropriate, efficient comprehension **strategies**. Some strategies are related to bottom-up procedures and others enhance the top-down processes. Following are ten such strategies, each of which can be practically applied to your classroom techniques.

1. Identify the purpose in reading.

How many times have you been told to read something and you don't know **why** you're being asked to read it? You end up doing only a mediocre job of retaining what you "read" and perhaps were rather slow in the process. Efficient reading consists of clearly identifying the purpose in reading something. By doing so, you know what you're looking for and can weed out potential distracting information. Whenever you are teaching a reading technique, make sure students know their purpose in reading something.

2. Use graphemic rules and patterns to aid in bottom-up decoding (for beginning level learners).

At the beginning levels of learning English, one of the difficulties students encounter in learning to read is making the correspondences between spoken and written English. In many cases, learners have become acquainted with oral language and have some difficulty learning English spelling conventions. They may need to be given hints and explanations about certain English orthographic rules and peculiarities. While in many cases you can assume that one-to-one grapheme-phoneme correspondences will be acquired with ease, other relationships might prove difficult. Consider how you might provide hints and pointers on such patterns as these:

- "short" vowel sound in VC patterns (bat, him, leg, wish, etc.)
- "long" vowel sound in VCe (final silent **e**) patterns (late, time, bite, etc.)
- "long" vowel sound in VV patterns (seat, coat, etc.)
- distinguishing "hard" **c** and **g** from "soft" **c** and **g** (cat vs. city, game vs. gem, etc.)

These and a multitude of other **phonics** approaches to reading can prove to be useful for learners at the beginning level and especially useful for teaching children and non-literate adults.

3. Use efficient silent reading techniques for relatively rapid comprehension (for intermediate to advanced levels).

If you are teaching beginning level students, this particular strategy will not apply because they are still struggling with the control of a limited vocabulary and grammatical patterns. Your intermediate to advanced level students need not be speed readers, but you can help them to increase efficiency by teaching a few silent reading rules:

- You don't need to "pronounce" each word to yourself.
- Try to visually perceive more than one word at a time, preferably phrases.
- Unless a word is absolutely crucial to global understanding, skip over it and try to infer its meaning through its context.

Aside from these fundamental guidelines, which if followed can help learners to be efficient readers, reading speed is usually not much of an issue for all but the most advanced learners. Academic reading, for example, is something most learners manage to accomplish by allocating whatever time they personally need in order to complete the material. If your students can read 250 to 300 words per minute, further concern over speed may not be necessary.

4. Skimming

Perhaps the two most valuable reading strategies for learners as well as native speakers are skimming and scanning. Skimming consists of quickly running one's eyes across a whole text (an essay, article, or chapter, for example) to get the gist. Skimming gives readers the advantage of being able to predict the purpose of the passage, the main topic or message, and possibly some of the developing or supporting ideas. This gives them a "head start" as they embark on more focused reading. You can train students to skim passages by giving them, say, 30 seconds to look through a few pages of material, have them close their books, and tell you what they learned.

5. Scanning

The second in the "most valuable" category is scanning, or quickly searching for some particular piece or pieces of information in a text. Scanning exercises may ask students to look for names or dates, to find a definition of a key concept, or to list a certain number of supporting details. The purpose of scanning is to extract certain specific information without reading through the whole text. For academic English, scanning is absolutely essential. In vocational or general English, scanning is important in dealing with genres like schedules, manuals, forms, etc.

6. Semantic mapping or clustering

Readers can easily be overwhelmed by a long string of ideas or events. The strategy of semantic mapping, or grouping ideas into meaningful clusters, helps the reader to provide some order to the chaos. Making such semantic maps can be done individually, but they make for a productive group work technique as students collectively induce order and hierarchy to a passage. Early drafts of these maps can be quite messy—which is perfectly acceptable. Figure 16.1, for example, shows a first attempt by a small group of students to draw a semantic map of an article by Rick Gore called "Between Fire and Ice: The Planets" (Brown, Cohen, O'Day, 1991:50–51), an article about a total solar eclipse as seen through the eyes of villagers in Patuk, Java.

Figure 16.1. Semantic Map.

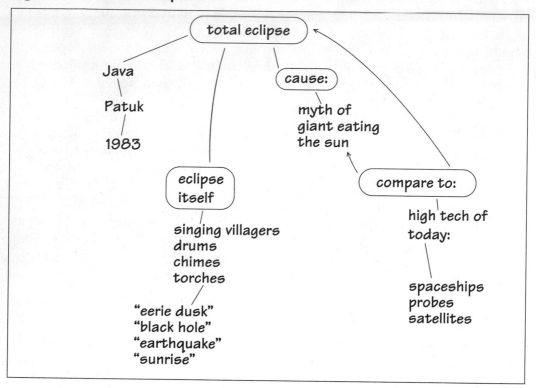

7. Guessing

This is an extremely broad category. Learners can use guessing to their advantage to:

- guess the meaning of a word,
- guess a grammatical relationship (e.g., a pronoun reference)
- guess a discourse relationship,
- infer implied meaning ("between the lines"),
- guess about a cultural reference,
- guess content messages.

Now, you of course don't want to encourage your learners to become haphazard readers! They should utilize all their skills and put forth as much effort as possible to be on target with their hypotheses. But the point here is that reading is, after all, a "guessing game" of sorts, and the sooner learners understand this game, the better off they are. The key to successful guessing is to make it reasonably **accurate**.

You can help learners to become accurate guessers by encouraging them to use effective **compensation strategies** in which they fill gaps in their competence by intelligent attempts to use whatever clues are available to them. Language based clues include word analysis (see #8 below), word associations, and textual structure. Nonlinguistic clues come from context, situation, and other schemata.

8. Vocabulary analysis

One way for learners to make guessing pay off when they don't immediately recognize a word is to analyze it in terms of what they know about it. Several techniques are useful here:

(a) look for prefixes (co-, inter-, un-, etc.) that may give clues

(b) look for suffixes (-tion, -tive, -ally, etc.) that may indicate what part of speech it is

(c) look for roots that are familiar (e.g., *intervening* may be a word a student doesn't know, but recognizing that the root, *ven* comes from Latin "to come" would yield the meaning "to come in between")

(d) look for grammatical contexts that may signal information

(e) look at the semantic context (topic) for clues

9. Distinguish between literal and implied meanings.

This requires the application of sophisticated top-down processing skills. The fact that not all language can be interpreted appropriately by attending to its literal, syntactic surface structure makes special demands on readers. Implied meaning usually has to be derived from processing **pragmatic** information, as in the following examples:

1. **Bill walked into the frigid classroom and immediately noticed Bob, sitting by the open window.**
   "Brrr!" he exclaimed, simultaneously eyeing Bob and the open windows, "It's sure cold in here, Bob."
   Bob glanced up from his book and growled, "Oh, all right, I'll close the window."
2. **The policeman held up his hand and stopped the car.**
3. **Mary heard the ice cream man coming down the street. She remembered her birthday money and rushed into the house...**

   (Rummelhart, 1977:265)

Each of these excerpts has implied information. The request in (1) is obvious only if the reader recognizes the nature of many indirect requests in which we ask people to do things without ever forming a question. We can't be sure in (2) if the policeman literally (physically) stopped the car with his hand, but the assumption is that this is a traffic policeman whose hand signal was obeyed by a driver. Rummelhart's classic example in (3) leads the reader, without any other context here, to believe Mary is going into the house to get money in order to buy some ice cream until the last few words are supplied:

. . . and locked the door!

10. Capitalize on discourse markers to process relationships.

There are many discourse markers in English that signal relationships among ideas as expressed through phrases, clauses, and sentences. A clear comprehension of such markers can greatly enhance learners' reading efficiency. Table 16.1 enumerates almost one hundred of these markers that learners of intermediate proficiency levels ought to be thoroughly familiar with.

Table 16.1. Types of Discourse Markers (Mackay, 1987:254).

Notional category/meaning	Marker
1. *Enumerative*. Introduce in order in which points are to be made or the time sequence in which actions or processes took place.	first(ly), second(ly), third(ly), one, two, three / a, b, c, next, then, finally, last(ly), in the first / second place, for one thing / for another thing, to begin with, subsequently, eventually, finally, in the end, to conclude
2. *Additive*	
2.1 Reinforcing. Introduces a reinforcement or confirmation of what has preceded.	again, then again, also, moreover, furthermore, in addition, above all, what is more
2.2 Similarity. Introduces a statement of similarity with what has preceded.	equally, likewise, similarly, correspondingly, in the same way
2.3 Transition. Introduces a new stage in the sequence of presentation of information.	now, well incidentally, by the way. O.K., fine
3. *Logical Sequence*	
3.1 Summative. Introduces a summary of what has preceded.	so, so far, altogether, overall, then, thus, therefore, in short, to sum up, to conclude, to summarize
3.2 Resultative. Introduces an expression of the result or consequence of what preceded (and includes inductive and deductive acts)	so, as a result, consequently, hence, now, therefore, thus, as a consequence, in consequence
4. *Explicative*. Introduces an explanation or reformulation of what preceded.	namely, in other words, that is to say, better, rather, by (this) we mean
5. *Illustrative*. Introduces an illustration or example of what preceded.	for example, for instance
6. *Contrastive*	
6.1 Replacive. Introduces an alternative to what preceded.	alternatively, (or) again, (or) rather, (but) then, on the other hand
6.2 Antithetic. Introduces information in opposition to what preceded.	conversely, instead, then, on the contrary, by contrast, on the other hand
6.3 Concessive. Introduces information which is unexpected in view of what preceded.	anyway, anyhow, however, nevertheless, nonetheless, notwithstanding, still, though, yet, for all that, in spite of (that), at the same time, all the same

Types of Classroom Reading Performance

Variety of reading performance in the language classroom is derived more from the variety of texts (refer to the list supplied earlier in this chapter) to which you can expose students than from the variety of overt types of performance. Consider the chart below.

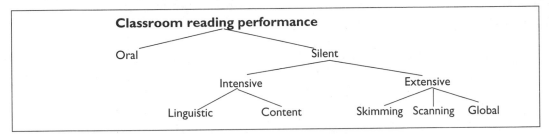

Occasionally, you will have reason to ask a student to read orally. At the beginning and intermediate levels, oral reading can:

(a) serve as an evaluative check on bottom-up processing skills,

(b) double as a pronunciation check,

(c) and it can serve to add some extra student participation if you want to highlight a certain short segment of a reading passage.

For advanced levels, usually only the latter advantage (c) can be gained by oral reading. As a rule of thumb, you want to use oral reading to serve these three purposes because the disadvantages of too much oral reading can easily come into play:

(a) oral reading is not a very authentic language activity;

(b) while one student is reading, others can easily lose attention (or be silently rehearsing the next paragraph!);

(c) it may have the outward appearance of "student participation" when in reality it is mere recitation.

Silent reading may be subcategorized into **intensive** and **extensive** reading. Intensive reading, analogous to intensive listening (described in Chapter 14), is usually a classroom-oriented activity in which students focus on the linguistic or semantic details of a passage. Intensive reading calls students' attention to grammatical forms, discourse markers, and other surface structure details for the purpose of understanding literal meaning, implications, rhetorical relationships, and the like.

As a "zoom lens" strategy for taking a closer look at a text, intensive reading also may be a totally content-related reading initiated because of subject-matter difficulty. A complex cognitive concept may be "trapped" inside the words of a sentence or paragraph, and a good reader will then very slowly and methodically extract meaning therefrom.

Extensive reading is carried out to achieve a general under-standing of a text. All pleasure reading is extensive. Technical, scientific, and professional reading can (and should) also be extensive. The latter, especially, sometimes involves skimming and scanning as strategies for gaining the general sense of a text. At other times, perhaps **after** students have done some pre-reading activity, skimmed for the gist, and scanned for some key details, extensive reading is quite simply a relatively rapid and efficient process of reading a text for **global** or general meaning.

Principles for Designing Interactive Reading Techniques

1. In an interactive curriculum, make sure that you don't over-look the importance of specific instruction in reading skills.

ESL students who are literate in their own language sometimes are "left to their own devices" when it comes to teaching them reading skills. We like to assume that they will simply learn good reading by absorption. In reality, there is much to be gained by your focusing on reading skills. This chapter has provided some guidelines on how to direct that focus.

It is important to make sure that your students have ample time for extensive reading. Sustained silent reading allows students to develop a sense of fluency. Also, silent reading then becomes an excellent method for self-instruction on the part of the learner.

2. Techniques should be intrinsically motivating.

What do you think makes for interesting and relevant reading for your students? Of that long list of texts towards the beginning of this chapter, how many of them will your students encounter in "real life"? Use those texts. What are your students' goals in learning to read English? Focus on those goals. Choose material that is relevant to those goals.

One very popular and intrinsically motivating approach to reading instruction is called the **Language Experience Approach (LEA)**. Developed initially for use in native language instruction of children, the LEA has now found its way into numerous ESL classes for both children and adults. The essence of this approach lies in students' self-generation of reading material. Instead of being handed some standard textbook, they create their own! For example, small groups might each be given the task of creating a story (either a true story or one they make up). Some members of the group collaborate on drafting a written version the story; one or two other students are prepared to pen the words themselves while another illustrates the story. The final products are shared among the groups, who read with great interest the products of their fellow classmates. The personalized nature of LEA along with the intrinsic pride that each student possesses in the creation of the original work almost always makes it an excellent learning experience.

3. Techniques should utilize authentic language and contexts.

By now, the importance of authentic language should be more than clear to you! But in teaching reading, one issue that has invited a bit of controversy is the advisability of what are called "simplified texts," in which an otherwise authentic text is edited to keep language within the proficiency level of a set of students. In order for you to make a decision on this issue, it is important (1) to distinguish between (a) simple texts and (b) simplified texts and (2) to understand sources of complexity in reading material.

Simple texts that are authentic can either be found out there in the real world or devised. From ads to labels to reports to essays, texts are available that are grammatically and lexically simple. Simplifying, or "doctoring up" an existing short story or description is therefore not only unnecessary but also is a disservice to students who are thereby deprived of original material with its natural redundancy, humor, wit, and other captivating features.

Second, you might ask yourself what "simplicity" is and then determine if a so-called simplified text is really simpler than its original. Sometimes simplified texts remove so much natural redundancy that they actually become difficult. And what you perceive as textual complexity may be more a product of background schemata than of linguistic complexity. Take another look at the list of characteristics of written language earlier in this chapter and you will no doubt see what it is that makes a text difficult. In light of those criteria, is a simplified text really simpler? The answer may be no.

4. Encourage the development of reading strategies.

Already in this chapter, ten different reading strategies have been discussed. To what extent are you getting your students to use all these strategies?

5. Include both bottom-up and top-down techniques.

In our craze for communicative, authentic language activity in the classroom, sometimes we forget that learners can indeed benefit from studying the fundamentals. Make sure that you give enough classroom time to focusing on the building blocks of written language— geared appropriately for each level.

6. Consider subdividing your techniques into pre-reading, during-reading, and after-reading phases.

It is tempting, especially at intermediate and advanced levels, to tell students, "Okay now, class, read the next two pages silently." No introduction, no hints on anything special to do while reading, and nary a thought about something to follow the silent reading period. A good rubric to try to keep in mind for teaching reading is the following three-part framework:

(a) **Before you read.** Spend some time introducing a topic, encouraging skimming, scanning, and activating schemata. Students can bring the best of their knowledge and skills to a text when they have been given a chance to "ease into" the passage.

(b) **While you read.** Not all reading is simply extensive-global reading. There may be certain facts or rhetorical devices that students should take note of while they read. This gives them a sense of purpose rather than just reading because the teacher ordered it.

(c) **After you read.** Comprehension questions are just one form of activity appropriate for post-reading. Consider vocabulary study, identifying the author's purpose, discussing the author's line of reasoning, examining grammatical structures, or steering students toward a follow-up writing exercise.

7. Build in some evaluative aspect to your techniques.

Because reading, like listening comprehension, is totally unobservable (we have to **infer** comprehension from other behavior), it is as important in reading as it is in listening to be able to accurately assess students' comprehension and development of skills. Consider some of the following overt responses (modeled after the list in Chapter 14 for listening) that indicate comprehension:

(1) doing—the reader responds physically to a command

(2) choosing—the reader selects from alternatives posed orally or in writing

(3) transferring—the reader summarizes orally what is read

(4) answering—the reader answers questions about the message

(5) condensing—the reader outlines or takes notes on a passage

(6) extending—the reader provides an ending to a story

(7) duplicating—the reader translates the message into the native language or copies it (beginning level, for very short passages only)

(8) modeling—the reader puts together a toy, for example, after reading directions for assembly

(9) conversing—the reader engages in a conversation that indicates appropriate processing of information

Two Reading Lessons

Following are excerpts from two different ESL textbooks designed to teach reading (and, in the case of the second book, writing) skills. The first excerpt is designed for beginners; the second is for advanced students.

Lesson 1 (Beginning level)

The following excerpt from *Basics in Reading* (Boone, Bennett, & Motai, 1988: 14–15) illustrates the use of natural, authentic language and tasks at the beginning level. Some attention is given to bottom-up skills, but not at the expense of top-down processing, even at this level.

RAIN FORESTS
by Scott Adelson

Have you ever seen a rain forest? Where do rain forest grow? What is unusual or unique about rain forests? Are they important to the world?

This text is about special forests in tropical areas of the world that are being cut down, and about a special group that is trying to save them.

 ## Vocabulary to Watch for

debt	—money you owe to another person
organization	—group
conservation	—saving the land and the animals
reserve	—a safe place for animals and nature
basin	—valley where there is a river
region	—area, large place
savannah	—dry, flat land; plain

 ## READ

In many tropical countries, people are cutting down rain forests to make room for farms. They hope that the farms will make money for them so that they can pay their **debts**. But a new **organization** is trying to help these countries save their forests. The name of this organization is **Conservation International.** Conservation International pays countries not to cut down their rain forests.

Their first agreement was with Bolivia, for a 4,000,000 acre **reserve** in the Amazon River **basin** in northeast Bolivia. The **region** has **savannahs**, deep woods, and rain forests. It is famous for the different plants and unusual wildlife that live there. Bolivia and Conservation International will take care of the reserve together.

This idea of helping countries make rain forest reserves is so unusual that Brazil and Ecuador, which are both interested in this program, are already having talks with Conservation International.

RESPOND

● Understanding the Details

Do you understand the text?
Try to answer the following questions. You may look in the text.
Practice *scanning* for important words or numbers.
Can you do this exercise in five minutes?

1. Why do some tropical countries cut down their rain forests?
2. What is the name of the organization that is helping to save rain forests?
3. What country did they do business with first?
4. How much land did they get for a reserve?
5. Where is the reserve located?
6. Why is this reserve interesting to save?
7. Who will take care of the reserve?
8. What other countries are interested in this program?

● The Big Picture: Reading for the Main Idea

What do you think is the <u>most</u> important idea in this text?

_____ a. Small countries need help to save their rain forests.
_____ b. Bolivia is taking care of its rain forests in the Amazon River Basin.
_____ c. Conservation groups are trying to help tropical countries save their rain forests.

DISCUSS

What Do You Think?

Are people in your country worried about conservation?
Do you think it is a good idea to pay countries <u>not</u> to cut down their forests?
What do you think is the most important conservation problem?

Lesson 2 (Advanced level)

The following excerpt from *Challenges: Process Approach to Academic English* (Brown, Cohen, O'Day, 1991: 7–18) illustrates the use of an article from a popular magazine for advanced level classes. Notice that mostly top-down processing is emphasized on the assumption that at this level, the greater need is for activating schemata (note the "Before You Read" sections) and understanding the organization and purpose of the article. In a topically related piece of authentic material, a sample of classified ads, scanning is practiced and followed up with a writing activity.

LESSON 2

OUR FUTURE STOCK

About the Selection:

In the first lesson you had an opportunity to explore some of your thoughts about change and about the future of your field or occupation. Now you will have a chance to compare your predictions for the future with those of experts who have studied these issues in depth. The following reading selection is from the popular science magazine *Omni.* In 1982 the editors of *Omni* gathered information from various U.S. government agencies and industry experts. They used this information to develop a picture of what the work force and the economy of the future may look like. This selection is an excerpt from the article reporting their predictions. As you read through it, consider whether the changes mentioned here are similar to those you wrote about in lesson 1.

The First Reading

Before You Read: Anticipating the Topic

Look at the title and graphics. *Stock* often refers to an investment or an accumulation of something for future use. Judging from the subtitles and the pictures, what do you think *stock* refers to in this case?

_____

What type of future developments does this excerpt seem to focus on?

_____

Based on the results of your brainstorming in lesson 1, write two to three sentences about the kinds of careers and workplace changes one could "put stock in" (expect; have faith in) for the future.

_____

_____

As You Read: Looking for the General Ideas

First read the article quickly to discover its main points and general organization. Then do the activities that follow. Later, in your second reading, you can go through the entire article more carefully or focus in on particular sections to pick up the specific details and development of the main points. You will see that two or three quick, purposeful readings will be more efficient and productive than one slow, detailed reading.

Don't worry about vocabulary! As you read, you will find words you do not know. Don't worry about these. Either guess their meanings or skip them entirely. _Do not_ look up any words in the dictionary at this time. To do so would only slow you down and prevent you from focusing on the key points. Vocabulary exercises will follow.

OUR FUTURE STOCK:
A Survey of Jobs, New Technology, and the World Economy in the Next Millenium

During the next 50 years an incredible array of new technologies is expected to move from the lab to the world of business. We are already seeing evidence of this today. Robots are replacing humans on the production lines. Microcomputers have become fixtures in offices. Biofactories are beginning to manufacture batches of engineered human insulin.... The coming decades promise to be especially volatile[1] and exciting for American business. The expected upheaval will profoundly change not only our lives but those of our children and grandchildren,

For the more deveoped nations, this era of turmoil will be marked by economic difficulties, problems with waste and pollution, and continually dwindling[2] resources. By contrast, the Third World countries will spearhead a new industrial age with the same fervor and energy that charcterized American industrial expansion in the days of Vanderbilt, Carnegie, Morgan and Rockefeller...

[1] volatile: changeable

[2] dwindling: becoming smaller and smaller (in amount)

Job Markets and Careers

The technological revolution that will prevail[3] for the remainder of this century will create jobs and professions that as little as five years ago were nonexistent. These newly developed markets will demand of workers an understanding of sophisticated technical communications systems as well as an increased technical expertise. By the year 2001 basic skills that once were vital to business will be rendered obsolete. The spot welder on the automobile production line, the clerk typist in an office, the field worker on a farm will go the way of the steamboat pilot and the blacksmith.

The most significant trend in years to come will be the shift from formation-type jobs (factory work, office typing, and general clerical work) to information-type jobs (programming, word processing, and supervising technical machinery).[4] The American economy will witness the demise

[3]**prevail:** occur as the most important feature

[4]**formation-type jobs:** jobs which result in the actual "formation" of a material product, such as a car, a manually typed report, and so on.

information-type jobs: jobs which focus on the electronic processing of information, whether that information is used in an office or business setting or used to control machines which then produce material goods and services. Note that this information may never take concrete material form, it can be processed and stored electronically in our computer systems, transmitted from one place to another by complex electronic telecommunications systems, and read on a computer screen rather than on separate sheets of paper.

of the blue-collar worker as automation and robotics become more prevalent, heralding the rise of the steel-collar worker. Such traditional blue-collar employers as General Motors and U.S. Steel have already begun to automate their factories—a fact reflected in the swollen[5] unemployment rolls in our industrial states.

By contrast, office and service jobs will be abundant, but only for those prepared to improve their technical skills. Again it will be automation that will displace many of the low-skilled and semi-skilled workers in the present economy.

In fact, the era of the paperless office has already begun. It has been promoted by two principal developments: computers that process business information and the explosive growth of telecommunications systems and products. This office revolution not only has changed how work is done and information is handled but has redefined the function of everyone who works in an office, from the corporate executive down to the lowliest clerk...

For the job hunter of 2020, scanning[6] classified ads will be a quick education in how drastically[7] the workplace will have changed. He or she is likely to see openings for such positions as biological historians, biofarming experts, computer art curators, fiberoptics technicians, robot retrainers, space traffic controllers, and teleconferencing coordinators, to cite but a few.

There will always be farms, but by the next century farmworkers as we know them will be scarcer. The business of farming will become ever more complex. With computerized operations and robot harvesters, there will be no need for unskilled labor. The farm will be a place for people with training as electronic technicians, bioengineers, and computer programmers. Indeed, the human farmworker someday may be simply the person with the phone number of the nearest robot repairman.

---

[5] **swollen**: enlarge; having got bigger
[6] **scanning:** looking over or reading quickly (often to find specific information)
[7] **drastically:** severely; suddenly

After You Read

• Identifying the Main Idea

DIRECTIONS: Choose the answer that best expresses the main idea.

1. Based on paragraphs 1 and 2, choose the statement that best expresses the main idea of the article.
    a. Industrialized nations will face many problems in the years ahead.
    b. New technological developments will greatly change our lives and the lives of our children.
    c. Robots will replace humans on factory production lines.
    d. Change is everywhere.

2. The main idea for the section "Job Markets and Careers" is:
    a. Our future world will be very different from today's world.
    b. Farmwork will be largely automated and computerized in the future.
    c. There will be more office jobs and fewer factory jobs in the future.
    d. New technology will create many new jobs and professions and will make many old ones outdated.

• Guessing Vocabulary from Context

When you encounter unfamiliar vocabulary in an English reading selection, what is your typical response? Do you bring out your bilingual or English monolingual dictionary to look up the word? Do you then spend precious moments looking through all the definitions to decide which one fits? Have you ever finally decided on a definition only to realize that you have forgotten what you were reading and must begin the sentence or paragraph all over again?

Over-reliance on a dictionary not only slows down your reading but may interfere with your comprehension as well. A better strategy is to use the **context,** the words and sentences surrounding a particular word, to help you **guess** that word's meaning. Usually the guesses you make will be accurate enough for you to understand the author's ideas. When they are not, or when the terms require an exact technical definition, you can use your English dictionary as a back-up resource.

DIRECTIONS: The following exercise contains words taken from the reading selection. Use the new context to select the most appropriate meaning.

1. Just as the invention of the automobile <u>rendered</u> horse-drawn carriages <u>obsolete</u> in modern cities, so the use of computers and word processors will make the common typewriter much <u>scarcer</u> in offices of the future.

    render obsolete: a. cause it to be outdated and no longer useful
                       b. cause it to increase in price
                       c. cause it to change

    scarcer: a. more common
              b. more efficient
              c. more rare

2. Because business computers are becoming more and more complex, many office workers have had to get new training to handle these <u>sophisticated</u> electronic systems.

    sophisticated: a. complex
                    b. business
                    c. worldly

3. Computers are even becoming more <u>prevalent</u> in American schools and homes; perhaps in another twenty years every school-age child in the United States will be able to operate a computer.

    prevalent: a. large
               b. common
               c. expensive

4. Some automobile factories have begun to <u>automate</u> their assembly lines by using robots instead of human workers. This <u>automation</u> will increase the amount of money needed for machinery but will decrease the cost of labor.

    automate: a. to increase the number of human workers
              b. to produce a greater variety of products
              c. to operate or control something by machine rather than by human labor

    automation: the noun form of *automate*, referring to the process of automating

5. Unlike white-collar workers, who usually work in an office, <u>blue-collar workers</u> may be found in many different work settings. For example, they may work outdoors to construct a new highway, or they may assemble new cars in an auto factory or repair damaged ones in a mechanic shop.

    blue-collar workers: a. business executives
                        b. secretaries
                        c. manual laborers

6. The early industrial revolution contributed to the <u>demise</u> of the feudal lords and the rise of the bourgeoisie. Likewise, the new technological revolution may <u>herald</u> major social and economic changes in the societies of the future.

    demise: a. creation
            b. loss of power
            c. gain in power
    herald: a. introduce
           b. end
           c. respond to

7. Blue-collar workers were originally given this name because of the blue workshirts they often wore. Given this information and the preceding vocabulary clues, reread paragraph 4. Can you guess what or who the "steel-collar workers" are who are replacing the blue-collar workers? Write you answer in the space provided.

    steel-collar worker: _____

The Second Reading
Before You Read: Knowing Your Purpose

In the first reading you were looking for the main ideas of the article; this time, your purpose is to see how these ideas are supported. You might want to think about the following questions as you read:

1. What is the main change that will take place in the work force?
2. What types of jobs will be affected by this change?
3. What are some specific examples of the jobs and careers we might expect to see in the future?

After You Read

● Understanding the Author's Plan

In order to better understand what you read, it is often helpful to consider the author's plan of organization and method of development. In the following exercise, the purpose of each paragraph in the section "Job Markets and Careers" is explained in the left-hand column.

DIRECTIONS: Read each explanation and then answer the comprehension questions to the right.

Authors' Plan

Paragraph 3: states the main idea for this section: The new technological revolution will create many new jobs and make old jobs obsolete.

Paragraph 4: expands the main idea by defining the principal trend in the job market.

Paragraphs 4-8: discuss specific types of work and the expected developments in each.

Paragraph 4: examines factory work.

Paragraphs 5-6: discuss office work.

Comprehension Questions

1. What kind of knowledge will the new jobs require workers to have?
2. What will happen to many of the existing jobs and skills?
3. Do the authors give examples of outdated jobs? What are they?
4. What is the most important change taking place in the American job market?
5. What will cause the "demise of the blue-collar worker?" Why?
6. What has been the result of the automation which has already occurred in General Motors and U.S. Steel factories?
7. Will office and service jobs be plentiful or scarce in the future?
8. What kind of workers will be needed to fill these positions?
9. What is meant by the "paperless office?"

10. What two major developments have contributed to the growth of the paperless office?

Paragraph 7: introduces other new occupations of the future.

11. How do the examples given in paragraph 7 show the "drastic" change in the workplace? Choose one example and explain.

Paragraph 8: discusses farmwork.

12. Why will farmworkers as we know them be scarcer in the next century?
13. Who will perform the unskilled labor on the farms?

We can see that the authors have established a specific purpose for each paragraph. Recognizing the function of each paragraph helps us to understand the ideas presented in a reading.

• A Deeper Look: Discussion Questions

DIRECTIONS: Discuss the following questions in small groups. Compare your answers with those of your classmates. '

1. The authors of "Our Future Stock" predict a greater demand for technically skilled labor and a decreased demand for unskilled labor. How do you think this will affect employment in industrialized nations? Have these effects already been seen in some areas?
2. How can the problem of displaced workers be resolved? Give examples.
3. In paragraph 2, the authors say, "the Third World countries will spearhead a new industrial age..." In a later section (not included in this textbook) they discuss several factors that will contribute to this advance in Third World countries. These factors include:
   —large populations
   —large amounts of unused resources
   —(in some cases) conservative governments that are opposed to labor legislation and antipollution laws.
   Do you agree that these factors may contribute to rapid economic development in many developing countries? Why or why not? If possible, give examples of specific countries to support your view.
4. Have the technological advances mentioned in this article affected your nation or area? In what ways? What will these changes mean for your future?
5. Some critics of the new technology argue that if humans rely on computers and robots, we will become mentally lazy; we will lose our artistic creativity and our ability or desire to invent new ways of doing things. Do you agree? Why or why not?

• Becoming an Efficient Reader: Scanning

To scan is to read quickly to locate specific information or details.

On the next page is an imaginary Help Wanted section of the classified ads for the year 2020. The jobs listed in this section are based on the predictions made in the previous article and on other sources. The form of this ad section is similar to that used in many U.S. newspapers.

DIRECTIONS: Answer the following questions by scanning the Help Wanted ads. First, observe how the information is organized in the ads. Then, read each question carefully to understand what is being asked. To locate the information you need, move your eyes quickly over the printed page, paying particular attention to bold headlines and key words. Finally, write the answers in the spaces provided.

1. What is the date of this ad section?
2. Where is there a position open for a space traffic controller? How many jobs are available?
3. In order to be hired as the robot psychologist at West Docks Engineering Corporation, what experience must you have? Is this same experience required for the position at Robopsyche Institute?
4. If you enjoy working on a team with other robot psychologists, which position would you apply for?
5. If you are looking for training in a space-related field, which position would you apply for?
6. What benefits are available for new sales people at Compu-Sales, Inc? Is on-the-job training offered for this position?
7. What job is listed as a temporary position? How long will the job last? Is there a possibility that there will be a permanent job with this company in the future?
8. If you are a teleconferencing coordinator (TC) and you speak several languages, where might you apply for a job? What languages are required?
9. Which TC position requires experience with TeleTech Systems?
10. What position is available at Hayward State University? What qualifications are needed?

HELP WANTED: JOB OPPORTUNITIES

ROBOT PSYCHOLOGIST

needed for scientific crew at West Docks Engineering Corp.

Responsibilities: to provide counseling and reprogramming to research robots suffering from directive overload and primary order conflict.

Qualifications: Must be independent and self-sufficient; able to get along without human companionship. B.S. in robotic psychology and experience with En500 Series robots required.

Process resume to CompuStation 6Z, Entry #435592.

Are you a
ROBOT PSYCHOLOGIST
looking for a CHANGE?

Are you tired of working in isolation for a single company? Join the qualified professional team at ROBOPSYCHE INSTITUTE, a recently established research facility located in sunny San Jose, California. Enjoy working with stimulating colleagues while you receive excellent salary and career advancement opportunities.

All you need is a Master's degree in robotic psychology and a cooperative, energetic personality. We will provide additional training and on-the-job ex-perience. Process your resume today to Robo-psyche Institute, CompuStation 5C, Entry#41156

TEMPORARY ROBOT RETRAINERS
NEEDED *NOW!*

600 Series-2Z3 Domestic Robots must be reprogrammed for new duties in a major San Francisco Hotel.

4-week deadline!

Programming degree and experience required. Good salary now with chance for permanent position to follow.

Call immediately: Elizabeth Cortex, personnel manager, 415-999-6443.

SALES/MARKETING: San Francisco-based firm is expanding business-computer operations. Needs 4 creative and energetic sales-people.

Qualifications: At least 2 years experi-ence in computer sales; knowledge of "Value Star" and related business soft-ware.

Duties: Responsible for initiating new sales contacts and handling existing valued clients.

Benefits: Base salary + commission, health and dental insurance.

Apply now: Send resume and current earnings statement to

COMPU-SALES, Inc.
CompuStation 9, Entry #6725

SPACE TRAFFIC CONTROLLER: 6 positions available for experiencedspace traffic con-trollers at the new space port in Santa Clara Valley. Excellent salary and benefits. Process resume to CompuStation 9, Entry #4413

SALES MANAGER: GFC, Inc. Agriculture Division. Knowledge of robot harvesters and agricultural operations software required. B.S. in Agricultural Management preferred. Send Resume and salary history to GFC, Inc.., CompuStation 15, Entry #2195.

LOOKING FOR ADVENTURE?

Become a Space Geographer! On Oct. 9 Astro Travel, Inc. will begin a 4-month train-ing session for space geographers: 3 months on-the-ground training in a classroom and 1 month actual space travel. Tuition includes travel expenses. Job placement guaranteed.
Call 773-1212 for more information.

TELECONFERENCING COORDINATOR is being sought by major L.A.-based law firm. Must have experience with TeleTech systems, and T.C. training certificate. Call (213) 592-6312 for details.

TELECONFERENCING COORDINATOR: Trans-Po Bank and Trust Co. Energetic, effi-cient T.C. needed for international business-conferences. Fluency in Spanish, Japanese, and English is a must. Experience with Tele-Tech systems preferred. Salary and benefits negotiable. Call (415) 599-6432.

UNIVERSITY PROFESSOR OF HISTORY FIELD: Early space exploration. Ph.D. in History with a concentration in international space programs. Send resume and related publications to History Dept., Hayward State University, CompuStation 7, E ##7924

Becoming a Proficient Writer

• Guided Writing: Considering Audience and Purpose

You have just scanned the classified ads and answered questions about them. Here is an exercise that will ask you to write about one of the ads.

DIRECTIONS: Look at the advertisement for a sales/marketing position. Imagine that you are the personnel manager for the company, Compu-sales, Inc. You need to send a note or memo (a short, informal letter, a memorandum) to the owner of the company describing the job that you are advertising. As you write, carefully consider the person to whom you are writing this note and the reason you are writing it. This will determine the style you use and the information you include. Your boss wants the description of this position to be written in paragraph form. You will need to include details about the required qualifications, and the duties and benefits of the job.

You might begin the memo like this:

```
To: Mr. John Wong, President
FROM: (your name), Personnel Manager

        Our software division is looking for four new sales-
people.We have placed an ad in the Herald describing the appli-
cants' qualifications and the duties and benefits of the job.
```

_____

_____

_____

_____

_____

_____

_____

_____

Now, imagine that you are an applicant for this job and you have just received a call from the personnel manager with the good news that you have been hired. Write a letter to a friend describing your new job. Notice that this time you are writing for a very different reason and to a very different person than you did in the first paragraph. This time you will not include the same kind of detailed information about the job. However, you should include more specific information about the company than in the previous paragraph. Remember, your friend has never heard of Compu-sales, Inc.

You might begin like this:

Dear _____
Guess what! I just got hired for a new job.

_____

_____

_____

_____

_____

_____

_____

_____

_____

You will notice that the two paragraphs that you just wrote are quite different. Think about the person to whom you were writing these paragraphs and about your reasons for writing them. In the first paragraph you were writing to your boss to describe a position that he knew something about already. In the second paragraph you were writing to a friend to describe a job that he knew nothing about. The differences in these two paragraphs are a result of having different audiences (intended readers) and different purposes for your writing. You can see that the considerations of audience and purpose are very important in the writing process. They affect to a great extent what you choose to include, what you can leave out, the tone and style of the piece, and other important aspects of writing that we will focus on later in this text. You need to think about these two aspects of writing before you actually begin composing, as you write, and when you revise what you have written. More than any other considerations, audience and purpose shape writing.

✻   ✻   ✻

In some ways this chapter has only begun to scratch the surface of information on the teaching of reading. Even more important may be the reading-writing connection, the second half of which we turn to in the next chapter.

TOPICS FOR DISCUSSION, ACTION, AND RESEARCH

1. In the discussion of the psycholinguistic guessing game (page 284) what does "data driven" mean? Give an example.

2. Think of an anecdote or joke that you could tell to your classmates, and write it down. Share copies of it with a small group of classmates. In your group, review the meaning of *content* and *formal* schemata, and then identify each type of schemata in the anecdotes of each person in the group.

3. On pages 286 and 287 many different *genres* of written language are listed. With a partner, brainstorm further genres of written language. Then, select three ESL contexts (e.g., adult, literacy level in the USA; high school EFL in Thailand; academic prep program) and decide which of the genres (already listed plus your new ones) are the most likely to be encountered in each context.

4. In small groups, choose a pair of contrasting types (from page 286) of written language and list their distinctive features, that is, what readers need to know about each. Focus especially on *formal* characteristics. Next, devise a technique that would teach the pair and demonstrate it to the rest of the class.

5. Review the meaning of skimming and scanning. What are the differences between them? What purposes does each serve? What hints would you give to a student who just doesn't seem to be able to skim a passage at all?

6. Ten reading strategies are discussed on pp. 292–296. Look at "Lesson 2" on page 302, and, with a partner, note which strategies are being encouraged in each activity. Can you think of other activities that would fill any gaps?

7. Review the discussion of semantic mapping on pages 293–294. Look at a short reading passage (supplied by your instructor) and draw a semantic map of it. Then, compare your map with a partner and talk about why you drew yours the way you did.

8. On page 294, **compensation strategies** were mentioned. What are these? Give some concrete examples. How might they be taught?

9. Look at the textbook lesson on rain forests (pp. 301 and 302). With a partner, critique it in terms of its adherence to principles of teaching interactive reading. What changes would you recommend, and why? Share your conclusions with the rest of the class.

10. Practice the following teaching activities with the sample textbook lesson beginning on page 304 ("Our Future Stock"). You may need to consider modifications for lower levels of proficiency since this is from an advanced textbook.

   (a) With a partner, discuss your connection to this subject. What do you know about it? What experience have you had with it?

   (b) Draw pictures or graphs to illustrate the story.

   (c) You are ___ (a person in the text). Tell the story from your point of view.

   (d) Choose one person, place, or object from the text. Describe it/her/him in detail.

   (e) Write a letter to one of the characters in the text.

FOR YOUR FURTHER READING

Carrell, Patricia L., and Eisterhold, Joan C. 1983. "Schema theory and ESL reading pedagogy." *TESOL Quarterly 17*(4), 553–573.

This article is of historical significance in clearly laying out the importance of background knowledge in a theory of second language reading. The relevance of schema theory, in which reading comprehension is seen as an interactive process between the text and the reader's prior knowledge, is shown through practical classroom applications.

Grabe, William. 1991. "Current developments in second language reading research." *TESOL Quarterly 25* (3), 375–406.

An excellent, comprehensive summary of a quarter century of research on reading a second language. Specific attention is given to current interactive approaches to reading and to differences between L1 and L2 reading. An exhaustive ten-page bibliography is included.

Williams, Eddie, and Moran, Chris. 1989. "Reading in a foreign language at intermediate and advanced levels with particular reference to English." *Language Teaching 22* (4), 217–228.

This is another in a series of "state of the art" summary articles published by this abstracting journal. In this article, current issues in reading pedagogy and research are very succinctly and cogently summarized.

Barnett, Marva. 1989. *More than Meets the Eye: Foreign Language Reading Theory in Practice.* Prentice Hall.

For a more complete treatment of reading research, this volume is well worth consulting. A host of research studies are summarized and analyze, pedagogical applications are provided, and issues for future research are probed.

Sage, Howard. 1987. *Incorporating Literature in ESL Instruction.* Prentice Hall.

A well-documented, positive rationale is offered for using literature in ESL classrooms. Principles and techniques are spelled out clearly for the teacher. The author addresses common objections to using literature in ESL and also makes a case for avoiding the use of simplified texts.

Chapter 17

Teaching Writing Skills

How is writing like swimming? Give up? Answer: The psycholinguist Eric Lenneberg (1967) once noted, in a discussion of "species specific" human behavior, that human beings universally learn to walk and to talk but that swimming and writing are culturally specific, learned behaviors. We learn to swim if there is a body of water available and usually only if someone teaches us. We learn to write if we are members of a literate society, and usually only if someone teaches us.

Just as there are non-swimmers, poor swimmers, and excellent swimmers, so it is for writers. Why isn't everyone an excellent writer? What is it about writing that blocks so many people, even in their own native language? Why don't people learn to write "naturally," as they learn to talk? How can we best teach second language learners of English how to write? What should we be trying to teach? Let's look at these and many other related questions as we tackle the last of the "four skills."

Research on Second Language Writing

Trends in the teaching of writing in ESL and other foreign languages have, not surprisingly, coincided with those of teaching of other skills, especially listening and speaking. You will recall from earlier chapters that as communicative language teaching gathered momentum in the 1980s, teachers learned more and more about how to teach fluency, not just accuracy, how to use authentic texts and contexts in the classroom, how to focus on the purposes of linguistic communication, and how to capitalize on learners' intrinsic motives to learn. Those same trends and the principles that undergirded them also applied to advances in the teaching of writing in second language contexts.

Three issues in this history will be highlighted for your consideration as you prepare to teach writing skills.

1. Process vs. product

A few decades ago writing teachers were mostly concerned with the final **product** of writing: the essay, the report, the story, and what that product should "look" like. Compositions were supposed to (a) meet certain standards of prescribed English rhetorical style, (b) reflect accurate grammar, and (c) be organized in conformity with what the audience would consider to be conventional. A good deal of attention was placed on "model" compositions that students would emulate and on how well a student's final product measured up against a list of criteria that included content, organization, vocabulary use, grammatical use, and mechanical considerations such as spelling and punctuation.

There is nothing inherently wrong with attention to any of the above criteria. They are still the concern of writing teachers. But in due course of time, we became better attuned to the advantage given to learners when they were seen as creators of language, when they were allowed to focus on content and message, and when their own individual intrinsic motives were put at the center of learning. We began to develop what is now termed the **process** approach to writing instruction. Process approaches do most of the following (adapted from Shih, 1986):

    (a) focus on the **process** of writing that leads to the final written product;

    (b) help student writers to understand their own composing process;

    (c) help them to build repertoires of strategies for prewriting, drafting, and rewriting;

    (d) give students time to write and rewrite;

    (e) place central importance on the process of revision;

    (f) let students discover what they want to say as they write;

(g) give students feedback throughout the composing process (not just on the final product) to consider as they attempt to bring their expression closer and closer to intention;

(h) encourage feedback both from the instructor and peers;

(i) include individual conferences between teacher and student during the process of composition.

Perhaps you can personally appreciate what it means to be asked to write something—say, a letter to an editor, an article for a newsletter, a paper for a course you're taking—and to allow the very process of putting ideas down on paper to transform thoughts into words, to sharpen your main ideas, to give them structure and coherent organization. As your first draft goes through perhaps several steps of revision, your thesis and developing ideas more and more clearly resemble something that you would consider a final product. If you have done this, you have used your own process approach to writing.

You may also know from firsthand knowledge what it is like to try to come up with a "perfect" final product without the above process. You may have experienced "writer's cramp" (mental blocks) that severely hampered any progress. You may have felt a certain level of anxiety welling up within you as you felt the pressure to write an in-class essay that would be judged by the teacher, graded, and returned with no chance in the future to revise it in any way. The process approach is an attempt to take advantage of the nature of the written code (unlike conversation, it can be planned and given an unlimited number of revisions before its "release") to give students a chance to think as they write. Another way of putting it is that writing is indeed a **thinking process**.

Peter Elbow (1973: 14–16) expressed this concept eloquently in his essay of two decades ago (he was a person well before his time!):

> **The common sense, conventional understanding of writing is as follows. Writing is a two-step process. First you figure out your meaning, then you put it into language: ...figure out what you want to say; don't start writing till you do; make a plan; use an outline; begin writing only afterward. Central to this model is the idea of keeping control, keeping things in hand. Don't let things wander into a mess.**

> **...I contend that virtually all of us carry this model of the writing process around in our heads and that it sabotages our efforts to write. ...This idea of writing is backwards. That's why it causes so much trouble. Instead of a two-step transaction of meaning-into-language, think of writing as an organic, developmental process in which you start writing at the very beginning—before you know your meaning at all—and encourage your words gradually to change and evolve. Only at the end will you know what you want to say or the words you want to say it with. You should**

expect yourself to end up somewhere different from where you started. Meaning is not what you start out with but what you end up with. Control, coherence, and knowing your mind are not what you start out with but what you end up with. Think of writing, then, not as a way to transmit a message but as a way to grow and cook a message. Writing is a way to end up thinking something you couldn't have started out thinking. Writing is, in fact, a transaction with words whereby you free yourself from what you presently think, feel, and perceive. You make available to yourself something better than what you'd be stuck with if you'd actually succeeded in making your meaning clear at the start. What looks inefficient—a rambling process with lots of writing and lots of throwing away—is really efficient since it's the best way you can work up to what you really want to say and how to say it. The real inefficiency is to beat your head against the brick wall of trying to say what you mean or trying to say it well before you are ready.

The new emphasis on process writing, however, must be seen in the perspective of a balance between process and product. As in most language teaching approaches, it is quite possible for you go to an extreme in emphasizing process to the extent that the final product diminishes in importance. Try not to let this happen! The product is, after all, the ultimate goal; it is the reason that we go through the process of prewriting, drafting, revising, and editing. Without that final product firmly in view, we could quite simply drown ourselves in a sea of revisions. Process is not the end; it is the means to the end.

2. Contrastive rhetoric

In 1966 an article was printed by Robert Kaplan that has been the subject of great debate and discussion ever since. Kaplan's thesis was that different languages (and their cultures) have different patterns of written discourse. English discourse, according to Kaplan(1966:14), was schematically described as proceeding in a straight line, Semitic writing in a zigzag formation, "Oriental" written discourse in a spiraling line, and so forth (see below).

Figure 17.1. Patterns of Written Discourse (Kaplan, 1966:14).

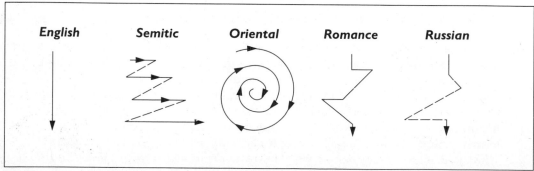

The point of his conclusions about how we write was, of course, that learners of English bring with them certain predispositions, which come from their native languages, about how to organize their writing. If English writers get "straight" to the point, and Chinese writers "spiral" around the point, then a Chinese speaker who is learning English will encounter some difficulty in learning to write English discourse.

There were serious problems with Kaplan's study. His diagrams and conclusions were simplistic and overgeneralized. Simplistic, because he based his conclusions about English discourse on style manuals rather than using data from actual writing in English. Overgeneralized, because one cannot conclude that English writers consistently use a "straight-line" attack on a thesis and certainly cannot make any generalization that applies, for example, to **all** Oriental languages. Furthermore, without a native-speaking English control group, one cannot determine if the "difficulty" of his sample data is simply the difficulty any inexperienced writer might encounter in learning to write.

Nevertheless, there was and still is a ring of truth to Kaplan's claims. No one can deny the effect of one's native culture, or one's predispositions that are the product of perhaps years of schooling, reading, writing, thinking, asserting, arguing, and defending. In our current paradigm of attending carefully to schemata and scripts, native language patterns of thinking and writing simply cannot be ruled out. A balanced position on this issue, then, would uphold the importance of your carefully attending to the rhetorical first language interference that may be at play in your students' writing. But rather than holding a dogmatic or predictive view (that certain writers **will** experience difficulty because of their native language), you would be more prudent to adopt a "weak" position (see *PLLT*, Chapter 8) in which you would consider a student's cultural/literary schemata as one possible source of difficulty.

In recent years new research studies have appeared that tackle the issue of contrastive rhetoric (see Leki, 1991). One important conclusion from this renewed wave of research is the significance of valuing students' native-language-related rhetorical traditions, and of guiding them through a process of understanding those schemata, but not attempting to eradicate them. That self-understanding on the part of students may then lend itself to a more effective appreciation and use of English rhetorical conventions.

3. Authenticity

A third issue in the teaching of writing surrounds the question of how much of our classroom writing is "real" writing. That is, how **authentic** are the classroom writing exercises that we ask students to perform? One could address this question by asking how much writing does the average, college-educated person in Western society do, and what kind of writing? I daresay very little, and that little amounts to filling out forms, writing telephone messages, and occasionally dashing off a letter or post card. In the era of electronic communication (video, phone, computer, etc.) we are less and less called upon to write. I was recently consulted by a friend of mine who is studying to be certified as a realtor. Part of his certification examination involved a simple one or two page written essay. The prospect frightened him!

So, why do we want students to write? In English for Academic Purposes (EAP), across the age-levels from elementary school through university graduate courses, we write in order to succeed in mastering the subject matter. In school, writing is a way of life. Without some ability to express yourself in writing, you don't pass the course. Academic writing ranges from short phrases (as in fill-in-the-blank tests), to brief paragraphs (as in "essay question" exercises and tests), to brief reports of many different kinds, to a full-length research paper. In vocational-technical English (where students are studying English in connection with a trade or occupation), students need to fill out forms, write simple messages, write certain conventional reports (for example, a bid on a contract, an inspection report), and at the most "creative" end of the continuum, write a brief business letter. In adult education and survival English classes, filling out simple forms and questionnaires may be as sophisticated as students' needs get. This leaves EAP as the major consumer of writing techniques, especially writing techniques that concern themselves with process, development of ideas, argument, logic, cause and effect, etc.

Another way to look at the authenticity issue in classroom writing is to distinguish between **real** writing and **display** writing. Real writing, as explained by Raimes (1991), is writing when the reader doesn't know the "answer" and genuinely wants information. In many academic/school contexts, however, if the instructor is the sole reader, writing is primarily for the "display" of a student's knowledge. Written exercises, short answer essays, and other writing in test situations are instances of display writing.

Should we as teachers incorporate more real writing in our classrooms? In some ways, yes. If ESL courses strive to be more content-based, theme-based, or task-based, students are more likely to be given the opportunity to convey genuine information on topics of intrinsic interest. But display writing is not totally unjustified by any means. Writing to display one's knowledge is a fact of life in the classroom, and by getting your students to perform well in display writing exercises, they can learn skills that will help them to succeed in further academic pursuits.

The bottom line for your teaching is that if you are to stay in line with the principles of learning and teaching already set forth in this book, and if you are to keep your teaching purposeful and intrinsically motivating, then you must discover why your students need to write, what form their writing will therefore take, and steer your techniques in the direction of those purposes and forms. Then, writing will be "real," meaningful, and communicative in the best sense of the term.

Types of Written Language

In the previous chapter, on pages 286–287, were thirty-some-odd types of written language "forms." As you consider an ESL class that you might be teaching, how many of these types of writing will your students be likely to **produce** themselves? Those types that they will indeed need, either for further study of English or for their ultimate academic/vocational goals, should then become the prime focus of "real" writing in your classroom.

Characteristics of Written Language: A Writer's View

Also in Chapter 16, some characteristics of written language, from the perspective of a reader, were set forth. Let's revisit those from a writer's viewpoint.

1. Permanence

Once something is written down and delivered in its final form to its intended audience, the writer abdicates a certain power: power to emend, to clarify, to withdraw. That prospect is the single most significant contributor to making writing a very scary operation! Student writers often feel that the act of releasing a written work to an instructor is not unlike putting yourself in front of a firing squad. Therefore, whatever you can do as a teacher and guide and facilitator to help your students to revise and refine their work before final submission will help to give them confidence in their work.

2. Production time

The good news is that, given appropriate stretches of time, a writer can indeed become a "good" writer by developing efficient processes for achieving the final product. The bad news is that many educational contexts demand student writing within time limits, or "writing for display" as noted in the previous section (examination writing, for example). So, one of your goals, especially if you are teaching in an EAP context, would be to train your students to make the best possible use of such time limitations. This may mean sacrificing some process time, but with sufficient training in process writing, combined with practice in display writing, you can help your students to deal with time limitations.

3. Distance

One of the thorniest problems writers face is anticipating their audience. That anticipation ranges from general audience characteristics to how specific words and phrases and sentences and paragraphs are going to be interpreted. The distance factor requires what I have called cognitive empathy (see *PLLT*, Chapter 6), in that good writers can "read" their own writing from the perspective of the mind of the targeted audience. Writers need to be able to predict the audience's general knowledge, cultural and literary schemata, specific subject-matter knowledge, and very importantly, how their choice of language will be interpreted.

4. Orthography

Everything from simple greetings to extremely complex ideas are captured through the manipulation of a few dozen letters and other written symbols. Sometimes we take for granted the mastering of the mechanics of English writing by our students. If students are non-literate in the native language, you must begin at the very beginning with fundamentals of reading and writing. For literate students, if their native language system is not alphabetic, new symbols have to be produced by hands that may have gotten too accustomed to another system. If the native language has a different phoneme-grapheme system (most do!), then some attention is due here.

5. Complexity

In the previous chapter, the complexity of written—as opposed to spoken—language was illustrated. Writers must learn how to remove redundancy (which may not jibe with their first language rhetorical tradition), how to combine sentences, how to make references to other elements in a text, how to create syntactic and lexical variety, and much more.

6. Vocabulary

As we noted in Chapter 16, writing places a heavier demand on vocabulary use than does speaking. Good writers will learn to take advantage of the richness of English vocabulary.

7. Formality

Whether a student is filling out a questionnaire or writing a full-blown essay, the conventions of each form must be followed. For ESL students, the most difficult and complex conventions occur in academic writing where students have to learn how to describe, explain, compare, contrast, illustrate, defend, criticize, and argue.

Microskills for Writing

Following the format from the previous three chapters, microskills for writing production can be enumerated:

1. Produce graphemes and orthographic patterns of English.
2. Produce writing at an efficient rate of speed to suit the purpose.
3. Produce an acceptable core of words and use appropriate word order patterns.
4. Use acceptable grammatical systems (e.g., tense, agreement, pluralization), patterns, and rules.
5. Express a particular meaning in different grammatical forms.
6. Use cohesive devices in written discourse.
7. Use the rhetorical forms and conventions of written discourse.
8. Appropriately accomplish the communicative functions of written texts according to form and purpose.
9. Convey links and connections between events and communicate such relations as main idea, supporting idea, new information, given information, generalization, and exemplification.
10. Distinguish between literal and implied meanings when writing.
11. Correctly convey culturally specific references in the context of the written text.
12. Develop and use a battery of writing strategies, such as accurately assessing the audience's interpretation, using pre-writing devices, writing with fluency in the first drafts, using paraphrases and synonyms, soliciting peer and instructor feedback, and using feedback for revising and editing.

Types of Classroom Writing Performance

While various genres of written texts abound, classroom writing performance is, by comparison, limited. Consider the following five major categories of classroom writing performance:

1. Imitative, or, writing down

At the beginning level of learning to write, students will simply "write down" English letters, words, and possibly sentences in order to learn the conventions of the orthographic code. Some forms of **dictation** fall into this category although dictations can serve to teach and test higher order processing as well. Dictations typically involve the following steps:

(1) Teacher reads a short paragraph once or twice at normal speed.

(2) Teacher reads the paragraph in short phrase units of three or four words each, and each unit is followed by a pause.

(3) During the pause, students write exactly what they hear.

(4) Teacher then reads the whole paragraph once more at normal speed so students can check their writing.

(5) Scoring of students' written work can utilize a number of rubrics for assigning points. Usually spelling and punctuation errors are not considered as severe as grammatical errors.

2. Intensive, or, controlled

Writing is sometimes used as a production mode for learning, reinforcing, or testing grammatical concepts. This intensive writing typically appears in controlled, written grammar exercises. This type of writing would not allow much, if any, creativity on the part of the writer.

A common form of **controlled** writing is to present a paragraph to students in which they have to alter a given structure throughout. So, for example, they may be asked to change all present tense verbs to past; in such a case, students may need to alter other time references in the paragraph.

Guided writing loosens the teacher's control but still offers a series of stimulators. For example, the teacher might get students to tell a story just viewed on a video tape by asking them a series of questions: Where does the story take place? Describe the principal character. What does he say to the woman in the car?...

Yet another form of controlled writing is a **dicto-comp**. Here, a paragraph is read at normal speed; then the teacher puts key words from the paragraph, in sequence, on the blackboard and asks students to rewrite the paragraph from the best of their recollection of the reading, using the words on the board.

3. Self-writing

A significant proportion of classroom writing may be devoted to self-writing, or writing with only the self in mind as an audience. The most salient instance of this category in classrooms is notetaking, where students take notes during a lecture for the purpose of later recall. Other notetaking may be done in the margins of books and on odd scraps of paper.

Diary or **journal** writing also falls into this category. However, in recent years more and more **dialogue journal** writing takes place, where students write thoughts, feelings, and reactions in a journal and an instructor reads and responds, in which case the journal, while ostensibly written for oneself, has two audiences.

Here is an entry from a journal written by an advanced ESL student from China. The teacher's response follows (from Vanett and Jurich, 1985).

Journal Entry:

    Yesterday at about eight o'clock I was sitting in front of my table holding a fork and eating tasteless noodles which I usually really like to eat but I lost my taste yesterday because I didn't feel well. I had a headache and a fever. My head seemed to be broken. I sometimes felt cold, sometimes hot. I didn't feel comfortable standing up and I didn't feel comfortable sitting down. I hated eveything around me. It seemed to me that I got a great pressure from the atmosphere and I could not breath. I was so sleepy since I had taken some medicine which functioned as an antibiotic.

    The room was so quiet. I was there by myself and felt very solitary. This dinner reminded me of my mother. Whenever I was sick in China, my mother always took care of me and cooked rice gruel, which has to cook more than three hours and is very delicious, I think. I would be better very soon under the care of my mother. But yesterday, I had to cook by myself even though I was sick, The more I thought, the less I wanted to eat, Half an hour passed. The noodles were cold, but I was still sitting there and thinking about my mother, Finally I threw out the noodles and went to bed.

                              Ming Ling, PRC

Teacher's Response: This is a powerful piece of writing because you really communicate what you were feeling. You used vivid details, like "…eating tasteless noodles…", "my head seemed to be broken…" and "…rice gruel, which has to cook more than three hours and is very delicious." These make it easy for the reader to picture exactly what you were going through. The other strong point about this piece is that you bring the reader full circle by beginning and ending with "the noodles."

    Being alone when you are sick is difficult. Now, I know why you were so quiet in class.

    If you want to do another entry related to this one, you could have a dialogue with your "sick" self. What would your "healthy" self say to the "sick" self? Is there some advice that could be exchanged about how to prevent illness or how to take care of yourself better when you do get sick? Start the dialogue with your "sick" self speaking first.

4. Display writing

It was already noted earlier that writing within the school curricular context is a way of life. For all language students, short answer exercises, essay examinations, and even research reports will involve an element of display. For academically bound ESL students, one of the academic skills that they need to master is a whole array of display writing techniques.

5. Real writing

While virtually every classroom writing task will have an element of display writing in it, nevertheless some classroom writing aims at the genuine communication of messages to an audience in need of those messages. The two categories of real and display writing are actually two ends of a continuum, and in between the two extremes lie some practical instances of a combination of display writing and real. Three subcategories illustrate how reality can be injected:

(a) **Academic.** The Language Experience Approach gives groups of students opportunities to convey genuine information to each other. Content-based instruction encourages the exchange of useful information, and some of this learning uses the written word. Group problem-solving tasks, especially those that relate to current issues and other personally relevant topics, may have a writing component in which information is genuinely sought and conveyed. Peer-editing work adds to what would otherwise be an audience of one (the instructor) and provides real writing opportunity. In certain ESP and EAP courses, students may exchange new information with each other and with the instructor.

(b) **Vocational/technical.** Quite a variety of real writing can take place in classes of students studying English for advancement in their occupation. Real letters can be written; genuine directions for some operation or assembly might be given; and actual forms can be filled out. These possibilities are even greater in what has come to be called "English in the Workplace" where ESL is offered within companies and corporations.

(c) **Personal.** In virtually any ESL class, diaries, letters, post cards, notes, personal messages, and other informal writing can take place, especially within the context of an interactive classroom. While certain tasks may be somewhat contrived, nevertheless the genuine exchange of information can happen.

Principles for Designing Writing Techniques

Out of all of these characteristics of the written word, along with microskills and research issues, a number of specific principles for designing writing techniques emerge.

1. Incorporate practices of "good" writers

This first guideline is sweeping. But as you contemplate devising a technique that has a writing goal in it, consider the various things that efficient writers do, and see if your technique includes some of these practices. For example, good writers:

- focus on a goal or main idea in writing
- perceptively gauge their audience
- spend some time (but not too much!) planning to write
- easily let their first ideas flow onto the paper
- follow a general organizational plan as they write
- solicit and utilize feedback on their writing
- are not wedded to certain surface structures
- revise their work willingly and efficiently
- patiently make as many revisions as needed

2. Balance process and product

In the first section of this chapter, a good deal was said about the process approach. Make sure that the application of the process principle does not detract from a careful focus on the product as well.

3. Account for cultural/literary backgrounds

Make sure that your techniques do not assume that your students know English rhetorical conventions. If there are some apparent contrasts between students' native traditions and those that you are trying to teach, try to help students to understand what it is, exactly, that they are accustomed to and then by degrees perhaps, bring them to the use of acceptable English rhetoric.

4. Connect reading and writing

Clearly, students learn to write in part by carefully observing what is already written. That is, they learn by observing, or reading, the written word. By reading and studying a variety of relevant types of text, students can gain important insights both about how they should write and about subject matter that may become the topic of their writing.

5. Provide as much authentic writing as possible

Whether writing is real writing or for display, it can still be authentic in that the purposes for writing are clear to the students, the audience is specified overtly, and that there is at least some intent to convey meaning. Writing that is shared with other students in the class is one way to add authenticity. Publishing a class newsletter, writing letters to people outside of class, writing a script for a skit or dramatic presentation, writing a resume, writing advertisements—all these can be seen as authentic writing.

6. Frame your techniques in terms of prewriting, drafting, and revising stages.

Process writing approaches tend to be framed in three stages of writing. The **prewriting** stage encourages the generation of ideas, which can happen in numerous ways:

- reading (extensively) a passage
- skimming and/or scanning a passage
- conducting some outside research
- brainstorming (see below)
- listing (in writing—individually)
- clustering (begin with a keyword, then add other words, using free association)
- discussing a topic or question
- instructor-initiated questions and probes
- freewriting (see below)

Examples of **brainstorming** and **freewriting**, from Brown, Cohen, and O'Day's (1991) *Challenges: A Process Approach to Academic English,* are given on pages 333 and 334.

Generating Ideas

• Brainstorming

Let's think about the future for a moment. Let's focus our attention on how it might affect your present or future job. Have you thought about the changes that might occur in your field? To help you think about this question, you are going to make two lists of ideas concerning changes in your field or in the field you plan to enter.

DIRECTIONS: Use your knowledge and imagination to follow these steps.

1. Prepare two sheets of paper with the following:
   a. What changes have occurred in my field in the last twenty years?
   > Your field—today's date
   b. What changes do I expect to occur in my field in the next twenty years?
   > Your field—the date twenty years from now
2. As quickly as possible, think of as many ideas as you can to answer the question on sheet a.
   a. Take between five and ten minutes to list every idea that comes to your mind.
   b. Do not evaluate your ideas. That will come later.
3. When you have written down everything you can think of, go over the list to evaluate what you have written. Cross out the ideas that don't fit.
4. Repeat this process (steps 2 and 3) for sheet b.

This process, called **brainstorming**, is a useful technique in writing because it permits you to approach a topic with an open mind. Because you do not judge your ideas as they emerge, you free yourself to come up with ideas that you might not even know you had. Brainstorming is one of several different ways to begin writing. In the following pages, we will introduce some other methods that will help you to explore ideas that you might want to write about.

• Working in a Group

In the preceding exercise you worked individually, using brainstorming to establish your own ideas, to follow your own train of thought. Another effective way to generate ideas is to work in a small group where you share your brainstormed ideas with the rest of the group members. By doing this, each of you will have an opportunity to further expand your own ideas.

DIRECTIONS: Form a small group (three to five people). Use the following guidelines for your group discussion.

1. Take turns reading your lists of changes in your field to each other.
2. Compare your classmates' lists to yours, looking for similarities and differences.
   a. Mark the changes on your list that are similar.
   b. Add to your list new ideas of changes that apply to your field.
3. As a group, select three changes that applied to the fields of each group member. If you have time, you can discuss these three ideas.
4. Choose a reporter from your group to share your three changes with the rest of the class.

Here is an example of what the compared lists of a group of three students might look like. (Notice that each list has some ideas that have been crossed out. These ideas had already been eliminated by the student in the last step of the brainstorming exercise because they did not fit.) The changes that were similar in each list have been labeled.

Teaching—Today	Sales—Today	Health Care—Today
attitudes toward teachers Ⓐ information explosion Ⓑ union activity more job security better benefits Ⓒ use of textbooks larger class size computers as teaching tools computers for record keeping Ⓓ competition for jobs greater student maturity higher diplomas	computerized inventory Ⓓ customers' bad attitudes Ⓐ distance from owners pressure meeting people incentive pay consumer action need to know more about products Ⓑ more responsibility more advancement changes fewer personnel time clocks students inceased knowledge better benefits Ⓒ	malpractice suits less respect Ⓐ hours pay educational demands pressure information increase Ⓑ consulting with others competion for clients advertising computerized business Ⓓ computerized diagnosis less paygreater benefits Ⓒ

• Freewriting

You have just begun to explore the question of changes in your field. Some of your ideas will interest you more than others. Now you will have an opportunity to develop your thinking about one of these ideas.

DIRECTIONS: Follow these steps to generate further ideas on this topic.

1. From your lists of changes, choose one idea that interested you.
2. Write that idea at the top of a clean sheet of paper.
3. For ten minutes, write about this topic without stopping. This means that you should be writing something constantly.
    a. Write down everything that comes to your mind.
    b. Do not judge your ideas.
    c. Do not worry about your spelling and grammar.
    d. If you run out of things to say, continue writing whatever comes to your mind.

This process is called **freewriting**. It is designed to help you free ideas that you might not realize that you have. An important aspect of freewriting is that you write without being concerned about spelling, punctuation, or grammar. Of course, these elements of writing are important, but students' concern about them can sometimes inhibit the free flow of their ideas. Freewriting is a technique to generate ideas; it should be used as a beginning, as an initial exploration of the ideas that you have about a topic.

You can use your freewriting to help you get started with related tasks. In fact, you might want to refer to this freewriting when you are doing other writing tasks later in this unit. Therefore, you should put this and all other freewriting that you do into a notebook that you can refer to when you are generating ideas for future assignments

The **drafting** and **revising** stages are the core of process writing. In traditional approaches to writing instruction, students either are given timed in-class compositions to write from start to finish within a class hour, or they are given a homework writing assignment. The first option gives no opportunity to students for systematic drafting, and the second assumes that if students did any drafting at all they would simply have to learn the tricks of the trade on their own. In a process approach, drafting is viewed as an important and complex set of strategies, the mastery of which takes time, patience, and trained instruction.

Several strategies and skills apply to the drafting/revising process in writing:

- getting started (adapting the freewriting technique)
- "optimal" monitoring of one's writing (without premature editing and diverted attention to wording, grammar, etc.)
- peer-editing (accepting/using classmates' comments)
- using the instructor's feedback
- "read aloud" technique (in small groups or pairs, students read their almost-final drafts to each other for a final check on errors, flow of ideas, etc.)
- proofreading

Beginning on page 336 is another sample from the student book of *Challenges* (1991:42–45), illustrating some of the above strategies, especially **peer-editing**, from the drafting and revising stages.

LESSON 3

COMPOSING ON YOUR OWN

In this unit you have read about the issues surrounding the predicted population explosion. You have also worked with important writing techniques such as showing and using facts and statistics. Let's now try to apply what you have learned to the writing process.

The First Draft

Choosing a Topic

DIRECTIONS: Choose one of the following topics to write about in a paragraph.

A. Explain the information introduced in the following bar graph.

B. In the final paragraphs of the article "The World's Urban Explosion," the author raises the question of what the effects of the population explosion might be in the future. Imagine your city, town, or village in the year 2025. Imagine that the population predictions did, in fact, come true. Place yourself in the scene, and describe what you see.

Note: Notice how different these topics are from one another. The first topic asks you to write an explanation which analyzes a graph. The second topic asks for

Figure 17.2. World Pupulation Explosion.

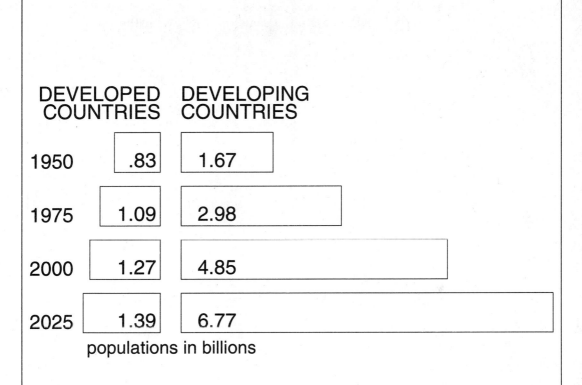

DEVELOPED COUNTRIES   DEVELOPING COUNTRIES

	DEVELOPED COUNTRIES	DEVELOPING COUNTRIES
1950	.83	1.67
1975	1.09	2.98
2000	1.27	4.85
2025	1.39	6.77

populations in billions

description. Think about the possible purposes of each topic. How do you think these purposes will affect the tone of each piece?

Generating Ideas

First, we need to find ways to unlock the hidden ideas we have in our minds. In this unit you have learned to use brainstorming, freewriting, and looping. Try these techniques in any combination that works for you. Reading also helps to generate ideas. As you write, keep in mind the information you learned about this topic in the readings.

Writing the First Draft

After exploring your ideas, put them into paragraph form, keeping in mind how showing and using facts and statistics makes writing powerful and convincing. Our task here is to discover how we can best express our ideas in the clearest manner possible so that our readers will receive the same message, with the same impact, that we intended.

Peerediting

What follows is an element of the writing process that is especially important: sharing what we have written with others, our readers, to see if we have been successful in conveying our intended meaning. This step can be a fascinating adventure. We step out of our own selves, to see what we have created through the eyes of others, to discover the impact of our words on the thoughts of our readers, so that we can then use the information to improve what we have written. We call this peerediting. Peerediting is a true sharing process. Not only do you get feedback from your classmates, but you also give feedback to them. It is a two-way street. You learn to be better writer and a better reader. In the following exercise you will work with several classmates, taking the roles of both reader and writer.

DIRECTIONS: Work with a group of four other classmates who chose to write on the same topic as you did.

1. Discuss the idea-generating techniques that you each used to write this composition.
2. Read each other's papers silently, and answer the following questions for each paper:
    a. What do you like the most about the writing?
    b. What is the main idea?
    c. Who is the audience, and what is the purpose?
    d. What convincing details does the writer use?
    e. Where could the writer add details to make the piece more convincing?
    f. What areas in the writing seem unclear?
    g. How could the writer make the piece clearer?
3. Now, for each paper, compare your notes on the questions to help the writer think of ways to improve the piece.

Revising

You have gotten feedback about your composition from several classmates. Now you can use what you learned about your writing to improve it, to make it clearer and more convincing. Writers call this step of the process revising. All good writers go through several steps of revision because they want to make their writing the best it can be. At this point they reconsider what they have written, get feedback from others, and then make changes.

Review your notes from your peerediting session. Think about the comments made by your peerreaders; in particular, comments they agreed on. If you agree with them, you can revise the piece. Remember, however, that you are the final judge as to what you want to include or eliminate in your writing.

Make corrections directly on your first draft. Do not be afraid to mark up this paper. You can scratch out unnecessary or irrelevant information, squeeze ideas that you want to add into the margin, and even cut up and repaste your paper to change the order or make additions. You might be surprised to see the revising process of professional writers. Their drafts will often be illegible to anyone but themselves!

The Second Draft

Writing the Second Draft and Proofreading

Once you have made the necessary changes in your paper, you can rewrite it legibly. As you are rewriting, you may think of more changes that you would like to make. Do not hesitate to continue revising during this step. Writing takes time and a lot of thought, so take advantage of this stage to keep improving what you have already done. After you have rewritten your paper, go over it carefully to see if the language sounds correct and if your message seems complete and understandable. Finally, submit your paper to your teacher.

Using Your Teacher's Feedback

When your paper is returned to you, spend time examining the comments your teacher made. This is a good time to compare your classmates' responses to your teacher's, taking into account the changes you made between the original draft and the revised paper. Did you improve on the parts of your original paper that your classmates encouraged you to work on? Did your teacher comment on aspects of your paper that your classmates did not comment on? Share this information with the classmates you did peerediting with. For each paper you looked at, compare the comments you made to the teacher's comments. Keep in mind the ideas you and your teacher had in common about each paper. Also, notice comments that your teacher made that you missed. This is valuable information. You'll use it the next time you write and the next time you do peerediting.

Keeping a Journal

In this unit we read about population growth, about changes that we expect to take place in the future that will affect our lives. For a moment, reflect back in time. Try to visualize a place from your distant past, any place that sticks out in your mind. Now roll the clock back up to the present. If the place looks very different in the present, you've found your journal topic. If not, start again until you come up with a scene that has changed over a period of time. When you've found this place that has changed, write about it. You can choose to describe it as it was in the past, in the present, or you can do both. You might want to write about how the changes in the place have affected you. Whatever aspect of the place you choose to write about, make sure that you have a single purpose, a central focus, and try to include detail that helps to develop that main point only. Remember that when you choose to write about something that is familiar and important to you, the task of writing is easier and more pleasurable.

7. Techniques should be as interactive as possible.

It is no doubt already apparent that a process-oriented approach to writing instruction is, by definition, interactive (as students work in pairs and groups to generate ideas and to peer-edit), as well as learner centered (with ample opportunities given to students to initiate activity and exchange ideas). Writing techniques that focus on purposes other than compositions (such as letters, forms, memos, directions, short reports) are also subject to the principles of interactive classrooms. Group collaboration, brainstorming, and critiquing are as easily and successfully a part of many writing-focused techniques. Don't buy into the myth that writing is solitary activity! Some of it is, to be sure, but a good deal of what makes a good writer can be most effectively learned within a community of learners.

8. Sensitively apply methods of responding to and correcting your students' writing.

In Chapter 15, some principles of error correction were suggested for dealing with learners' speech errors. In the case of writing, error correction must be approached in a different manner. Because writing, unlike speaking, often includes an extensive **planning** stage, error treatment can begin in the drafting and revising stages, during which time it is more appropriate to consider errors among several features of the whole process of **responding** to student writing. As a student receives responses to written work, errors—just **one** of several possible things to respond to—are rarely changed outright by the instructor; rather, they are treated through self-correction, peer-correction, and instructor-initiated comments.

As you respond to your students' writing, remember that you are there as an ally, as a guide, as a facilitator. When the final work is "turned in," you may indeed then have to assume the position of judge and evaluator (see below for some comments on evaluation), but until then, the role of consultant will be the most productive way to respond. Ideally, your responses—or at least some them—will be written **and oral** as you hold a conference, however short, with a student. Under less than ideal conditions, written comments may have to suffice.

Here are some guidelines for responding to the **first draft**:

(a) Resist the temptation to treat minor ("local") grammatical errors; major ("global") errors within relevant paragraphs—see (e) below— can at this stage be indicated, either directly (say, by underlining) or quite indirectly (for example, by a check next to the line in which an error occurs).

(b) Generally resist the temptation to rewrite a student's sentences.

(c) Comment wholistically, in terms of the clarity of the overall thesis and the general structural organization.

(d) Comment on the introductory paragraph.

(e) Comment on features that appear to be irrelevant to the topic.

(f) Question clearly inadequate word choices and awkward expression within those paragraphs/sentences that are relevant to the topic.

For the **subsequent drafts**, your responses can include all of the above except that (a) now may change its character some:

(g) Minor ("local") grammatical and mechanical (spelling, punctuation) errors should be indicated, but not corrected for the student.

(h) Comment on the specific clarity and strength of all main ideas, supporting ideas, and on argument and logic.

(i) Comment on any further word choices and expressions that may not be "awkward" but are not as clear or direct as they could be.

(j) Check cohesive devices within and across paragraphs.

(k) In academic papers, comment on documentation, citing sources, evidence, and other support.

(l) Comment on the adequacy and strength of the conclusion.

9. Clearly instruct students on the rhetorical, formal, conventions of writing.

Each type of writing has its formal properties. Don't just assume that students will pick these up by absorption. Make them explicit. A reading approach to writing is very helpful here. For academic writing, for example, some of the features of English rhetorical discourse that writers use to explain, propose solutions, debate, and argue are as follows:

- a clear statement of the thesis or topic or purpose
- use of main ideas to develop or clarify the thesis
- use of supporting ideas
- supporting by "telling:" describing
- supporting by "showing:" giving evidence, facts, statistics, etc.
- supporting by linking cause and effect
- supporting by using comparison and/or contrast

10. Make your final evaluation of student writing consistent with your overall approach.

The evaluation of writing, especially in a process-oriented classroom, is a thorny issue. If you are a guide and facilitator of students' performance in the ongoing process of developing a piece of written work, how can you also be the judge? What do you judge?

The answer to the first question—how can you be a judge and a guide at the same time—is one of the primary dilemmas of all teachers. Juggling this dual role requires wisdom and sensitivity. The key to being a judge is fairness and explicitness in **what** you take into account in your evaluation.

Six general categories are often the basis for the evaluation of student writing (adapted from J.D. Brown, 1991):

Content
- thesis statement
- related ideas
- development of ideas through personal experience, illustration, facts, opinions
- use of description, cause/effect, comparison/contrast
- consistent focus

Organization
- effectiveness of introduction
- logical sequence of ideas
- conclusion
- appropriate length

Discourse
- topic sentences
- paragraph unity
- transitions
- discourse markers
- cohesion
- rhetorical conventions
- reference
- fluency
- economy
- variation

Syntax

Vocabulary

Mechanics
- spelling
- punctuation
- citation of references (if applicable)
- neatness and appearance

You will find a bit of disagreement among the "experts" on the system of weighting each of the above categories, that is, which of the six is most important, next, and so on. However, the order in which the six are listed here at the very least emphasizes the importance of content over syntax and vocabulary, which traditionally might have had high priority.

In your evaluation of student writing, the most instructive evaluative feedback you can give is your comments, both specific and summative, regarding the student's work. The six-category list above can serve as the basis for such evaluations. If numerical scores are either pedagogically or administratively important to you, then you can establish a point scale (say, 0 to 5) for each of the above categories, and return papers with six different scores on them. By avoiding a single overall score you can help students to focus on aspects of writing to which they need to give special attention. If you still need to assign a single "grade" or score to each paper, then consider weighting the first few categories more heavily. You can thereby emphasize the content-based flavor of your evaluation. Such a weighting scale might look like this:

Content:	0 - 24
Organization:	0 - 20
Discourse:	0 - 20
Syntax:	0 - 12
Vocabulary:	0 - 12
Mechanics:	0 - 12
TOTAL	100

A key, of course, to successful evaluation is to get your students to understand that your grades, scores, and other comments are varied forms of **feedback** from which they can all benefit. The final evaluation on one composition simply creates input to the learner for the next composition.

❋   ❋   ❋

Writing instruction in a communicative, interactive language course should be deeply rooted in the twelve principles of language learning and teaching that have formed a train of thought throughout this book. As you think about each principle, you can make the connections. Automaticity, for example, is gained as students develop fluency in writing, which can best be promoted through the multiple stages of a process writing approach. Meaningful learning is paramount as you try to get your students involved in topics of interest and significance for them and in authentic writing tasks. Perhaps you can continue down the list yourself.

TOPICS FOR DISCUSSION, ACTION, AND RESEARCH

1. Explain how the **process** approach to teaching writing could become (or may have already become) yet another "bandwagon" that teachers blithely jump onto. How can you put the process approach into a perspective? What can be said for **product** oriented approaches?

2. If possible, read Kaplan (1966) in preparation for this activity. In a group, review the comments on cross-cultural differences and contrastive rhetoric (p. 322). Then, discuss the validity of Kaplan's diagrams. How do writing conventions differ between or among cultures that you are familiar with? In your group, pick one other culture to contrast English writing to, and sketch out salient differences between the two sets of rhetorical conventions. What does this say about what to teach in an ESL writing class?

3. With a partner, pick an ESL audience. Brainstorm reasons or purposes for that group to write. Talk about how you would teach toward those purposes by getting students to do as much "real" writing as possible?

4. In pairs, turn back to pages 286 and 287 and review the types of written language listed there. Pick several familiar audiences or contexts and decide which of the genres your students will actually need to *produce*. Prioritize them and share your conclusions with the rest of the class.

5. Rivers & Temperley (1978:265), listed 4 types or stages of classroom writing performance:
   (a) Writing down (learning the conventions of the code)
   (b) Writing the language (learning the potential of the code)
   (c) Production (practicing the construction of fluent expressive sentences and paragraphs)
   (d) Expressive writing (using the code for purposeful communication)

   Compare these four to the five types of written performance listed in this book (pp 327–330). Are they compatible? Combinable? Are there omissions in either list?

6. On page 331, things that "good" writers do were listed. Do you agree with the list? Can you add to the list? In what way do the other suggestions that follow implement these behaviors? Discuss your opinions, additions, and classroom implications in a small group.

7. On page 335, some specific steps for guiding students through stages of drafting and revising a composition are listed. Review those steps again. If possible, sit in on a teacher-student *conference* in which the student's essay is being discussed. Notice the interaction between student and teacher. Was the session effective? Why?

8. Carefully look through the guidelines on methods of responding to written work (pp. 340–341). With a sample first draft (supplied by your instructor), try to provide some written responses that would stimulate the writer to make some appropriate revisions. Compare your responses with a partner. Discuss differences as a whole class.

9. There are many different scales and inventories for rating/evaluating written work. The one presented here (pp. 342–343) is not exhaustive by any means. Can you think of things you would add to the inventory? Look at an actual student's composition (supplied by your instructor) and try to rate the student's performance on the basis of the taxonomy. To do so, you might want to experiment with assigning a numerical weighting scale (p. 343). Compare your "diagnosis" with a partner. How well did the scale serve its purpose?

10. If possible, observe an ESL writing class. Use the list of ten principles (pp. 331–342) for designing writing techniques to evaluate what you see. Discuss your observations in a small group.

FOR YOUR FURTHER READING

Zamel, Vivian. 1982. "Writing: The process of discovering meaning." *TESOL Quarterly 16* (2), 195–209.

> This was one of the first comprehensive overviews of the process writing approach for second language learners. Written in the early 1980s, it still stands as an effective statement of the philosophy underlying an approach which has now been revised and refined into standard practice in many institutions.

Raimes, Ann. 1991. "Out of the woods: Emerging traditions in the teaching of writing." *TESOL Quarterly 25* (3), 407–430.

> This is another in a series of comprehensive summaries carried in the twenty-fifth anniversary volume of the *TESOL Quarterly*. Raimes describes and comments on five "thorny" issues in the teaching of writing: topics for writing, "real" writing, writing in the academic arena, contrastive rhetoric, and responding to writing.

Leki, Ilona. 1991. "Twenty-five years of contrastive rhetoric: Text analysis and writing pedagogies." *TESOL Quarterly 25* (1), 123–143.

The specific issue of contrastive rhetoric is addressed here and looked at from the historical perspective of some twenty-five years of concern over differences in the way various languages and cultures define effective writing.

Kroll, Barbara (Ed.). 1990. *Second Language Writing: Research Insights for the Classroom.* Cambridge University Press.

This anthology is a gold mine of references to the teaching of writing to second language learners. Summaries of research studies are offered, practical applications are clearly spelled out, and challenges for further research are offered.

Chapter 18

Teaching Grammar and Vocabulary

The teaching of grammar and vocabulary has always been a central aspect of foreign language teaching. For centuries, in fact, the only activity of language classrooms was the study of grammar and vocabulary. The twentieth century, especially the last half, has changed all that dramatically. Now, as we speed toward the twenty-first century, language teachers are often confused by a swarm of mixed messages about the place of grammar and vocabulary in the communicative language classroom. Can we teach grammar in our CLT framework? Or should it just be somehow absorbed without direct teaching? How should we treat vocabulary? These and other questions about the "bits and pieces" of language are crucial to rounding out an interactive, communicative approach to language teaching. We'll take a look at the questions and some practical answers here. First, grammar.

The Place of Grammar

So that we know just what it is we are talking about when we use the word **grammar**, a definition is in order. Grammar is a system of rules governing the conventional arrangement and relationship of words in a sentence. In place of "words," I could, for more specificity, have said "morphemes," but for the moment just remember that the components of words (prefixes, suffixes, roots, verb and noun endings, etc.) are indeed a part of grammar. And, when we use the word grammar, we refer to sentence-level rules. Be careful not to confuse the term grammar with rules governing the relationship **among** sentences, which we refer to as **discourse** rules.

In the widely accepted definition of communicative competence which was reviewed in Chapters 2 and 5 (see also *PLLT*, Chapter 9), grammatical competence occupies a prominent position as a major component of communicative competence. **Organizational** competence is an intricate, complex array of rules, some of which govern the sentence (grammar), while others govern how we string sentences together (discourse). Without the structure that organizational constraints impose on our communicative attempts, our language would simply be chaos.

Grammatical competence is **necessary** for communication to take place, but not **sufficient** to account for all production and reception in language. As Larsen-Freeman (1991) pointed out, grammar is one of three dimensions of language that are interconnected. Grammar gives us the **form** or the structures of language themselves, but those forms are literally meaningless without a second dimension, that of **meaning/semantics**, and a third dimension, **pragmatics**. In other words, grammar tells us how to construct a sentence (word order, verb and noun systems, modifiers, phrases, clauses, etc.). Semantics tells us something about the meaning of words and strings of words—or, I should say, meanings, because there may be several. Then pragmatics tells us about which of several meanings to assign given the **context** of a sentence. Context takes into account such things as:

- who the speaker/writer is,
- who the audience is,
- where the communication takes place,
- what communication takes place before and after a sentence in question,
- implied vs. literal meanings,
- styles and registers,
- the alternative forms among which a producer can choose.

It is important to grasp the significance of the interconnectedness of all three dimensions: no one dimension is sufficient.

So, no one can tell you that grammar is irrelevant, or grammar is no longer needed in a CLT framework. No one doubts the prominence of grammar as an organizational framework within which communication operates.

To Teach or Not to Teach Grammar

The next question, then, is whether or not to teach grammar in language classes, and if so, how to teach it. Varied opinions on the question can be found in the literature on language teaching. Historically, grammar has been central. But in recent decades, a few extremists have advocated no teaching of grammar whatsoever. Reason, balance, and the experience of teachers in recent CLT tradition tell us that judicious attention to grammatical form in the **adult** classroom is not only helpful, if appropriate techniques are used, but essential to a speedy learning process. Appropriate grammar focusing techniques:

- are embedded in meaningful, communicative contexts.
- contribute positively to communicative goals.
- promote accuracy within fluent, communicative language.
- do not overwhelm students with linguistic terminology.
- are as lively and intrinsically motivating as possible.

For adults, the question is not so much whether to teach or not to teach grammar, but rather, what are the optimal conditions for overt teaching of grammar. Marianne Celce Murcia (1991) offered six easily identifiable variables that can help you to determine the role of grammar in language teaching (see Table 18.1). Notice that for each variable, the continuum runs from less to more important; however, it does not say that grammar is **un**important for any of the six variables.

Table 18.1. Variables That Determine the Importance of Grammar (Celce-Murcia, 1991:465).

	Less Important ← Focus on Form → More Important		
Learner Variables			
Age	Children	Adolescents	Adults
Proficiency level	Beginning	Intermediate	Advanced
Educational background	Preliterate no formal education	Semiliterate some formal education	Literate well educated
Instructional Variables			
Skill	Listening, reading	Speaking	Writing
Register	Informal	Consultative	Formal
Need/Use	Survival	Vocational	Professional

1. Age

Clearly, due to normal intellectual developmental variables, young children can profit from a focus on form only if the focus is very, very simple and stated or illustrated in concrete form. Adults, with their abstract intellectual capabilities, can use grammatical pointers to advance their communicative abilities.

2. Proficiency level

If too much grammar focus is forced on to beginning level learners, you run the risk of blocking the acquisition of fluency skills. At this level, grammatical focus is helpful as an occasional "zoom lens" with which we zero in on some aspect of language that is currently being practiced, but not helpful if it becomes the major focus of class work. At the advanced level, grammar is not necessarily "more important," as Celce-Murcia would suggest by her chart, but rather, it is less likely to disturb communicative fluency. It may or may not be more important, depending on the accuracy already achieved by learners.

3. Educational background

Students who are non-literate or who have no formal educational background may find it difficult to grasp the complexity of grammatical terms and explanations. Highly educated students, on the other hand, are cognitively more receptive to grammar focus and may insist on error correction to help refine their already fluent skills.

4. Language skills

Because of the permanence of writing and the demand for perfection in grammatical form in written English, grammar work may be more suitable for improving written English than for speaking, reading, and writing.

5. Register

Informal contexts often make fewer demands on a learner's grammatical accuracy. In conversation classes, for example, form may be less of an issue than in a class on formal writing.

6. Needs and goals

If learners are headed toward professional goals, they may need to stress formal accuracy more so than learners at the survival level.

These six categories should be looked on as **general** guidelines for judging the need for conscious grammatical focus in the classroom, but none of these suggestions here are absolute! For example, you can probably already think of numerous situations where it is quite important indeed to focus on form with beginners, or to get learners away from too intense a grammatical focus in a context of a formal register.

Issues About How to Teach Grammar

There is still a good deal of current debate on the particular approach that teachers should take in offering grammatical instruction. Four primary issues characterize this ongoing professional discussion:

1. Should grammar be presented inductively or deductively?

Do learners benefit from an inductive approach where various language forms are practiced but where the learners are left to discover or induce rules and generalizations on their own? Or would they be better off being given a rule/generalization by the teacher or textbook and then allowed to practice various instances of language to which the rule applies? These two approaches are often contrasted with each other when questions about grammar teaching arise.

Generally, an inductive approach is currently more in favor because

(a) it is more in keeping with natural language acquisition (where rules are absorbed subconsciously with little or no conscious focus),

(b) it conforms more easily to the concept of interlanguage development in which learners progress through possible stages of rule acquisition,

(c) it allows students to get a communicative "feel" for some aspect of language before getting possibly overwhelmed by grammatical explanations, and

(d) it builds more intrinsic motivation by allowing students to discover rules rather than being told them.

There may be occasional moments, of course, when a deductive approach—or a blend between the two—is indeed more appropriate. In practice, the distinction is not always apparent. Consider the following excerpt from a low intermediate classroom (S1 is concluding an account of a recent unpleasant airplane ride):

> **S1:** And so, you see, I tell the, eh, uh, stewardess, to bring me hot tea! Well, she doesn't!
>
> **S2:** Yes, eh, well, I am also very, eh, frustrated last week. When I, eh, travel in the airplane, I get no sleep...
>
> **T:** Okay, Kamal, before you go on, since we need to review the past tense anyway, try to use the past tense—so you want to say "I was frustrated," "I got no sleep," "I told the stewardess." Okay, class, let's look at some verbs.

The teacher then put those and a few other verbs on the board, listed their past tense forms, and had students practice them. Eventually, the teacher came back to Kamal and had him finish his story. While you might question the appropriateness of the interruption here, the point is that the teacher's focus on the past tense was deductive by virtue of the way she presented it. But it was inductive in that the focus on the past actually was triggered by students' meaningful performance.

2. Should we use grammatical explanations and technical terminology in a CLT classroom?

Our historical roots (in Grammar Translation methodology) placed a strong emphasis on grammatical explanations (in the mother tongue) and on the terminology necessary to carry out those explanations. Many foreign language learners in the United States have remarked that their first and only encounter with grammatical concepts was not in English (language arts classes) but in a foreign language class. It was there that they learned about subjects and predicates and direct objects and intransitive verbs.

In CLT classes now, the use of grammatical explanation and terminology must be approached with care. We teachers are sometimes so eager to display our hard-earned metalinguistic knowledge that we forget that our students are busy enough just getting the language itself that the added load of complex rules and terms is too much to bear. But clearly, adults can benefit from a bit of explaining from time to time. Following a few simple (but not always easily interpreted) rules of thumb will enhance any grammatical explanations you undertake:

(a) Keep your explanations brief and simple. Use the mother tongue if students cannot follow an explanation in English.

(b) Use charts and other visuals whenever possible to graphically depict grammatical relationships.

(c) Illustrate with clear, unambiguous examples.

(d) Try to account for varying cognitive styles among your students (for example, analytical learners will have an easier time picking up on grammatical explanations than will wholistic learners).

(e) Do not get yourself (and students!) tied up in knots over so-called "exceptions" to rules.

(f) If you don't know how to explain something (e.g., if a student asks you about a point of grammar and you are not sure of the rule), do not risk giving false information (that you may have to retract later, which will cause even more embarrassment); rather, tell students you will research that point and bring an answer back the next day.

3. Should grammar be taught in separate "grammar only" classes?

The collective experience of the last two decades or so of CLT practice combined with the research on the effectiveness of grammatical instruction (see Eisenstein, 1980; Long, 1983) indicates the advisability of embedding grammatical techniques into general language courses, rather than singling grammar out as a discrete "skill" and treating it in a separate course. Grammatical information, whether consciously or subconsciously learned, is an enabling system, a component of communicative competence like phonology, discourse, the lexicon, etc. Therefore, as courses help students to pursue relevant language goals, grammar is best brought into the picture as a contributor toward those goals.

In some curricula, however, certain class hours, workshops, or courses are set aside for grammar instruction. In a language teaching paradigm that stresses communicative, interactive, meaningful learning, such courses may appear to be anachronisms. However, under certain conditions, they can provide a useful function, especially for high intermediate to advanced learners, where a modicum of fluency is already in place. Those conditions are:

(a) The grammar course is explicitly integrated into the total curriculum so that students can readily relate grammatical pointers to their other work in English.

(b) The rest of the curriculum (or the bulk of students' use of language outside of the grammar class) controls the content of the grammar course, and not vice versa. That is, the grammar course "serves" (enhances) the curriculum. For example, a significant portion of the agenda for the grammar class should come from students' work in other courses.

(c) Grammar is contextualized in meaningful language use.

(d) The course is tailored as much as possible for particular individual problems students are experiencing. For example, grammar "workshops" for intermediate and advanced students are often effective ways to individualize grammar instruction. In such workshops, grammatical topics come from the students' own performance in other classes, rather than being pre-set by a curriculum or textbook.

(e) Sometimes grammar modules in a standardized test preparation course serve as helpful reviews of certain grammatical principles that may be incorporated into the test.

(f) The ultimate test of the success of such courses is in the improvement of students' performance outside of the grammar class, not in their score on discrete-point grammar tests.

Under these conditions, then, grammar assumes its logical role as one of several supporting foundation stones for communication.

4. Should teachers correct grammatical errors?

Error correction has already been treated in detail in Chapter 15. Many student errors in speech and writing performance are grammatical. Interestingly, we have no research evidence that specifically shows that overt grammatical correction by teachers in the classroom is of any consequence in improving learners' language. But we do have evidence that various other forms of **attention** to and **treatment** of grammatical errors have an impact on learners. Therefore, it is prudent for you to engage in such treatment, as long as you adhere to principles of maintaining communicative flow, of maximizing student self-correction, and of sensitively considering the affective and linguistic place the learner is in.

Grammar Techniques

Following are some sample techniques for teaching grammar, using Sandra McKay's (1985) six-fold classification:

1. Using Charts

Charts and graphs are useful devices for clarifying relationships. Consider the following chart on frequency adverbs:

EXERCISE 1

Read the paragraphs on page 98 again. Then choose the appropriate adverb of frequency.

	never	seldom	sometimes	often	usually	always
1. Keiko works hard.						✔
2. She is on time for work.						
3. She is late or sick.						
4. She is early for work.						
5. She types letters.						
6. She files.						
7. She makes copies.						
8. She makes mistakes when she types.						
9. She answers the phone politely.						
10. She is angry.						

Now say the complete sentences.

> 1. Keiko always works hard.
> 2. She is always on time for work.

3. _____   7. _____
4. _____   8. _____
5. _____   9. _____
6. _____   10. _____

Another grammatical system that lends itself well to charts is the verb system. David Cross (1991:29–30) offers the following commonly used system of depicting some verb tenses:

Introducing tenses

A visual representation can often be clearer than a verbal one to intoduce a tense. This is especially true where students do not have similar tense systems in their mother tongue. Time can be shown by a line across the board. An arrow pointing down indicates this moment now. To the left of the arrow is past time, to the right is the future. A cross indicates a single event, a row of dots denotes an action that lasted or will last for a period of time. The uses of most tenses can be shown and contrasted pictorially on such a time line, as shown in the following examples.

1 *He used to smoke* (in the past, not any more).

$$\downarrow$$

. . . .

2 *She works in the market* (did in the past and will continue in the future).

$$\downarrow$$

. . . .

3 *He is having his supper* (eating now, having started a short while ago in the past, but this will not continue for any appreciable length of time).

$$\downarrow$$

. . .

4 *He got up at six o'clock* (in the past, a single event).

$$\downarrow$$

X

5 *I've been teaching for a long time* (started in the past, still doing it today).

$$\downarrow$$

. . . .

6 *We'll travel by plane* (in the future).

_____

↓

. . .

7 *We were out walking when it started to rain* (a continuous past action interrupted by a single event).

_____

↓

. . . . . . X. . . .

8 *It's 6 o'clock now, I shall have finished by 8 o'clock* (a task started earlier and which will continue for 2 more hours).

. X

This is by no means the full range of tenses, but once you have grasped the idea you will be able to use the technique to introduce others the same way. You can also use a time scale to show concepts like *for 2 months, since April* and *from April to mid June.* This is done in the following example.

Jan.   Feb.   March.   April   May   June   July   Aug.   Sept.   Oct.   Nov.   Dec.
. . . .

2. Using objects

Objects brought into the classroom not only liven up the context but provide some kinesthetic, hands-on dimension to your teaching. To teach the possessive to beginning level students, for example, bring in a few things like:

- **a necklace**
- **a purse**
- **some glasses**

Then ask students each to put two or three of their own things on their desks. Then do something like the following three exercises from *Vistas* (Brown, 1992):

Review the vocabulary on page 10. Then talk about possessions.

This (that) is **my** handbag.
This (that) is Gina**'s** sweater.
These (those) are Oscar**'s** glasses.

backpack

notebook   pen

bracelet

jacket

earrings

necklace

handbag   ring

wallet

money

glasses   watch

Work with a group. Ask questions about things in the classroom. 🔲

A: Excuse me. Is this your *handbag*?
B: No, it's *Lucy's*. **(Yes, it is. Thank you.)**

A: Excuse me. Are these your *papers*?
B: No. They're *Pravit's*. **(Yes, they are. Thank you.)**

Listen and match the people with the things. 🔲

1. Lucy   a. glasses
2. Tony   b. English book
3. Gina   c. handbag
4. Mrs. Brennan   d. gloves
5. Lynn   e. money
6. Carlos   f. briefcase
7. Olga   g. wallet
8. Tetsuo   h. earrings

3. Using maps and other simple drawings

Maps, also mentioned earlier in Chapter 11, make for practical and simple visual aids in the classroom. Useful for jigsaw, information gap, and other interactive techniques, they can also serve to illustrate certain grammatical structures. For example, maps can stimulate learners' use of

- prepositional phrases (up the street, on the left, over the hill, etc.)
- question formation (where, how do I get to, can you tell me, is this, etc.)
- imperatives (go, walk, look out for, etc.)

McKay (1985:61) suggests using drawings of circles, squares and other familiar shapes to teach locative words:

SIMPLE DRAWINGS

With Prepositional Phrases of Location   **To Describe Locations**
                                               To Give Directions

Drawings of simple shapes can be used to provide practice in stating locations and giving directions. In order to do this, you might begin by using the following drawing, modeling the expressions which follow.

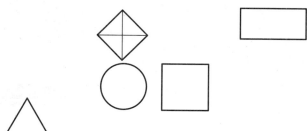

The circle is *in the corner of the paper*.
The diamond is *directly above* the circle.
The square is *to the right of* the circle
The rectangle is *in the upper right-hand corner*.
The triangle is *in the lower left-hand corner*.

After you have introduced these terms tell the students to take out a piece of paper. Give them a series of commands and have them draw these on this paper. (E.g., Draw a square in the upper left hand corner. Draw a circle inside the square.)

Later you might use this same technique to introduce more technical vocabulary of shapes along with the relative proportion (Eg., Draw a triangle in the center of the paper. Draw a circle above the triangle. The diameter of the circle should be the same length as the base of the triangle.)

---

4. Using dialogues

Dialogues are of course an age-old technique for introducing and practicing grammatical points. Consider the dialogue on page 360, with the suggestions for teachers that follow on page 361.

5. Using written texts

At the very simple, mechanical level, a text might be used to get at a certain verb tense, for example, as in the passage on page 362.

Or simply to illustrate a grammatical category as on page 363.

What are you doing next week?

Look at the picture. Then listen as you read the conversation.

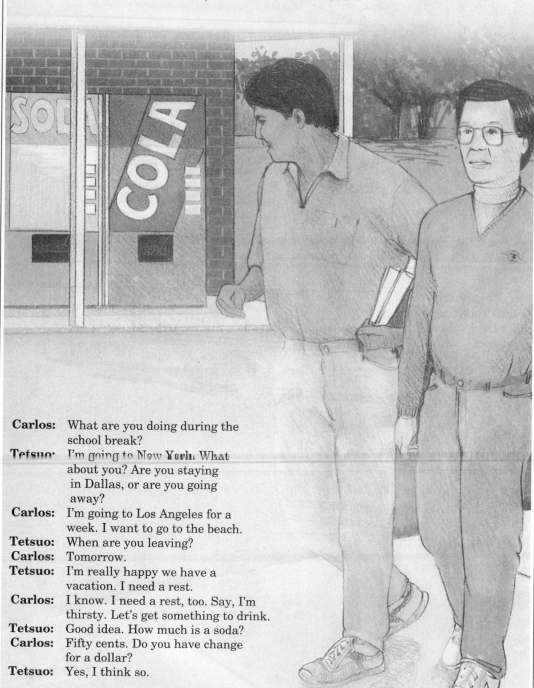

Carlos: What are you doing during the school break?

Tetsuo: I'm going to New York. What about you? Are you staying in Dallas, or are you going away?

Carlos: I'm going to Los Angeles for a week. I want to go to the beach.

Tetsuo: When are you leaving?

Carlos: Tomorrow.

Tetsuo: I'm really happy we have a vacation. I need a rest.

Carlos: I know. I need a rest, too. Say, I'm thirsty. Let's get something to drink.

Tetsuo: Good idea. How much is a soda?

Carlos: Fifty cents. Do you have change for a dollar?

Tetsuo: Yes, I think so.

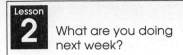

Preparing the students

A. Introduce future time expressions and the future with the present continuous tense. On the board, write the following sentence. Underline *is* and *-ing*:

Mark <u>is</u> driv<u>ing</u> to Colorado tomorrow.

Tell the students that you want them to help you continue to write a story about Mark. Write another sentence on the board:

He's leaving early in the morning, and he's taking a friend with him.

Now have the class suggest other lines for the story. Write them on the board. Finally, call on students to underline all the examples of the present continuous tense.

B. Review the word *let's* used in making suggestions or invitations. Have the students perform actions which you suggest. For example, with appropriate gestures, say "Let's stand up and stretch." (The students stand up and stretch.) Make several other suggestions and have the class carry out the actions. Be sure that you participate.

Presentation: Conversation

A. Have the students look at the picture. Establish the context—Carlos and Tetsuo are talking about a school break. Read the conversation or play the cassette. Have the students listen as they read along silently in their books.

B. Answer any questions students have about vocabulary or structures. Introduce or review the words *during, break, stay, go away, beach, vacation*, and *rest*. Then have the students close their books. Ask them questions about the conversation. For example:

Do Carlos and Tetsuo have a break soon?
Are they both staying in Dallas?
Where are they going?
Why's Carlos going to Los Angeles?
When's he leaving?
Do they think they need a rest?
Are they both going to drink a soda?
How much does a soda cost?

C. In pairs, have the students practice the conversation. Encourage them to use their own ideas by changing the names of places, times, and activities. Call on several pairs to present their conversations to the class.

What does Lucy do every day? What is she doing now'? Choose the correct form of the verb.

"Lucy Mendoza is a nurse. She is never bored because she is always busy. She usually (**1.** works/is working) in a hospital, but sometimes she (**2.** works/is working) in a special home for old people. Lucy (**3.** enjoys/is enjoying) her work every day, and she never (takes/is taking) a day off. She is always happy. She is never sad. Today she (**4.** doesn't work/isn't working) in the hospital. She (**5.** works/is working) in the home for old people. Right now she (**6.** talks/is talking) to a woman. The woman is very lonely because her children never (**7.** visit/are visiting)."

> **What about you?**
> What do you usually do every day?
> What are you doing right now?

Keiko always works hard.

Look at the picture. Then listen as you read the paragraphs.

Keiko is a secretary. She enjoys her work, and she always works hard. She is always on time for work. In fact, she is often early. She is never late, and she is never sick.

Keiko usually types letters and answers the telephone. She sometimes files and makes copies. She seldom makes mistakes when she types or files. She always answers the phone politely.

Keiko is intelligent, and she has a good sense of humor. She is never angry. Everybody in the office likes Keiko.

Grammar Sequencing in Textbooks and Curricula

Grammatical sequencing received a great deal of attention in the 1950s and '60s as curricula and textbooks were organized around grammatical categories. Some language professionals were of the opinion that difficulty could be predicted (especially if the native language is taken into consideration) and that therefore grammar in a curriculum should be sequenced in a progression of easier to more difficult items. No one had been able to empirically verify such hierarchies of difficulty when the debate over grammatical sequencing whimpered to a halt as situational and notional-functional curricula assumed popularity. At that point the question shifted more to whether or not there was an optimal functional sequence!

In recent years, we have witnessed a return to a more balanced viewpoint in which grammar is seen as one of several organizational aspects of communicative competence, all of which should be considered in programming a textbook or a curriculum. In this perspective, the question of an optimal sequence of grammatical structures is not irrelevant, but with our current disciplinary maturity, we seem to agree that:

- Grammatical categories are one of several considerations in curricular sequencing.
- There is a logical sequence of basic grammatical structures that would be prudent to follow (for example, introduce the past perfect tense after the past tense, relative clauses after question formation) that is more a factor of frequency and usefulness than of some abstract concept of linguistic difficulty.
- Beyond those basic structures, a few permutations here and there will make little difference in the eventual success of students, as long as language is being learned in the context of a communicative (content-based, task-based, interactive) curriculum.

In Chapter 7 (pp. 107–110) the sequence of grammatical **and** communication skills of the *Vistas* series was given. Please turn back to those pages to refresh your memory. This "scope and sequence" chart is illustrative of a typical sequence of grammatical structures in a basal ESL series. An attempt has been made to use the principles of simplicity and frequency in arranging the order of structures. Therefore, the more "complex" tenses and clause formations come later in the series. While one could quibble with certain elements and suggest alternative permutations, nevertheless learners' success in a course like this seems to be more a factor of (a) clear, unambiguous presentation of material, and (b) opportunity for meaningful, interactive practice, than a factor of a grammar point presented a week earlier or later.

A "Word" About Vocabulary Teaching

Some attention has already been given in this book to vocabulary learning under other topics in previous chapters: Reading (Chapter 16), Speaking (15), Strategies (12), and others. At this time, then, let me just offer a "word" or two of commentary about these lexical units of our language.

In the days when grammar was the major center of attention in language classes, vocabulary was also the focus of drills, exercises, and memorization efforts. Then, as grammar fell into some disfavor a few decades ago, vocabulary instruction tended to go with it. Currently, in our attention to communicative classrooms that are directed toward content, tasks, or interaction, we are once again giving vocabulary the attention it deserves. But this attention now comes from quite a different perspective: rather than viewing vocabulary items as a long and boring list of words, vocabulary is seen in its central role in contextualized, meaningful language. Below are some guidelines for the communicative treatment of vocabulary instruction.

1. Allocate specific class time to vocabulary learning.

In the hustle and bustle of our interactive classrooms, sometimes we get so caught up in lively group work and meaningful communication that we don't pause to devote some attention to words. After all, words are basic building blocks of language; in fact, survival level communication can take place quite intelligibly when people simply string words together — without any grammatical rules applying at all! So, if we're interested in being communicative, words are among the first orders of business.

2. Help students to learn vocabulary in context.

The best internalization of vocabulary comes from encounters (comprehension or production) with words within the context of surrounding discourse. Rather than isolating words and/or focusing on dictionary definitions, attend to vocabulary within a communicative framework in which items appear. Students will then associate new words with a meaningful context to which they apply.

3. Play down the role of bilingual dictionaries.

A corollary to the above is to help students to resist the temptation to overuse their bilingual dictionaries. In recent years, with the common availability of electronic pocket dictionaries, students are even more easily tempted to punch in a word they don't know and get an instant response.

Unfortunately, such practices rarely help students to internalize the word for later recall and use.

4. Encourage students to develop strategies for determining the meaning of words.

Included in the discussion of learning strategies in Chapter 12 are references to learning words. A number of "clues" are available to learners to develop "word attack" strategies. Kruse (1987:315–316) offers a detailed taxonomy of such strategies with examples (pp. 367–368).

A PROGRAM FOR TEACHING VOCABULARY DEVELOPMENT SKILLS

1. *Goals*
   a To improve the reading vocabulary skills of ESL students.
   b. To teach ESL students word-building skills.
   c. To teach ESL students to guess word meanings from context clues.

2. *Word building*
   a. *Suffixes:* It may be a good idea simply to give a list of these to the student for memorization. Roots used for this section should be familiar.
      (1) Practice in suffix recognition, i.e., simple exercises in isolation of suffixes:

      go(od)*ness*   famili (ar) (ly)

      (2) Lesson and practice in noting grammatical changes effected by suffixes. Word tables might be very useful here.

      Adj. (good)+ness=N (goodness)
      Adj. (gloomy)+ly=Adv. (gloomily)

      (3) Practice in word *formation* through exercises in which the student adds and subtracts suffixes. Again the word table is useful. The student fills in the appropriate forms of a word by manipulating suffixes. It is of great importance to group words by the way they form variations so that all words being studied at one time add the same suffixes in the same manner and regularity of change can be emphasized.
   b. *Prefixes* These are more varied and less regular and therefore should not be presented until after suffixes have been mastered. A list of these can also be memorized.
      (1) Practice in prefix recognition.
      (2) Lesson and practice in meaning changes resulting from the use of prefixes, e.g., *in + formal* = not formal=casual. This is fairly difficult. The examples used should be straightforward in the early stages. Here again, the groupings must be of words that add the same prefixes in the same manner to achieve the same type of meaning. Groupings like UN in *untie* and UN in *unfair* must be avoided. As these are mastered, more difficult items requiring progressively higher degrees of interpretation may be introduced.
      (3) Practice in word formation:
         (a) Addition of prefixes. These exercises should progress in difficulty. E.g., Make a word meaning "not natural" (*unnatural*).
         (b) Addition of prefixes and suffixes.
   c. *Roots*. These are quite difficult, and should not be taught at all unless the student is fairly advanced and flexible in his approach to word forms. For a good list of Latin and Greek roots, refer to Dechant (1970, Ch. 12).
      (I) Recognizing roots. Isolation of root forms.
      (2) Effect of prefixes and suffixes on root forms.

3. *Definition clues*
   a. *Parentheses and footnotes* X (Y); X* $_y$
      (1) A lesson would first be given on these two types of clues stressing their physical structure and how to read them correctly.
      (2) Practice in recognizing these clues. E.g. Draw a line under the words in parentheses: *The panther* (<u>a large black animal related to a cat</u>) *is very dangerous and deadly.*
      (3) Practice in using the clue. Here exercises of the following sort are useful: *The principal* (main) *reason for wearing clothes is to keep warm.* What is the meaning of *principal* in the sentence?

b. *Synonyms and antonyms.* Most students have studied and enjoy learning words with similar and opposite meanings. The task is to get them to recognize the definitional role these often play.

(1) X *is* Y; X, *that is*, Y. Students can be taught that an unfamiliar word is often defined in a sentence using the copula *be* and a synonym.

  (a) Clue recognitions, both of signal words and synonyms. E.g. Underline the signal word <u>is</u> or, <u>that is</u>: *A birthday party is an obser-vance,* <u>that is</u> *a remembrance of someone's day of birth.*

  (b) Practice in using the clue. Again exercises in producing or recognizing a synonym are useful.

(2) X—Y—; X, *which* is Y; X. *or* Y; X, Y. Appositival constructions. This can be approached in essentially the same manner as the *is* and *that is* clues were.

4. *Inference clues*

These types of clues require a higher level of analytical skill and practice than previous types dealt with. They should be approached slowly, moving from obvious answers to increasingly vague exercises. The ESL student should never be expected to do the same kind of inferring that a native speaker could do, but should be encouraged to go as far as possible as long as the guessing is not allowed to become wild. For all three types of clues (example, summary, and experience) the same method of practice in (i) recognition of clue elements and (ii) obtaining meaning from the elements, can be followed.

a. *Example:*

(1) Specific clues: X, *e.g.* Y; X, *ie.* Y; X, *for example,* Y

E.g. *Iran is trying to* <u>restore</u> *many of its ancient monuments. Persepolis for example, is being partly rebuilt by a group of Italian experts.*

(2) No physical clue.

E.g. *Roberta Flack, Aretha Franklin, and Olivia Newton-John are popular female* <u>vocalists.</u>

b. *Summary:*

(1) Restatement

  (a) With a physical clue: . . . X. This Y . . .; . . . X. X is Y.

E.g. *Many products are sold to stop* <u>perspiration</u>. *This wetness that comes from your body whenever you are too warm, work very hard, or are afraid, usually doesn't smell very good.*

  (b) Without physical clue.

Either: The same meaning. X, Y. Eg. *He's a really good* <u>athlete</u>. *He plays sports well.*

Or: Opposite meaning. X. (neg) Y. E.g. *He's* <u>bound</u> *to win. He can 't lose.*

(2) Information. E.g. *The* <u>forsythia</u> *was covered with the golden flowers that bloom early in the spring.*

c. *Experience:* The reader must decide from his own experiences what is probably meant by a word. E.g. *The old dog* <u>snuffled</u> *and* <u>moped</u> *as he slowly walked from the room.*

5. Engage in "unplanned" vocabulary teaching.

In all likelihood, most of the attention you give to vocabulary learning will be unplanned: those moments when a student asks about a word or when a word has appeared that you feel deserves some attention. These impromptu moments are very important. Sometimes, they are simply brief little pointers; for example, the word "clumsy" once appeared in a paragraph students were reading and the teacher volunteered:

> T: Okay, "clumsy." Does anyone know what that means? [writes the word on the board]
>
> Ss: [silence]
>
> T: No one? Okay, well, take a look at the sentence it's in. "His clumsy efforts to imitate a dancer were almost amusing." Now, was Bernard a good dancer? [Mona raises her hand.] Okay, Mona?
>
> S1: Well, no. He was a very bad dancer, as we see in the next sentence.
>
> T: Excellent! So, what do you think "clumsy" might mean?
>
> S2: Not graceful.
>
> T: Good, what else? Anyone?
>
> S3: Uncoordinated?
>
> T: Great! Okay, so "clumsy" means awkward, ungraceful, uncoordinated. [writes synonyms on the board] Is that clear now?
>
> Ss: [most Ss nod in agreement]

Sometimes, such impromptu moments may be extended: the teacher gives several examples, and/or encourages students to use the word in other sentences. Make sure that such unplanned teaching, however, does not detract from the central focus of activity by going on and on, ad nauseam.

Unfortunately, professional pendulums have a disturbing way of swinging too far one way or the other, and sometimes the only way we can get enough perspective to see these overly long arcs is through hindsight. Hindsight has now taught us that there was some overreaction to the almost exclusive attention that grammar and vocabulary received in the first two thirds of the twentieth century. So-called "natural" approaches in which grammar was considered damaging were overreactive. Advocating the "absorption" of grammar and vocabulary with **no** overt attention whatsoeve to language forms went too far. We now seem to have a healthy respect for the place of grammar and vocabulary, as basic "bits and pieces" of a language, in an interactive curriculum. And now we can pursue the business of finding better and better techniques for getting these bits and pieces into the communicative repertoires of our learners.

TOPICS FOR DISCUSSION, ACTION, AND RESEARCH

1. Sometimes grammatical knowledge isn't sufficient to understand "hidden" or implied meanings of what people say or write. Look at the following:

    (a) "Oh! That's just great!"

    (b) "Good to see you again, Helen. You've lost some weight, haven't you?"

    (c) "Brrrr! It's sure cold in this house."

    The "surface" grammatical meaning differs from potential "deep" structure meanings. What are those meanings? Can you think of other examples? In pairs, devise a few techniques that could be used to teach such **pragmatic** aspects of English, and share your ideas with the rest of the class.

2. Observe a class in which the teacher uses some grammar-focusing techniques. Evaluate their effectiveness using the five criteria on page 349. Share your observations with a group or the whole class.

3. Review the six guidelines proposed by Celce-Murcia for determining when to use grammar-focusing techniques in the classroom (p. 349). Do you agree with all six points? If you take exception to any, explain why. For example, non-literate students might profit greatly from a certain focus on grammar; does this invalidate point #3?

4. In a small group, try to come up with examples of a **deductive** approach to a grammar point and describe students for which such an approach is justified. Observe a class and note the extent to which deductive or inductive approaches are taken, and why.

5. On page 351, an example of a teacher's intervention is given. Was the teacher's interruption warranted? Would such an interruption be appropriate in all ESL contexts?

6. On page 353 some reasons are offered that justify separate grammar classes. Do you agree with all the reasons? Do you know of any institutions that offer such courses? Do they follow all the criteria listed here? If not, do you have any suggestions for improving the situation?

7. Review the section on error correction in Chapter 15 (pp. 262–265) Observe a class and try to determine if all the principles of error correction were followed. How, specifically, did the teacher treat grammatical (as opposed to vocabulary, pronunciation, etc.) errors?

8. A number of grammar focusing techniques are illustrated at the end of the chapter. Pick one or two to peer teach in your class. You might wish to work in pairs. When others are peer teaching, take note of what you think worked especially well and discuss why.

9. Look back at the grammar sequence chart in Chapter 7 (pp. 107–110). Are all the grammatical items in an appropriate sequence? Which items could be placed significantly earlier or later in the course without posing undue difficulty for the students?

10. Review sections of Chapters 12, 15, and 16 that deal with vocabulary acquisition. Refer to Kruse's taxonomy (p. 367–368) and, with a partner, figure our what word-attack skills are appropriate for a context with which you are familiar.

FOR YOUR FURTHER READING

Celce-Murcia, Marianne. 1991. "Grammar pedagogy in second and foreign language teaching." *TESOL Quarterly 25*(3), 459–480.

In the series of "state of the art" articles published in the twenty-fifth anniversary volume of the TESOL Quarterly, Celce-Murcia offers some perspective on current issues and challenges concerning the role of grammar in communicative language teaching.

Terrell, Tracy D. 1991. "The role of grammar instruction in a communicative approach." *Modern Language Journal 75*(1), 52–63.

Terrell, once a strong proponent of Krashen's "restricted" role of explicit grammar instruction, here, in somewhat of an about-face, demonstrates the utility of grammar instruction as advance organizers and as a meaning-form focus in communicative activities. Practical classroom illustrations are offered.

McKay, Sandra. 1985. *Teaching Grammar: Form, Function, and Technique*. Pergamon Press (Prentice Hall).

This very practical handbook for teachers brings together classroom proven techniques for teaching grammatical structures. Techniques are designed to give some attention both to form and to function.

Ur, Penny. 1988. *Grammar Practice Activities: A Practical Guide for Teachers*. Cambridge University Press.

Celce-Murcia, Marianne, and Hilles, Sharon. 1988. *Techniques and Resources in Teaching Grammar*. Oxford University Press.

Both of these practical teacher's resource books demonstrate how to combine grammar teaching with a communicative approach. These collections of dozens of lively and motivating techniques are both enhanced by the specification of general guidelines for effective teaching toward grammatical points.

Taylor, Linda. 1990. *Teaching and Learning Vocabulary.* Prentice Hall.

Allen, Virginia French. 1983. *Techniques in Teaching Vocabulary.* Oxford University Press.

These two handbooks are collections of numerous techniques for teaching vocabulary. And both give the teacher some background on the place of vocabulary teaching within communicative frameworks.

Chapter 19

Creating Interactive, Intrinsically Motivating Tests

Tests are a way of life in the educational world. In every learning experience there comes a time to pause and take stock, to put our focal processes to their best use and to demonstrate—either to self or others—accumulated skills or knowledge. Tests can serve positive, intrinsically motivating aims as they spur you to muster all of your abilities for a particular performance and then provide feedback on your progress toward goals.

Unfortunately, tests have gotten a bad rap in recent years. And not without reason. More often than not, tests are seen by learners as dark clouds hanging over their heads, upsetting them with thunderous anxiety as they anticipate the lightning bolts of questions they don't know, and worst of all, a flood of disappointment if they don't make the grade. Students tend to feel "prodded, jostled, or dragged by an establishment bent on spoiling what might otherwise be a pleasant student life." (Mueller, 1987:124)

So that this chapter doesn't just become a theoretical exercise for you, before reading on, take one minute (time yourself!) and without consulting a dictionary, try to respond to the test on the next page. Circle the correct meaning for each word.

1. **KREUZER**
   a. A German maker of cheeses
   b. German pastry made in the shape of a cross
   c. Scandinavian word for a ship's navigator
   d. a small coin of low value formerly in currency in Austria and Germany

2. **KWACHA**
   a. the basic monetary unit of Zambia equal to 100 ngwee
   b. any of a number of tropical diseases resulting in acute anemia, swelling of the lower intestinal tract, and engorged glands
   c. South African rhythmic dance to accompany flutes and bongos
   d. a nut of the betelnut family found in the lowlands of Peru and Bolivia; the hull is used in the dying of cloth and the meat is an edible protein

3. **MEALIE**
   a. a microscopic organism that enhances the excretory process of mucous membranes
   b. burrowing animal of the rodent family usually found in tropical regions
   c. in Appalachian dialect, a derogatory term for someone who eats too much
   d. South African word for an ear of corn

4. **PROPTOSIS**
   a. forward displacement of an organ, such as an eyeball
   b. a trigonometric function denoting the tendency of certain hyperbolic curves to reach a state of linearity
   c. in dream analysis, the underlying factor in the individual's world view that gives credence to the majority of dream subjects
   d. a systematic disease of the roots of various coniferous trees found mainly in North America

5. **LATICIFEROUS**
   a. pertaining to plants predisposed to climb fences or walls
   b. secreting or exuding latex
   c. pertaining to animals lacking in climbing ability
   d. trees which grow parallel to the ground

6. **QUADROON**
   a. a small featherless bird usually found in swampy areas
   b. a person having one quarter Negro ancestry
   c. four sailing ships in tandem
   d. old English gold coin worth one quarter of a pound

Now, how did that make you feel? It probably didn't puff you up with pride. Well, that's the way many learners feel when they take today's typical standardized, timed, multiple choice, tricky, artificial tests. Oh, you want to know the answers? Ah, in six weeks, we will mail you... Okay, just because you're so special, you get the answers right away: 1-d, 2-a, 3-d, 4-a, 5-b, 6-b. If you got more than two of these right, you have exceeded the average!

Can tests be positive experiences? Can they build a person's confidence? Can they be part of an ongoing dialogue between teacher and learners? Can they bring out the best in students? The answer is a resounding YES! But creating tests that are constructive instruments of feedback takes some care and effort on your part. Let's look at how your tests might become more intrinsically motivating and **interactive**.[1]

Testing and Teaching

First, it is important to understand what the difference is between testing and teaching. In some ways the two are so interwoven and interdependent that it is difficult to tease them apart. Every instructional sequence, if it is of any worth at all, has a testing component to it, whether the tests themselves are formal or informal. That is, teachers measure or judge learners' competence all the time and, ideally, learners measure and judge themselves. Whenever a student responds to a question or tries out a new word or structure, you might be testing that student. Written work is a test. Oral work is a test. Reading and writing performance are tests. How, then, are testing and teaching different?

The difference lies in what we'll call formal and informal testing. The above examples referred to **informal** testing: unplanned assessments that are made as a course moves along toward its goals. Most informal testing is what testing experts call **formative** evaluation: assessing students in the process of "forming" their competencies and skills with the goal of helping them to continue that growth process. Our success as teachers is greatly dependent on this constant informal assessment for it tells us how well learners are progressing toward goals and what the next step in the learning process might be. **Formal** tests are exercises or experiences specifically designed to tap into an extensive storehouse of skills and knowledge, usually within a relatively

---

[1] You may be anticipating a "complete" treatment of language testing in this chapter. Unfortunately, the field is so large with so many complex issues, both theoretical and practical, that one chapter in a textbook on teaching methodology cannot possibly treat everything you need to know about testing. For such a treatment, I recommend that you consult books like:

Hughes, Arthur. 1989. *Testing for Language Teachers*. Cambridge University Press.

Weir, Cyril J. 1990. *Communicative Language Testing*. Prentice Hall.

I also strongly recommend that you read Chapter 11 of *PLLT* for information and terminology on language testing.

short time limit. They are systematic, planned sampling techniques constructed to give teacher and student an appraisal, as it were, of their achievement. Such tests are often **summative**, as they occur at the end of a unit, module, or course, and therefore attempt to measure, or summarize, what a student has grasped.

Pedagogically, it is very important for you to make the distinction between teaching and formal testing, especially from the point of view of principles of intrinsic motivation. For optimal learning to take place, students must have the freedom in the classroom to experiment, to try things out, to "test" their **own** hypotheses about language **without** feeling that their overall competence is being "judged" in terms of these trials and errors. In the same way that, say, tournament tennis players must have the freedom to practice their skills—with no implications for their final placement—before the tournament itself begins, so also must your learners have ample opportunities to "play" with language in your classroom without being formally graded.

Teaching, then, sets up the practice games of language learning, the opportunities for learners to listen and think and take risks and set goals and process feedback and cycle and recycle through whatever it is that they are trying to set in place. While we cannot escape from the informal testing that naturally ensues while we teach, formal testing places a different set of expectations on students. Formal tests are the tournament games, or the "recitals," that periodically occur in the learning process.

Signs of Hope in Language Testing

For many of us, tests conjure up images of people walking into a classroom with jangled nerves and fingernails already chewed to the quick, sitting hunched over a test booklet and score sheet for too short a time while a clock ticks away ominously, their minds suddenly as empty as the vastness of space, vainly attempting to "multiple guess" their way through the ordeal. In many cases these images are the reality. But there is good news. There are signs of hope in our educational testing mentality.

1. New views on intelligence

Intelligence was once viewed strictly as the ability to perform (a) linguistic and (b) logical-mathematical problem solving. This "IQ" concept of intelligence has permeated the Western world and its way of testing. Since "smartness" in general is measured by timed, discrete point tests consisting of hundreds of little items, then why shouldn't every field of study be so measured? So, today we live in a world of standardized, norm-referenced tests that are:

- timed
- multiple choice
- tricky
- long
- artificial

However, new research on intelligence by psychologists like Howard Gardner and Robert Sternberg are turning the psychometric world upside down. Gardner (1983), for example, extends the traditional view of intelligence to **seven** different components (For a summary of Gardner's theory of intelligence, see *PLLT*, Chapter 4.). He accepts the traditional conceptualizations of intelligence on which standardized IQ (Intelligence Quotient) tests are based, that is:

(1) linguistic intelligence

(2) logical-mathematical intelligence

But he adds five other "frames of mind" to round out his theory of intelligence:

(3) spatial intelligence (the ability to find your way around an environment, to form mental images of reality)

(4) musical intelligence (the ability to perceive and create pitch and rhythmic patterns)

(5) bodily-kinesthetic intelligence (fine motor movement, athletic prowess)

(6) interpersonal intelligence (the ability to understand others, how they feel, and to interact effectively with them)

(7) intrapersonal intelligence (the ability to understand oneself and to develop a sense of self-identity)

Robert Sternberg (1988) is also charting new territory in intelligence research in recognizing people's **creative** thinking and **manipulative** strategies as part of intelligence. All "smart" people aren't necessarily adept at fast, reactive thinking. They may be very innovative in being able to think beyond the normal limits imposed by existing tests, and may need a good deal of processing time to enact this creativity. And other forms of smartness are found in those who know how to manipulate their environment, especially people in their environment. Debaters, politicians, successful salespersons, "smooth" talkers, and con artists are all smart in their own manipulative way.

These new conceptualizations of intelligence give us both freedom and responsibility in our testing agenda. We are free from **only** using timed, discrete point, analytical tests in measuring language. We are liberated from the tyranny of "objectivity" and its accompanying impersonalness. But we are responsible for **also** tapping into whole language skills, learning processes, and the ability to negotiate meaning. We must therefore test interpersonal, creative, communicative, interactive skills, and in doing so place some trust in our subjectivity, our intuition.

2. Performance-based testing

Tests that tackle the latter responsibility are beginning to be developed in educational settings around the world. Instead of just offering paper-and-pencil single-answer tests of possibly hundreds of discrete items, performance-based testing of typical school subjects involves:

- open-ended problems
- hands-on projects
- student portfolios
- experiments
- labs
- essay writing
- group projects

To be sure, such testing is time consuming and therefore expensive, but the losses in practicality are made up for in higher validity. Students are tested as they actually **perform** the behavior itself. In technical terms (see *PLLT*, Chapter 11), higher **content** validity is achieved as learners are measured in the process of performing the criterion behavior.

In the ESL context, performance-based testing means that you may have a difficult time distinguishing between formal and informal testing. If you do a little less setting aside of formally structured times labeled as "tests" and a little more formative evaluation during students' performance of various tasks, you will be taking some steps toward meeting some of the goals of performance-based testing.

3. Interactive language tests

The language version of performance-based testing comes in the form of various interactive language tests. Such tests are constructed in the spirit of Gardner's and Sternberg's theories of intelligence as students are assessed in the process of creatively interacting with people. This means that tests have to involve people in actually performing the behavior that we want to measure. Paper and pencil multiple choice tests certainly do not involve test takers in speaking, requesting, responding, interacting, and in combining listening and speaking, or reading and writing. Interactive testing involves them in all of the above rather than relying on the assumption that a good paper and pencil test taker is a good overall language performer.

What you are being asked to do is to "take the audacious step of making testing truly interactive: ...a lively exchange of stimulating ideas, opinions, impressions, reactions, positions or attitudes. Students can be actively involved and interested participants when their task is not restricted to providing the one and only correct answer." (Mueller, 1987:124)

Consider the example of the functional dialogue tests described by Wesche (1983) and summarized in *PLLT*, Chapter 11. This test puts students into imaginary situations in which they play an assigned role and are asked to accomplish certain functions like asking for information, persuading, etc. Within a set of themes (personal life, daily schedules, holidays, etc.) specific speech acts (greeting, introducing, thanking, departing, etc.) have to be carried out. The test requires one examiner for each student, so it takes a good deal of time for a classroom teacher to administer it to each student separately, but surely this is the direction we must move in.

Merrill Swain (1990) has been developing a test battery that includes a paper and pencil multiple-choice format as **one** component of the three part test; the other two parts measure oral communication skills and written proficiency. Each of these parts is subdivided into grammatical, discourse, and

Table 19.1. Operationalization of Traits in Second Language Proficiency.
     (Swain, 1990:403).

Trait Method	GRAMMAR focus on grammatical accuracy within sentences	DISCOURSE focus on textual cohesion and coherence	SOCIOLINGUISTIC focus on social appropriateness of language use
ORAL	*structured interview* scored for accuracy of verbal morphology, prepositions, syntax	*story telling and* *argumentation/suasion* detailed rating for e.g. identification, logical sequence, time orientation, and global ratings for coherence	*role-play of speech acts:* *requests,offers, complaints* scored for ability to distinguish formal and informal register
MULTIPLE CHOICE	*sentence-level 'select* *the correct form'* *exercise* (45 items) involving verb morphology, prepositions, and other items	*paragraph-level 'select the* *coherent sentence' exercise* (29 items)	*speech act-level 'select* *the appropriate utterance'* *exercise* (28 items)
WRITTEN COMPOSITION	*narrative and letter* *of suasion* scored for accuracy of verb morphology, prepositions, syntax	*narrative and letter* *of suasion* detailed ratings much as for oral discourse, and global rating for coherence	*formal request letter* *and informal note* scored for the ability to distinguish formal and informal register

sociolinguistic skills. Table 19.1 describes the 3 X 3 design of the test. Of course, for a classroom teacher, and even more so for large test administrations, this format takes time to administer because of the individualization involved, but time well invested in the interactive process that we profess to be teaching.

For many years the ILR/FSI oral interview (see Chapter 10, *PLLT*) has been a widely used interactive oral proficiency test. Its current scoring

Table 19.2. Oral Proficiency Test Scoring Categories.

	I	II	III
Grammar	Errors in grammar are frequent but can be understood by a native speaker used to dealing with foreigners attempting to speak his language.	Can usually handle elementary constructions quite accurately but does not have thorough or confident control of the grammar.	Control of grammar is good. Able to speak the language with sufficient structural accuracy to participate effectively in most formal and informal conversations on practical, social and professional topics.
Vocabulary	Speaking vocabulary inadequate to express anything but the most elementary needs.	Has speaking vocabulary sufficient to express himself simply with some circumlocutions.	Able to speak the language with sufficient vocabulary to participate effectively in most formal and informal conversations on practical, social and professional topics. Vocabulary is broad enough that he rarely has to grope for a word.
Comprehension	Within the scope of his very limited language experience can understand simple questions and statements allowing for slowed speech, repetition, or paraphrase.	Can get the gist of most conversations of non-technical subjects (i.e., topics which require no specialized knowledge).	Comprehension is quite complete for a normal rate of speech.
Fluency	(No specific fluency description. Refer to other four language areas for implied level of fluency.)	Can handle with confidence but not with facility most social situations including introductions and casual conversations about current events as well as work, family and autobiographical information.	Can discuss particular interests of competence with reasonable ease. He rarely has to grope for words.
Pronunciation	Errors in pronunciation are frequent but can be understood by a native speaker used to dealing with foreigners attempting to speak his language.	Accent, though often quite faulty, is intelligible.	Errors never interfere with understanding and rarely disturb the native speaker. Accent may be obviously foreign.
Task	Can ask and answer questions on topics very familiar to him, Able to satisfy routine travel needs and minimum courtesy requirements. (Should be able to order a simple meal, ask for shelter or lodging, ask and give simple directions, make purchases and tell time.)	Able to satisfy routine social demands and work requirements, needing help in handling any complication or difficulties.	Participate effectively in most formal and informal conversation on practical, social and professional topics.

IV	V
Able to use the language accurately on all levels normally pertinent to professional needs. Errors in grammar are quite rare.	Equivalent to that of an educated native speaker.
Can understand and participate in any conversation within the range of his experience with a high degree of precision of vocabulary.	His speech on all levels is fully accepted by educated native speakers in all its features including breadth of vocabulary and idioms, colloquialisms and pertinent cultural references.
Can understand any conversation within the range of his experience.	Equivalent to that of an educated native speaker.
Able to use the language fluently on all levels normally pertinent to professional needs. Can participate in any conversation within the range of his experience with a high degree of fluency.	Has complete fluency in the language such that his speech is fully accepted by educated native speakers.
Errors in pronunciation are quite rare.	Equivalent to and fully accepted by educated native speakers.
Would rarely be taken for a native speaker but can respond appropriately even in unfamiliar situations. Can handle informal interpreting from and into language.	Speaking proficiency equivalent to that of an educated native speaker.

process involves a complex wholistic evaluation. A previous version of its scoring rubric, however, is one that can serve as a practical guideline for classroom teachers to consult when devising an oral test (see Table 19.2, pp. 380–381). By identifying which one of five score levels your interviewee is in for each of the six major categories, a total rating might be roughly calculated.

Intrinsically Motivating Language Tests

Interaction is one ideal to strive for in your classroom tests, an ideal that will take time, but the results of which will be rewarding. Another important consideration in this new era of testing is the principle of intrinsic motivation. In the old, traditional view of testing there was surely no such thing as an "enjoyable test," and that still may be a lofty ideal. But an intrinsically motivating test is not at all unrealistic, especially within classroom (as opposed to large-scale, standardized) settings.

An intrinsically motivating test involves students in cooperative group preparation. Students embrace the test as a valid and fair means of measuring their competence. It brings out their best performance, not their worst. It has authentic language and tasks. It provides optimal feedback to the students. And it may involve students in some phase of evaluation.

Here are two candid attempts from a classroom teacher to follow some of these ideals. Both of these classroom tests come from Tim Murphey, an instructor in EFL in Nagoya, Japan.

The first is a description of a test; the second is an actual test that used some rather challenging cooperative techniques.

Test 1: Cooperative item construction

It is one of the most satisfying things in the world to me, to see my students busy learning, interacting intensively with each other, occasionally consulting with me, but taking the responsibility themselves and being energetically involved.

I wanted to give a test last week over the different vocabulary and structures that we had covered the last few weeks. But I decided to share the task with the students and see how we might do it interactively. I asked the students in pairs to brainstorm all the things that they thought they had learned and that should be in a test. I forbade them to look into their books. It had to be from memory.

Next they had to go into groups of fours and exchange their papers and discuss whether they agreed with what the other pairs suggested be on the test. Some ideas were crossed off, some were added on, and there was a lot of negotiation going on. I collected the lists, condensed them into one list, and distributed copies to each person at the next class, instructing them to formulate the actual test questions. They each did so, and then in pairs verified that there were no mistakes in the questions, occasionally asking me as I circulated around the room.

Then I told them that in the next class a certain number of their questions would be on the actual test. In the remaining quarter of an hour they were permitted to read every other student's test and to ask the author the answer if they didn't know it. Needless to say, it was an intense fifteen minutes. What is more, I learned they had learned things that I was unaware of teaching or doing in class, and not learned things, at least in their conscious memory, that I thought I had taught.

I am convinced that the exercise of listing items to test, making the questions themselves, and then discussing them with each other initiated many more "opportunities for learning" (Allwright) than would have occurred if I had simply given them a test. And of course, if I had made the test alone I would have tested what I, one person alone, thought was and should have been learned. Together they taught each other, and me, much more, and the test was ultimately much more reliable as a mirror of what was actually covered very thoroughly in the test preparation phase as the students were convinced that it was a useful and testable item.

Test 2: Cooperative pair work and self-evaluation
English II Oral test
Name:
Part A: filled out by you

grades: A+ A B C F   ENGLISH ONLY ALL THE TIME

1. Based upon what you think you know for the test, what grade would you give yourself now before you take it?

grade/score:_____

2. Based upon **how much time and effort you spent studying** for the test, what grade would you give yourself now before you take it?

grade/score:_____

Now, give your study list of words to your partner and your partner will give you theirs. Also exchange this sheet of paper with your partner.

Part B: Filled out by your partner

Go outside (if it is pretty) and ask your partner the following (The partner who is the tallest should answer first and the other should ask, then switch):

3. Call out words that he/she marked on their sheet as being difficult and ask them to explain them and/or use them in an example. Do at least 10 words. If they marked more than 10 words, just pick the last ten on their list that they marked. If they marked less than ten, choose some others that you found difficult. But do only ten.

They should start to answer immediately. If they don't start answering after five seconds hit the buzzer BBBBEEEEEEEPPPP. Time's up. But give them all the time they need to answer completely after they have started.

Write here how many out of ten they could explain adequately:

grade/score:_____

If you went first, it is now your partner's turn to ask you questions.

4. When both of you have finished #3 above:
Ask your partner to describe some object at home without naming the object so that you know what it is. They should be able to tell you at least five things about it that allow you to know what it is. Count the number of things they tell you. Give them a score of one to five depending on how many things they told you about the object. Then exchange roles.

grade/score:_____

5. The partner with the highest student number should choose one of the following to explain:
       a) the 4 dimensions of learning
       b) steps in learning how to juggle
       c) telling 2 stories that they heard Mr. Murphey tell.
The second person speaking must not choose what the first one chose.
Give a grade of 1(poor) to 5(excellent).

grade/score:_____

6. The partner whose student number is lowest should name 5 ways to improve your oral English outside of class as Mr. Murphey has asked you to do. Write their answers below and give them a score.

grade/score:_____

The other partner must name 5 songs and one word they have learned from each song. Write these below and give them a score.

grade/score:_____

Minus points every time you spoke Japanese.   _____
Total number of points out of 25 possible: _____
Now return this paper to the owner.

Part C: Filled out by the same person as in A
After having taken this test, what kind of grade do you think you should get?
Do you think this test gave a fair picture of what you know? Was it easy, fun or what? Would you like to take other tests like this? Was it useful? Could it be improved in any way? Write some feedback below.
Thank you very much.

The first test is an excellent example of cooperative involvement in the actual construction of the test. Students were able to feel that they had invested something in the test, that it wasn't going to be just a barrage of strange items. The second test utilizes interactive work with a partner, peer evaluation, and promotes respect between teacher and learner in the grading process.

How can you take steps to create intrinsically motivating tests? Consider the following four major principles:

1. The principle of giving students advance preparation.

This may sound simple, but much too often teachers do little to help students to prepare for a test. Tests, by their very nature, are anxiety-raising experiences. Students don't know what to expect. And they may not be aware of test-taking strategies that could help them. So, your first task in creating intrinsically motivating tests is to be an ally in the preparation process. Tim Murphey's first test, in which students actually constructed items, was an excellent example of bringing students into the preparation process. But you can do even more:

- Provide information about the general format of a test
- Provide information about types of items that will appear
- Give students opportunities to practice certain item types
- Encourage a thorough review of material to be covered
- Offer advice on strategies for test preparation
- Offer advice on strategies to use during the test itself
- Give anxiety-lowering reassurance

2. The principle of face validity

Sometimes students don't know **what** is being tested when they tackle a test. Sometimes they feel, for a variety of possible reasons, that a test isn't testing what it is "supposed" to test. Face validity means that the students, as they perceive the test, feel that it is valid. You can help to foster that perception with:

- a carefully constructed, well thought-out format
- items that are clear and uncomplicated
- directions that are crystal clear
- tasks that are familiar, that relate to their course work
- a difficulty level that is appropriate for your students
- test conditions that are **biased for best**—that bring out students' best performance

3. The principle of authenticity

Make sure that the language in your test is as natural and authentic as possible. Also, try to give language some **context** so that items aren't just a string of unrelated language samples. Thematic organization of items may help in this regard. Or, consider a story line that may run through your items.

Also, the tasks themselves need to be tasks that they have practiced and feel comfortable with. A classroom test is not the time to introduce brand new tasks, because you won't know if student difficulty is a factor of the task itself or of the language you are testing.

4. The principle of "washback"

"Washback" is the benefit that tests offer to learning. When students take a test, they should be able, within a reasonably short period of time, to utilize the information about their competence that test feedback offers. Formal tests must therefore be learning devices through which students can receive a diagnosis of areas of strength and weakness. Their incorrect responses can become windows of insight about further work. Your **prompt** return of written tests with your feedback is therefore very important to intrinsic motivation.

One way to enhance washback is to provide **narrative evaluations** of test performance. Many teachers, in our overworked (and underpaid) lives, are in the habit of returning tests to students with a letter grade or a number score on it, and considering our job done. In reality, letter grades and a score showing the number right or wrong give absolutely no information of intrinsic interest to the student whatsoever. Grades and scores reduce a mountain of linguistic and cognitive performance data to an absurd minimum. At best they give a **relative** indication of a formulaic judgment of performance as compared to others in the class—which fosters competitive, not cooperative learning.

So, when you return a written test, or even a data sheet from an oral production test, consider giving more than a number or grade or phrase as your feedback. Even if your evaluation is not a neat little paragraph appended to the test, at least you can respond to as many details throughout the test as time will permit. Give praise for strengths—the "good stuff"—as well as constructive criticism of weaknesses. Give strategic hints on how a student might improve certain elements of performance. In other words, take some time to make the test performance an intrinsically motivating experience through which a student will feel a sense of accomplishment and challenge.

Finally, washback also implies that students have ready access to you to discuss the feedback and evaluation you have given. I'm sure you have known teachers in your life with whom you wouldn't dare "argue" about a grade. In an interactive, cooperative, intrinsically motivating classroom, one could hardly promote such a tyrannical atmosphere. For learning to continue, learners need to have a chance to feed back on your feedback, to seek clarification of any issues that are fuzzy, and to appropriately set new goals for themselves for the days and weeks ahead.

Some Practical Steps to Test Construction

If you haven't already had an occasion to create and administer a classroom test, your time is coming soon! As you have read about testing issues in this chapter and considered the guidelines that have been offered on making interactive, intrinsically motivating tests, you may be thinking that you now must go out there and devise a wonderfully innovative instrument that will garner the accolades of your colleagues and the admiration of your students. Don't worry. First of all, traditional testing techniques can, with a little tinkering, be altered to adhere to the spirit of an interactive, communicative language curriculum. Second, entirely new, innovative testing formats take a lot of effort to design and a long time to refine through the process of trial and error. Your best tack as a new teacher is to work **within** the guidelines of accepted, known, traditional testing techniques to give an intrinsically motivating, interactive flavor to your tests. Slowly, with experience, you can get bolder in your attempts.

In that spirit, then, here are some practical steps to take in constructing classroom tests.

1. Test toward clear, unambiguous objectives.

You need to know as specifically as possible **what** it is you want to test. Sometimes teachers give tests simply because it's Friday or it's the third week of the course, and after hasty glances at the chapter(s) covered during the period, they dash off some test items so that students will have something to do during that period. This is no way to approach a test. Carefully list every-thing that you think your students should "know" or be able to "do," based on the material that students are responsible for.

Your "objectives" can, for testing purposes, be as simple as the following list of grammatical structures and communicative skills in a unit that, let's say, you have recently taught:

> **Grammar:**
> **Tag questions**
> **Simple past tense in:**   (a) **negative statements**
>   (b) **information questions**
>
> **Irregular past tense verbs**
> **Who as subject**
> *Anyone, someone,* and *no one*
> **Conjunctions** *so* **and** *because*
>
> **Communication skills:**
> **Guessing what happened**
> **Finding out who did something**
> **Talking about family and friends**
> **Talking about famous people and events**
> **Giving reasons**
> **Asking for confirmation**

2. From your objectives, draw up test specifications.

Now, this sounds like you're supposed to be some sort of psychometri-cian with a Ph.D. in statistics. Wrong. Test specifications for classroom use can be a simple and practical **outline** of your test.[2] Let's say you are testing the above unit. Your specifications will indicate how you will divide up the 45-minute test period, what skills you will test, what the items will look like. Your "specs" may look something like this:

> **Listening** (15 minutes)
>   Part 1: Minimal sentence pairs (choose the sentence that you
>   think you hear) [10 pairs, 2 themes]
>
>   Cover: tag questions
>   negative statements
>   guessing what happened
>   finding out who did something
>
>   Part 2: Conversation (choose the correct answer) [5 items]
>
>   Cover: information questions
>   talking about family and friends

---

[2]Note that for standardized, large-scale tests that are intended to be widely distributed and therefore widely generalized, test specifications are much more formal and detailed.

Multiple Choice (10 minutes) [15 items in a story-line (cloze) format]

Cover:	simple past tense
	past irregular verbs
	anyone, someone, and **no one**

Writing production (15 minutes) [topic: why I liked/didn't like a recent movie]

Cover:	conjunctions **so** and **because**
	giving reasons

These informal classroom oriented specifications give you an indication of (a) which of the topics (objectives) you will cover, (b) what the item types will be, (c) how many items will be in each section, and (d) how much time is allocated for each. Notice that a couple of communication skills and one grammatical structure are not tested—this may be a decision based on the time you devoted to these objectives or on simply the finite number of minutes available to administer the test. Notice, too, that this course quite likely has a good deal of oral production in it, but for reasons of practicality (perhaps oral testing was done separately?) oral production is not included on this test.

3. Draft your test.

A first draft will give you a good idea of what the test will look like, how students will perceive it (face validity), the extent to which authentic language and contexts are present, the length of the the listening stimuli, how well a story line comes across, how things like the cloze testing format will work, and other practicalities.

Your items may look like these:

Listening, Part 1 (theme: last night's party)

1. Teacher says:	They sure made a mess last night, didn't they?
Student reads:	(a) They sure made no mess last night, did they?
	(b) They sure made a mess last night, didn't they?

Listening, Part 2 (theme: talking about family and friends)

2. Teacher says:[3]	A. Mary, who was that gorgeous man I saw you with yesterday?
	B. Oh, Nancy, that was my brother!

---

[3]Ideally, for the sake of authenticity, you should enlist the aid of a colleague and make a tape in which you read the different parts in items like this so that students will readily perceive that there are two people speaking. If time, equipment, and colleagues don't permit this, then make sure that when you read the two parts, you differentiate clearly (with voice and also by bodily facing in two different directions) between the two characters.

Student reads: (a) Mary's brother is George.

(b) Nancy saw Mary's brother yesterday.

(c) Nancy's brother is gorgeous.

Multiple choice   (theme: last week's crazy weather)

Student reads: Then we ___3___ the loudest thunder you have ever heard! And of course right away lightning ___4___ right outside my window!

3. (a) heared   (b) did hear   (c) heard
4. (a) struck   (b) stricken   (c) strack

As you can see, these items are quite traditional. In fact, you can justifiably object to them on the grounds that they ask students to rely on short-term memory and on spelling conventions. But the thematic format of each section, the authentic language, and the contextualization adds face validity, interest, and intrinsic motivation to what might otherwise be quite a mundane test. And the essay section adds some creative production to help compensate for the lack of an oral production component.

4. Revise your test.

At this stage, you will work through all the items you have devised and ask a number of important questions:

(1) Are the directions to each section absolutely clear?

(2) Is there an example item for each section?

(3) Does each item measure a specified objective?

(4) Is each item stated in clear, simple language?

(5) Does each multiple choice item have appropriate **distractors**, that is, are the wrong items clearly wrong and yet sufficiently "alluring" that they aren't ridiculously easy?

(6) Does the difficulty of each item seem to be appropriate for your students?

(7) Does the sum of the items and and test as a whole adequately reflect the learning objectives?

5. Final-edit and type the test.

Ideally, you would try out all your tests on some students before actually administering it. In our daily classroom teaching, the tryout phase is virtually impossible. And so you must do what you can to bring to your students an instrument that is, to the best of your ability, practical, reliable, and valid. So, after careful completion of the drafting phase, a final edit is in order.

In your final editing of the test before typing it for presentation to your class, imagine that you are one of your students taking the test. Go through each set of directions and all items slowly and deliberately. Time yourself as you do so. Often we underestimate the time students will need to complete a test. If the test needs to be shortened or lengthened, make the necessary adjustments. Then make sure your test is neat and uncluttered on the page, reflecting all the care and precision you have put into its construction.

In the case of the test example above, the listening component has to be carefully treated. Make sure **your** script is clear, or that tape playing equipment is in working order.

6. Utilize your feedback after administering the test.

After you give the test, you will have some information about how easy or difficult it was, about the time limits, and about your students' affective reaction to it and their general performance. Take note of these forms of feedback and use them for making your next test.

7. Work for washback.

As you evaluate the test and return it to your students, your feedback should reflect the principles of washback discussed earlier. Use the information from the test performance as a springboard for review and/or for moving on to the next unit.

Tests Can Aid Learning!

It is quite obvious by now, I hope, that tests have a useful place in an interactive, communicative curriculum. Tests need not violate any of the principles of cooperation and student-centeredness. They in fact become indispensable components of a curriculum. Tests can aid learning in a number of ways:

(1) Tests can increase motivation as they serve as milestones of student progress.

(2) Tests can spur learners to set goals for themselves, both before and after a test.

(3) Tests can aid the retention of information through the feedback they give on learners' competence.

(4) Tests can provide a sense of periodic closure to various units and modules of a curriculum.

(5) Tests can encourage students' self-evaluation of their progress.

(6) Tests can promote student autonomy as they confirm areas of strength and areas needing further work.

(7) Tests can aid in evaluating teaching effectiveness.

TOPICS FOR DISCUSSION, ACTION, AND RESEARCH

1. Teachers are called upon to play dual roles in the classroom. One is the role of a "coach" or "guide," and the other is the role of a "judge" who administers tests and assigns grades. Describe these two roles further. Are they conflicting roles? With a partner, brainstorm some ways that you as a teacher lessen the potential conflict. Then, share your ideas with the rest of the class.

2. Review the meaning of **informal, formal, formative,** and **summative** testing. Is it fair to say that informal testing is really "testing" rather than simply an evaluative facet of teaching? In a group, discuss ways that summative tests might provide constructive feedback to the student.

3. Following traditional views of intelligence, we would have to say that numerous highly "intelligent" people fail to learn a foreign language. How do Howard Gardner's and Robert Sternberg's views on intelligence shed new light on such an apparent paradox?

4. Look again at the two tests devised by Tim Murphey (pp. 382–384). How does each manifest principles of intrinsic motivation? Do you see any weaknesses in either test? How practical are such tests for contexts that you are familiar with?

5. Can you think of some examples of how you would construct a test that is **biased for best**? Illustrate with an actual classroom test, if possible.

6. From your experience taking tests, what are some test taking strategies that you would offer to your students? Consider two categories: (1) strategies that apply to the preparation phase, and (2) those that one would use during the actual taking of the test. Make lists of these strategies and compare them with classmates in a small group. A whole-class goal might be to devise a composite list of test-taking strategies, which then will become a useful tool for your own teaching.

7. As a group project, devise an oral test for a specified purpose and audience that you are familiar with. How would you elicit spoken language from a learner? What kinds of questions would you ask? What other stimuli might you use (pictures, for example)? How would you make sure that the four phases of warm-up, level check, probe, and wind-down would be adequately represented? If possible, try out your test format on some actual learners. Then, share your format and results with the rest of the class.

8. Think of a classroom language test you know and possibly have recently taken. Describe it. Evaluate it on the four principles of intrinsically motivating tests offered in this chapter. Use a scale of 1–5 (1 poor, 5 excellent) for each criterion. Then, describe some ways in which it could have been more intrinsically motivating. In a small group, do the same for a test you all know in common. Compare evaluations. Then, discuss some ways in which it could have been more intrinsically motivating.

FOR YOUR FURTHER READING

Brown, James Dean. 1992. "Classroom-centered language testing." *TESOL Journal 1*(4), 12–15.

> In this very quick, practical primer on classroom language testing, the author gives teachers the bare essentials on how to create effective tests and how to improve existing tests.

Bachman, Lyle F. 1991. "What does language testing have to offer?" *TESOL Quarterly 25* (4), 671–704.

> This is one of the silver anniversary "state of the art" articles in the *TESOL Quarterly*. The author gives a comprehensive survey of the last 25 years of language testing research with a focus on current issues in testing research. In spite of its theoretical focus, some practical implications can be gleaned from this excellent summary.

Shohamy, Elana. 1992. *An Introduction to Language Testing*. Oxford University Press.

> This is a clear, step-by-step guide to preparing, administering, and evaluating communicative language tests in the classroom. It includes many stimulating ideas, accompanied by illustrative examples, for testing all four skills.

Hughes, Arthur. 1989. *Testing for Language Teachers*. Cambridge University Press.

Weir, Cyril J. 1990. *Communicative Language Testing*. Prentice Hall.

Madsen, Harold. 1983. *Techniques in Testing*. Oxford University Press.

> All three of these books are quite practical in their attention to classroom testing techniques. Teachers are given numerous examples of tests covering varying skills and proficiency levels. In all three, general guidelines and principles are also offered, so that the teacher isn't simply an item-writing machine. Madsen's book is especially practical with clear directions and examples for the teacher who has not had the benefit of a formal course in language testing.

Part Four

✳✳✳

Classroom
Practicalities

Chapter 20

How to Plan
a Lesson

We now begin a series of three chapters that deal with the practicalities of classroom teaching from an administrative, managerial point of view. That is, you are a teacher faced with the reality that tomorrow (or sometime in the near future) you will step into a classroom, and theoretically, you will be putting everything that has been covered in the previous 19 chapters into practical application. I'm sure a battery of questions comes to your mind: How do I plan a lesson? How do I follow a curriculum? How can I become an excellent classroom manager? How do I make the best use of the textbook and other instructional aids? What do I do when things go wrong? How do I know if my lesson is successful? And more.

We'll begin to answer these questions with what is probably your most pressing need right now: how to plan a lesson. The term "lesson" is popularly considered to be a unified set of activities that cover a period of classroom time, usually ranging from 40 to 90 minutes. These classroom time units are administratively significant for teachers because they represent "steps" along a curriculum before which and after which you have a hiatus (of a day or more) in which to evaluate and prepare for the next lesson. Sometimes your whole life seems to be caught up in a never-ending series of lesson plans. But those lessons, from the point of view of your own and students' time management, are practical, tangible units of effort that serve to provide a rhythm to a course of study.

Format of a Lesson Plan

While variations are plentiful, seasoned teachers generally agree on what the essential elements of a lesson plan should be. For examples of each, turn to the sample lesson plan at the end of this chapter.

1. Goal(s)

You should be able to identify an overall purpose or goal that you will attempt to accomplish by the end of the class period. This goal may be quite generalized, but it serves as a unifying theme for you. Thus, in the sample lesson plan, "understanding telephone conversations" generally identifies the lesson topic.

2. Objectives

It is very important to state explicitly what you want students to gain from the lesson. Explicit statements here help you to:

(a) be sure that you indeed know what it is you want to accomplish,

(b) preserve the unity of your lesson,

(c) predetermine whether or not you are trying to accomplish too much, and

(d) evaluate students' success at the end of, or after, the lesson.

Objectives are most clearly captured in terms of stating what students will **do**. However, many language objectives are not overtly observable and therefore you may need to depart from strictly behavioral terms for some objectives. Try to **avoid** vague, unverifiable statements like:

    *Students will learn about the passive voice.

    *Students will practice some listening exercises.

    *Students will do the reading selection.

    *Students will discuss the homework assignment.

You would be unable to **confirm** the realization of any of these sorts of abstruse, loosely stated objectives. The objectives in the sample lesson plan at the end of the chapter are the sorts of statements that you can turn back to after a lesson and determine, to some extent anyway, how well students accomplished the objectives.

In stating objectives, distinguish between **terminal** and **enabling** objectives. Terminal objectives are final learning outcomes that you will need to measure and evaluate. Enabling objectives are interim steps that build upon each other and lead to a terminal objective. Consider the following examples:

    Terminal lesson objective:

      • Students will successfully request information about air-
        plane arrivals and departures.

Enabling objectives:
- Students will comprehend and produce the following ten new vocabulary items.
- Students will read and understand an airline schedule.
- Students will produce questions with **when, where,** and **what time**..
- Students will produce appropriate polite forms of requesting.

You may be able to identify a number of other enabling objectives that will vary depending upon what students' proficiency level is and what they have already learned in the course. For another example, notice the difference between terminal and enabling objectives in the sample lesson plan.

3. Materials and equipment

It may seem a trivial matter to list materials needed, but good planning tactics always indicate the importance of knowing what you need to take with you or to arrange to have in your classroom. It is easy, in the often harried life of a teacher, to forget to bring a tape recorder or a poster or some handouts you left on your desk or the workbooks that students gave you the night before.

4. Procedures

At this point, lessons clearly have tremendous variation. But, as a start, and as a very general set of guidelines for planning, you might think in terms of making sure your plan includes:

(a) an opening statement or activity as a "warm up"

(b) a set of activities and techniques in which you have considered appropriate proportions of time for:

   (i) whole class work

   (ii) small group and pair work

   (iii) teacher talk

   (iv) student talk

(c) closure

5. Evaluation

Next, how are you going to determine whether or not your objectives have been accomplished? If your lesson has no evaluative component, you can easily find yourself simply making assumptions that are not informed by careful observation or measurement. Now, you must understand that every lesson does not need to end up with a little quiz. Nor does evaluation need to be a separate element of your lesson. Evaluation can take place in the course of "regular" classroom activity. Some forms of evaluation may have to wait a day or two until certain abilities have had a chance to build. But evaluation is an assessment, formal or informal, that you make after students have sufficient opportunities for learning, and without this component, you have no means for (a) assessment of the success of your students or (b) making adjustments in your lesson plan for the **next** day.

6. Extra-class work

Sometimes misnamed "homework" (students don't necessarily do extra-class work only at home), extra-class work, if it is warranted, needs to be planned carefully and communicated clearly to the students. Whether you are teaching in an EFL or ESL situation, you can almost always find applications or extensions of classroom activity that will help students to do some learning beyond the class hour.

Guidelines for Lesson Planning

1. How to begin planning

In most normal circumstances, especially for a teacher without much experience, the first step of lesson planning will already have been performed for you: choosing what to teach. No doubt you will be—or have already been—given a textbook and told to teach from it, with either a suggestion or a requirement of how many chapters or units you should cover. As you look over the chapter you are to cover for a class hour, you might go through the following sequence:

(a) Assuming that you are already familiar with (a) the curriculum your students are following (see "Adapting to an established curriculum" below in this section), and (b) the overall plan and "tone" of the textbook(s), look over the textbook chapter.

(b) Based on (a) your view of the whole curriculum and (b) your perception of the language needs of your students, determine what the topic and purpose of the lesson will be and write that down as the overall **goal**.

(c) Again considering the curriculum and the students' needs, draft out perhaps one to three explicitly stated **terminal** objectives for the lesson.

(d) Of the exercises that are in the textbook, decide which ones you will do, change, delete, and add to, all based on the objectives you have drafted.

(e) Draft out a skeletal outline of what your lesson will look like.

(f) Carefully anticipate step by step procedures for carrying out all techniques, especially those that involve changes and additions. State the purpose(s) of each technique and/or activity as **enabling** objectives.

For teachers who have never taught before, it is often very useful to write a **script** of your lesson plan in which your exact anticipated words are written down and followed by exactly what you would anticipate students to say in return. Scripting out a lesson plan helps you to be more specific in your planning and can often prevent classroom pitfalls where you get all tangled up in explaining something or students take you off on a tangent. Writing a complete script for a whole hour of teaching is probably too laborious and unreasonable, but more practical and instructive (for you) are **partial scripts** that cover:

(a) introductions to activities

(b) directions for a task

(c) statements of rules or generalizations

(d) anticipated interchanges that could easily bog down or go astray

(e) oral testing techniques

(f) conclusions to activities and to the class hour.

2. Variety, sequencing, pacing, and timing

As you are drafting out step-by-step procedures, or afterward, you need to look at how the lesson, as a whole, holds together. Four considerations come into play here:

(a) Is there sufficient **variety** in techniques to keep the lesson lively and interesting? Most successful lessons give students a number of different activities during the class hour. This keeps minds alert and enthusiasm high.

(b) Are your different techniques or activities **sequenced** logically? Ideally, elements of a lesson will build progressively toward accomplishing the ultimate goals. Easier aspects will no doubt be better placed at the beginning of a lesson. Tasks that require knowledge gained from previous exercises should be appropriately sequenced.

(c) Is the lesson as a whole **paced** adequately? Pacing can mean a number of things. First, it means that activities are neither too long nor too short. You could, for example, have too much variety with so many short activities that just as students are getting the "feel" for one activity, they get bounced to the next. Second, you need to anticipate how well your various techniques "flow" together. You would not, for example, find a smooth flow in a class that had five minutes each of whole-class work, pair work, whole-class work, group work, pair work, whole-class work, etc. Nor would you normally plan for two silent reading activities in a row. Third, good pacing also is a factor of how well you provide a transition from one activity to the next. For example:

> T: Okay, you've just had a good chance to listen to the way a lecturer signals various segments of a class lecture. Now we're going to use this information to look at a reading passage about space exploration and figure out...

(d) Is the lesson appropriately **timed**, considering the number of minutes in the class hour? This is one of the most difficult aspects of lesson planning to control. It's not unusual for new teachers to plan a lesson so tightly that they actually complete their lesson plan early, but after just a little experience the most common occurrence is that we don't complete our lessons within the planned time allotment. The latter is not a cardinal sin, by any means, for most likely it means you have given some time to students for genuine inter-action and creative use of language. But timing is an element that you should build into a lesson plan: (i) if your planned lesson ends early, have some backup activity ready to insert; (ii) if your lesson isn't completed as planned, be ready to gracefully end a class on time and on the next day pick up where you left off.

3. Gauging difficulty

Figuring out in advance how easy or difficult certain techniques will be is something that usually must be learned by experience. It takes a good deal of cognitive empathy to put yourself in your students' shoes and anticipate their problem areas. Some difficulty is caused by tasks themselves; therefore, make your directions crystal clear by writing them out in advance (note the comments on "scripting" lessons, above). I have seen too many classes where teachers have not clearly planned exactly what they will say by way of direc-tions for a task. Writing them ahead of time gives you a chance to be more objective in determining if everything is clear. And then, either give an **example** yourself or solicit an example of a subtask within a technique.

Another source of difficulty, of course, is linguistic. If you can follow the **i+1** principle of providing material that is just a little above, but not too far above, students' ability, the linguistic difficulty should be optimal. The main problem here lies in the heterogeneity of a classroom full of learners whose proficiency range is very broad. Individual attention, feedback, and small group work can sometimes bring balance into the classroom.

4. Individual differences

For the most part a lesson plan will aim at a majority of students in the class who comprise the "average" ability range. But your lesson plan should also take into account what you already know about the variation of ability in your classroom, especially individuals who are well below or well above the classroom norm. Several steps can be taken to account for individual differ-ences:

(a) Design techniques that have easy and difficult aspects or items.

(b) Solicit responses to easier items from students who are below the norm and to harder items from those above the norm.

(c) Try to design techniques that will involve **all** students actively.

(d) Use judicious selection to assign members of small groups so that each group has either (i) a deliberately heterogeneous range of ability or (ii) a homogeneous range (to encourage equal participation).

(e) Use small group and pair work time to circulate and give extra attention to those below or above the norm (see Chapter 11 on Group Work principles).

5. Student talk and teacher talk

Give careful consideration in your lesson plan to the balance between student talk and teacher talk. Our natural inclination as teachers is to talk too much! As you plan your lesson, and as you perhaps script out some aspects of it, see to it that students have a chance to talk, to produce language, and even to **initiate** their own topics and ideas.

6. Adapting to an established curriculum

Because this book is aimed at teachers in training, specific information about curriculum development and revision is not included here. The assumption is that your primary task is not that of writing a new curriculum or of revising an existing one but rather of following an established curriculum and adapting to it in terms of your particular group of students, their needs, and their goals, as well as your own philosophy of teaching.

As you plan lessons, your first concern is that this class hour must contribute to the goals that a curriculum is designed to pursue. Perhaps your institution will not have a curriculum that is spelled out in a document; in other words, it is a "textbook driven" curriculum that, in practice, simply tells you to teach everything in a textbook. Or, somewhere in the description of the institution and/or the course in particular, you may find certain specifications for the course you are about to teach. At best, you would be presented with a document that clearly delineates the goals of the curriculum and offers suggestions on how to meet those goals in terms of weekly or even daily lesson objectives.

If you do not have such overall course goals, then it would be wise to informally devise some for yourself so that you can keep your course focused on attainable, practical ends. To do so, consider the following two factors that contribute to curriculum planning:

Learner factors:

(a) Who are the students (age, education, occupation, general purpose in taking English, entering proficiency level)?

(b) What are the specific language needs of your students (e.g., to read English scientific texts, to serve as a tour guide, to survive minimally in an English speaking country)? Break those needs down into as many specific subcategories as feasible.

Institutional factors:

(c) What are the practical constraints of the institution you are teaching in (consider budget, equipment, classroom space and size, philosophy of the institution, etc.)?

(d) What supporting materials (textbooks, audio-visual aids, overhead projector, and other equipment) are available?

By paying primary attention to the learner factors above, you will have a good chance of pointing your students toward pragmatic, **communicative** goals in which their real-life needs for English will be met. You will focus on the learners and their needs rather than on your needs or your institution's needs. However, taking the institutional factors seriously will add some administrative practicality to your goals. After all, every educational institution is limited in some way in its capacity to deliver the very best.

Your course goals might look like the following goals of an advanced pre-university listening comprehension course:

(1) Students will understand the teacher's instructions and demonstrate that understanding.

(2) Students will understand the teacher's explanations and show that comprehension.

(3) Students will understand classroom peers in discussions, activities, and oral reports.

(4) Students will understand academic lectures given by different speakers.

(5) Students will identify topics and topic development.

(6) Students will infer relationships among topics.

(7) Students will recognize different points of view.

(8) Students will identify key information as signaled by vocabulary.

(9) Students will recognize key information as signaled by stress and intonation.

(10) Students will identify key information as signaled by grammatical structure.

7. Classroom lesson "notes"

A final consideration in your lesson planning process is a very practical one: What sort of lesson "notes" will you actually carry into the classroom with you? If you have pages and pages of notes and reminders and scripts, you could get too focused on details and never free yourself for spontaneity. Most teachers operate well with no more than **one page** of a lesson outline and notes. Some prefer to put lesson notes on a series of index cards for easy handling. By reducing your plans to such a physically manageable minimum, you will reduce the chances of getting bogged down in all the details that went into the planning phase, and yet there is enough there in writing to provide order and clarity as you proceed.

Sample Lesson Plan[1]

Class Description

This is an intermediate level pre-university class at the American Language Institute at San Francisco State University. The 16 students in the class range in age from 18 to 25. Their general goals are academically oriented. Their native languages are Japanese, Korean, Mandarin, Indonesian, Thai, and Arabic.

1. Goal

Students will increase their familiarity with conventions of telephone conversations.

2. Objectives

Terminal objectives:

(1) Students will develop inner "expectancy rules" that enable them to **predict** and **anticipate** what someone else will say on the phone.

(2) Students will solicit and receive information by requesting it over the telephone.

Enabling objectives:

(1) Students will comprehend a simple phone conversation (played on a tape recorder).

(2) In the above conversation, students will identify who the participants are, what they are going to do, and when.

(3) Students will comprehend and produce necessary vocabulary for this topic.

---

[1] I am grateful to Karen Tenney for allowing me to adapt one of her lesson plans here.

(4) Students will comprehend cultural and linguistic schemata regarding movies, theaters, and arranging to see a movie with someone.

(5) Students will infer what a second speaker is saying on the phone by "eavesdropping" on one speaker only.

(6) Each student will ask someone to go to a movie with him or her and respond appropriately to a reciprocal request.

(7) Students will get "live" movie information over the phone.

3. Materials and equipment

Materials/equipment needed are:
1. tape recorder with taped conversation
2. a telephone (if possible) or a toy facsimile
3. movie advertisements, 8 different ones
4. movie Guide page for extra-class work

4. Procedures

(See next page.)

1. PRE-LISTENING

(The teacher places a phone on the front table. It will be used later.)

To point the students' thinking in the right direction for this lesson, we will start off with the following "model" phone conversation on tape. It is very short and very easy, well below the students' level. There is no question that they will understand it fully; its purpose is to set up a framework for the lesson.

2. LISTENING TO THE TAPE

Please listen:

Phone:	Ring!
Tom:	Hullo?
Jack:	Tom, this is Jack. D'ya wanna go to th' movies?
Tom:	Mmm … When?
Jack:	Tonight. I have free passes.
Tom:	Uh, OK, sure. What time?
Jack:	Eight o'clock. I'll—I'll meet ya there, OK?
Tom:	Fine. See ya then.

(This tape may be played twice.)

3. WHOLE-CLASS DISCUSSION

T:	Did Tom call Jack?
Ss:	No, Jack called Tom.
T:	Right. What are they going to do?
Ss:	Go to the movies.
T:	Good! When are they going?
Ss:	Tonight (and/or) Eight o'clock.
T:	Right! What are free passes?
S1:	Free tickets.
T:	Yes! Who has free passes?
S2:	Jack.
T:	Exactly. What movie are they going to?
Ss:	It doesn't say.
T:	Hmm …. What could that mean?
S1:	There's only one theater in their town.
S2:	They always meet at the same place.
	etc.
T:	Good! Any of those things are possible. It sounds like they know each other very well. Maybe they go to the movies often together.

A general discussion about movie-going (and phoning to arrange it) will involve students personally and will introduce one new term.

4. SCHEMATA-BUILDING DISCUSSION

T:	Who's been to the movies lately?
S1:	(raises hand)
T:	S1, what did you see?
S1:	Harlem Nights.
T:	Harlem Nights—was it good?
S1:	Yes.
T:	Did you go with a friend?
S1:	Yes.
T:	Did you call him/her to arrange it?
S1:	She called me.

(This conversation will continue to include other Ss. The main subjects to come back to are what movies they saw, if they arranged it with a friend by phone, and whether they went to a bargain matinee.)

*Note: During all interactions the teacher LISTENS with interest, to student comments. The teacher gives feedback after each comment, making sure to let the students realize that they *do* already know a lot.

5. LISTENING ACTIVITY #1

T: (Indicates the phone on the front desk)   My friend Debbie is going to call me in a few minutes. Of course, you won't hear Debbie talking to me; you'll just hear me, right?

I want you to listen carefully and try to figure out two things (write these on the board as you say them):

One—What does Debbie want to do? [repeat]

Two—When? [repeat]

Ok, listen for what Debbie wants to do and when. (Indicating questions on board.)

(Pause. The phone rings.)

T:	Hullo?
Gap 1	_____
T:	This is Karen.
Gap 2	_____
T:	Oh, hi Deb, how're you?
Gap 3`	_____
T:	The movies? (Look at watch) When?
Gap 4	_____
T:	Um, OK, this afternoon's fine. Whadda ya wanna see?
Gap 5:	_____
T:	Well, I'll only go to Batman if it's a bargain matinee.
Gap 6	_____

T:	There is? One o'clock? Great! I'll meet you there. 'Bye.
T:	What does Debbie want to do?
Ss:	Go to the movies.
T:	Right! When?
Ss:	This afternoon (and/or) One o'clock.
T:	Excellent! She wants to go to the movie this afternoon.

Now you're going to hear the same phone call again. This time try to figure out three things:

(1) What movie does Debbie suggest?

(2) Am I willing to pay full price?

(3) Does Debbie tell me I will have to pay full price?

(Erase the first two questions from the board and put the three new questions up on the board.) (Repeat the phone call.)

T:	What movie does Debbie suggest?
S1:	Batman.
T:	Right! Was I willing to pay full price?
S2:	No. You wanted to go to a bargain matinee.
T:	Yes! And what does Debbie tell me? Will I have to pay full price?
S3:	No. She tells you that there is a bargain matinee.
T:	At what time?
S3:	One o'clock
T:	OK, good! Now you're going to hear the phone call one last time. This time I'll stop every time Debbie should be speaking, and I want you to tell me what Debbie might have said. Many different answers may be correct.
T:	(goes back to phone) Hullo?
S1:	Hullo?...
S2:	Is Karen there?
S3:	Is Karen home?
T:	(smiles and nods to show answers are good) This is Karen.
S4:	It's Debbie.
S5:	This is Debbie.
T:	Oh, hi Deb, how're you?
S6:	Fine...
S7:	Do you want to go to the movies?
S8:	Do you have time to see a movie?

(This format continues until the conversation is completed and all students have participated.)

6. POST-LISTENING ACTIVITY

Teacher passes out eight different movie ads to eight students (see samples on ad page). Teacher puts a second phone on the front table.

> T: Ok, everyone with an ad, please get a partner who does *not* have an ad. S1 and S2 (one pair-group) please come up to these phones. S1 has a newspaper ad for a movie. She will call S2 and ask him to go to that movie with her. Be sure to arrange the following things in your phone conversation (write these on the board):

1. What movie?

2. What time?

3. Which theater?

The students come up in pairs and have very short phone conversations to arrange going to a movie together. If there is not time for each pair to come to the front and use the phones, pairs can work on their conversations at their desks.

7. EXTRA-CLASSWORK ASSIGNMENT

Teacher passes out DATEBOOK/MOVIE GUIDE page to each student.

> T: Everyone please choose a theater from this page. (Make sure each student chooses a different theater.)
>
> Circle the theater and the phone number on your handout.
>
> Choose a movie at your theater.
>
> Circle the movie.
>
> Circle the times next to it.

Repeat these directions and demonstrate with your own movie list. Go around and make sure that everyone has circled:

1. a theater.

2. the right phone number.

3. a movie at their theater.

4. the times it's showing.

> T: Tonight when you go home, please call the theater you've chosen. Listen to the recording.
>
> Find out two things:
>
> 1) Is "your" movie still playing?
>
> 2) Are the times the same?
>
> Please write these questions on the back of your handout (write them on the board):
>
> 1) Is the movie you've chosen still playing?
>
> 2) Are the times the same?
>
> Remember that you can call the theater as many times as you want. These are local calls.

5. Evaluation

Terminal objective (1) and enabling objectives (1) through (5) are evaluated as the activities unfold without a formal testing component. The culminating pair-work activity is the evaluative component for terminal objective (2) and enabling objective (6). As pairs work together, T circulates to monitor students and to observe informally whether or not they have accomplished the terminal objective. The success of the extra-class assignment (enabling objective [7]) will be informally observed on the next day.

❋   ❋   ❋

This chapter has focused specifically on the **planning** stage of classroom teaching. When you walk into the classroom, all that planning—you hope!— works to your advantage. We turn to that crucial step in the next chapter.

TOPICS FOR DISCUSSION, ACTION, AND RESEARCH

1. Following are some curricular **goals** sampled from various English language programs:

   > Understand academic lectures
   > Write a business letter
   > Use greetings and "small talk"
   > Request information in a restaurant
   > Read informal essays

   For each of the above, briefly describe a specific audience for which the goal might be appropriate, then (a) transform the goal into **terminal objective(s)**, and (b) state a number of **enabling objectives** that would have to be reached in order to accomplish the terminal objective.

2. In a group, practice stating other lesson objectives for a course everyone is familiar with. In your group, discuss the extent to which you could objectively **evaluate** students' achievement of the objectives. Share your group's conclusions with the rest of the class.

3. Observe an ESL class in which you look especially for manifestations of variety, sequencing, pacing, and timing, or the lack thereof. Write down your observations and share them in a group and/or with the whole class.

4. Accounting for individual differences is not as easy as it sounds. Describe some dimensions of student differences you have experienced or observed. How would you ensure, in each case, that students on both ends of the continuum are "reached" in some way? Small groups sometimes provide a means for accounting for differences. What are some other ways (see p. 401) to systematically divide the class into small groups? Justify each.

5. Look at the sample lesson plan (pp. 403–409). Use the six guidelines for lesson planning (pp. 398–403) to evaluate the plan. Would you make any changes?

6. Transform the lesson plan (pp. 403–409) into some practical "lesson notes"—on a few index cards perhaps—that you could carry into the classroom with you. What decisions did you have to make? On what basis did you decide to create your notes the way you did? Share your notes with others in a small group and discuss your reasons for doing what you did.

7. A needs analysis normally considers such questions as who the learners are, why they are learning English, in what context(s) they they use it, etc. Identify a group of learners you are familiar with, and devise a list of specific questions that you could use to analyze needs and, in turn, to determine how a curriculum or a set of lessons should be designed. Share your list with a partner or small group and design a consensus list.

8. Find a teachers' manual or instructor's edition of an ESL textbook. Look at a chapter or unit and read through the "plan" or "suggestions" for teaching. Using the principles cited in this and in previous chapters, evaluate it for an audience that you specify. How would the suggestions need to be changed or added to?

FOR YOUR FURTHER READING

Purgason, Katherine Barnhouse. 1991. "Planning lessons and units." In Celce-Murcia, Marianne (Ed.), *Teaching English as a Second or Foreign Language.* Second Edition. Newbury House.

This is one of the few readily accessible single articles in the field dealing with principles and practical guidelines for planning lessons. Sample lesson notes are included as an appendix.

Gower, Roger, and Walters, Steve. 1983. *Teaching Practice Handbook: A Reference Book for EFL Teachers in Training.* Heinemann. [Chapter 4, pp. 60–83].

Cross, David. 1991. *A Practical Handbook of Language Teaching.* Cassell. [Chapter 11, pp. 138–150].

Both of these handbooks for teachers offer some practical guidelines for lesson planning in the respective chapters referenced.

Brown, H. Douglas. 1992. *Vistas: An Interactive Course in English. Teacher's Edition.* Prentice Hall.

The Teacher's Edition of *Vistas* will give you quite a number of ideas of how various techniques combine to form cohesive classroom lessons. Each unit has explicit directions for teachers which can be used as lesson plans or as general guidelines which can be adapted for various audiences.

Chapter 21

Classroom Management

Is teaching an art or a science? Are teachers born or made? Is the learning-teaching connection poetic or predictable? These questions are commonly found swirling about in the minds of educators, not so much as "either-or" questions but rather as "both-and" questions. I think you can easily agree that teaching is both an art and a science, that some innate ability complements learned teaching skills, and that with all of our best laid lesson plans there still remains an intangible aura surrounding acts of learning. But how do the two traditions coexist in practice? How do art and science mingle in the principles and approaches and techniques and plans of ESL teachers?

One answer to these questions lies in what we call **classroom management,** which encompasses an abundance of factors ranging from how you physically arrange the classroom to teaching "styles" to one of my favorite notions: classroom energy. By understanding what some of the variables are in classroom management, you can take some important steps to sharpening your skills as a language teacher. And then, as you improve some of those identifiable, overtly observable skills, you open the door to the intangible, to art, to poetics, to the invisible sparks of energy that kindle the flames of learning.

The Classroom Itself

One of the simplest principles of classroom management centers on the physical environment for learning: the classroom itself. Consider three categories:

1. Sight, sound, and comfort

As trivial as it may first appear, in the face of your decisions to implement language teaching principles in an array of clever techniques, students are indeed profoundly affected by what they see, hear, and feel when they enter the classroom. If you have any power to control the following, then it will be worth your time to do so:

- The classroom is neat, clean, and orderly in appearance.
- Blackboards are erased.
- Chairs are appropriately arranged (see below).
- If the room has bulletin boards and you have the freedom to use them, can you occasionally take advantage of visuals?
- The classroom is as free from external noises as possible (machinery outside, street noise, etc.).
- Acoustics within your classroom are at least tolerable.
- Heating or cooling systems (if applicable) are operating.

Granted, you may be powerless to control some of the above. I have been in classrooms in tropical countries where there is no air conditioning, the concrete walls of the classroom echo so badly you can hardly hear anyone, and jackhammers are rapping away outside! But if these factors can be controlled, don't pass up the opportunity to make your classroom as physically comfortable as possible.

2. Seating arrangements

You may have had the experience of walking into a classroom and finding the movable desks all lined up in columns (not rows) that are perpendicular to the front wall of the room. Neat and orderly, right? Wrong. If you won't get fired from your teaching post by doing so, change the pattern immediately! Students are members of a team and should be able to see one another, to talk to one another (in English!), and not made to feel like they just walked into a military formation.

If your classroom has movable desk-chairs, consider patterns of semi-circles, U-shapes, concentric circles, or—if your class size is small enough—one circle so that students aren't all squarely facing the teacher. If the room has tables with two to four students at each, try to come up with configurations that make interaction among students most feasible. Give some thought to how students will do small group and pair work with as little chaos as possible.

Should you determine who sits next to whom? Normally, students will soon fall into a comfortable pattern of self-selection in where they sit. You may not need to tamper with this arrangement unless you feel the need to force a different "mix" of students. In some ESL contexts, where students come from varied native language backgrounds, English will be more readily practiced if students of the same native language are not sitting next to each other. And if some adjacent students are being disruptive, you may decide to selectively move a few people. When assigning small groups, as noted already in Chapter 11, you may of course want to do so with a certain plan in mind.

3. Blackboard use

The blackboard is one of your greatest allies. It gives students added visual input along with auditory. It allows you to illustrate with words and pictures and graphs and charts. It is always there and it is recyclable! So, take advantage of this instant visual aid by profusely using the blackboard. At the same time, try to be neat and orderly in your blackboard use, erasing as often as appropriate; a messy, confusing blackboard drives students crazy.

4. Equipment

The "classroom" may be construed to include any equipment you may be using. If you're using electrical equipment (say, an overhead projector or a video player), make sure that:

- The room has outlets,
- The equipment fits comfortably in the room.
- Everyone can see it (and/or hear it),
- You leave enough time before and after class to get the equipment and return it to its proper place.,
- The machine actually works,
- You know how to operate it, and
- There is an extra light bulb or battery or whatever else you'll need if a routine replacement is in order.

You would be surprised at how many lesson plans get thrown out the window because of some very minor practicality surrounding the use of equipment.

Your Voice and Body Language

Another fundamental classroom management concern has to do with YOU and the messages you send through your voice and through your body language.

One of the first requirements of good teaching is good voice projection. You do not have to have a loud booming voice, but you need to be heard clearly by all the students in the room. When you talk, project your voice so that the person sitting farthest away from you can hear you clearly. If you are directing comments to a student in the first row sitting right in front of you, remember that in whole-class work, **all** the rest of the students need to be able to hear that comment. As you speak, articulate clearly; remember these students are just learning English and they need every advantage they can get.

Should you slow down your normal rate of delivery? For beginning level classes, yes, but only slightly so, and not to the point that the rate of delivery is downright silly. Keep as natural a flow to your language as possible. Clear articulation is usually more of a key to comprehension than slowed speech.

Your voice isn't the only production mode available to you in the classroom. Nonverbal messages are very powerful. In language classes, especially, where students may not have all the skills they need to decipher verbal language, their attention is drawn to nonverbal communication. Here are some pointers:

- Let your body posture exhibit an air of confidence.
- Your face should reflect optimism, brightness, and warmth.
- Use facial and hand gestures to enhance meanings of words and sentences that might otherwise be unclear.
- Make frequent eye contact with **all** students in the class.
- Do not "bury yourself" in your notes and plans.
- Do not plant your feet firmly in one place for the whole hour.
- Move around the classroom, but not to distraction.
- Follow the conventional rules of proxemics (distance) and kinesthetics (touching) that apply for the culture(s) of your students.
- Dress appropriately considering the expectations of your students and the culture in which you are teaching.

Unplanned Teaching: Midstream Lesson Changes

Now that you have considered some of the factors in managing the physical space and your physical self, imagine that you have entered the classroom and begun your lesson. The warm-up has gone well. You have successfully (with clear unambiguous directions) introduced the first major technique, which, let's say, has to do with different countries' forms of government. Students are clear about why they are doing this task and have launched themselves into it. Then one student asks about the political campaign happening right now. Another student responds, and then another, and before you know it, students are engaged in a very interesting, somewhat heated debate about current political issues. This theme is related to your lesson, but the discussion is not what you had in mind. Nevertheless, students are all alert, interested, participating, and using fairly complex English in the process. You realize that your lesson will have to change in some way.

This scene is commonplace. What would you do now? Should you have cut off the conversation early and nipped it in the bud? Or were you wise to let it continue and to discard some other activities you had in mind? Classroom management involves decisions about what to do when:

- your students digress and throw off the plan for the day
- **you** digress and throw off the plan for the day
- an unexpected but pertinent question comes up
- some technicality prevents you from doing an activity (e.g., a machine breaks down or your handout is illegible)
- a student is disruptive in class
- you are asked a question you don't know the answer to (e.g., a grammatical point)
- there isn't enough time at the end of a class period to finish an activity that has already started

And the list could go on. In short, you are daily called upon to deal with the **unexpected**. You have to engage in what we'll call unplanned teaching that makes demands on you that were not anticipated in your lesson plan. One of the initiation rites that new teachers go through is experiencing these unexpected events and learning how to deal with them gracefully. And the key is **poise**. You will keep the respect of your students and your own self-confidence by staying calm, assessing the situation quickly, making a midstream change in your plan, and allowing the lesson to move on.

Teaching Under Adverse Circumstances

Under the rubric of "adverse circumstances" are a number of management concerns of widely divergent nature. What is implied here is that no teaching-learning context is perfect. There are always imperfect institutions, imperfect people, and imperfect circumstances for you to deal with. How you deal with them is one of the most significant factors contributing to your professional success.

1. Teaching large classes

I was once asked by a student in a teacher education course about how to deal with large classes. I began to list the kinds of adjustments he could make with classes of 50 to 75 students, when he said that he meant **really** large classes: somewhere in the neighborhood of 600 students! As I caught my breath, my only response was to ask him how he would teach 600 people to swim in one swimming pool without displacing all the water in the pool!

Ideally, language classes should have no more than a dozen people or so: large enough to provide diversity and student interaction and small enough to give students plenty of opportunity to participate and to get individual attention. Unfortunately, educational budgets being as paltry as they are, most language classes are significantly larger. Classes of 50 to 75 are not uncommon across this globe. While you need to keep reminding administrators (who too often believe that languages are learned by rote memorization) of the diminishing returns of classes in excess of 25 or 30, you nevertheless may have to cope with the reality of a large class for the time being. Large classes present some problems:

- Ability across students varies widely.
- Individual teacher-student attention is minimized.
- Student opportunities to speak are lessened.
- Teacher's feedback on students' written work is limited.

Some solutions to these problems are available. Consider the following that apply to one or several of the above challenges:

(a) Try to make each student feel important (and not just a "number") by learning names and using them. Name tags or desk "plates" serve as reminders.

(b) Get students to do as much interactive work as possible, including plenty of "get-acquainted" activities at the beginning, so that they feel a part of a community and are not just lost in the crowd.

(c) Optimize the use of pair work and small group work to give students chances to perform in English. In grouping, consider the variation in ability levels.

(d) Do more than the usual number of listening comprehension activities, using tapes, video, and yourself. Make sure students know what kind of response is expected from them. Through active listening comprehension, students can learn a good deal of language that transfers to reading, speaking, and writing.

(e) Use peer editing, feedback, and evaluation in written work whenever appropriate.

(f) Give students a range of extra-class work, from a minimum that all students must do to challenging tasks for the better students in the class.

(g) Don't collect written work from all of your students at the same time; spread it out in some systematic way both to lighten your load and to give students the benefit of a speedy return of their work.

(h) Set up small "learning centers" in your class where students can do individualized work.

(i) Organize informal conversation groups and study groups.

2. Compromising with the "institution"

Another adverse circumstance is one that most teachers have to deal with at some time in their careers, teaching under institutional conditions that do not meet your ideal standards or philosophy of education. Sometimes such circumstances focus on an individual in charge, a director or principal. And sometimes they center on administrative constraints that are beyond the scope and power of one individual. Some examples:

- classes that are far too large to allow for the kind of results that the administration expects (see above)
- physical conditions in the classroom that are onerous
- administratively imposed constraints on **what** you have to teach in your course (the curriculum, possibly in great detail)
- administratively imposed constraints on **how** you should teach (a specific methodology that you disagree with is required)
- courses that satisfy an institutional foreign language requirement, in which students simply want a passing grade
- courses that are test-focused rather than language-focused

All these and more adverse circumstances are part of the reality of teaching and ultimately of classroom management because they all impinge in some way on what you can do in your lessons. Your handling of such situations will almost always demand some sort of compromise on your part. You must, as a professional "technician" in this field, be ready to bring professional diplomacy and efficiency to bear on the varying degrees of hardship.

3. Discipline

Many volumes of research and practical advice have been written on the subject of classroom discipline. If all of your students were hard-working, intrinsically motivated, active, dedicated, intelligent learners—well, you would **still** have what we could label as "discipline" problems! Without making this section a whole primer on discipline, I will simply offer some pointers here and let you make the applications to specific instances.

- Learn to be comfortable with your position of authority.
- Gain the respect of your students by treating them all with equal fairness.
- State clearly and explicitly to your students what your expectations are regarding their behavior in class (speaking, turntaking, respect for others, group work, individual work, test taking, etc.), attendance (tardiness and absence policy), and any extra-class ("homework") obligations.
- Be firm but warm in dealing with variances to these expectations.

- If a reminder, reprimand, or other form of verbal disciplinary action is warranted, do your best to preserve the dignity of the student (in spite of the fact that you could be frustrated enough to want to humiliate the student in front of class-mates!).
- Try, initially, to resolve disciplinary matters outside of class time (ask to see a student after class and quietly but firmly make your observation and let the student respond) so that valuable class minutes aren't spent focusing on one student.
- In resolving disciplinary problems, try to find the source of the problem rather than treating symptoms (for example, if a student isn't paying attention in class, it could be because of a lack of sleep caused by trying to work a late night shift, in which case you could suggest a different shift or a different time bracket for the English class).
- If you cannot resolve a recurring disciplinary problem, then consult your institution's counselor or administrator.

4. Cheating

Cheating is a special disciplinary matter that warrants careful treatment. For the sake of definition, we will say **cheating** is a surreptitious violation of standards of individualized responses to tests or other exercises. The first step to solving a perceived problem of cheating is to ascertain a student's own perception: Did he or she honestly believe they were doing something wrong? There is a good deal of cultural variation in defining what is or isn't cheating, and for some, what you may think is cheating is merely an intelligent utiliza-tion of resources close at hand. In other words, if the answer that is written on the test is correct, then the means used to come up with the correct answer are justified. Once you have adequately ascertained a student's perception, then follow the disciplinary suggestions above as a guide to a solution.

Minimizing opportunities to cheat—that is, prevention—may prove to be more fruitful than trying to tangle with the mixture of emotions that ensues from dealing with cheating after the fact. Why do students cheat? Usually because of pressure to "excel." So if you can lower that pressure (see Chapter 19 on Testing), you may reduce the chance that someone will write notes on a fingernail or glance across the aisle. Remind students that you and the test are there to help them and to give them feedback, but if you don't see their "real" selves, you won't be able to help them. If the classroom size permits, get stu-dents spread out as much as possible (this "elbow room" also promotes some physical relaxation). Then, consider an "A" and "B" form of a test in which items are in a different order for every other person thereby making it more difficult for someone to spot an answer.

Teachers' Roles and Styles

In these final sections on classroom management, we turn a little more centrally to the affective or emotional side of being and becoming a good teacher.

1. Roles

A teacher has to play many **roles**, as was pointed out in Chapter 10. Think of the possibilities: authority figure, leader, knower, director, manager, counselor, guide, and even such roles as friend, confidante, and parent. Depending on the country you are in, on the institution in which you are teaching, on the type of course, and on the makeup of your students, some of these roles will be more prominent than others, especially in the eyes of your students.

Two rules of thumb in growing comfortable and confident in playing multiple roles is **a willing acceptance** of many ways that students will perceive you, and **a consistent fairness** to all students equally. Know yourself, your limitations, your strengths, your likes and dislikes, and then accept the fact that you are called upon to be many things to many different people. Then, as you become more comfortable with, say, being an authority figure, be consistent in all your dealings with students. There is something quite unsettling about a teacher who is a sympathetic friend to some students and a dispassionate authority figure to others. Such waffling in playing out your roles can set students against each other, with many feeling shut out from an inner circle of "teacher's pets."

2. Styles

Your teaching **style** is another affective consideration in the development of your professional expertise. Teaching style will almost always be consistent with your personality style, which can vary greatly from individual to individual. As you consider the teaching styles below, remember that each represents a **continuum** of possibilities:

shy	gregarious
formal	informal
reserved	open, transparent
understated	dramatic
rational	emotional
steady	variety of moods
serious	humorous
restrictive	permissive

Where do you place yourself on these continua? Do you feel it is necessary to lean toward one end in order to be an effective teacher? If you do, you may be succumbing to a stereotype that doesn't jibe with your most effective "self" in the classroom. I have seen excellent teachers on both sides of these style continua. As you grow more comfortable with your teaching roles in the classroom, make sure your style of teaching is also consistent with the rest of you and with the way you feel you can be most genuine in the classroom; then, learn how to capitalize on the strengths of your teaching style.

3. Cultural expectations

Western cultures emphasize nondirective, nonauthoritarian roles and teaching styles in the right hand column in the list above. One major consideration, therefore, in the effectiveness of playing roles and developing styles is the **culture** in which you are teaching, and/or the culture of your students.

Listed below are a number of cultural expectations of roles and styles as they relate to teachers and students and schools (adapted from Hofstede, 1986):

• Teachers are expected to have all the answers	• Teachers are allowed to say "I don't know"
• Teachers are expected to suppress emotions (and so are students)	• Teachers are allowed to express emotions (and so are students)
• Teachers interpret intellectual disagreement as personal disloyalty	• Teachers interpret intellectual disagreement as a stimulating exercise
• Teachers reward students for accuracy in problem solving	• Teachers reward students for innovative approaches to problem solving
• Students admire brilliance in teachers	• Students admire friendliness in teachers
• Students should speak in class only when called on by the teacher	• Students are encouraged to volunteer their thoughts
• Teachers should never lose face; to do so loses the respect of students	• Teachers can admit when they are wrong and still maintain students' respect
• Students expect the teacher to show them "the way"	• Teachers expect students to find their own way

Wherever you find yourself teaching, the above forces will come into play as you attempt to be an effective teacher. If you feel that one column is more "you" than another, then you should be cautious in developing a relationship with students and colleagues who may come from a different tradition. Always be sensitive to the **perceptions** of others but then do what you feel is appropriate to negotiate changes in attitude. Be ready to compromise your ideal self to some extent, especially when you begin a teaching assignment. There is little to be gained by coming into a teaching post like gangbusters and alienating all those around you and finding yourself unemployed a couple of months later. If you have convictions about what good teaching is, it pays to be patient in slowly reaching your goals. After all, you might learn something from **them**!

Creating a Positive Classroom Climate

The roles you play and the styles that you develop will merge to give you some tools for creating a classroom climate that is positive, stimulating, and energizing.

1. Establish rapport

"Rapport" is a somewhat slippery but important concept in creating positive energy in the classroom. Rapport is the relationship or connection you establish with your students, a relationship that is built on trust and respect and that leads to students' feeling capable, competent, and creative. How do you set up such a connection? By:

- showing interest in each student as a person,
- giving feedback on each person's progress,
- openly soliciting students' ideas and feelings,
- valuing and respecting what students think and say,
- laughing **with** them and not **at** them,
- working **with** them as a team, and not **against** them, and
- developing a genuine sense of vicarious joy when **they** learn something or otherwise succeed.

2. Praise and criticism

Part of the rapport you create is based on the delicate balance that you set between praise and criticism. Too much of either one or the other renders it less and less effective. Genuine praise, appropriately delivered, enables students to welcome criticism and to put it to use. Here are some guidelines for effective praise contrasted with ineffective praise (adapted from Brophy, 1981):

Effective Praise	Ineffective Praise
• shows genuine pleasure and concern	• is impersonal, mechanical, and "robotic"
• shows verbal and nonverbal variety	• shows bland uniformity
• specifies the particulars of an accomplishment so students know exactly what was performed well	• is restricted to global comments; so students are not sure what was perform well
• is offered in recognition of noteworthy effort on difficult tasks	• is offered equally strongly for easy and difficult tasks
• attributes success to effort, implying that similar success can be expected in the future	• attributes success to ability, luck, or other external factors
• fosters intrinsic motivation to continue to pursue goals	• fosters extrinsic motivation to perform only to receive more praise
• is delivered without disrupting the communicative flow of ongoing interaction	• disrupts the communicative flow of ongoing interaction

3. Energy

What is classroom **energy**? I like to use this term for a force that is unleashed in a classroom, perceivable only through a "sixth sense," if you will, that is acquired in the experience of teaching itself. Energy is what you react to when you walk out of a class period and say to yourself, "Wow! That was a great class" or "What a great group of students!" Energy is the electricity of many minds caught up in a circuit of thinking and talking and writing. Energy is an aura of creativity sparked by the interaction of students. Energy drives students toward higher attainment. Students (and teachers) take energy with them when they leave the classroom and bring it back the next day.

How do you create this energy? Not necessarily by being dramatic or flamboyant, witty or wise. Sometimes energy is unleashed through a quiet, reserved, but focused teacher. Sometimes energy forces gather in the corporate intensity of students focused on rather mundane tasks. But you are the key. Because students initially look to you for leadership and guidance, you are the one to begin to get the creative sparks flying. And through whatever role or style you accomplish this, you do so through solid preparation, confidence in your ability to teach, a genuinely positive belief in your students' ability to learn, a sense of joy in doing what you do, and you also do so by overtly manifesting that preparation, confidence, positive belief, and joy when you walk into the classroom.

TOPICS FOR DISCUSSION, ACTION, AND RESEARCH

1. Plan a brief demonstration or role-play of **bad** nonverbal communication—what you should not do in the classroom. Present your demonstration to your classmates. They can then comment on what they saw and on what aspects of your simulation would not be recommended.

2. Look again at the list of things (p. 415) that can go "wrong" in a classroom. Can you add some other things to the list? In a small group, brainstorm some possible "solutions" to each problem. Then report your group's ideas to the rest of the class which in turn can discuss their relative merits and come up with a composite list of solutions.

3. Consider the list of solutions to problems encountered in large classes. Are the solutions practical? Do they apply to actual circumstances that you or your classmates may be familiar with? What are some further measures that can be taken to maximize student opportunity for practice in large classes?

4. Suppose you have been assigned to teach in a language institute for adults in [you name the country]. The director insists that students will learn best through the Grammar Translation Method, mainly because that's the way he learned three foreign languages. He has asked you to use this method and the textbooks for the course are a grammar reference guide and a book of readings with vocabulary words listed at the end of each reading. Your class is a group of intermediate-level young adults, all currently employed in various places around the city. They want to learn English in order to get into a university. What would you do? How would you resolve the difference between what you believe your students need and the dictates of your director? (You need the money, so you don't want to get fired!)

5. Look again at the section on discipline. What are some discipline problems you have—or might—encounter? Talk about these in a small group and share ideas about how you would solve the problems.

6. What is cheating? Has anyone ever tried to cheat in a class you have been a student in? Describe the situation in a small group. What did the teacher do, if anything? What would you have done had you been the teacher?

7. Can you think of other "adverse circumstances" of teaching? Describe them. How would you deal with them?

8. Rate yourself on the continua of teacher styles on page 419. Use four boxes in between each factor and check the one that appropriately describes yourself. Do you feel that you need to change some of those natural styles when you enter a classroom? If not, why do you feel that your present styles are adequate? Are there any tendencies that might work against you? What should you do to prevent such a problem?

9. Consider the society you are teaching in, or anticipate teaching in. Where does that society fall on the list of continua describing cultural expectations of students? Are there other expectations you would add

to the list? Consider each factor and discuss specific ways in which you would deal with a conflict of expectations between yourself and your students.

10. In your own words, describe "energy." Share your description with a partner. Observe a class and see if you can identify things that the teacher **does** or the that students **do** that makes you feel that the class is "energized." Share your observations with others in your class.

FOR YOUR FURTHER READING

Crookes, Graham, and Chaudron, Craig. 1991. "Guidelines for classroom language teaching." In Celce-Murcia, Marianne (Ed.), *Teaching English as a Second or Foreign Language*. Second Edition. Newbury House.

A number of classroom management issues are dealt with here as the authors focus primarily on various classroom techniques (referred to in Chapter 9). Of special interest is a section on "classroom climate."

Hofstede, Geert. 1986. "Cultural differences in teaching and learning." *International Journal of Intercultural Relations 10*, 301–320.

A study of cultural expectations in fifty different countries with various implications for classroom management. Constructs like power distance and collectivism are described in some detail, with illustrations of how teacher and student behavior needs to be interpreted in their cultural contexts.

Lawrence, Gordon. 1984. *People Types & Tiger Stripes: A Practical Guide to Learning Styles*. Center for Applications of Psychological Type.

This fascinating little book outlines implications of the various Myers-Briggs personality types for educational settings. Teachers are introduced to Jung's theory of psychological types. They are then given practical guidelines for understanding the roles of teachers and learners, and for developing classroom activities that maximize learning.

Wright, Tony. 1990. "Understanding classroom role relationships." In Richards, Jack C., and Nunan, David (Eds.), *Second Language Teacher Education*. Cambridge University Press.

The author takes an in-depth look at the teacher and student roles in the second language classroom. Students' expectations and values are seen as important considerations in planning lessons, choosing materials, and managing the classroom.

Chapter 22

Lifelong Learning: Continuing Your Teacher Education

One of the most invigorating things about teaching is that you never stop learning. The complexity of the dynamic triangular interplay between teachers and learners and subject matter continually gives birth to an endless number of questions to answer, problems to solve, issues to ponder. Every time you walk into a classroom to teach something, you face some of those issues and if you are a **growing** teacher, you learn something. You find out how well a technique works, how a student processes language, how classroom interaction can be improved, how to assess a student's competence, how emotions enter into learning, or how your teaching style affects learners. The discoveries go on and on—for a lifetime.

As you embark on this journey into the teaching profession, how can you best continue to grow professionally? How can you most fruitfully meet the challenges that lie ahead? Are there some practical goals that you can pursue? So far, as you have worked through the material of this book, you have already begun to tackle some major professional goals (adapted from Pennington, 1990:150):

- a knowledge of the theoretical foundations of language learning and language teaching
- the analytical skills necessary for assessing different teaching contexts and classroom conditions
- an awareness of alternative teaching techniques and the ability to put these into practice
- the confidence and skill to alter your teaching techniques as needed
- practical experience with different teaching techniques
- informed knowledge of yourself and your students
- interpersonal communication skills
- attitudes of flexibility and openness to change

These eight different goals can provide continuing career growth for many, many years as you strive to a better and better job of teaching. But you must be patient! Don't expect to become a "master" teacher overnight. Right now, as you begin your teaching career, set some realistic, practical goals that you can focus on without being overwhelmed by everything you have to attend to when you teach. Just as beginning language learners are in a **controlled** mode of operation (see *PLLT*, Chapter 9, for a summary of McLaughlin's controlled vs. automatic processing) at the outset, able to manage only a few bits of information at a time with capacity-limited systems, so it is with your teaching as well. If you try to focus on everything in the classroom all at once (all the management issues, techniques, delivery, body language, feedback, individual attention, lesson goals and mid-lesson alterations, etc.) you may end up doing nothing well. In due course of time, however, the abundance of cognitive/emotional phenomena in the classroom will be sufficiently **automatic** that you will indeed manage to operate on many planes at once.

As you read on here, you will find some ideas that you can immediately put to work and others that may apply to you after you have gained some experience.

Peak Performers

Are you doing the best you can do? Are you being all that you can be— "self-actualized," in Maslow's terms? Or are you satisfied with getting by? In the stressful world of teaching, it's easier than you might imagine to slip into a pattern of just keeping a step ahead of your students as you struggle through long working hours and overly large classes. This pattern is the beginning of a downward spiral that you should avoid at all costs. How do you do that? In part by practicing the behaviors of **peak performers**, people who are reaching their fullest potential and therefore who, in turn, reap success. Consider the following four rules (among many) of peak performers that you might apply to yourself, even at this early stage in your career:

1. Set realistic goals

Peak performers, first of all, know their limitations and strengths and their feelings and needs and then set goals that will be realistic within this framework. They set their own goals and don't let the world around them (their colleagues, supervisors, friends, etc.) dictate goals to them. If you have a sense of overall purpose in your career as a mission, then this mission will unfold in the form of daily, weekly, monthly, or annual goals.

It would not be a bad idea right now for you to write down some short-term and long-term goals. Be realistic in terms of what you can accomplish. Be specific in your statements. Here are some examples to get the wheels turning:

- Read three teacher resource books this year.
- Use intrinsically motivating techniques on my next test.
- Observe five other teachers this semester.
- Monitor my error treatments in the classroom.
- Attend two professional conferences/workshops this year.

2. Set priorities

It is important that you have a sense of what is most important and what is least important, and everything in between, in your professional goals and tasks. If you don't, you can end up spending too much time on low priority tasks that rob you of the time you should be spending on higher priorities. Priority setting requires a sense of your whole life, professional and personal, and how you are going to use your waking hours.

3. Take risks

Peak performers don't play it safe all the time. They are not afraid to try new things. Nor are they put off by limiting circumstances—what cannot be done, or "the way" things are done. They don't linger in the safety of a "comfort zone"; instead they reach out for new challenges.

The key to risk taking as a peak performance strategy, however, is not simply in taking the risks. It is in **learning from your "failures."** When you risk a new technique in the classroom, or a new approach to a difficult student, or a frank comment to a supervisor, you must be willing to accept the possible "failure" in your attempt. Then, you assess all the facets of that failure and turn it into an experience that teaches you something about how to calculate the next risk.

4. Practice principles of stress management

Contrary to some perceptions from outside our profession, teaching is a career with all the makings for high stress conditions. Think of some of the sources of stress in this business:

- long hours
- large classes
- low pay
- pressure to "perform" in the classroom
- high student expectations
- demands beyond the classroom
- emotional connections with students' lives
- bureaucracies
- pressure to keep up with a rapidly changing field
- information overload

Managing those potential stress factors is an important key to keeping yourself fresh, creative, bright, and happy.

One of the cardinal rules of stress management is setting priorities, which has already been dealt with above. Another rule was also touched on above: Know your limitations. Other rules follow—don't take on too many extra little duties; take time for yourself; and balance your personal and professional time. Peak performers don't spend 18 hours a day working. They don't get so consumed with their profession that the rest of their life is a shambles. They work hard but stop to play. They know how to relax and do so regularly. And they develop fulfilling personal relationships with family and friends that provide enrichment and renewal.

As you begin a teaching career, you may feel the weight of heavy demands. And teaching is not one of those careers where you can necessarily leave all the cognitive and emotional load in the office. So, you can expect to be the proverbial overworked and underpaid laborer. But in the midst of those demands, try to balance your life, and take everything in perspective .

The "Good" Language Teacher

One way to begin setting goals and priorities is to consider the qualities of successful language teachers in particular. Numerous "experts" have come up with their lists of attributes and they all differ in a variety of ways. The eight goals for continuing career growth cited at the beginning of this chapter are one example of a list of attributes of a "good" language teacher. Harold B. Allen (1980) once offered the following down-to-earth list of characteristics of good ESL teachers:

1) Competent preparation leading to a degree in TESL

(2) A love of the English language

(3) The critical faculty

(4) The persistent urge to upgrade oneself

(5) Self-subordination

(6) Readiness to go the extra mile

(7) Cultural adaptability

(8) Professional citizenship

(9) A feeling of excitement about one's work

There's a good deal of grist for the professional growth mills in those nine items. How would you rate yourself on all nine? Any room for improvement on any of them? If so, you have some goal setting to do.

I offer the following checklist as a composite of several unpublished sources along with TESOL's *Guidelines for the Certification and Preparation of Teachers of English to Speakers of Other Languages.* You may wish to use this checklist to do a self-check to determine some areas for continued professional growth, to prioritize those areas, and to state specific goals that you will pursue. Try rating yourself for each item on a scale of 1 (poor) to 5 (excellent) and see how you come out.

Good Language Teaching Characteristics

Technical Knowledge

1. Understands the linguistic systems of English phonology, grammar, and discourse.
2. Comprehensively grasps basic principles of language learning and teaching.
3. Has fluent competence in speaking, writing, listening to, and reading English.
4. Knows through experience what it is like to learn a foreign language.
5. Understands the close connection between language and culture.
6. Keeps up with the field through regular reading and conference/workshop attendance.

Pedagogical Skills

7. Has a well thought out, informed **approach** to language teaching.
8. Understands and has experience using a wide variety of techniques.
9. Efficiently designs and executes lesson plans.
10. Monitors lessons as they unfold and makes effective mid-lesson alterations.
11. Effectively perceives students' linguistic needs.
12. Gives optimal feedback to students.
13. Stimulates interaction, cooperation, and teamwork in the classroom.
14. Uses appropriate principles of classroom management.
15. Uses effective, clear presentation skills.
16. Creatively adapts textbook material and other audio, visual, and mechanical aids.
17. Innovatively creates brand new materials when needed.
18. Uses interactive, intrinsically motivating techniques to create effective tests.

Interpersonal Skills

19. Is aware of cross-cultural differences and sensitive to students' cultural traditions.
20. Enjoys people, shows enthusiasm, warmth, rapport, and appropriate humor.
21. Values the opinions and abilities of students.
22. Is patient in working with students of lesser ability.
23. Offers challenges to students of exceptionally high ability.
24. Cooperates harmoniously and candidly with colleagues (fellow teachers).
25. Seeks opportunities to share thoughts, ideas, and techniques with colleagues.

Personal Qualities

26. Is well organized, conscientious in meeting commitments, and dependable.
27. Is flexible when things go awry.
28. Maintains an inquisitive mind in trying out new ways of teaching.
29. Sets short-term and long-term goals for continued professional growth.
30. Maintains and exemplifies high ethical and moral standards.

Classroom Observation

One the most neglected areas of professional growth among teachers is the mutual exchange of classroom observations. Once you get into a teaching routine, it is very difficult to make time to go and see other teachers and to invite the same in return. Too often, teachers tend to view observations as necessary while "in training" but unnecessary thereafter unless a supervisor is forced by regulations to visit your class in order to write up a recommendation for rehiring. If one of your colleagues comes up to you and says, "Hey, guess what? I was observed today," your answer might be something like "Oh, no! How bad was it?"

Fortunately, in an era of **action research** (see below, this chapter), the prevailing attitude toward observations is changing. Teachers are coming to understand that seeing one's actions through another's eyes is an indispensable tool for classroom research as well as potentially enlightening for both observer and observee. Before you get into the nasty habit of filling your time with everything **else**, why don't you carve out some time in your work schedule to visit other teachers and to invite reciprocity? As long as such visits pose no undue complication in schedules and other institutional constraints, you will reap rewarding benefits as you gain new ideas, keep fresh, and sharpen your own skills.

A second form of observation, which can be very effective in different ways, is self-observation. Actually, self-observation is no more than a systematic process of monitoring yourself, but it's the **systematic** part that is crucial. It requires discipline and perseverance, but the results are worth it. How do you go about observing yourself?

(1) Select an element of your teaching to "keep an eye out for" as you teach. Make sure it's one finite element, like teacher talk, eye contact, teaching predominantly to one side of the classroom, or blackboard work. If you try to take in too many things, you could end up becoming too self-conscious to the detriment of the rest of the lesson.

(2) Monitor that particular element during the class period. If you can, video tape yourself (or have someone come in and operate the camera).

(3) After class, set aside a few moments to give these elements careful assessment.

The most common and instructive means to go about observing oneself or others is to use an **observation checklist**. Dozens of such instruments are in active use by teacher trainers, supervisors, and teachers across the profession. Two such checklists are found on pages 432–436. The first is a checklist for observing other teachers; the second is designed for self-observation.

Teacher Observation Form A: Observing other teachers

Please try to keep in mind the following criteria when observing a teacher. Circle or check each item in the column that most clearly represents your evaluation: 4 excellent, 3 above average, 2 average, I unsatisfactory, N/A not applicable. *In addition* or *in lieu of* checking a column, you may write comments in the space provided.

I.　PREPARATION

Degree to which ...

1.　The teacher was well-prepared and well-organized in class.

N/A 4 3 2 I

Comment:

2.　The lesson reviewed material and looked ahead to new material.

N/A 4 3 2 I

Comment:

3.　The prepared goals/objectives were apparent.

N/A 4 3 2 I

Comment:

II.　PRESENTATION

Degree to which ...

4.　The class material was explained in an understandable way.

N/A 4 3 2 I

Comment:

5.　The lesson was smooth, sequenced, and logical.

N/A 4 3 2 I

Comment:

6.　The lesson was well-paced.

N/A 4 3 2 I

Comment:

7.　Directions were clear and concise and students were able to carry them out.

N/A 4 3 2 I

Comment:

8.　Material was presented at the students' level of comprehension.

N/A 4 3 2 I

Comment:

9.　An appropriate percentage of the class was student production of the language.

N/A 4 3 2 I

Comment:

10.　The teacher answered questions carefully and satisfactorily.

N/A 4 3 2 I

Comment:

11.　The method/s was/were appropriate to the age and ability of students.

N/A 4 3 2 I

Comment:

12.　The teacher knew when the students were having trouble understanding.

N/A 4 3 2 I

Comment:

13.　The teacher showed an interest in, and enthusiasm for, the subject taught.

N/A 4 3 2 I

Comment:

III.   EXECUTION/METHODS

Degree to which...

14.   There were balance and variety in activities during the lesson.

N/A 4 3 2 1

Comment:

15.   The teacher was able to adapt to unanticipated situations.

N/A 4 3 2 1

Comment:

16.   The material was reinforced.

N/A 4 3 2 1

Comment:

17.   The teacher moved around the class and made eye contact with students.

N/A 4 3 2 1

Comment:

18.   The teacher knew students' names.

N/A 4 3 2 1

Comment:

19.   The teacher positively reinforced the students.

N/A 4 3 2 1

Comment:

20.   Student responses were effectively elicited (i.e., the order in which the students were called on).

N/A 4 3 2 1

Comment:

21   Examples and illustrations were used effectively.

N/A 4 3 2 1

Comment:

22.   Instructional aids or resource material was used effectively.

N/A 4 3 2 1

Comment:

23.   Drills were used and presented effectively.

N/A 4 3 2 1

Comment:

24.   Structures were taken out of artificial drill contexts and applied to the real contexts of the students' culture and personal experiences.

N/A 4 3 2 1

Comment:

25.   Error perception.

N/A 4 3 2 1

Comment:

26.   Appropriate error correction.

N/A 4 3 2 1

Comment:

IV.   PERSONAL CHARACTERISTICS

27.   Patience in eliciting responses.

N/A 4 3 2 1

Comment:

28.   Clarity, tone, and audibility of voice.

N/A 4 3 2 1

Comment:

29. Personal appearance.

  N/A 4 3 2 1

  Comment:

30. Initiative, resourcefulness, and creativity.

  N/A 4 3 2 1

  Comment:

31. Pronunciation, intonation, fluency, and appropriate and acceptable use of language.

  N/A 4 3 2 1

  Comment:

V. TEACHER/STUDENT INTERACTION

Degree to which …

32. Teacher encouraged and assured full student participation in class.

  N/A 4 3 2 1

  Comment:

33. The class felt free to ask questions, to disagree, or to express their own ideas.

  N/A 4 3 2 1

  Comment:

34. The teacher was able to control and direct the class.

  N/A 4 3 2 1

  Comment:

35. The students were attentive and involved.

  N/A 4 3 2 1

  Comment:

36. The students were comfortable and relaxed, even during intense intellectual activity.

  N/A 4 3 2 1

  Comment:

37. The students were treated fairly, impartially, and with respect.

  N/A 4 3 2 1

  Comment:

38. The students were encouraged to do their best.

  N/A 4 3 2 1

  Comment:

39. The teacher was relaxed and matter-of-fact in voice and manner.

  N/A 4 3 2 1

  Comment:

40. The teacher was aware of individual and group needs.

  N/A 4 3 2 1

  Comment:

41. Digressions were used positively and not over-used.

  N/A 4 3 2 1

  Comment:

Teacher Observation Form B: Self-observation (Christison & Bassano, 1984)

Thoughtfully consider each statement. Rate yourself in the following way:
3=Excellent   2=Good   1=Needs Improvement   0=Not Applicable

Write your ratings in the blanks. When you've finished, give overall consideration to the various areas.

I. Learning Environment
   A. Relationship to Students

_____ 1. I establish good eye contact with my class. I do not talk over their heads, to the blackboard, or to just one person.

_____ 2. If I tend to teach predominantly to one area of the classroom, I am aware of this. I make a conscious effort at all times to pay attention to all students equally.

_____ 3. I divide my students into small groups in an organized and principled manner. I recognize that these groups should differ in size and composition, varying with the objective of the group activity.

   B. The Classroom

_____ 1. If possible, I arrange the seating in my class to suit the class activity for the day.

_____ 2. I consider the physical comfort of the room such as heat and light.

_____ 3. When I need special materials or equipment, I have them set up before the class begins.

   C. Presentation

_____ 1. My handwriting on the blackboard and charts is legible from all locations in the classroom. It is large enough to accommodate students with vision impairments.

_____ 2. I speak loudly enough to be heard in all parts of the classroom and I enunciate clearly.

_____ 3. I vary the exercises in class, alternating rapid and slow paced activities to keep up the maximum interest in the class.

_____ 4. I am prepared to give a variety of explanations, models, or descriptions for all students.

_____ 5. I help the students form working principles and generalizations.

_____ 6. Students use new skills or concepts long enough so that they are retained and thus future application is possible.

_____ 7. I plan for "Thinking time" for my students so they can organize their thoughts and plan what they are going to say or do.

   D. Culture and Adjustment

_____ 1. I am aware that cultural differences affect the learning situation.

_____ 2. I keep the cultural background(s) of my students in mind when planning daily activities and am aware of cultural misunderstandings that might arise from the activities I choose.

_____ 3. I promote an atmosphere of understanding and mutual respect.

II. The Individuals
   A. Physical Health

_____ 1. I know which students have visual or aural impairments and have seated them as close to my usual teaching positions as possible.

_____ 2. I am aware that a student's attention span varies from day to day depending on mental and physical health and outside distractions. I pace my class activities to accommodate the strengths. I don't continue with an activity that may exhaust or bore them.

_____ 3. I begin my class with a simple activity to wake students up and get them working together.

_____ 4. I am sensitive to individual students who have bad days. I don't press a student who is incapable of performing at the usual level.

_____ 5. I try to challenge students who are at their best.
_____ 6. If I am having a bad a day and feel it might affect my normal teaching style, I let my students know it so there is no misunderstanding about my feelings for them.

B. Self-concepts
_____ 1. I treat my students with the same respect that I expect them to show me.
_____ 2. I plan "one-centered" activities that give all students an opportunity at some point to feel important and accepted.
_____ 3. I like to teach and have a good time teaching—on most days.

C. Aptitude and Perception
_____ 1. I am aware that my students learn differently. Some students are visual-receptive, some are motor receptive, and others are audio-receptive.
_____ 2. My exercises are varied; some are visual, aural, oral, and kinesthetic. I provide models, examples, and experiences to maximize learning each of these areas.
_____ 3. I know basic concepts in the memory process. When applicable, I use association to aid students in rapid skills acquisition.

D. Reinforcement
_____ 1. I tell students when they have done well, but I don't let praise become mechanical.
_____ 2. I finish my class period in a way that will review the new concepts presented during the class period. My students can immediately evaluate their understanding of those concepts.
_____ 3. My tests are well-planned and produced.
_____ 4. I make my system of grading clear to my students so that there are no misunderstandings of expectations.

E. Development
_____ 1. I keep up to date on new techniques in the ESL profession by attending conferences and workshops and by reading pertinent professional articles and books.
_____ 2. I realize that there is no one right way to present a lesson. I try new ideas where and when they seem appropriate.
_____ 3. I observe other ESL teachers so that I can get other ideas and compare them to my own teaching style. I want to have several ideas for teaching one concept.

III. The Activity
A. Interaction
_____ 1. I minimize my role in _conducting_ the activities.
_____ 2. I organize the activities so they are suitable for _real_ interactions among students.
_____ 3. The activities maximize student involvement.
_____ 4. The activities promote spontaneity or experimentation on the part of the learner.
_____ 5. The activities generally transfer attention away from "self" and outward toward a "task."
_____ 6. The activities are organized to insure a high success rate, leaving enough room for error to make the activity challenging.
_____ 7. I am not always overly concerned with error correction. I choose the appropriate amount of correction for the activity.

B. Language
_____ 1. The activity is focused.
_____ 2. The content of the skill presented will be easily transferrable for use outside the class.
_____ 3. The activity is geared to the proficiency level of my class or slightly beyond.
_____ 4. The content of the activity is not too sophisticated for my students.
_____ 5. I make the content of the activity relevant and meaningful to my students' world.

Classroom Research

Research is a scary word for many of us. It is something that we are just as happy leaving in someone else's hands because it involves statistics (which we hate), experimental design (which we don't know), and the interpretation of ambiguous results (which we think is best left to the "experts"). Unfortunately, leaving all the research in the hands of researchers is an upside-down policy, as Meek (1991:34) recently noted:

> **The main thing wrong with the world of education is that there's this one group of people who do it—the teachers—and then there's another group who think they know about it—the researchers. The group who think they know about teaching try to find out more about it in order to tell the teachers about teaching—and that is total reversal.**
>
> **Teachers are the ones who do it and, therefore, are the ones who know about it. It's worth getting teachers to build on what they know, to build on what questions they have, because that's what matters—what teachers know and what questions they have. And so anybody who wants to be a helpful researcher should value what the teachers know and help them develop that.**

Actually, research does not have to be a scary prospect at all. You are researching ideas all the time, whether you know it or not. If, as a growing teacher, one of your goals is to improve the quality of your teaching, then you will ask some relevant questions, hypothesize some possible answers or solutions, put the solutions to a practical tryout in the classroom, look for certain results, and weigh those results in some manner to determine whether your hypothesized answer held up or not. That's research. Some classroom research is an informal, everyday occurrence for you. You divide up small groups in a different way to stimulate better exchange of ideas; you modify your usual non-directive approach to getting students to study harder and take a bold, direct, no-nonsense approach; you try a video tape as a conversation stimulus; you try a deductive approach to presenting a grammar point instead of your usual inductive approach. Other classroom research may be more of a long-term process covering a term or more. In this mode, still in an informal manner, you may try out some learner strategy training techniques to see if students do better at conversation skills; you may do a daily three-minute pronunciation drill to see if students' pronunciation improves; you may assign specific extra-class reading to see if reading comprehension improves.

This kind of "action research," better known simply as **classroom research**, is carried out not so much to fulfill a thesis requirement or to publish a journal article as to improve your own understanding of the teaching-learning process in the classroom. The payoff for treating your teaching-learning questions seriously is, ultimately, your becoming a better teacher. And, yes, you might also find that what you have learned is worth sharing with other teachers, either through informal chats in the teacher's lunchroom or through a conference presentation.

David Nunan (1989) suggested that classroom research may be categorized into four different aspects: the developmental features of learner language, interaction in the second language, classroom tasks, and learning strategies. The list below (Nunan 1989b:36) offers some examples of research questions in each category.

Learner Language: Developmental Features

1. In my teaching, I generally provide an application task to follow up a formal presentation. Which language items do learners actually use in the application task?

2. Do learners learn closed class items (e.g., pronouns/demonstratives) when these are presented as paradigms, or when they are taught separately over a period of time?

Learner Language: Interaction

3. In what ways do turn taking and topic management vary with variations in the size and composition of learner groups?

4. Are learners more effective at conversational management when techniques such as holding the floor, bringing in another speaker, etc., are consciously taught?

Tasks

5. Which tasks stimulate more interaction?

6. Which tasks work best with mixed-ability groups?

Strategies

7. Is there a conflict between the classroom activities I favor and those my learners prefer?

8. Do my best learners share certain strategy preferences that distinguish them from less efficient learners?

You still may be feeling a little queasy about labeling some of your teacher inquisitiveness as "research": Can I really ask the "right" questions? How do I know if my research methodology is sound? How will I deal with numerical results (statistics)? Will my conclusions be valid? Good questions. First of all, I recommend that you consult one or both of two excellent recent teacher resource books on classroom research:

Allwright, Dick, and Bailey, Kathleen M. 1991. *Focus on the Language Classroom: An Introduction to Classroom Research for Language Teachers.* Cambridge University Press.

Nunan, David. 1989b. *Understanding Language Classrooms: A Guide for Teacher-Initiated Action.* Prentice Hall.

Second, consider the following pointers to get yourself started on some simple but potentially effective action research.

1. Convert your "ideas" into specific questions.

You may have quite a few "ideas" about things that you could investigate in the classroom. That's good; keep those creative juices flowing. But in order to be able to draw conclusions, your ideas have to be converted into questions that you can answer. Sometimes those questions are too broad: Is communicative language teaching effective? How useful is reading aloud in class? Does process writing work? So, make sure that your questions are specific enough that you can look back after your investigation and really come up with an answer. The questions do not have to be long and drawn out, just specific, like the eight questions listed above on page 438. As an example here, we will consider the following question:

Given a selection of six commonly used techniques, how do they compare with each other in terms of stimulating interaction?

2. Operationally define the elements of your question.

Next, take your question and operationally define all the elements in it. "Operational" means that you have a measurable means for determining something. So, for example, the word "techniques" appears in our example question. You know what a technique is, but for the purpose of your research you have selected six **small-group** techniques (jigsaw, role-play, etc.). You will simply limit your investigation to those six. Interaction then has to be defined. Suppose you define interaction as the total number of **turns** taken in each group. And, just for a possibly interesting additional statistic, suppose you total up the number of **minutes** of student talk as well.

3. Determine how you will answer your question.

Now, you are ready to launch the investigation. How will you answer the question? Your research **methodology** may call for several weeks of data collecting and, in this particular case, some tape recorders, since you will not be able to record data for several small groups at once and also attend to the techniques as well. For each of the six designated techniques you will have a tape recorder placed in each small group and running during the entire technique. (Yes, the tape recorders may inhibit some students, but that's the risk you have to take.) You will (perhaps with the help of a colleague?) then listen to each tape and tally the number of turns for each and add up minutes of talk as well. Assuming that all the groups have been allowed an equal number of total minutes within each technique, then you can come up with a grand total of turns and minutes for each technique. The number of turns for each technique will determine its rank order among the six.

4. Interpret your results appropriately.

According to your findings (see below), technique A stimulates the most interaction, B is next, and so on. But your conclusion may not be so simple. Every research study has its necessary caveats, so before you make a sweeping generalization about your findings, it will help to state, even if only for yourself, some of the limitations on your results.

Here are the results you came up with:

Technique	Turns	Minutes
		Student talk/Total time
A	137	73/90
B	133	85/90
C	116	79/90
D	111	69/90
E	102	71/90
F	91	79/90

First, can you be sure that Technique A stimulated **significantly** more turns than Technique B? And B more than C, etc.? Ask a statistician to help you to determine how probable it is that your results stemmed from the technique rather than from just random possibilities. This way you will be able to determine the statistical significance of your findings.

Second, notice that the number of minutes of student talk didn't correspond, meaning that in some techniques (A for example) there was some relatively rapid turn taking interspersed with student silence, and in other techniques (F for example) certain students talked for longer stretches of time. This may give you cause to redefine interaction or at least to interpret your results accordingly.

Finally, results need to be seen in terms of other limitations in the study itself: the choice and number of tasks, number of students, the operational definitions chosen, your particular group of students. You may be tempted to generalize results of classroom research to the world at large. Beware. Your safest conclusion is one that reports what you found for your class, and to invite others to **replicate** your study if they wish to see if similar results are obtained.

Classroom research is ideally suited to current practice in language teaching where we are **not** in the business of buying into one of the "designer" methods with their prescriptions of what teachers should do in the classroom. Instead our communicative, interactive language teaching **approach** is one that asks every teacher to assess his or her own classroom full of students and to design instructional techniques that work under those particular conditions, for those particular learners, who are pursuing particular purposes in learning the English language. Nunan (1989b:97–98) comments:

> In contrast with the "follow the method" approach, a teacher-as-classroom-researcher orientation encourages teachers to approach methods and ideas with a critical eye, and to adopt an experimental approach to incorporating these ideas into their classrooms. Rather than adopting new methods, materials, or ideas and judging their efficacy on intuitive grounds, it is far more satisfactory, and professionally rewarding, to establish a small-scale classroom experiment to monitor, observe, and document the effect of the new methods or materials on learner language, learning outcomes, classroom climate, [and] patterns of group interaction. …In addition, this alternative orientation seeks to derive principles for teaching from the close observation and documentation of what actually happens in the classroom rather than uncritically importing and applying ideas from outside.

Agents for Change

A few years ago, Alastair Pennycook, in a very stimulating essay on language teaching, power, and politics, reminded us that teachers are "transformative intellectuals" who must see ourselves "as professionals who are able and willing to … connect pedagogical theory and practice to wider social issues, and who work together to share ideas, exercise power of the conditions of our labor, and embody in our teaching a vision of a better and more humane life." (Pennycook, 1989:613)

Teaching is a **political act**. You have a set of beliefs about how the people of this world should behave toward one another. You have convictions about the quality of life, the shape of liberty, and the pursuit of happiness. You have perhaps more than an inkling of how your skills as a teacher might be utilized to create empathy and unity in a world full of misunderstandings. You are therefore engaged in a political, empowering act when you teach English. You will no doubt be very careful not to push a particular "philosophy" or a particular morality on your students, but you will nevertheless be acting from your deepest convictions when you teach people to speak tactfully, to negotiate meaning harmoniously, to read critically, and to write persuasively.

You are not merely a language teacher. You are much more than that. You are an **agent for change** in a world in desperate need of change: change from competition to cooperation, from powerlessness to empowerment, from conflict to resolution, from prejudice to understanding.

And what could be more intrinsic to the spirit of all language teachers around the world than to finely tune our ability to become agents for change? Our professional commitment drives us to help the inhabitants of this planet to communicate with each other, to negotiate the meaning of peace, of goodwill, and of survival on this tender, fragile globe. We must, therefore, with all the professional tools available to us, passionately pursue these ultimate goals.

TOPICS FOR DISCUSSION, ACTION, AND RESEARCH

1. If you have been systematically reading and studying the chapters of this book, then you have by now picked up a reasonably comprehensive picture of principles and issues in language teaching and how they apply to the classroom. With that background information, go back now to Chapter 1 and look through the lesson that was described there. Then, look at the 30 questions posed in the subsequent section ("Beneath the Lesson," pp. 10 to 12). In pairs or small groups, share your answers to those questions. What aspects of this class hour would you change, and why? Present your rationale for changes to the whole class.

2. Look again at the 12 principles of language learning and teaching outlined in Chapter 2. Restate them in your own words. Which principles are more applicable to your own context(s) of teaching English?

3. Over the next six months, see what you could do to be more of a "peak performer" as a teacher. Set some goals for yourself, and write them down in an order of priority or in a chronological order. Resolve to take some risks, and, if you think you need to do so, do some specific things to lower stress in your life. Consider writing a journal to keep track of your progress.

4. Look again at the list of 30 characteristics of a "good language teacher" (p. 430). Pick two or three that you think you would like to work on (see exercise #3 above). Share your resolutions with a partner, friend, or colleague and see if you can keep each other "on track."

5. Use Observation Form B for self-observation the next time you teach. What did you learn? Use Form A to observe another teacher and go over your notes with the teacher. Encourage reciprocity in the latter.

6. Look at the list of research questions suggested on page 438. Select one. In a group discuss how you might go through steps 1 through 4 that were suggested on pages 439 to 441. Share your plan with the rest of class.

7. Using the list on pages 438 as a starting point, brainstorm in a group some other researchable ideas. (Use a blackboard or poster paper to write the ideas down.) Pick several ideas that you, individually, or a small team of teachers might carry out. Make plans for some action research that you might someday share in a presentation at a professional conference.

8. Explain how teaching is a political act. Just how is it that politics enters in? What kind of an "agent" are you? What **changes** would your teaching lead to in a student? in a society in general?

FOR YOUR FURTHER READING

Allwright, Dick, and Bailey, Kathleen M. 1991. *Focus on the Language Classroom: An Introduction to Classroom Research for Language Teachers.* Cambridge University Press.

Nunan, David. 1989b. *Understanding Language Classrooms: A Guide for Teacher-Initiated Action.* Prentice Hall.

Both of these books provide comprehensive overviews of what classroom centered research is, principles and procedures involved, and exemplary classroom research studies. They serve as excellent manuals to guide teachers as they carry out various kinds of research in their own classrooms.

Bailey, Kathleen M. 1990. "The use of diary studies in teacher education programs." In Richards, Jack C., and Nunan, David (Eds.), *Second Language Teacher Education.* Cambridge University Press.

One of the best ways for teachers to observe their own professional growth is through the use of a diary or log of candid reflections on their teaching. The author gives specific guidance on writing such diaries and on the benefits thereof to the teacher.

Pennycook, Alastair. 1989. "The concept of method, interested knowledge, and the politics of language teaching." *TESOL Quarterly 23* (4), 589–618.

Pennycook argues here that linguistics, sociolinguistics, and language teaching all have important political ramifications that we too often overlook. Teachers, especially language teachers, are "agents for change" in this political arena.

Bibliography

ACTFL Proficiency Guidelines. 1986. American Council on Teaching Foreign Languages.

Allen, Harold B. 1980. "What it means to be a professional in TESOL." Lecture presented at the conference of TEXTESOL, April.

Allen, Virginia French. 1983. *Techniques in Teaching Vocabulary.* Oxford University Press.

Allwright, Dick, and Bailey, Kathleen M. 1991. *Focus on the Language Classroom: An Introduction to Classroom Research for Language Teachers.* Cambridge University Press.

Anthony, Edward. 1963. "Approach, method, technique." *English Language Teaching 17*, 63–67.

Asher, James. 1977. *Learning Another Language Through Actions: The Complete Teacher's Guidebook.* Los Gatos, CA: Sky Oaks Productions.

Au, S.Y. 1988. "A critical appraisal of Gardner's social-psychological theory of second language learning." *Language Learning 38*, 75–100.

Ausubel, David A. 1963. "Cognitive structure and the facilitation of meaningful verbal learning." *Journal of Teacher Education 14*, 217–221.

Ausubel, David A. 1968. *Educational Psychology: A Cognitive View.* Holt, Rinehart and Winston.

Bachman, Lyle F. 1991. "What does language testing have to offer?" *TESOL Quarterly 25*(4), 671–704.

Bailey, Kathleen M. 1985. "Classroom-centered research on language teaching and learning." In Celce-Murcia, Marianne (Ed.), *Beyond Basics: Issues and Research in TESOL*. Newbury House.

Bailey, Kathleen M. 1990. "The use of diary studies in teacher education programs." In Richards, Jack C., and Nunan, David (Eds.), *Second Language Teacher Education*. Cambridge University Press.

Barnett, Marva. 1989. *More than Meets the Eye: Foreign Language Reading Theory in Practice*. Prentice Hall.

Bassano, Sharon, and Christison, Mary Ann. 1984. "Teacher self-observation." *TESOL Newsletter 18,* 17–19.

Bell, J., and Burnaby, B. 1984. *A Handbook for ESL Literacy*. Agincourt, Ontario: Dominie Press.

Bloom, Benjamin C. 1956. *Taxonomy of Educational Objectives: Cognitive Domain*. David McKay.

Boone, Eleanor, Bennett, Joseph, and Motai, Lyn. 1988. *Basics in Reading An Introduction to American Magazines*. Lateral Communications.

Bowen, J. Donald. 1972. "Contextualizing pronunciation practice in the ESOL classroom." *TESOL Quarterly 6*(1), 83–94.

Bowen, J. Donald, Madoon, Harold, and Hilferty, Ann. 1985. *TESOL Techniques and Procedures*. Newbury House.

Breen, Michael. 1987. "Learner contributions to task design." In Candlin, Christopher, and Murphy, D. (Eds.), *Language Learning Tasks*. Prentice Hall.

Brinton, Donna M., Snow, Marguerite Ann, and Wesche, Marjorie B. 1989. *Content-based Second Language Instruction*. Newbury House.

Brinton, Donna M., and Neuman, R. 1982. *Getting Along*. Book 2. Prentice Hall.

Brock, Cynthia A. 1986. "The effects of referential questions on ESL classroom discourse." *TESOL Quarterly 20*(1), 47–59.

Brophy, J. 1981. "Teacher praise: A functional analysis." *Review of Educational Research 51*, 5–32.

Brown, Gillian, and Yule, George. 1983. *Teaching the Spoken Language.* Cambridge University Press.

Brown, H. Douglas. 1972. "Cognitive pruning and second language acquisition." *Modern Language Journal 56*, 218–222.

Brown, H. Douglas. 1989. *A Practical Guide to Language Learning.* McGraw Hill.

Brown, H. Douglas. 1991a. *Breaking the Language Barrier.* Intercultural Press.

Brown, H. Douglas. 1991b. "TESOL at twenty-five: What are the issues?" *TESOL Quarterly, 25*(2), 245–260.

Brown, H. Douglas. 1992. *Vistas: An Interactive Course in English.* Books 1, 2, 3, 4. Prentice Hall Regents.

Brown, H. Douglas. 1994. *Principles of Language Learning and Teaching.* Third Edition. Prentice Hall Regents.

Brown, H. Douglas, Cohen, Deborah, and O'Day, Jennifer. 1991. *Challenges A Process Approach to Academic English.* Prentice Hall Regents.

Brown, James Dean. 1991. "Do English faculties rate writing samples differently?" *TESOL Quarterly 25*(4), 587–603.

Brown, James Dean. 1992. "Classroom-centered language testing." *TESOL Journal 1*(4), 12–15.

Brown, Raymond. 1991. "Group work, task difference, and second language acquisition." *Applied Linguistics 12*(1), 1–12.

Bruner, Jerome S. 1962. *On Knowing: Essays for the Left Hand.* Harvard University Press.

Campbell, Russell. 1978. "Notional-functional syllabuses 1978: Part I." In Blatchford, Charles H., and Schachter, Jacqueline (Eds.), *On TESOL 78: EFL Policies, Programs, Practices.* Washington, DC: Teachers of English to Speakers of Other Languages.

Carrell, Patricia L., and Eisterhold, Joan C. 1983. "Schema theory and ESL reading pedagogy." *TESOL Quarterly 17*(4), 553–573.

Cazden, Courtney, and Snow, Catherine. 1990. *English Plus: Issues in Bilingual Education.* (Annals of the American Academy of Political and Social Science No. 508). Sage Publications.

Celce-Murcia, Marianne. 1991a. "Grammar pedagogy in second and foreign language teaching." *TESOL Quarterly 25*(3), 459–480.

Celce-Murcia, Marianne (Ed.). 1991b. *Teaching English as a Second or Foreign Language.* Second Edition. Newbury House.

Celce-Murcia, Marianne, and Goodwin, Janet M. 1991. "Teaching pronunciation." In Celce-Murcia, Marianne (Ed.), *Teaching English as a Second or Foreign Language.* Second Edition. Newbury House.

Celce-Murcia, Marianne, and Hilles, Sharon. 1988. *Techniques and Resources in Teaching Grammar.* Oxford University Press.

Chamot, Anna Uhl, and McKeon, Denise. 1984. *Second Language Teaching.* Rosslyn, VA: National Clearinghouse for Bilingual Education.

Chamot, Anna Uhl, O'Malley, Michael, and Kupper, Lisa. 1992. *Building Bridges: Content and Learning Strategies for ESL.* Books 1, 2, 3. Heinle & Heinle.

Christenbury, L., and Kelly, P. 1983. *Questioning: A Path to Critical Thinking.* National Council of Teachers of English.

Christison, Mary Ann, and Bassano, Sharon. 1984. "Teacher self-observation." *TESOL Newsletter* (August), 17–19.

Claire, Elizabeth. 1988. *ESL Teacher Activities Kit.* Prentice Hall.

Clark, Herbert H., and Clark, Eve V. 1977. *Psychology and Language: An Introduction to Psycholinguistics.* Harcourt Brace Jovanovich, Inc.

Clark, John L.D., and Clifford, Ray T. 1988. "The FSI/ILR/ACTFL proficiency scales and testing techniques." *Studies in Second Language Acquisition 10,* 129–147.

Clarke, Mark A., and Silberstein, Sandra. 1977. "Toward a realization of psycholinguistic principles for the ESL reading class." *Language Learning 27*(1), 135–154.

Coffey, Margaret Pogemiller. 1983. *Fitting In: A Functional/Notional Text for Learners of English.* Prentice Hall.

Cohen, Andrew. 1990. *Language Learning: Insights for Learners, Teachers, and Researchers.* Newbury House.

Coleman, Algernon. 1929. *The Teaching of Modern Foreign Languages in the United States: A Report Prepared for the Modern Language Study.* Macmillan Company.

Cook, Vivian J. 1969. "The analogy between first and second language learning." *International Review of Applied Linguistics 7*, 207–216.

Crookes, Graham, and Chaudron, Craig. 1991. "Guidelines for classroom language teaching." In Celce-Murcia, Marianne (Ed.), *Teaching English as a Second or Foreign Language.* Second Edition. Newbury House.

Crookes, Graham, and Schmidt, Richard W. 1991. "Motivation: Reopening the Research Agenda." *Language Learning*, 41(4), 469–512.

Cross, David. 1991. *A Practical Handbook of Language Teaching.* Cassell (Prentice Hall).

Curran, Charles A. 1972. *Counseling-Learning: A Whole Person Model for Education.* Grune and Stratton.

Deci, Edward L. 1975. *Intrinsic Motivation.* Plenum Press.

DiPietro, Robert J. 1987. *Strategic Interaction: Learning Languages through Scenarios.* Cambridge University Press.

Doff, Adrian. 1988. *Teach English: A Training Course for Teachers.* Teacher's Handbook. Cambridge University Press.

Doughty, Catherine. 1991. "Second language instruction does make a difference: Evidence from an empirical study of SL relativization." *Studies in Second Language Acquisition 10*, 245–261.

Doughty, Catherine, and Pica, Teresa. 1986. "'Information gap' tasks: Do they facilitate second language acquisition?" *TESOL Quarterly 20*(2), 305–325.

Dunkel, Patricia. 1991. "Listening in the native and second/foreign language: Toward an integration of research and practice." *TESOL Quarterly 25*(3), 431–457.

Ehrman, Madeline. 1990. "The role of personality type in adult language learning: An ongoing investigation." In Parry, Thomas, and Stansfield, Charles (Eds.), *Language Aptitude Reconsidered.* Prentice Hall Regents.

Eisenstein, Miriam R. 1980. "Grammatical explanations in ESL: Teach the student, not the method." *TESL Talk 11*(4), 3–11.

Elbow, Peter. 1973. *Writing Without Teachers.* Oxford University Press.

Ellis, Gail, and Sinclair, Barbara. 1989. *Learning to Learn English: A Course in Learner Training.* Cambridge University Press.

Enright, D. Scott. 1991. "Supporting children's English language development in grade-level and language classrooms." In Celce-Murcia, Marianne (Ed.), *Teaching English as a Second or Foreign Language.* Second Edition. Newbury House.

Epstein, Jim. 1983. "Intonation." *CATESOL News,* December, 7.

Eyring, Janet L. 1991. "Experiential language learning." In Celce-Murcia, Marianne (Ed.), *Teaching English as a Second or Foreign Language.* Second Edition. Newbury House.

Finocchiaro, Mary, and Brumfit, Christopher. 1983. *The Functional-Notional Approach: From Theory to Practice.* Oxford University Press.

Flanders, N.A. 1970. *Analyzing Teaching Behavior.* Addison-Wesley.

Freire, Paolo. 1970. *Pedagogy of the Oppressed.* Seabury Press.

Fries, Charles C. 1945. *Teaching and Learning English as a Foreign Language.* The University of Michigan Press.

Gardner, Howard. 1903. *Frames of Mind: The Theory of Multiple Intelligences.* Basic Books.

Gardner, Robert C. 1985. *Social Psychology and Second Language Learning.* Edward Arnold.

Gardner, Robert C., and Lambert, Wallace E. 1972. *Attitudes and Motivation in Second Language Learning.* Newbury House.

Garvie, Edie. 1990. *Story as Vehicle: Teaching English to Young Children.* Clevedon, U.K.: Multilingual Matters.

Gattegno, Caleb. 1972. *Teaching Foreign Languages in Schools: The Silent Way.* Second Edition. New York: Educational Solutions.

Gibbons, John. 1985. "The silent period: An examination." *Language Learning 35*, 255–267.

Gilbert, Judy. 1978. "Gadgets: Nonverbal tools for teaching pronunciation." *CATESOL Occasional Papers 4*, 68–78.

Golebiowska, Aleksandra. 1990. *Getting Students to Talk: A Resource Book for Teachers*. Prentice Hall.

Goodman, Kenneth S. 1970. "Reading: A psycholinguistic guessing game." In Singer, H., and Ruddell, R.B. (Eds.), *Theoretical Models and Processes of Reading*. Newark, DE: International Reading Association.

Gower, Roger, and Walters, Steve. 1983. *Teaching Practice Handbook: A Reference Book for EFL Teachers in Training*. Heinemann.

Grabe, William. 1991. "Current developments in second language reading research." *TESOL Quarterly 25*(3), 375–406.

Haverson, Wayne, and Haynes, J. 1982. *Literacy Training for ESL Adult Learners*. Prentice Hall (Center for Applied Linguistics).

Hendrick, Judith Carl, and Butler, Marilyn Smith. 1992. *Interaction Activities in ESL*. Second Edition. University of Michigan Press.

Hendrickson, James M. 1980. "Error correction in foreign language teaching: Recent theory, research, and practice." In Croft, Kenneth (Ed.), *Readings on English as a Second Language*. Second Edition. Winthrop.

Higgs, Theodore, and Clifford, Ray. 1982. "The push toward communication." In Higgs, Theodore (Ed.), *Curriculum, Competence, and the Foreign Language Teacher*. Lincolnwood, IL: National Textbook Company.

Hockman, B., Lee-Fong, K., and Lew, E. 1991. "Earth saving language." Workshop presented at the convention of Teachers of English to Speakers of Other Languages (TESOL), New York, March.

Hofstede, Geert. 1986. "Cultural differences in teaching and learning." *International Journal of Intercultural Relations 10*, 301–320.

Howatt, A. 1984. *A History of English Language Teaching*. Oxford University Press.

Hughes, Arthur. 1989. *Testing for Language Teachers*. Cambridge University Press.

Hunt, J. McV. 1971. "Toward a history of intrinsic motivation." In Day, H.I., Berlyne, D.E., Hunt, D.E. (Eds.), *Intrinsic Motivation: A New Direction in Education*. Holt, Rinehart and Winston of Canada.

Jerald, Michael, and Clark, Raymond C. 1989. *Experiential Language Teaching Techniques*. Pro Lingua Associates.

Judd, Elliot. 1987. "Teaching English to speakers of other languages: A political act and a moral question." *TESOL Newsletter 21*(1), 15–16.

Kachru, Braj B. 1985. "Standards, codification, and sociolinguistic realism: The English language in the outer circle." In Quirk, R., and Widdowson, Henry (Eds.), *English in the World: Teaching and Learning the Language and Literatures*. Cambridge University Press.

Kachru, Braj B. 1992. "World Englishes: Approaches, issues, and resources." *Language Teaching 25* (1), 1–14.

Kaplan, Robert B. 1966. "Cultural thought patterns in intercultural education." *Language Learning 16*(1), 1–20.

Keeton, Morris, and Tate, Pamela (Eds.). 1978. *New Directions for Experiential Learning*. Council for the Advancement of Experiential Learning.

Keirsey, David, and Bates, Marilyn. 1984. *Please Understand Me: Character and Temperament Types*. Del Mar, CA: Prometheus Nemesis Book Company.

Kenning, Marie-Madeleine. 1990. "Computer assisted language learning." *Language Teaching 23*(2), 67–76.

Kenworthy, J. 1987. *Teaching English Pronunciation*. Longman.

Kinsella, Kate. 1991. "Promoting active learning and classroom interaction through effective questioning strategies." Workshop presented at San Francisco State University, September 14.

Klippel, Friederike. 1984. *Keep Talking: Communicative Fluency Activities for Language Teaching*. Cambridge University Press.

Kohn, Alfie. 1990. "Rewards hamper creativity." *San Francisco Chronicle* (June 21), B3–B4.

Krashen, Stephen D. 1982. *Principles and Practice in Second Language Acquisition*. Pergamon Press.

Krashen, Stephen D. 1985. *The Input Hypothesis*. Longman.

Krashen, Stephen D. 1986. "Bilingual education and second language acquisition theory." In California State Department of Education, *Schooling and Language Minority Students: A Theoretical Framework*.

Krashen, Stephen D., and Terrell, Tracy D. 1983. *The Natural Approach: Language Acquisition in the Classroom*. Pergamon Press.

Kroll, Barbara (Ed.). 1990. *Second Language Writing: Research Insights for the Classroom*. Cambridge University Press.

Kruse, Anna Fisher. 1987. "Vocabulary in context." In Long, Michael H., and Richards, Jack C. (Eds.), *Methodology in TESOL: A Book of Readings*. Newbury House.

Ladousse, Gillian Porter. 1987. *Role Play*. Oxford University Press.

Lamendella, John. 1969. "On the irrelevance of transformational grammar to second language pedagogy." *Language Learning 19*, 255–270.

Larsen-Freeman, Diane. 1986. *Techniques and Principles in Language Teaching*. Oxford University Press.

Larsen-Freeman, Diane. 1991. "Teaching grammar." In Celce-Murcia, Marianne (Ed.), *Teaching English as a Second or Foreign Language*. Second Edition. Newbury House.

Larsen-Freeman, Diane, and Long, Michael H. 1991. *An Introduction to Second Language Acquisition Research*. Longman.

Lawrence, Gordon. 1984. *People Types and Tiger Stripes: A Practical Guide to Learning Styles*. Center for Applications of Psychological Type.

Legutke, Michael, and Thomas, Howard. 1991. *Process and Experience in the Language Classroom*. Longman.

Leki, Ilona. 1991. "Twenty-five years of contrastive rhetoric: Text analysis and writing pedagogies." *TESOL Quarterly 25*(1), 123–143.

Lenneberg, Eric H. 1967. *The Biological Foundations of Language*. John Wiley and Sons.

Littlewood, William. 1981. *Communicative Language Teaching: An Introduction.* Cambridge University Press.

Long, Michael H. 1977. "Teacher feedback on learner error: Mapping conditions." In Brown, H. Douglas, Yorio, Carlos, and Crymes, Ruth (Eds.), *Teaching and Learning English as a Second Language: Trends in Research and Practice.* Washington, DC: Teachers of English to Speakers of Other Languages.

Long, Michael H. 1988. "Instructed language development." In Beebe, Leslie M. (Ed.), *Issues in Second Language Acquisition: Multiple Perspectives.* Newbury House.

Long, Michael H., and Crookes, Graham. 1992. "Three approaches to task-based syllabus design." *TESOL Quarterly 26* (1), 27–56.

Long, Michael H., and Porter, Patricia. 1985. "Group work, interlanguage talk, and second language acquisition." *TESOL Quarterly 19*(2), 207–228.

Long, Michael H., and Richards, Jack C. (Eds.) 1987. *Methodology in TESOL: A Book of Readings.* Newbury House.

Long, Michael H., and Sato, Charlene. 1983. "Classroom foreigner talk discourse: Forms and functions of teacher questions." In Seliger, Herbert W. and Long, Michael H. (Eds.), *Classroom Oriented Research in Second Language Acquisition.* Newbury House.

Lozanov, Georgi. 1979. *Suggestology and Outlines of Suggestopedy.* Gordon and Breach Science Publishers.

Lund, R. 1990. "A taxonomy for teaching second language listening. *Foreign Language Annals 23*(1), 105–115.

Madsen, Harold. 1983. *Techniques in Testing.* Oxford University Press.

Marckwardt, Albert D. 1972. "Changing winds and shifting sands." *MST English Quarterly 21*, 3–11.

Marshall, Terry. 1990. *The Whole World Guide to Language Learning.* Intercultural Press.

Maslow, Abraham H. 1970. *Motivation and Personality.* Second Edition. Harper and Row.

McDonald, Marguerite G. 1989. "Oral dialogue journals: Spoken language in a communicative context." *TESL Reporter 22*(2), 27–31.

McKay, Ronald. 1987. "Teaching the information-gathering skills." In Long, Michael H., and Richards, Jack C. (Eds.), *Methodology in TESOL: A Book of Readings.* Newbery House Publishers.

McKay, Sandra. 1985. *Teaching Grammar: Form, Function, and Technique.* Pergamon (Prentice-Hall).

McLaughlin, Barry. 1987. *Theories of Second Language Learning.* Edward Arnold.

McLaughlin, Barry. 1990. "'Conscious' versus 'unconscious' learning." *TESOL Quarterly 24*, 617–634.

McLaughlin, Barry, Rossman, Tamimi, and McLeod, Beverly. 1983. "Second language learning: An information-processing perspective." *Language Learning 33*, 135–158.

Meek, Anne. 1991. "On thinking about teaching: A conversation with Eleanor Duckworth." *Educational Leadership* (March), 34.

Morley, Joan. 1991a. "Listening comprehension in second/foreign language instruction." In Celce-Murcia, Marianne (Ed.), *Teaching English as a Second or Foreign Language.* Second Edition. Newbury House.

Morley, Joan. 1991b. "The pronunciation component in teaching English to speakers of other languages." *TESOL Quarterly 25*(3), 481–520.

Moskowitz, Gertrude. 1971. "Interaction analysis: A new modern language for supervisors." *Foreign Language Annals 5*, 211–221.

Moskowitz, Gertrude. 1976. "The classroom interaction of outstanding foreign language teachers." *Foreign Language Annals 9*, 125–157.

Mueller, Marlies. 1987. "Interactive testing: Time to be a test pilot." In Rivers, Wilga (Ed.), *Interactive Language Teaching.* Cambridge University Press.

Nilsen, Don L.F., and Nilsen, Alleen Pace. 1971. *Pronunciation Contrasts in English.* Regents/Simon and Schuster.

Nolasco, Rob, and Arthur, Lois. 1987. *Conversation.* Oxford University Press.

Nunan, David. 1988. *The Learner-Centered Curriculum.* Cambridge University Press.

Nunan, David. 1989a. *Designing Tasks for the Communicative Classroom452*. Cambridge University Press.

Nunan, David. 1989b. *Understanding Language Classrooms: A Guide for Teacher-Initiated Action.* Prentice Hall.

Nunan, David. 1991a. "Communicative tasks and the language curriculum." *TESOL Quarterly 25*(2), 279–295.

Nunan, David. 1991b. *Language Teaching Methodology: A Textbook for Teachers.* Prentice Hall.

Oller, John W. 1983. "Story writing principles and ESL teaching." *TESOL Quarterly 17*(1), 39–53.

Omaggio, Alice C. 1981. *Helping Learners Succeed: Activities for the Foreign Language Classroom.* Washington, DC: Center for Applied Linguistics.

Omaggio, Alice C. 1986. *Teaching Language in Context.* Heinle & Heinle.

Ostrander, Sheila and Schroeder, Lynn. 1979. *Superlearning.* Dell Publishing Company.

Oxford, Rebecca. 1990. *Language Learning Strategies: What Every Teacher Should Know.* Newbury House.

Paulston, Christina B., and Bruder, Mary N. 1976. *Teaching English as a Second Language: Techniques and Procedures.* Winthrop.

Pennington, Martha C. 1990. "A professional development focus for the language teaching practicum." In Richards, Jack C., and Nunan, David (Eds.), *Second Language Teacher Education.* Cambridge University Press.

Pennington, Martha C., and Richards, Jack C. 1986. "Pronunciation revisited." *TESOL Quarterly 20*(2), 207–225.

Pennycook, Alastair. 1989. "The concept of method, interested knowledge, and the politics of language teaching." *TESOL Quarterly 23*(4), 589–618.

Peterson, Pat Wilcox. 1991. "A synthesis for interactive listening." In Celce-Murcia, Marianne (Ed.), *Teaching English as a Second or Foreign Language.* Second Edition. Newbury House.

Prabhu, N.S. 1990. "There is no best method — why?" *TESOL Quarterly 24*(2), 161–176.

Prator, Clifford H. and Celce-Murcia, Marianne. 1979. "An outline of language teaching approaches." In Celce-Murcia, Marianne, and McIntosh, Lois (Ed.), *Teaching English as a Second or Foreign Language*. Newbury House.

Purgason, Katherine Barnhouse. 1991. "Planning lessons and units." In Celce-Murcia, Marianne (Ed.), *Teaching English as a Second or Foreign Language*. Second Edition. Newbury House.

Raimes, Ann. 1991. "Out of the woods: Emerging traditions in the teaching of writing." *TESOL Quarterly 25*(3), 407–430.

Richards, Jack C. 1983. "Listening comprehension: Approach, design, procedure." *TESOL Quarterly 17*(2), 219–239.

Richards, Jack C., and Nunan, David (Eds.). 1990. *Second Language Teacher Education*. Cambridge University Press.

Richards, Jack C., and Rodgers, Theodore. 1982. "Method: Approach, design, procedure." *TESOL Quarterly 16*, 153–168.

Richards, Jack C., and Rodgers, Theodore. 1986. *Approaches and Methods in Language Teaching*. Cambridge University Press.

Rigg, Pat. 1991. "Whole language in TESOL." *TESOL Quarterly 25*(3), 521–542.

Rigg, Pat, and Enright, D. Scott. 1982. *Children and ESL: Integrating Perspectives*. Washington, DC: Teachers of English to Speakers of Other Languages.

Rivers, Wilga M. 1964. *The Psychologist and the Foreign Language Teacher*. University of Chicago Press.

Rivers, Wilga M., and Temperley, Mary S. 1978. *A Practical Guide to the Teaching of English as a Second or Foreign Language*. Oxford University Press.

Rivers, Wilga M. (Ed.). 1987. *Interactive Language Teaching*. Cambridge University Press.

Robinett, Betty Wallace. 1978. *Teaching English to Speakers of Other Languages: Substance and Technique*. University of Minnesota Press.

Rogers, Carl. 1983. *Freedom to Learn in Eighties*. Charles E. Merrill Publishing Company.

Rost, Michael. 1991. *Listening in Action: Activities for Developing Listening in Language Teaching.* Prentice Hall.

Rubin, Joan, and Thompson, Irene. 1982. *How to Be a More Successful Language Learner.* Heinle and Heinle.

Rumelhart, D. 1977. "Toward an intractive model of reading." In S. Dornic (Ed.), *Attention and Performance IV.* Academic Press.

Sage, Howard. 1987. *Incorporating Literature in ESL Instruction.* Prentice Hall.

Savignon, Sandra J. 1991. "Communicative Language Teaching: State of the Art." *TESOL Quarterly, 25*(2), 261–277.

Scovel, Thomas. 1979. "Review of Suggestology and Outlines of Suggestopedy by Georgi Lozanov." *TESOL Quarterly 13*, 255–266.

Shih, May. 1986. "Content-based approaches to teaching academic writing." *TESOL Quarterly 20(*4), 617–648.

Shoemaker, Connie L., and Shoemaker, F. Floyd. 1991. *Interactive Techniques for the ESL Classroom.* Newbury House.

Shohamy, Elana. 1992. *An Introduction to Language Testing.* Oxford University Press.

Skierso, Alexandra. 1991. "Textbook selection and adaptation." In Celce-Murcia, Marianne (Ed.), *Teaching English as a Second or Foreign Language.* Second Edition. Newbury House.

Smith, Stephen M. 1984. *The Theater Arts and the Teaching of Second Languages.* Addison-Wesley.

Stern, H.H. 1983. *Fundamental Concepts of Language Teaching.* Oxford University Press.

Sternberg, Robert J. 1988. *The Triarchic Mind: A New Theory of Human Intelligence.* Viking Press.

Stevick, Earl. 1989. *Success with Foreign Languages.* Prentice Hall.

Swain, Merrill. 1990. "The language of French immersion students: Implications for theory and practice." In Alatis, James E. (Ed.), *Georgetown University Round Table on Languages and Linguistics.* Georgetown University Press.

Taylor, Linda. 1990. *Teaching and Learning Vocabulary*. Prentice Hall.

Terrell, Tracy D. 1991. "The role of grammar instruction in a communicative approach." *Modern Language Journal 75*(1), 52–63.

Ur, Penny. 1984. *Teaching Listening Comprehension*. Cambridge University Press.

Ur, Penny. 1988. *Grammar Practice Activities: A Practical Guide for Teachers*. Cambridge University Press.

Van Ek, J.A., and Alexander, L.G. 1975. *Threshold Level English*. Pergamon Press.

Vanett, Lauren, and Jurich, Donna. 1985. "The missing link: Connecting journal writing to academic writing." Paper presented at the conference of CATESOL, April 19.

Ventriglia, L. 1982. *Conversations with Miguel and Maria: How Children Learn a Second Language*. Addison-Wesley.

Vigil, Neddy A., and Oller, John W. 1976. "Rule fossilization: A tentative model." *Language Learning 26*, 281–295.

Wardhaugh, Ronald. 1970. "The contrastive analysis hypothesis." *TESOL Quarterly 4*, 123–130.

Weir, Cyril J. 1990. *Communicative Language Testing*. Prentice Hall.

Wenden, Anita, and Rubin, Joan. 1987. *Learner Strategies in Language Learning*. Prentice Hall International.

Wenden, Anita. 1992. *Learner Strategies for Learner Autonomy*. Prentice Hall.

Wesche, Marjorie B. 1983. "Communicative testing in a second language." *The Modern Language Journal 67*, 41–55.

Wilkins, David A. 1976. *Notional Syllabuses*. Oxford University Press.

Williams, Eddie, and Moran, Chris. 1989. "Reading in a foreign language at intermediate and advanced levels with particular reference to English." *Language Teaching 22*(4), 217–228.

Wong, Rita. 1987. *Teaching Pronunciation: Focus on English Rhythm and Intonation*. Prentice Hall Regents.

Wright, Tony. 1987. *Roles of Teachers and Learners.* Oxford University Press.

Wright, Tony. 1990. "Understanding classroom role relationships." In Richards, Jack C., and Nunan, David (Eds.), *Second Language Teacher Education.* Cambridge University Press.

Zamel, Vivian. 1982. "Writing: The process of discovering meaning." TESOL Quarterly 16(2), 195–209.

Subject Index

Name Index